LOS PAISANOS

Spanish Settlers on the Northern Frontier of New Spain

OAKAH L. JONES, JR.

University of Oklahoma Press

Norman and London

By Oakah L. Jones, Jr.

Pueblo Warriors and Spanish Conquest (Norman, 1966)
My Adventures in Zuñi (editor) (Palo Alto, 1970)
Federal Control of the Western Apaches, 1848–1886 (editor) (Albuquerque, 1970)
The Spanish Borderlands: A First Reader (Los Angeles, 1974)
Los Paisanos: Spanish Settlers on the Northern Frontier of New Spain (Norman, 1979)
Guatemala in the Spanish Colonial Period (Norman, 1994)

For
Marcia, Kathy, and Chris,
that someday they too may learn to
appreciate another culture

Library of Congress Cataloging-in-Publication Data

Jones, Oakah L.
Los paisanos : Spanish settlers on the northern frontier of New
Spain / Oakah L. Jones, Jr.
p.   cm.
Originally published: Norman : University of Oklahoma Press,
1979. With new pref.
Includes bibliographical references and index.
ISBN 0-8061-2885-2 (alk. paper)
1. Southwest, New—History—To 1848.   2. Mexico—History—To
1810.   3. Spaniards—Southwest, New—History.   I. Title.
F799.J75   1996
979—dc20   96-17090
                                                                              CIP

The paper in this book meets the guidelines for permanence and durability of the Committee on Production Guidelines for Book Longevity of the Council on Library Resources, Inc. ∞

2   3   4   5   6   7   8   9   10   11

Contents

Illustrations

Maps

Preface to the Paperback Edition

Nearly fifty years ago I first visited New Mexico and immediately became interested in its Indian and Hispanic cultures. Since then I have returned at least once a year except when I was overseas. Over the years my interest has deepened and expanded to encompass the entire Spanish Southwest and northern Mexico. In more recent years I have devoted myself to an intensive study of Spanish society in this region. My research interests brought me in contact with repositories of documents and sources of the written word and a much closer association with the Spanish-speaking people of the region who have a Spanish or Mexican heritage. This concentration of interest and research has led to an appreciation of their cultural inheritance, their points of view, their beliefs, and particularly why they live and act as they do.

It is the thesis of this book that Spanish settlers on the northern frontier of New Spain were more numerous than has been supposed and that they not only developed a culture distinct from those in other parts of the viceroyalty but contributed markedly to the development and permanent occupation of a ten-state region on the northern frontier of New Spain. These settlers were everyday people who created a culture reflecting institutions brought from Europe, yet modified to meet the challenge of different environmental conditions. This culture became the nucleus of the present Mexican society in the northern states of that republic and the Spanish-speaking lifestyle in the southwestern states of the United States of America.

Yet few historians have studied the role of the settlers in these frontier provinces. Instead, they have contributed important works on government officials and institutions, the presidial system and military affairs, and the work of explorers, conquistadores, and missionaries. I have chosen to concentrate on the civilian settler—the farmer, day laborer, stockman, and artisan—to depict his importance in the frontier expansion of New Spain from the settlement of Culiacán in 1531 to the achievement of Mexican independence in 1821.

An effort has been made to portray the settlers as they were, not as they have been disparaged by Anglo-American observers of the nineteenth century or romanticized in a "fantasy heritage," as Carey McWilliams so aptly stated in his book *North from Mexico*. Three general subjects have been emphasized: the establishment of civil settlements; the settlers themselves; and the lifestyle, achieve-ments, and problems of these frontier people.

The real settlers of northern New Spain were the *paisanos* (countrymen and women), not aristocrats, government officials, missionaries, or presidial soldiers, except when they became permanent residents of frontier communities. Many terms could be used to describe these settlers, including *pobladores* and *colonos*. I have used *paisanos*, however, for a variety of reasons. The term accurately describes the settlers as those who were attached to the land and the environment, who worked the land, and raised livestock. Furthermore, it seems to convey the idea of the everyday people who settled in remote communities on the frontier. Also, my personal observations are that the term is used by Spanish-speaking people today to demonstrate a common origin, association, and cultural heritage.

This work is *not* intended to be a comprehensive examination of the entire Spanish Borderlands and all their frontier institutions. It touches upon missions, presidios, governmental agencies, American Indians, and military problems only tangentially. It stresses the founding of communities and the organization of civilian settlers themselves—who they were, where they originated, why they came to particular regions, how many they were at selected times, what classes and races composed the population, and how they occupied themselves. It also describes their way of life, achievements, everyday life, diversions, educational developments, folk arts, and their problems, ranging from transportation and communications to health, land systems, and crime and punishment, as well as external threats and isolation.

Although Herbert Eugene Bolton and his two generations of graduate students have viewed the northward advance of Spain in North America as a three-pronged expansion, I have altered this approach slightly. The Northeastern Frontier here includes Coahuila, Nuevo León, Texas, and Nuevo Santander (modern Tamauli-pas). The North Central Frontier concentrates upon Nueva Vizcaya (modern Durango and Chihuahua) and New Mexico, which includes the region of El Paso del Norte now in Texas and Chihuahua. The Northwestern Frontier, unlike that proposed by Bolton, includes only Sinaloa and Sonora, of which Pimería Alta (northern Sonora and southern Arizona now) was a part, not a separate entity. The Pacific Frontier includes both Baja and Alta California. The approach and point of view, then, is through the eyes and experiences of Spanish settlers and governmental officials. The frontier is seen as a continuous northward expansion spanning three centuries, and no attempt is made to draw an arbitrary boundary between Mexico and the United States.

My research has taken me to widely dispersed archival materials, as well as major primary and secondary sources. I have concentrated mainly upon provincial and state archives because they seem to have more documents relating to local affairs, people of the settlements, and everyday occurrences. Census reports listing numbers, families, ages, names, occupations, servants, and in-laws were consulted both extensively and intensively. Probation of wills and inheritances and records of births, baptisms, marriages, and deaths have also been used. Local regulations and written reports dealing with everyday events and problems have also been examined.

Since the publication of the first edition of *Los Paisanos*, in 1979, the field of research and publication pertaining to the Spanish frontiers in North America (Spanish Borderlands) has grown and changed. More and more scholars are devoting their studies to the Spanish-speaking people in the Southwest and the northern Mexican states. They stress the social and cultural aspects of colonial society, the people and their ways of life, and interdisciplinary approaches. Instead of concentrating upon heroic individuals and institutions, new studies examine the region using documentary research and methodologies of other disciplines (e.g. anthropology, archaeology, ethnohistory, sociology, and geography). Research today is no longer restricted to the Spanish colonial period but ranges into the Mexican period (1821–48) and the Anglo-American period (1848 to the present). Undoubtedly, these changes have been sparked by the ever-growing Hispano population of the United States, the increasing population and new border problems of Mexico and the United States, and the pressing need for cultural and historical awareness of the Spanish-speaking people, who will soon become the largest minority in the United States.

Frequent articles in professional journals, presentations of research papers, sessions at professional conferences, and public speeches all have been indicative of this increased interest and research about Spanish frontiers. Some have introduced new questions and viewpoints and controversial topics. Others focus on narrow, specialized topics and avoid earlier works and narrative history. Still more are secondary works that explain all or parts of Spain's extensive northern frontiers (those in present-day Mexico and the United States), including specific regions or special topics. Finally, a boon to researchers has been the publication of Spanish primary documents from archives in English and Spanish editions.

Many of the studies published since the mid-1970s complement the focus of *Los Paisanos*, and I shall discuss them below as they pertain to the Spanish period covered in this volume. Because all borders or frontiers involve at least two sides, I include major works that deal with northern Mexico and those whose focus is the southwestern United States. Most of these studies focus upon the Spanish settlements, their people, and their social and cultural history. (Other works, which cover explorers, missionaries, government, the economy, and related topics, also have been valuable contributions to the overall study of Spanish frontiers in North America.)

Of the many general works stressing Spanish frontiers, six are especially notable. David J. Weber, *The Spanish Frontier in North America* (Yale Univ. Press, 1992), is one of the most recent and most comprehensive. Soundly researched and lucidly written, it is an up-to-date study of the Spanish Borderlands from Florida to the Southwest and Alta California. While it contains information about each region and chapters on frontier people and the Spanish legacy for the United States, it does not include much information on frontiers in the present northern Mexican states. One masterful work that does encompass both regions is Peter Gerhard, *The North Frontier of New Spain* (Princeton Univ. Press, 1982; rev. ed. Univ. of Oklahoma Press, 1993). It is an indispensable study of Nueva Galicia, Nueva Vizcaya, Sinaloa, Sonora, Baja California, Alta California, Nuevo México, Coahuila, Texas, Nuevo León, and Nuevo Santander (modern Tamaulipas). It examines a variety of topics, such as Spanish-Indian contacts, *encomiendas*, the Catholic Church, settlements and communities by province, population, and government, and it includes maps, tables, and suggested sources for each province and region.

Three other studies concern only the Southwest. Elizabeth A. H. John, *Storms Brewed in Other Men's Worlds: The Confrontation of Indians, Spanish, and French in the Southwest*, 1540–1795 (Texas A & M Univ. Press, 1975; 2d ed., Univ. of Oklahoma Press, 1996), is a vividly written product of intensive archival research and familiarity with published works, emphasizing the complex people of the region, their interrelationships, and the problems they faced. David H. Thomas, ed., *Columbian Consequences*, vol. 1, *Archaeological and Historical Perspectives of the Spanish Borderlands West* (Smithsonian Institution Press, 1989), is a comprehensive study of only the Southwest and Pacific Coast, with individual chapters written on specific topics by notable scholars. Arthur L. Campa, *Hispanic Culture in the Southwest* (Univ. of Oklahoma Press, 1979), not only provides a study of Spanish exploration, conquest, and settlement of the Southwest, but also focuses upon Hispano customs, traditions, beliefs, language, arts and crafts, folk drama, and music.

An excellent research tool is Thomas C. Barnes, Thomas H. Naylor, and Charles W. Polzer, *Northern New Spain: A Research Guide* (Univ. of Arizona Press, 1981), which devotes special emphasis to documents and documentary collections, especially the Documentary Relations of the Southwest at the University of Arizona. It is a highly valuable reference for all the northern provinces of New Spain, not only for its useful summaries and observations concerning settlements but also for special topics, such as the structures of colonial government, political evolution, money and currency, weights and measures, names of Indian groups, lists of colonial officials, maps, and bibliographical references.

For the northeastern frontiers of New Spain (Coahuila, Nuevo León, Texas, and Nuevo Santander), Texas understandably has received the most attention. The best single volume on colonial Texas is unquestionably Donald L. Chipman, *Spanish Texas*, 1519–1821 (Univ. of Texas Press, 1992). In readable prose, Chipman comprehensively and accurately covers the land and people and chronologically relates the explorations, conquests, settlements, and developments. He also examines foreign threats and Spanish-Indian relations, concluding with a thoughtful analysis of the Spanish legacies for Texas.

Four other studies examine the establishment of civilian towns and ranches, their people, and the growing sense of community in eighteenth-century Texas. Gerald E. Poyo and Gilberto M. Hinojosa, eds., *Tejano Origins in Eighteenth-Century San Antonio* (Univ. of Texas Press, 1991), is an important collection of essays by seven noted experts, who examine how diversified settlers became imbued with a sense of community in the presidio, missions, and civil community of San Antonio and San Fernando de Béxar. This sense of community is also the focus of Jesús F. de la Teja, *San Antonio de Béxar: A Community on New Spain's Northern Frontier* (Univ. of New Mexico Press, 1995). Based upon intensive and extensive archival research in Spanish documents, de la Teja's work clearly explains how Spanish colonists of diversified backgrounds developed into a single cohesive community by the end of the eighteenth century. Gilbert R. Cruz, *Let There Be Towns: Spanish Municipal Origins of the American Southwest, 1610–1810* (Texas A & M Univ. Press, 1988), focuses upon the establishment of Spanish settlements and the *cabildo* (town council) as a municipal institution. While the principal emphasis is upon San Antonio and Laredo, it also examines four civil communities and the civilians' lifestyle in Alta California and New Mexico. Spanish ranching, the livestock industry, and the trade of Tejanos with neighboring provinces are the topics treated by Jack Jackson, *Los Mesteños: Spanish Ranching in Texas, 1721–1821* (Texas A & M Univ. Press, 1986), which provides detailed, well-researched information on the development of the cattle and horse industries, entrepreneurs, problems, and commercial ties between Texas and other provinces.

Several works on the Spanish frontier period of the northeastern present-day states of Nuevo León, Coahuila, and Tamaulipas have been published. Charles H. Harris III, *A Mexican Family Empire: The Latifundio of the Sánchez Navarro Family, 1765–1867* (Univ. of Texas Press, 1975), provides an intensive study, based upon research in public and private documents, of the *hacienda* system in Coahuila, emphasizing across the Spanish and Mexican periods the second largest ranching and commercial estate of the province established and managed by generations of the Sánchez Navarros. Juan Bautista Chapa, ed. by William C. Foster, *Texas and Northeastern Mexico, 1650–1690* (Univ. of Texas Press, forthcoming), makes important connections among seventeenth-century Coahuila, Nuevo León, and Texas, using information from such primary sources as the reports of Alonso de León and Juan Bautista Chapa. Concerning frontier Nuevo Santander's only civil community north of the Río Grande and its people, Gilberto Miguel Hinojosa, *A Borderlands Town in Transition: Laredo, 1755–1870* (Texas A & M Univ. Press, 1983), is an excellent study based upon the Laredo Archives and other documentary repositories. Hinojosa effectively interweaves demographic analysis with a narrative development of Laredo across the Spanish, Mexican, and Anglo-American periods.

For the north central frontier of New Spain (Nueva Vizcaya and New Mexico), or what Herbert Eugene Bolton once called "the heart of the north," two new works have significantly advanced our knowledge of Spanish frontiers in the region. Oakah L. Jones, Jr., *Nueva Vizcaya: Heartland of the Spanish Frontier* (Univ. of New Mexico Press, 1988), provides a comprehensive chronological and topical view of New Spain's most important northern frontier from exploration and conquest to colonization and independence. It emphasizes civil settlements, population, colonizers, and problems of defense against Indian hostilities. Michael M. Swann, *Tierra Adentro: Settlement and Society in Colonial Durango* (Westview Press, 1983), is a regional study emphasizing eighteenth-century population change—as well as social, economic, and political factors—in colonial Durango and other settlements within the larger province of Nueva Vizcaya.

New Mexico in the Spanish colonial period has received more attention from historians, ethnohistorians, geographers, and anthropologists than any other single region of the northern frontier. Easily the best overall history of the El Paso region (which belonged to New Mexico during the colonial period) in the Spanish, Mexican, and Anglo-American eras is W. H. Timmons, *El Paso: A Borderlands History* (Univ. of Texas at El Paso, 1990), a product of the author's lifelong teaching, research, and residence in the area. Of special interest is Part I, "The Legacy of the Spanish-Mexican North," which pertains to the explorers, conquistadores, settlements, and settlers of the El Paso area. Similarly, Richard L. Nostrand employs his expertise as an historical geographer to examine a specific region in *The Hispano Homeland* (Univ. of Oklahoma Press, 1992). Nostrand concentrates upon the Spanish-speaking people of the mountains and river valleys of northern New Mexico from colonial years to the late twentieth century, emphasizing their relationships with Pueblos, other Indians, Anglo-Americans, and Mexican-Americans in the forging of a special place, or homeland. Marc Simmons, *Coronado's Land: Essays on Daily Life in Colonial New Mexico* (Univ. of New Mexico Press, 1991), is a collection of well-written essays by the author on everyday life and customs of Spaniards and Indians.

Two other works emphasize the religious life of New Mexicans in Spanish communities. Marta Weigle, *Brothers of Light, Brothers of Blood: The Penitentes of New Mexico* (Univ. of New Mexico Press, 1976), is the finest, most comprehensive, and authoritative work dealing with the *penitentes* and their *cofradías*—theories of their origins, their history from the colonial period to the mid-twentieth century, and their organizations and activities. A similar study is William Wroth, *Images of Penance, Images of Mercy: Southwestern Santos in the Late Nineteenth Century* (Univ. of Oklahoma Press, 1991). Although the focus is upon late nineteenth-century religious images, this beautifully illustrated and intensively researched book also explains penances in the Christian tradition of Europe, Spain, colonial Mexico, and colonial New Mexico, in addition to describing *santos, santeros,* and the *penitente* brotherhood.

Marc Simmons, *The Last Conquistador: Juan de Oñate and the Settling of the Far Southwest* (Univ. of Oklahoma Press, 1991), is an up-to-date biography of New Mexico's colonizer, explorer, and conquistador. It is more than a biography because it also focuses on the original settlers, and describes how America's first settlement west of the Mississippi River relates to national and international development of the late sixteenth century and beyond. Finally, three major works concentrate upon Spanish institutions in the Southwest. Two of these are by Charles R. Cutter: *The Protector de Indios in Colonial New Mexico, 1659–1821* (Univ. of New Mexico Press, 1986), which focuses on the Indians' use of the Spanish legal system; and *The Legal Culture of Northern New Spain, 1700–1821* (Univ. of New Mexico Press, 1995), for which Cutter conducted extensive documentary research in Spain, Mexico, New Mexico, and Texas. Both studies focus on the people, legal culture in the Spanish period, the theories and practices of law, and judicial procedures. Lastly, Victor Westphall, *Mercedes Reales: Hispanic Land Grants in the Upper Río Grande Region* (Univ. of New Mexico Press, 1983), is a thorough study of Spanish and Mexican land grants (*mercedes reales*) and settlement patterns in northern New Mexico and southern Colorado.

For the northwestern frontier (Sinaloa and Sonora) in the Spanish and Mexican periods, the best study published to date is James E. Officer, *Hispanic Arizona, 1536–1856* (Univ. of Arizona Press, 1987), a comprehensive, soundly researched study of southern Arizona and northern Sonora (Pimería Alta). Henry F. Dobyns, *Spanish Colonial Tucson: A Demographic History* (Univ. of Arizona Press, 1976), is an anthropological-historical case study of colonial Tucson, its nearby Jesuit and later Franciscan missions, its presidio, and its civil settlers. Joseph P. Sánchez, *Spanish Bluecoats: The Catalonian Volunteers in Northwestern New Spain, 1767–1810* (Univ. of New Mexico Press, 1990), is an important study of the Catalonian soldiers, their campaigns against hostile Indians in Sonora, and their later roles as explorers and garrison forces in Alta California and at Santa Cruz de Nutka, Vancouver Island. Sánchez emphasizes the function of Catalonians as frontier colonizers in chapter 9, giving perspective to their twin roles as soldiers and frontier settlers. Daniel T. Reff, *Disease, Depopulation, and Culture Change in Northwestern New Spain, 1518–1764* (Univ. of Utah Press, 1991), is an ethnohistorical study of the impact of disease upon Indians during the Spanish conquest and settlement of Sinaloa, Sonora, and western Nueva Vizcaya. Many of his observations are subject to question and controversy, and unfortunately the coverage does not extend to the end of the colonial period. Evelyn Hu-DeHart, *Missionaries, Miners, and Indians: Spanish Contact with the Yaqui Nation of Northwestern New Spain, 1533–1820* (Univ. of Arizona Press, 1981), concentrates upon Spanish relations with the Yaqui people over the course of three centuries, and also explains the presence of miners as civil settlers.

For the Pacific frontier (Baja California and Alta California), most of the major contributions in the last seventeen years or so have pertained to Alta California. One major study has been published, however, on the little-known and infrequently examined province of Baja California. Harry Crosby, *Antigua California:*

Mission and Colony on the Peninsular Frontier, 1697–1768 (Univ. of New Mexico Press, 1994), provides an intensive, readable, and soundly researched study of Baja California, from its permanent occupation to the expulsion of the Jesuits, including information about its settlements, presidios, soldier-settlers in the vicinities of presidios and missions, the Jesuits, and problems experienced by those who resided on this difficult, remote frontier.

Alta California (the modern state) and the far northwest of North America have received more attention from scholars both before publication of *Los Paisanos* and since. Among the recent major studies of this frontier region is Doyce B. Nunis, ed., *Southern California's Spanish Heritage: An Anthology* (Historical Society of Southern California, 1992), which is a collection of nineteen articles reprinted from the *Southern California Quarterly*. Although not a comprehensive history of Spanish California, it does include experts who have written on a wide variety of topics, such as explorers, missionaries, presidios, *rancho* land grants, and settlements. Two other major contributions relate to Spanish visits to Alta California and observations concerning people, settlements, and conditions on this frontier and the Northwest Coast. Iris H. W. Engstrand, *Spanish Scientists in the New World: The Eighteenth-Century Expeditions* (Univ. of Washington Press, 1981), is a masterful study of the Royal Scientific Expedition and the voyage of Alejandro Malaspina to Alta California and the Northwest Coast. Based on archival research in Spain and Mexico, the book depicts the observations of the Enlightenment era on plant, animal, and mineral species, while also recording conditions in Alta California and describing Indian life and customs. A similar volume by Donald C. Cutter, *California in 1792: A Spanish Naval Visit* (Univ. of Oklahoma Press, 1990), concentrates upon the firsthand observations of Spanish naval officers visiting Monterey. Their comments describe conditions in California and include information on the little-known Runsien and Esselen Indians and their vocabulary and catechism. George W. Phillips, *Indians and Intruders in Central California, 1769–1849* (Univ. of Oklahoma Press, 1993), and Albert L. Hurtado, *Indian Survival on the California Frontier* (Yale Univ. Press, 1988), treat the topic of Spanish-Indian relations and the impact of Spaniards and Mexicans upon the Indians in the Spanish and Mexican periods, but neither work contains much information on civil settlers and settlements.

It would be remiss of me not to mention important documentary studies of the frontiers of New Spain that have recently appeared. Two of these emanated from the Vargas Project at the University of New Mexico. John L. Kessell and Rick Hendricks, eds., *By Force of Arms: The Journals of Don Diego de Vargas, 1691–1693* (Univ. of New Mexico Press, 1992), and Kessell, Hendricks, and Meredith D. Dodge, eds., *To the Royal Crown Restored: The Journals of Don Diego de Vargas, 1692–1694* (Univ. of New Mexico Press, 1995), contain useful information about the two *entradas* of the reconquest of New Mexico, the civil settlers rescued by the Spaniards from Pueblo Indians, the colonists in the 1693 expedition, and the settlements reestablished in the province. Future volumes in the series should be equally valuable.

Four other documentary works are also significant additions for the study of Spanish frontiers, communities, and settlers. Thomas H. Naylor and Charles W. Polzer, comps. and eds., *The Presidio and the Militia on the Northern Frontier of New Spain: A Documentary History*, vol. 1: 1570–1700 (Univ. of Arizona Press, 1986), is an excellent summary of the early frontiers of New Spain. It contains numerous documents in Spanish and English translation on the Chichimeca wars, rebellions of Indians, Spanish defenses, and frontier civilians. Naylor and Polzer, comps. and eds., *Pedro de Rivera and the Military Regulations for Northern New Spain, 1724–1729: A Documentary History of His Frontier Inspection and the Reglamento de 1729* (Univ. of Arizona Press, 1988), in addition to being a study of Rivera's inspection and royal military regulations, contains bilingual documents about frontier communities and civil settlers. Polzer and Thomas E. Sheridan, comps. and eds., *The Presidio and the Militia on the Northern Frontier of New Spain: A Documentary History*, vol. 2, part 1: 1700–1765 (Univ. of Arizona Press, forthcoming), continues the series of military activities along with censuses and other documents containing information on civil communities and settlers in Baja California and Sonora. Finally, in this category is Donald C. Cutter, ed. and trans., *The Defenses of Northern New Spain: Hugo O'Conor's Report to Teodoro de Croix, July 22, 1777* (Southern Methodist Univ. Press and DeGolyer Library, 1994). In a handsomely printed and effectively annotated volume, Cutter provides the original document and a translation relating O'Conor's far-flung activities as *comandante inspector* on the northern frontiers.

Since *Los Paisanos* first appeared, it is evident that scholars have devoted considerable attention to the social and cultural history of settlements, settlers, and their lifestyle on the northern frontiers of New Spain during the Spanish colonial period. With the added contributions of those of other disciplines, historians have benefited from fresh topics, new methodologies, and challenging points of view. Yet, the importance of *Los Paisanos* has not diminished, as is apparent by its numerous citations in the works of others and many requests for a paperback reprint edition since the original went out of print.

As José E. Espinosa once wrote, New Mexicans "were frontiersmen, with all the moral virtues and weaknesses, all the practical gifts, and intellectual shortcomings of any group living on the fringes of civilization." (*Saints in the Valleys: Christian Sacred Images in the History, Life, and Folk Art of Spanish New Mexico*, rev. ed., Univ. of New Mexico Press, 1967, 82). As *Los Paisanos* demonstrates, this was true not only of New Mexicans, but also of Hispanos living in communities and rural areas everywhere on northern frontiers of New Spain. This sense of community established and maintained by *paisanos* was a signal achievement among the many Spanish contributions for both present-day northern Mexico and the southwestern United States. I hope that this study of *Los Paisanos* will continue to build understanding and appreciation for Spanish settlements, civil settlers, and their way of life, as well as respect for their customs, traditions, and beliefs, for this is the heritage of those whose beginnings were with the *paisanos* of the northern frontiers of New Spain.

OAKAH L. JONES, JR.

Albuquerque, New Mexico
January 1996

LOS PAISANOS

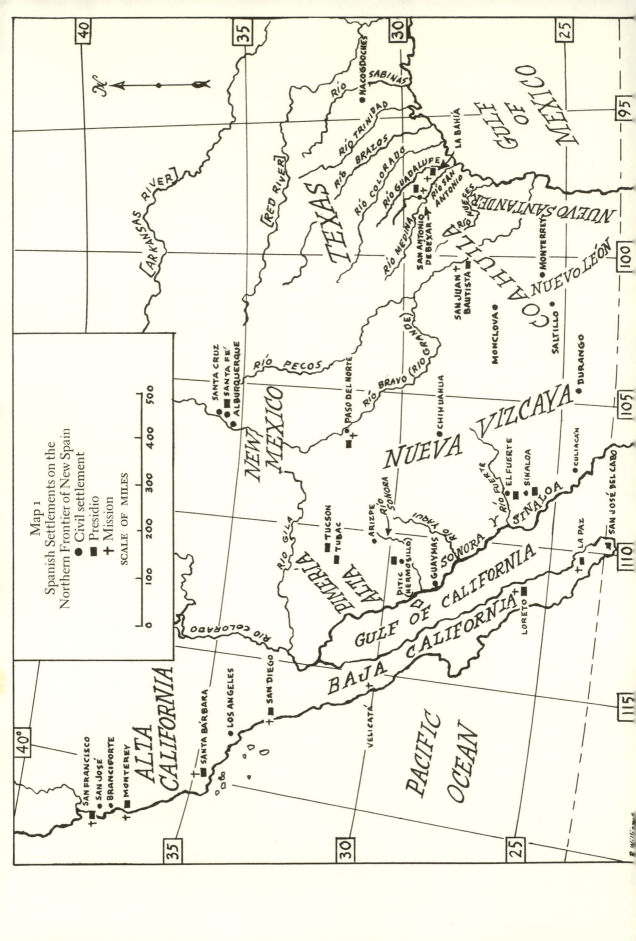

Map 1
Spanish Settlements on the
Northern Frontier of New Spain
● Civil settlement
■ Presidio
✚ Mission

SCALE OF MILES

0   100   200   300   400   500

Introduction

Spanish settlement of the northern frontier of New Spain was more than a military-missionary venture. Over the course of nearly three centuries, from the founding of Culiacán in 1531 to the establishment of Mexican independence in 1821, there were always some civil communities on the frontier. Missionaries, presidial soldiers, and government officials constituted the initial elements of Spanish contact with the various Indian nations of this extensive region. Civilian settlers, often called *pobladores, colonos,* and *vecinos,* were not far behind. Many soldiers became permanent settlers of communities, missionaries and soldiers became dependent upon supplies from nearby civil settlements, and the three institutions—presidio, mission, and civil community—became interdependent in many ways. Yet the number of settlers on almost all frontiers came to exceed those of the missionaries and soldiers combined. Whereas men of the cloth came to be numbered in the tens and soldiers in the hundreds, settlers swelled into the thousands. This was true of all the frontier provinces in this study except Baja California and the Pimería Alta region of Sonora.

These communities became the focal points in the permanent occupation of northern New Spain. They re-enforced Spain's claim by actual occupation of territory reaching from the Gulf of Mexico to the Pacific Ocean, supplementing the original Spanish claims based upon papal bulls, treaties, discovery, and exploration. Many types of permanent communities were founded and maintained on the northern frontier. These included various urban-oriented settlements, such as the *ciudades* (chartered major cities with their own governments, privileges, and responsibilities), *villas* (chartered frontier settlements with more limited self-government, obligations, and privileges), and *pueblos* or *poblaciones* (unchartered communities with direct royal control, appointed officials, and usually attached to other major settlements for administrative purposes). In addition, there were *reales de minas* (mining districts or jurisdictions), *haciendas* (large ranching and farming enterprises, usually privately owned), and *ranchos* (smaller stock farms, also under private control), where settlers resided mostly in a rural environment associated with a nearby urban center.

This urban orientation was not a new experience for Spanish-speaking people.

3

It was a well-developed institution transplanted from Spain and adapted to the peculiar conditions encountered on each frontier. The development of these communities partially refutes the *leyenda negra* (Black Legend) of the English, according to which Spaniards were not true colonizers. Only the English-speaking people planted permanent colonies, it was maintained, and Spaniards brought few, if any, lasting benefits of civilization to the New World. Rather than being settlers, they were interested solely in "glory, God, and gold." Furthermore, they were exceptionally cruel in the conquest of the Americas, and they had a peculiar national character of bigotry, pride, hypocrisy, and other undesirable attributes; in addition, they refused to work or till the soil.[1] Such an attitude arose among Anglo-Saxons in the sixteenth century, and is still present, even among some historians. One recent world-history textbook, for example, maintains that the Spanish colonies differed from the English ones because the former were inhabited by "mostly soldiers, members of the clergy, government officials, and a few necessary craftsmen."[2] According to this view, Spaniards had the labor of the Indians to depend upon while the English did their own work, clearing land themselves, living by their own efforts as farmers, fishermen, and traders, and developing communities that were exclusively European in composition.[3]

Such a thesis cannot be supported by an intensive study of the civil community, the thousands of settlers, and the lifestyle of northern New Spain. There urban-oriented, everyday settlers had to work for themselves. Frequently there were no tractable Indians to employ when the settlements were established. It is true that Indians, Negroes, mixed bloods, Spaniards, and Creoles (those of Spanish heritage born in the New World) came to settle the frontier and some were employed as domestic servants. Yet the numbers of these servants were always small and their proportion to the over-all population was very low. How did the situation differ from the use of indentured servants in the English colonies of North America? They may be considered as settlers, whether voluntary or involuntary. The fact is that the large majority of the people on the Spanish frontier in the colonial period consisted of real settlers, established in formal communities, and absolutely dependent upon tilling the soil and raising livestock for their livelihood. Since they were so close to the land, and indeed were true people of the country they inhabited, they may be called *paisanos* (countrymen), a term which is still widely used among Spanish-speaking people of the southwestern United States.[4]

Because the towns were the focal points for these settlers, it is necessary to know something about the origins of the urban community in the Iberian Peninsula. Also, the reader must become somewhat familiar with the detailed planning that went into the establishment of these frontier communities. Finally, he must be aware of the different types of settlements, the changes and variations in them made necessary by environmental circumstances, and their over-all importance to the frontier in general.

The Spanish preoccupation with community living began in the Iberian Peninsula centuries before America was discovered. Phoenicians, Carthaginians, and Romans established the first cities of Spain in such places as Cádiz, Cartagena, and Segovia. During the long period of the *Reconquista* (Reconquest) from the Moslem people—extending as some maintain from 711 A.D., when the Moors first invaded the Iberian Peninsula, to 1492, when they were evicted from Granada and southern Spain—the Spanish city-state became a highly developed institution. Granted certain rights and privileges such as exemption from tribute, special titles, and some self-government in return for their assistance against rival kingdoms or the hated infidels, these cities became social, economic, and political centers of the provinces, especially those of Castile and León. Once granted these privileges, the cities jealously guarded them against any centralizing tendencies of monarchs. To this day many Spaniards think of themselves first as residents of a particular community and province first and as Spaniards second. It is no wonder that this regionalistic attitude and the institution of the civil community were both evident early in the colonization of the New World.

Towns were established in the Americas as a part of the Spanish conquests, as early as 1493–1543, not as afterthoughts or institutions created once the pacification of resisting Indian nations had been completed. La Navidad, Isabella, and Santo Domingo—the last being the first permanent Spanish settlement in the New World—were founded on the island of Española during the first three years of Spanish-Indian contact. Santiago de Cuba and La Habana were both established during the conquest of Cuba, by 1515. One of the first acts of Hernán Cortés after landing in New Spain in 1519 was to create the town of Villa Rica de Vera Cruz, thereby establishing a degree of autonomy with a separate *cabildo*, or town council, independent from the jurisdiction of the governor of Cuba. Once the Aztec Confederation had been finally conquered in 1521, Cortés built Mexico City right on top of the Aztec capital of Tenochtitlán. Before the middle of the sixteenth century Spaniards had founded additional towns at Guadalajara, Puebla de los Angeles, Guanajuato, and Zacatecas, each with its special titles as well as privileges in return for colonizing, military, and other services rendered by its settlers to the Crown of Castile.

It should be emphasized that civil settlements were not confined to the Caribbean Islands and to New Spain. Spaniards established towns in Central and South America also. Two small communities were founded on the Gulf of Urabá (Darién) as early as 1510 and were combined into the single settlement of Santa María la Antigua del Darién, Panamá's first important urban community. Pedro Arias de Ávila (Pedrarias) established Panamá City ("Panamá Viejo," not the present city) in 1519, and Guatemala had three successive capitals during the colonial period. Spanish colonizers carried the civil settlement into South America from Panamá and directly from Europe. Francisco Pizarro built La Ciudad de los Reyes (The City of the Kings—present Lima) in 1535. Three years later an Extremaduran, Gonzalo Jiménez de Quesada, founded Santa Fé de Bogotá in modern Colombia. The decade of the 1540s saw the founding of Charcas (also called Chuquisaca and La Plata), the present Bolivian city of Sucre, as well as Santiago de Chile, Concepción, and Valparaíso by Pedro de Valdivia as part of the conquest of Chile. Caracas (1567), Nuestra Señora de Buen Aire (Buenos Aires—founded in 1536 but abandoned soon afterwards and re-established in 1580), and Asunción (1537) are only a few examples.

From all of this evidence it is apparent that everywhere Spaniards went the civil settlement was an early institution in the permanent colonization of America. Settlements were not made in helter-skelter fashion. According to one leading urban historian, "To a far greater degree than any other colonizing powers in the New World the Spanish followed a system of land settlement and town planning formalized in written rules and regulations."[5]

In the beginning there were few written rules concerning the establishment of towns, and founders relied principally upon models from the Iberian Peninsula. La Navidad was the first military outpost in America, and Santo Domingo had a rectangular street system, a pattern widely employed thereafter in the New World;[6] both settlements borrowed from Spain. The town of Santa Fé in southern Spain had a rectangular square and a gridiron system of streets. It may have been the model adopted for the later regularization of town planning in the Laws of the Indies.[7] But the early Spanish town was much more than its name implies. It was a self-contained rural-urban unit. The land allocated to each community had both house lots (*solares*) within the town itself and farming lots (*suertes*) adjacent to the settlement. Both were part of the royal grants (*mercedes*) initially measuring ten thousand *varas* (about five and one-quarter miles) on each side.[8] The standard grant in New Spain, however, became four square leagues (about eighteen thousand acres), usually made to a group of settlers numbering from one to ten *vecinos* (heads of families or citizens). To maintain possession, settlers had to occupy and use the land.[9] Thus, the municipality—*ciudad*, *villa*, *pueblo*, *población*, or whatever name it was known by—replaced the feudal lord in America.[10]

Although Spain issued many regulations to promote, regularize, and control the establishment of colonies in the Americas, three comprehensive sets of laws provide an understanding of the nature of civil settlements in New Spain. The first is collectively known as "The Royal Ordinances Concerning the Laying Out of Towns," originally disseminated by King Philip II in 1573. The second is the huge, multivolume codification of Spanish law published in 1681 and known as the *Recopilación de leyes de los reynos de las Indias*, or more popularly as the "Laws of the Indies." The third is the lesser-known but important series of regulations for frontier communities known by its short title as the "Instructions for the Establishment of the New Villa of Pitic in the Province of Sonora." These regulations collectively prescribed the ideal system and practices for promoting colonization and laying out civil settlements, but a closer look at each will provide a basis for understanding the detailed planning that went into the founding of communities in America.

Philip II's royal ordinances were issued at San Lorenzo on July 3, 1573, and are part of his general regulations concerning discoveries, settlements, and methods of pacification. They codify some colonization practices already in existence, but for the first time provide uniform standards and procedures for the laying out of towns, use of newly opened lands, and regulation of the living conditions of settlers.[11] However, it should be remembered that these instructions provided only for the ideal community; in reality settlements were frequently modified to fit their environment. It would indeed be hard to find any single settlement that adhered to all of these laws. Furthermore, the regulations themselves changed with the passage of time and issuance of additional laws.[12]

According to Philip's ordinances, towns should be founded only where vacant lands existed or where Indians had consented freely to their establishment. They should be located on an elevated site if possible, surrounded by an abundance of good land for farming and pasturage, as well as an ample supply of fresh water, fuel, timber, and a nearby native people, presumably for labor purposes. In addition, sufficient space should be left in the original townsite for it to grow. Before constructing the town it was always necessary to draw up a plan showing the location of its principal buildings, lots, streets, and plaza.[13]

The principal plaza of the town was the initial point in planning the over all community. It was located near the landing place for coastal towns and in the center of the community for inland ones. The plaza was laid out first and the entire town oriented from it. Of rectangular form, its length was one and one-half times the width, largely because this was considered best for the movement of traffic and holding fiestas. Variations of size were permitted from a minimum of two hundred by three hundred feet to three hundred by eight hundred feet. An ideal standard plaza was considered to measure four hundred by six hundred feet. The corners of the plaza were to face the four principal winds, and arcades were to be built on the streets adjacent to the plaza so that merchants would have a place to sell their wares.[14]

Four principal streets, one radiating from the middle of each side, were run at right angles from the plaza, while two more were joined at each corner. Other streets were arranged in gridiron, or checkerboard, fashion throughout the remainder of the town. Smaller plazas were placed here and there as needed. Important buildings were also located within the community. The cathedral in coastal towns was in a prominent place where it could be seen from the ocean and also serve as a center of defense. Lots for the cathedral, parish church, monastery, *casas reales* (royal council), and *cabildo*, customhouse, and arsenal were allocated first, and hospitals were established in suitable, healthful places. Cathedrals in inland towns were not placed on the plaza, but at some distance from it and preferably on an elevation so that they could be seen readily from all points in or near the settlement. Furthermore, towns should be built on the northern banks of navigable rivers where possible, and all trades causing filth and nauseous odors should be on the opposite side downriver from the settlement.[15]

After the ecclesiastical and royal lots were assigned, settlers were to draw lots for building sites (*solares*). Beyond these a common plot (*ejido*) was provided for the future growth of the settlement and the common use of settlers for recreation and pasturage of livestock. Farm lands were then assigned each settler, with as many such lots as there were building lots in the town. The remaining land in the grant was reserved for the crown. Merchant shops and temporary houses were built first, while settlers set up tents or built huts for temporary residences. Then they were to construct a palisade or ditch around the plaza for defense against Indian attack. Settlers were to plant seeds they had brought with them and begin breeding cattle immediately. Subsequently, they could build their permanent houses with strong foundations and walls, rooms exposed to southerly and northerly winds for health purposes, and corrals for work animals. Buildings were of one style, to enhance the beauty of the town, and they were arranged uniformly so that they could serve as a defense against invaders. Settlers were to avoid all contact with the nearby Indians while constructing the town because it was supposed that the settlement itself would serve as an object of wonderment for the natives.[16]

The "Laws of the Indies," particularly the fourth and seventh books of the second volume, also provided extensive instructions for the establishment and regulation of civil settlements. In fact, they included the earlier laws of Philip II and added others. No person could on his own initiative make discoveries, go on expeditions, or found new settlements without first obtaining a royal license. Violators would lose all of their material possessions and were subject to the death penalty. Viceroys, *audiencias* (district governing bodies as well as courts), and governors of kingdoms already discovered and pacified, however, were granted the right to issue such licenses as needed in their jurisdictions.[17] Reminiscent of Philip II's original instructions are the provisions that towns be established only on vacant lands or those permitted by nearby Indians; instructions for laying out plazas, streets, and building lots; and suggested topographical sites for settlements.[18] Having selected a site, the governor would specify whether the settlement was to be a *ciudad*, *villa*, or *lugar* (small place). However, the authority to grant the first two titles was held only by the Royal Council of the Indies in Sevilla, Spain, since each community was granted its own coat of arms for use on pennants, flags, standards, and seals as a reward for its loyal service to the crown.[19] Colonizers were instructed to establish communities only in regions considered useful for commerce or defense; they were not to locate the new settlements too close to rivers that might flood.[20]

Once authorized to establish a town and having selected its location, governors were instructed to reserve certain sections for royal and ecclesiastical building lots, a commons, and the *dehesa,* or common pasture land. The remainder was divided into four parts, one for the founder of the community and the other three for the settlers' agricultural lands.[21] Then the building lots and agricultural lands were divided among the new settlers, using the system of *peonías* and *caballerías* for measurement. A *peonía* was a house lot measuring fifty by one hundred feet, while a *caballería* was twice the length and width of a *peonía* and included five times as large an agricultural plot.[22] Settlers were obligated to build homes, live in them with their families, and begin the cultivation of their lands as well as the raising of livestock. Possession of such lands had to be taken within three months following the grant, and the settler had to live on, work, and improve the land for a total of four continuous years before he gained full title to it. Thereafter he could sell either the land or his home. Failure to carry out the terms of this agreement resulted in a fine and loss of the grant itself.[23] Plazas were laid out in locations and with dimensions specified earlier by Philip II, except that the maximum size was increased to 530 by 800 feet.[24]

Settlers were closely regulated by these laws. They were not to build their houses within three hundred paces (*pasos*) of the walls for the defense of the settlement, nor were they to build permanent homes at all until the first crops had been sown.[25] Single residents were encouraged to marry if they were of age and otherwise qualified.[26] Gambling and gambling houses were prohibited. Vagabonds could not live in either Spanish or Indian settlements. In fact, they were forced to work whether they were Spaniards, mixed bloods, or others; failure to do so resulted in their being sent to the Philippines, Chile, or "other parts" of the Spanish kingdoms. All gypsies were to be expelled from the Indies. Negroes and mulattoes were declared free and had to pay tribute to the king. All blacks who did not have jobs were to work in the mines, and free Negroes were prohibited from working for Indians. Negroes could not walk through city streets at night and were forbidden to carry arms at any time, while *mestizos* (mixed bloods) might do so only if they possessed a license.[27]

In return for their services, frontier settlers were always granted certain privileges, such as exemption from paying the *alcabala* (an excise tax, or one paid when goods changed hands) for a period of twenty years. Neither were they required to pay the *almojarifazgo* (an export-import duty) for a period of ten years. People in mining districts were required to pay only one-tenth of their profits instead of the normal *quinto real* (royal fifth). Settlers were allowed to carry arms for defense, and community leaders along with their children were declared *hijosdalgo* (*hidalgos,* or members of the lesser aristocracy), with all honors and privileges of such titles extended to them as though they resided in Spain. Sons of original *vecinos* were permitted to inherit the positions, titles, responsibilities, and privileges of their parents.[28]

With the promulgation of the "Instructions for the Establishment of the New Villa of Pitic in Sonora," approved by the king in 1789, regulations concerning civil communities in northern New Spain not only were updated but were made more realistic in light of actual frontier experience. The twenty-four paragraphs of this document outlined procedures for the foundation of frontier *villas*. The full title of the document included the statement that it was not only for Pitic but for "other Projected Villas to Be Established in This General Commandancy" and showed the continuing nature of the instructions. Indeed, the establishment of Pitic (present Hermosillo) was to serve as a model for later *villas*. In fact, this legislation did serve as a standard for the foundation of settlements in Texas and Alta California, although these towns were not exact copies of the earlier one in Sonora.[29]

According to the new rules, the governor of a province could decide whether to designate the new settlement a *ciudad, villa,* or *lugar,* along with selecting a proper name.[30] *Villas* were granted four leagues of land, either square or rectangular in form, and as soon as there were thirty heads of families the people could elect their own *cabildo,* or town council. Commissioners were appointed at the outset to survey and mark the land, then distribute it to the settlers of the community. Spaniards and Indians who settled the *villa* were to share in common the pastures, woods, water rights, fishing, hunting, stone quarries, and fruit trees outside the four-square-league limit of the *villa.*[31] A town plan showing the location of public buildings, house lots, and symmetrical arrangement of streets was to be drawn up in advance, that for Pitic being made by Don Manuel Mascaró.[32] The size of building lots, unlike that in early legislation, was not fixed. The commissioner was authorized to grant a whole, half, quarter, or eighth of a block, according to the size of a man's family or the quantity of his material possessions.[33]

Initial settlers were to draw lots for assignment of lands within the *villa.* Beyond the limits of the settlement itself commons were laid out in all directions for recreation, pasturage of stock, and future distribution to new settlers. Agricultural plots were assigned to settlers, who had to start cultivation and build a house within two years of the date of the grant. Each settler was allotted three plots. Lands were granted in the name of the king and were intended to be forever, descending by right of inheritance. However, settlers were obligated to keep arms and mounts for the defense of the *villa,* and they were required to live on their grants for at least four years. During this time they could not alienate, mortgage, transfer, or sell their lands. They had to cultivate their plots and at least begin the construction of permanent homes or lose their assigned properties. Absolute title to their allotment was permitted at the end of this four-year probationary period. Even after they had obtained title, they were not permitted to sell their property to any ecclesiastical body or individual who, it was feared, might hold it in mortmain.[34]

Villas and *pueblos* became the principal civil settlements on the frontier. They served as centers of farming and trade.[35] Seldom were all existing laws pertaining to such communities applied, mainly because they were impractical, and distances, isolation, and peculiar problems made it necessary to modify the regulations to meet existing conditions. San Agustín, Florida, had an irregular grid plan for its streets with flush house fronts and abundant areas in the rear for gardens, patios, and confinement of stock.[36] San Fernando de Béxar (modern San Antonio, Texas) was first a *pueblo*, then a *villa*, and finally a *ciudad*. It had a grid of rectangular blocks neatly arranged around a central plaza, on which were located a church and royal buildings. But the houses were a mixture of stone, mud, and wood, all poorly constructed, according to Fray Juan Agustín de Morfi, who visited the settlement in 1777.[37] Santa Fé, New Mexico, was described a year earlier by Fray Francisco Atanasio Domínguez as a *villa* of small *ranchos* (small privately owned subsistence farms, or ranches) at various distances from one another and having no central plan. There was a semblance of streets in the *villa*, but no orderly row or blocks of houses.[38] When it was established in 1781, the *pueblo* of Los Angeles in Alta California had a plaza two hundred feet wide by three hundred feet long and house lots measuring sixty by one hundred and twenty feet.[39]

These civil settlements were not the only communities on the frontier where Spanish-speaking people resided. Jesuit and Franciscan missions, military presidios, *haciendas* usually exceeding 2,500 acres in size (few of these were ever established in that part of New Spain now within the southwestern United States), and *ranchos* (both of stockfarming and agricultural nature) existed in almost all of the ten provinces considered in this book. Mining districts (*reales de minas*) abounded in such provinces as Nueva Vizcaya and Sonora, but were scarce in New Mexico and Texas. They were usually controlled by a small group of well-to-do miners and offered little opportunity for the individual prospector except as an employee of the great silver-producing families.[40] The large majority of the settlers in all ten provinces lived in civil settlements such as the *ciudad, villa, pueblo,* and *población* described in the following chapters.

Before turning to the study of these communities and their inhabitants, something should be said about social history, population analysis, and the nature of Spanish society in New Spain.

Social history, as defined by one prominent Latin American historian at a recent professional meeting, deals with "the informal, the unarticulated, the daily and ordinary manifestations of human existence."[41] Although it uses conventional sources such as manuscripts, documents, and political/economic studies, it depends heavily upon notarial records, land titles, litigations, estate papers,[42] and census returns. In any demographic study census returns are helpful in determining the status of society at a particular point in history or over a period of years. A noted scholar of demographic studies pointed out recently that "a census is almost always the best source of demographic information . . . [and that censuses should] always be taken as more reliable sources for demographic study than registers of vital events. . . ."[43] With their limitations of comprehensiveness, accuracy, duplication, nonstandard preparation procedures, and recognizable errors, the censuses for New Spain, especially after the middle of the eighteenth century, along with ecclesiastical records of baptisms, marriages, and wills provide valuable insights into the study of Spanish frontier society. So do contemporary reports, diaries, and letters of Spanish officials who visited various parts of the frontier.

Sherburne F. Cook and Woodrow Borah, distinguished professors of the University of California, Berkeley, have become the leading experts of our time on the population history of New Spain. Their recent work is concerned primarily with the people of central New Spain and only in a peripheral way with those of the northern frontier.[44] Nevertheless, their comments and evaluation of sources and definitions can be applied to the experience of Spanish settlers in the northern areas. On the general subject of "historical demography," Cook and Borah note that it is a piecing together of records and circumstances before the expanded censuses began in the year 1890 for the United States.[45] They further note that eighteenth century records show a "movement toward fuller and more accurate keeping and reporting of vital statistics," and in particular that the northward advances in New Spain "provide another series of courts and records which are extraordinarily useful for historico-demographic study."[46] The present work follows the lines suggested by Cook and Borah. It endeavors to piece together the story of the Spanish-speaking people in the civil settlements of the frontier using whatever records are available, particularly the census returns from the last half of the eighteenth century through the first quarter of the nineteenth.

Although there were scattered census listings of families and statistical summaries earlier, the first comprehensive, systematic returns appear after 1776, and particularly in the period 1780–1800. King Carlos III issued a *cédula* (decree) from San Lorenzo in Spain on November 10, 1776, instructing viceroys to prepare and send forward *padrones* (censuses) with information on numbers of people, social classes, races, sex, and marital status for their jurisdictions. These were prepared subsequently on an irregular basis (supposedly they were to be completed yearly) in every parish and are considered "remarkably careful listings of all persons within a parish, with division by household. . . ."[47] A careful family-by-family analysis of these *padrones* for New

Mexico, Texas, Nuevo Santander, Nueva Vizcaya, Alta California, and Sonora reveals that this is indeed true.

Local and regional censuses also provide information on the numbers of people within each community, their ages, sex, sizes of families, servants integrated into certain families, settlement patterns, occupations, classes of settlers, origins of some, and population growth or decline over a period of years. For example, a *vecino* in the census returns is obviously the head of a particular household. The entire family unit may consist of several families living together; a modern anthropologist or sociologist would immediately recognize the existence of the extended rather than the nuclear family. Therefore, the term *vecino* can never be used to give a definite figure for the total population. A *vecino* was a citizen or resident of a town, a householder,[48] and might be any sort of person—male, female, married or single, a widow or widower, a growing young man, or older person without family.

Similarly, the term *castas* could be employed to mean those of Negro, part Negro, or other colored descent. In a broader sense it might mean all mixed bloods. Whatever the case, the *gente de razón* meant all non-Indians or those practicing a European culture,[49] including the *castas* (castes, or mixed bloods). This was especially true by the latter eighteenth century all over the frontier. Finally, it should be noted that the average number of persons in each household exceeded the ratio of four to one,[50] including not only fathers, mothers, and direct offspring, but all sorts of relatives and servants as well. In fact, the census listings reveal that the ratio was more nearly five to one.

Lyle N. McAlister, of the University of Florida, noted that colonial society in New Spain was *not* static and ponderously stable as it has often been reported to be. It was really characterized by "continuous though unspectacular change," and it possessed qualities of flexibility, openness in the social stratification of people, and a certain degree of upward and downward mobility.[51] Furthermore, according to McAlister, social change in the eighteenth century was accelerated by population growth, miscegenation, expansion of the areas of settlement, economic development, an increase in wealth, administrative and military reforms, and the infiltration of egalitarian doctrines from abroad.[52] Although he did not visit the northern provinces while he was in New Spain in 1803 and 1804, Alexander von Humboldt also reported some of these characteristics in the societal composition of New Spain. He listed the total population of the intendency of Durango as 159,700, enough to rank it ninth among the twelve intendencies; he reported Sonora to have 121,000 persons.[53] Humboldt added that the area of settlement had reached Nueva Vizcaya and had "increased there with rapidity everywhere," replacing a nation of shepherds with one of "agricultural colonists."[54] He reported that in 1794 the population of Durango was 122,866; Sonora, 93,396; New Mexico, 30,953; and the two Californias, 12,666. Together with his low estimate of 13,000 for Coahuila, the total number of people on the frontiers of New Spain reached 272,881, or about 6 per cent of New Spain's total of 4,483,559 people in 1794.[55] Thus, McAlister's observations concerning the spread of the population and its growth in numbers are borne out by Humboldt's figures.

In addition, Humboldt noted that the population of New Spain was composed of three basic classes: whites, or Europeans, Indians, and castes.[56] Although there was hatred between *gachupines* (Spaniards born in Spain) and *criollos* (Creoles—Spaniards born in America), he emphasized that in the north "almost all of the inhabitants . . . pretend[ed] to be of pure European extraction."[57] According to Humboldt, the *gente de razón* was composed of all whites, mestizos, and mulattoes.[58] Professor McAlister agrees, emphasizing that for official purposes there were indeed only three primary classes: Spaniards, castes, and Indians.[59] Furthermore, there were all sorts of arbitrary names and internal divisions within each of these groups,[60] classifications being influenced greatly by cultural factors. A "Spaniard" could include a person of pure Spanish origin as well as a mixed blood of legitimate descent, free from the supposed taint of Negro blood, and persons who "lived like Spaniards."[61] Census returns from the northern provinces bear out many of McAlister's contentions. They show that class definition meant very little except for the existence of many local terms of hazy meaning, usually employed solely for reporting purposes. Some census listings go no further with class breakdowns than the simple listing of the three primary classes.

Few persons on the frontier might have been considered upper class by modern standards. Presidial captains, missionaries, government officials, and perhaps a few professionals would belong in this group, judged according to contemporary standards. Artisans, farmers, merchants, and owners of small *ranchos* might have been considered middle class. Laborers, servants, and vagabonds—mostly castes and Indians—might have made up the lower class, which was nowhere near the majority of the population.[62] However, it should be remembered that such a system of upper, middle, and lower class really did not exist during the colonial period; this categorization is only a modern effort to classify the people to facilitate comprehension of the nature of colonial society.

Spanish expansion northward followed four general lines of advance—a northeastern thrust, a north central expansion, a northwestern advance, and finally one into a Pacific frontier.[63] It was a gradual movement extending over the course of nearly three centuries. It was not a uniform advance, nor did it take place in all provinces at once. Thus Sinaloa was settled before Sonora and Pimería Alta, Baja California before Alta California, Coahuila and Nuevo León before Texas, and southern Nueva Vizcaya before the northern portion of that province. Only New Mexico and Nuevo Santander are exceptions. New

Mexico was settled in a great leap northward after 1598, bypassing an unsettled region in between. Nuevo Santander was not colonized until the mideighteenth century, a southward step from Texas, although most of its settlers came from Nuevo León and Coahuila.

We now turn to this expansion of the northern frontier in the four major thrusts mentioned earlier. Our emphasis is upon the civil settlement, particularly the founding of such communities, the settlers themselves, and the principal characteristics depicting their way of life.

PART I
The Northeastern Frontier

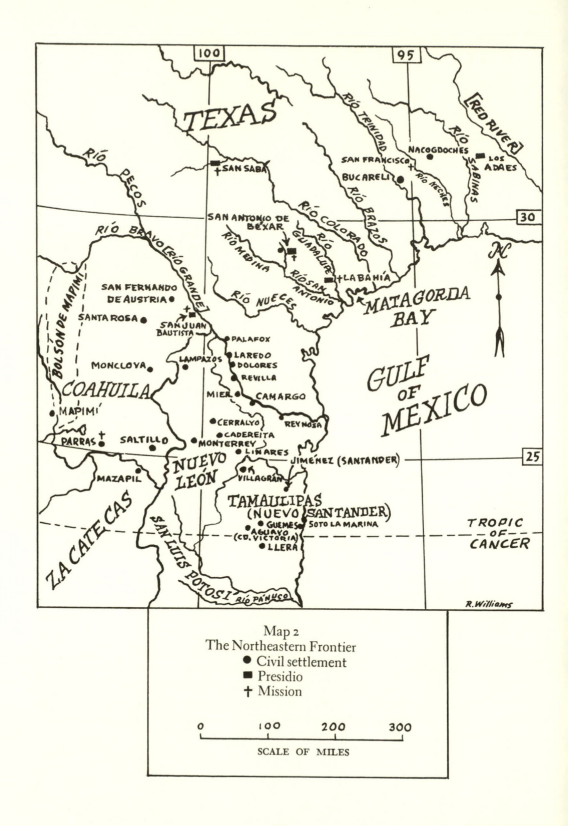

Map 2
The Northeastern Frontier
● Civil settlement
■ Presidio
✝ Mission

```
0          100        200        300
SCALE  OF  MILES
```

Introduction

Spanish expansion northward from Mexico City made an early thrust to the Río Pánuco when Nuño de Guzmán founded a settlement there at the end of the first decade following the conquest of Mexico. However, the frontier halted and a gradual process of expansion from Nueva Vizcaya and the Central Plateau became the norm. From the last quarter of the sixteenth century to the end of Spanish administration over the Viceroyalty of New Spain, portions of this northeastern frontier of Spanish civil settlement remained in a primitive and sparsely settled state.

Four provinces eventually constituted this region. Not all were initially settled at the same time, but by the late eighteenth century each had some civilian settlers. Coahuila (sometimes called Nueva Estremadura after the province in Spain) and Nuevo León (officially titled Nuevo Reino de León) led the way with the establishment of civil communities before the end of the sixteenth century. Coahuila, in fact, then included only the region north of the twenty-sixth parallel and between the Bolsón de Mapimí on the west and the Río Grande del Norte on the east. It did not contain the Saltillo-Parras communities until they were transferred from Nueva Vizcaya after 1787. Nuevo León, east of Coahuila, was thought to have extended from the Río Pánuco northward originally for two hundred leagues (about 2.6 miles were equivalent to a league). It was settled about the same time as Saltillo and Parras, but a century earlier than the northern communities of Coahuila. Spanish Texas was not permanently occupied until the first quarter of the eighteenth century. It was much smaller than the present state of Texas. The Río Medina separated it from Coahuila and the Río Nueces from Nuevo Santander (present Tamaulipas). These were its southwestern boundaries, while the eastern one extended to the Arroyo Hondo east of the Sabine River. Spanish Texas was the most sparsely inhabited province on New Spain's northeastern frontier. Finally, the province of Nuevo Santander, the last occupied by civilian settlers in this direction, extended from the Río Pánuco northward to the Río Nueces and was bounded on the west by the province of Nuevo León. It, therefore, included settlements on both banks of the Río Grande, some of which are located today within the state of Texas.

Here was probably the most confused collection of states or provinces on

New Spain's entire northern frontier. Geographic uncertainties and overlapping boundaries blurred jurisdictional matters and led to frequent disputes as well as lack of unity in Spanish efforts to colonize the region. The desire to convert resisting Indian nations; the need to protect missionaries, civilian settlers, and dispersed ranches against marauding Indians; and the necessity of defending Spanish possessions against foreign incursions all promoted the settlement of this frontier. Furthermore, the economic necessity of feeding and maintaining the local population, as well as supplying food, clothing, and equipment for miners on the Central Plateau and inhabitants of Mexico City contributed to the emphasis on livestock raising in all four provinces, particularly in Coahuila and Texas.

Early settlement took place from two centers, Nueva Vizcaya and the Río Pánuco. Saltillo and Parras were prosperous Spanish civil communities before the end of the sixteenth century. Properly speaking, they were part of Nueva Vizcaya, not Coahuila, but they are considered part of Coahuila here for a variety of reasons. First, they were physically separated by vast distances from the rest of the province. Second, they were ultimately attached to Coahuilan territory toward the end of the eighteenth century and are part of that state today. Third, their economy and social development were more closely associated with the northeastern frontier than with the north central one. Other civil establishments in Coahuila proper were not made until the end of the seventeenth century, and the great ranching period in the province did not occur until the following century. Nuevo León, on the other hand, was settled primarily from the Río Pánuco in the last two decades of the sixteenth century and therefore is technically the oldest province on the northeastern frontier. Spanish Texas and Nuevo Santander, the youngest frontier provinces of this region, were settled mostly for defensive purposes in the eighteenth century.

Four settlements became the foci of Spanish civil settlers on this frontier before the end of the seventeenth century: Saltillo, Parras, and Monclova, in present Coahuila, along with Monterrey in Nuevo León. These were supplemented by numerous smaller settlements, *haciendas*, and *ranchos*. San Antonio de Béxar, La Bahía, and Nacogdoches were the centers of Spanish settlement in Texas by the end of the eighteenth century. Nuevo Santander had many scattered communities at the same time, but there were two principal centers of population: the interior of the province and along the lower Río Grande. Franciscan missions and military presidios were also present in all of these provinces at one time or another.

Spanish society on the northeastern frontier was largely pastoral and agricultural by nature. There was some mining activity in Coahuila and Nuevo León, but it was sporadic and of little importance when compared to that of Nueva Vizcaya. Large *haciendas* devoted to the raising of livestock dominated the scene in Coahuila, although there were also many *ranchos*. Parras became a center for the production of fine wines in demand throughout New Spain during colonial times. Wheat, corn, vegetables, garden crops, and some fruit were also grown.

The people who settled this region mostly migrated from other frontier communities rather than from Europe directly, although Texas came to have a considerable number of foreign immigrants by the early nineteenth century, some from the Canary Islands. The large majority of the population, however, was made up of Spaniards born in New Spain (called Creoles elsewhere but commonly *españoles* on the frontier) and various mixed bloods, known collectively as mestizos, or castes. These people, along with the Tlaxcaltecan Indians imported from the city-state of Tlaxcala in central Mexico at the end of the sixteenth century, constituted the *gente de razón* or *gente decente*, both meaning civilized people. Living on this remote frontier, they developed a culture that blended their European background with their environment, adapting to circumstances in each area of settlement.

Two of the provinces—Coahuila and Texas—became involved in the Mexican War for Independence in the period from 1810 to 1821. Coahuila's conservatively oriented large landowners and military caudillos (political leaders) played an important role in the capture of Father Miguel de Hidalgo as he fled northward in 1811. Texas was the most rebellious, unstable, and tumult-ridden of all of New Spain's northern provinces during the war for independence. The presence of large numbers of foreigners, especially in East Texas, filibustering expeditions from the United States, and remoteness from the centers of Spanish political and military control insured that Texas was a *tierra de guerra* (battleground) throughout most of the decade preceding the establishment of Mexican independence from Spain in 1821.

1. Coahuila and Nuevo León

The province of Coahuila, or Reino de la Nueva Estremadura as it was first known, was not settled until the last quarter of the seventeenth century. It consisted then of the region north of the twenty-sixth parallel extending to the Río Grande on the north and northeast, the Bolsón de Mapimí on the west, and the older province of Nuevo León on the east. However, the settlements of Saltillo and Parras, as well as their adjacent communities, were founded a century earlier as part of the settlement of Nueva Vizcaya. After 1787 they became part of the colonial province of Coahuila and today are included within that modern Mexican state. Furthermore, Coahuila's northern boundary in the late colonial era was no longer limited to the Río Grande, but extended beyond it to the Río Medina in the present state of Texas.[1]

Santiago de Saltillo, a small community of soldier-settlers, was founded in 1575 by one Alberto del Canto. At first there were only some twenty residents, who pursued agricultural, pastoral, and military lives. Apparently these earliest inhabitants came from other regions in Nueva Vizcaya. By 1592 this small Spanish village had been elevated to the official status of a *villa* with the right to have its own *ayuntamiento* (town council). For some years it was the most northerly of Spanish settlements on the northeastern frontier.[2] Thus it was the first Spanish settlement in the present state of Coahuila and for some sixteen years the only one.

On September 13, 1591, the Indian *pueblo* of San Esteban de Nueva Tlaxcala was officially established in the immediate vicinity of Santiago de Saltillo, but as an entirely separate community.[3] This settlement was part of a plan developed by Viceroy Luis de Velasco II and Don Gregorio Nanciaceno, chief of the Tlaxcalan Republic in central New Spain, to move four hundred married men and their families to the northern frontier. These Tlaxcaltecans were to settle at various designated points to induce the wild northern Indian nations to accept the Spaniards and to establish pacified communities. King Philip II of Spain approved the *capitulación* (contract or agreement) with the Tlaxcaltecans, granting them extensive privileges in return for their resettlement. They were considered *caballeros* and *hidalgos* (gentlemen and noblemen), permitted to use the title of *Don* before their given names, authorized to ride horses, and allowed to carry firearms. Furthermore, they were exempt from all tribute and personal services. They were given land to work and also had their own council, from which all Spaniards and other Indians were excluded.[4]

Four hundred Indian families totaling 1,591 persons left Tlaxcala in the summer of 1591 and were escorted northward by royal soldiers. They founded colonies at Tlaxcalilla, San Luis Potosí, San Miguel Mexquitic, Colotlá, San Jerónimo del Agua Hedionda, El Venado, and finally the northernmost at San Esteban de Nueva Tlaxcala, the only community within the region of this work.[5]

Eighty of these families established the second civil settlement of Coahuila. In September, 1591, lots were set aside for the construction of a church, convent, and public buildings. Indians were given possession of their own commons, and plots were allocated for residences and farm lands. The people of nearby Saltillo seem to have appreciated the presence of the Tlaxcaltecans, and they evidently reached a tacit agreement whereby Spaniards raised livestock, supplied artisans, and performed the role of merchants, while the Tlaxcaltecans raised agricultural products. No *encomiendas* (grants of Indians for labor purposes made to deserving Spanish settlers) were permitted in this region, contrary to the practice elsewhere in New Spain at this time.[6]

Of utmost importance is the role played by this community of Nueva Tlaxcala. Not only did it consolidate Spanish control over a sparsely settled region and serve as an attraction to the Chichimeca tribes to seek peace, but it became the "mother colony" for other settlements on the northern frontier. From Nueva Tlaxcala Indian settlers spread to Santa María de las Parras by 1598, and later to Monclova, San Juan Bautista, Texas, and Nuevo Santander, especially after 1746. Although there was no formal colonization plan for New Mexico, it is evident that some Tlaxcaltecans even reached that distant province before the Pueblo Indian revolt of 1680, and a few may have returned with the Spanish settlers after the reconquest.[7]

The third civil settlement in this vicinity developed around the Jesuit mission of Santa María de las Parras after its establishment in 1594. In a very fertile valley well adapted to agriculture, especially vineyards, a small community of Spaniards and Tlaxcaltecans was founded before 1598. Francisco de Urdiñola and others established *haciendas* between Parras and Saltillo, thus beginning a prosperous livestock industry which was to dominate the entire province by the end of the eighteenth century.[8]

Before the end of the sixteenth century, then, Spaniards and friendly Tlaxcaltecans had established civil communities in the region south of the twenty-sixth parallel. Saltillo, Nueva Tlaxcala, and Parras had become the first permanent settlements of what is today the state of Coahuila.

Occupation of the northern portion took place a century later. It was prompted by fear of French incursions on Spain's northern frontier, especially with the reported possibility that France might colonize the region about the time of the expedition led by Jean Cavalier, sieur de La Salle.

The *villa* and presidio of Santiago de Monclova was officially established on
August 12, 1689, although there had been earlier missions and a presidio near
the site selected.[9] A proposal to found a *villa* at a place called Santiago de
Paredes had failed to materialize.[10] Captain Alonso de León, the newly appointed governor of the province, made efforts as early as 1687 to locate soldier-
settlers at Monclova.[11] In August, 1689, after his expedition to Bahía del
Espíritu Santo in Texas, he succeeded in establishing the *villa* with twenty-nine
vecinos. He set aside plots for a parish church, designated house lots for the
original settlers, and ordered that all of them had to have their homes built
by January 1, 1690. De León prohibited the settlers from moving elsewhere at a
penalty of four months' hard labor with the presidial forces of the frontier. By
December, he had established the civil government of the *villa* with its council
and other public officials.[12] Monclova became the first capital of the province
of Coahuila and was the principal base for the later settlement of Texas.[13]

Gradually during the eighteenth century other Spanish settlements were
founded, but the population did not grow markedly until the end of the period.
Furthermore, there was little mining development to serve as an inducement
for rapid population growth, Indian raids deterred the dispersal of the people,
and land was held by a few *hacendados* (large land-owners), thus limiting the
availability of suitable farming lands for individuals. Yet some progress was
made. *Haciendas*, *ranchos*, and a few missionary settlements were maintained,
although the Franciscans apparently had little success in converting the nomadic, rebellious Indian tribes of the region. Viceroy Juan Francisco de
Güemes y Horcasitas, the first conde de Revilla Gigedo, ordered the founding
of a *villa* at San Fernando de Austria in 1749, although it did not occur until
February 1, 1753.[14] This community was to support and protect settlers at San
Juan Bautista and Presidio del Río Grande, the origins of which extended back
to the year 1699, when the mission was established on the south bank of the
Río Grande.[15] At San Fernando de Austria the governor of Coahuila established a plaza with a church, a building for the council, and a jail fronting on
the plaza. He divided the land and waters among the original settlers and provided twenty-one soldiers to protect them.[16] Two other *villas* were founded,
largely for defensive reasons, at San Pedro de Gigedo in 1753, and at San Carlos
in 1774.[17]

When Nicolás de Lafora visited the province of Coahuila in 1767 as part of
the general inspection of the northern frontier led by the Marqués de Rubí,
there were only three small *villas*—Santiago de Monclova, San Fernando de
Austria, and San Pedro de Gigedo—along with two *pueblos* and "several
haciendas."[18] Half a century later there were only twelve Spanish communities
even after the southern region had been transferred from Nueva Vizcaya to
Coahuila. By the early nineteenth century the largest and most prosperous communities were Monclova, Saltillo, Parras, and Santa Rosa.[19]

The ruins of San José de Palafox, Coahuila, now on the north bank of the Río Grande in Texas. *Courtesy University of Texas Archives.*

About 1810 the governor of Coahuila, Don Antonio Cordero y Bustamente, founded the *villa* of San José de Palafox, named for a Spanish patriot who had led the fight against Napoleon Bonaparte during the French invasion of Spain.[20] Colonized by Coahuilan settlers, it was on the north bank of the Río Grande, midway between San Juan Bautista and the ranching community of Laredo in the province of Nuevo Santander.[21] Settlers were allotted land fronting on the river and extending inland; they were exempt from paying taxes on their crops and livestock for a period of five years.[22] Officially founded on April 27, 1810, the *villa* was dependent upon the presidio of Río Grande near the mission of San Juan Bautista.[23] By 1814 there were thirty-six families residing at San José de Palafox, and an official census of June 6, 1815, showed sixty-two families consisting of 203 persons.[24] A census for December, 1816, revealed that there were 277 people in the *villa*,[25] but it was abandoned after 1818 when hostile Indians, thought to be Comanches, drove off the settlers' stock, set fire to the community, and broke up the settlement.[26]

Population growth of the two regions—Saltillo and Parras being one and Coahuila proper centered around Monclova the other—was relatively slow until the end of the eighteenth century. Until 1689 the only Spanish settlers lived in the southern portion of Coahuila, largely in the Parras-Saltillo district. Thereafter for a century this southern region and the northern one grew almost equally, but each hardly exceeded ten thousand people by 1785. After the two regions were combined, the population of Coahuila grew more rapidly.

Very little growth of population at Santiago de Saltillo may be noted in the first thirty years of its existence. Approximately twenty soldier-settlers made up the original complement of the town in 1575. Alonso de la Mota y Escobar noted in the early seventeenth century that there were between fifteen and twenty Spanish *vecinos* there. Francisco de Urdiñola's census for Nueva Vizcaya in 1604 revealed that there were only twenty-two *vecinos* in the whole jurisdiction of Saltillo, with eighteen of them in the *villa* itself, three at Parras, and one at the *hacienda* of Los Patos. Of this total, eleven were married, eight were bachelors, and three were widowers.[27] This would seem to indicate that the total population of the entire jurisdiction was somewhere near sixty-five people.

By 1677 there were fifty-four *vecinos* capable of bearing arms at Saltillo, and the number of residents approached three hundred persons in all. Fifteen years later there were 147 families at Parras, of which 87 were Tlaxcaltecan Indians, 21 were *coyotes naturales del país* (native mixed bloods), 18 were Indians married to Tlaxcaltecans, 8 were pacified Chichimecas, 7 were Toboso Indians, 3 were mestizos, and 3 were *coyotes* married to Tlaxcaltecans. At Nueva Tlaxcala in 1703 there were 179 families, including 600 soldiers.[28] From these scanty figures at widely separated intervals, it may be estimated that the total population of this southern district at the turn of the eighteenth century may have been as much as 1,900 persons. At the same time, Monclova, the only Spanish community of the northern district, had 29 heads of families, or approximately 125 to 150 people, after its founding in 1689.[29] A total of two thousand people is, therefore, a reasonable estimate for the Spanish, mixed-blood, and pacified-Indian population of Coahuila at the beginning of the eighteenth century.

Fortunately, in that century population figures for Coahuila are more numerous and detailed. Hubert Howe Bancroft reported four hundred families, of which one hundred and fifty were Spaniards, living at Monclova in 1744 to 1745,[30] but the first fairly detailed statistics are in the report of Bishop Pedro Tamarón y Romeral and the bishop of Guadalajara's observations in the early 1760s. Bishop Tamarón found 3,813 Spanish and mestizo settlers living at Parras alone in 1761, along with 1,559 Indians.[31] The bishop of Guadalajara's figures for the province of Coahuila (not including Saltillo and Parras) showed a total of 1,072 families, composed of 4,568 persons, or 4.26 persons per family, in the province.[32] These figures undoubtedly included friendly Indians, Spaniards, and mixed bloods. Nicolás de Lafora noted that Santiago de Monclova alone had a company of 36 soldiers in addition to 100 families of settlers; he also emphasized that there were 777 families of Spaniards, mestizos, and mulattoes in the entire province during his visit there in 1767.[33] Using the approximate number of persons per family developed by Sherburne Cook and Woodrow Borah from the bishop of Guadalajara's figures, this would indicate that there were some 3,310 persons in frontier Coahuila by the decade of the 1760s.

By 1780 this population had nearly doubled, increasing to 8,319 persons.[34] Of course, these figures still did not include the statistics for Parras and Saltillo to the south. They did include the new *villa* of San Fernando de Austria with its seventy-six families in 1778 when Fray Juan Agustín de Morfi visited it and wrote in his diary that it was nothing more than a miserable village with houses of sticks and roofs of grass.[35]

The census returns for Saltillo in 1785 show a total of 8,174 people residing in the *villa* and suburbs, the Indian *pueblo* of San Esteban de Nueva Tlaxcala, thirteen nearby *haciendas*, and one *rancho*. Unfortunately, there are no statistics for Parras shown. Nevertheless, there were 2,709 people (men, women, boys, girls, and slaves of both sexes) living in the *villa* of Saltillo and its *barrios* (wards or districts), while there were 2,510 people at Nueva Tlaxcala. These two settlements comprised nearly sixty-five per cent of the total population in this region.[36]

On July 27, 1787, the southern jurisdictions of Parras and Saltillo were annexed to the province of Coahuila. At that time there were 8,244 people living in the Saltillo region and 7,028 in Parras and its environs. The total of 15,272 people[37] was much higher than the 8,319 people indicated seven years earlier for Coahuila proper. Thus, there were approximately twenty-five thousand people living in the combined province of Coahuila by the end of the 1780s.

The *Tribunal del Consulado* estimated the population at 40,000 in 1803; by 1810 it had risen to 42,397, consisting of 12,285 Spaniards, 17,215 castes, and 12,437 pacified Indians. Saltillo had about twelve thousand people, Parras ten thousand, and Monclova six thousand at the beginning of the second decade of the nineteenth century.[38] By 1810, then, there were 30,500 Spaniards and mestizos in Coahuila, representing seventy-two per cent of the total population. Although figures are lacking for the year 1821, when Spain lost control over the province, it would be safe to estimate that the population of Coahuila may have approached forty-five thousand people in all.

Very few of the settlers on this frontier were actually "Spaniards" in the sense that they had come to Coahuila from Spain or other parts of Europe. Luis Navarro García notes that only a few dozen families in Coahuila and Texas really originated in Spain.[39] Nor was there any mass migration to the province after the initial settlements were founded. "Spaniards"—actually those of a Spanish culture or heritage born elsewhere in New Spain and called Creoles elsewhere—and various castes came to constitute the vast majority of the population. Negroid strains were represented by the presence of mulattoes. Mixed bloods intermarried among themselves and with various Indian groups, further complicating the nature of what has been supposed to be an ordered, static society. The presence of large numbers of Tlaxcaltecans in Coahuila was an unusual factor in the settlement and over-all composition of society in this particular province. At Parras, for example, there were Spanish mixtures, Tlaxcaltecans, some Tobosos, and some pacified Chichimecas, all living in close proximity. Frontier society was, therefore, much more flexible than in central New Spain. In Coahuila, as elsewhere on the frontier, class distinction often became more pronounced in theory than in fact.

Also, these were working people, doing their own manual labor. They raised crops and livestock, became tradesmen and merchants, and performed the dual role of soldiers and settlers, particularly in the early years of Spanish occupation. The large majority, however, farmed and raised livestock. This is readily apparent as early as 1604, when Urdiñola's census showed that the twenty-two *vecinos* in Saltillo and Parras possessed sixteen wheat and corn fields, ten stock-raising *estancias* (livestock ranches) for cattle and horses, and five herds of mules. Nine *vecinos* were employed entirely in raising crops and/or livestock, three were mule drivers or carters, three were government officials, five worked for others, one was a shoemaker, and another was a tailor.[40]

Coahuila was not only more heavily populated than its neighboring province of Texas in the eighteenth century, but it was agriculturally and pastorally more productive. Its livestock industry, in fact, may have been one of the origins of the later one in Texas. Furthermore, Coahuila had developed an important industry with the production of wine and *aguardiente* (brandy), both export products much in demand from Mexico City to Chihuahua.

Perhaps the distinguishing institution in the development of frontier Coahuila was the *hacienda*. It was prevalent by the early seventeenth century in the region between Saltillo and Parras, and a century later visitors noted that it dominated the province. Although in both sectors, its influence was most pronounced in the southern region. The *hacienda* was not just a landholding system, for it affected the social and economic affairs of the entire province as well as political matters. Indeed, it influenced the entire life style of the settlers.

Private land grants (*mercedes*) in northern New Spain were made by the governors of the provinces to individual applicants after payment of specified fees. These allotments were in the name of the king and were in perpetuity so long as the owner actually occupied and used his land. This was the only requirement to maintain clear title. Two types of grants were made for raising livestock. The *sitio de ganado mayor* was intended for cattle, horses, or mules, and a single such allotment usually was in the shape of a square, 5,000 *varas* (one *vara* equaled about 33 inches) on a side and encompassing an area of approximately 4,428 acres. The *sitio de ganado menor* was intended for sheep and goats, and it was necessarily smaller, being 3,333 *varas* on a side and encompassing about 1,920 acres. Often two or three such *sitios* were granted to an applicant, who could supplement these holdings by purchasing those of others. No limit was placed upon how much land a single individual might possess.[41] Such holdings differed from those in the civil settlements, since the government did not furnish the owner livestock, seed, or any other form of financial aid. He had to supply these himself.

In Coahuila land grants to individuals were made in the early period of settlement of Saltillo and Parras. Francisco de Urdiñola developed *haciendas* in the vicinity of Los Patos by the early seventeenth century; they were subsequently incorporated into the extensive holdings of the Marqués de San Miguel de Aguayo. Fray Juan Agustín de Morfi described three enormous *latifundios* (large landholdings), each consisting of numerous *haciendas* under one owner, during his visit to the Saltillo-Parras region in the late 1770s. The largest belonged to the Marqués de San Miguel de Aguayo. It covered the area from Mapimí in the west to Saltillo in the east, a distance of almost 300 kilometers, or approximately 185 miles. From north to south it extended from a point just south of Monclova to Mazapil, a distance of perhaps 225 kilometers, or about 140 miles. Of irregular boundaries, the entire *latifundio* amounted to more than 26,000 square miles. Morfi estimated that the marqués possessed about one-half of the total land then comprising the province of Coahuila. Two other *latifundios* in the province belonged respectively to the College of the Jesuits of Parras to the west of the property held by the marqués and to the *cura* (parish priest) José Miguel Sánchez Navarro to the north and east of Monclova.[42]

The Sánchez Navarro holdings provide an interesting example of how such large *latifundios* came into being. Although Juan Sánchez Navarro was among the original founders of the *villa* of Saltillo in 1575, the landed estate and power of the family did not really develop until sometime after 1755, when José Miguel Sánchez Navarro became *cura* of Monclova.[43] He was really more of an entrepreneur than a religious official. Land and commerce were the sources of his wealth. After purchasing a store in Monclova, he invested the profits from that enterprise in land. He then purchased sheep at local prices and sold them at great profit in central New Spain, especially in Mexico City. With this capital he bought additional land and purchased goods to improve the stock of his store, which had a value of 20,000 pesos by 1775. Two years later he had achieved a virtual monopoly over commerce in Monclova. José Miguel Sánchez Navarro also directed his personal attention to the administration of his *haciendas* and his store; he was not an absentee landlord.[44] By the time of his death in 1821, he possessed over 800,000 acres of land, 80,000 head of sheep, and left an estate valued at 250,000 pesos for his nephew.[45] Thereafter his successors expanded the land holdings to encompass seventeen *haciendas* and over sixteen million acres, including those of the Marquesado de San Miguel de Aguayo, which were purchased for a price of 326,000 pesos in 1840.[46]

Not only were the size and economic power of the *latifundios* important, but their political influence was often great. The Marqués de San Miguel de Aguayo virtually underwrote the permanent occupation of Spanish Texas after 1719. José Sánchez Navarro and his nephew both helped to organize the counterrevolution for the royalist cause in Coahuila that ended with the capture of Father Hidalgo near Bazán in 1811. Ignacio Elizondo, the principal conspirator who engineered the capture of the priest, owed ten thousand pesos to José Miguel.[47]

Haciendas in Coahuila were also sizable communities of Spaniards, mestizos, and Indians. In 1785 the census of the *villa* of Saltillo revealed that there were thirteen *haciendas* in the vicinity of that civil settlement, ranging in size from 24 to 481 inhabitants, with a total of 2,822, which amounted to nearly thirty-five per cent of the population for the entire district.[48]

Yet livestock raising was not the only important economic activity in Coahuila. Agriculture was also significant, and *hacienda* grants were made for farming. Wheat was cultivated, and that of the Saltillo region was considered of such excellent quality that it was exported to Texas, Nuevo León, Nuevo Santander, and mining districts in Nueva Vizcaya. Corn, beans, *piñones*, fruits, peppers, melons, squash, and cotton were raised in the province. Mota y Escobar noted that some of these crops were among the finest in all of New Spain; he particularly emphasized the *haciendas* near Saltillo and those between the *villa* and Parras where both livestock and crops such as wheat and corn were raised in great quantity.[49]

Of particular importance was the cultivation of vineyards near Parras and the production of fine wines and brandy. Although royal regulations prohibited the local manufacture of wines, Coahuila not only developed the industry extensively but even exported its products elsewhere in New Spain. The vines themselves probably were introduced into the Parras district shortly after 1597 by the Jesuits. Since Spaniards were accustomed to drinking wine regularly and much was consumed in the celebration of the Catholic Mass, there was a steadily increasing demand. Parras enjoyed a virtual monopoly on the production of wine until the latter part of the eighteenth century, when it had to compete with the fine wines produced in the Paso del Norte district of New Mexico. Although much wine was imported from Spain, *vino de Parras* was always cheaper and more easily obtainable than *vino de Castilla*.[50]

Although wine was produced on many *haciendas* in Coahuila, considered best was that of San Lorenzo de Abajo, the largest producer in the region. Some

900 barrels of *aguardiente* (brandy) and 250 of wines were being shipped from Parras to the Zacatecas mines alone by the early eighteenth century.[51] Exports of these two products evidently reached Mexico City and other parts of New Spain. All wines were sold over the counter by the bottle, not by the drink. There were no saloons on the Coahuilan-Nueva Vizcayan frontier.[52]

Important minerals were exploited in neither Coahuila nor Texas during the colonial period.[53] The economy of the northeastern frontier was founded on the principle that the provinces there should produce staple goods which would be exchanged for manufactured articles. Yet the production of wines and fine textile goods indicated that some manufacturing existed. By the eighteenth century there were approximately forty looms in Saltillo for the weaving of cotton products; Tlaxcaltecans had sixty looms at Nueva Tlaxcala for woolen goods, and it is evident that their women produced fine tablecloths and *serapes* (woolen shawls).[54]

Spanish social and cultural life in frontier Coahuila was very different from that in the principal centers of the Viceroyalty of New Spain.[55] Here, as elsewhere on the distant northern frontier, the "Spaniards had to work the land with their own hands to maintain and clothe themselves."[56] Their constant need for work precluded the development of an extensive cultural life.

Education remained rudimentary, and public education was almost non-existent. Only in Saltillo and Monterrey, the capital of Nuevo León, were there sparse endowments to maintain primary teachers (*maestros de primeras letras*) by the end of the eighteenth century. Schools in the *villas* and presidios were maintained here, as in the other northern provinces, by voluntary contributions from heads of families and funds of the presidial companies. Reading, writing, simple arithmetic, and the Christian doctrine were taught in these schools. In addition, there were schools at individual *haciendas*, where the sons of the owners and a few others could be given this same fundamental education. Higher learning did not exist in the province. To obtain it students could continue their studies elsewhere in New Spain, especially in Guadalajara, or in Europe. Two of Coahuila's most highly educated leaders of the early nineteenth century, Dr. Miguel Ramos Arizpe and Juan Antonio de la Fuente, followed this procedure to obtain their advanced education.[57]

By the beginning of the eighteenth century Saltillo became the emporium for the northeastern provinces. Its central location on the route from Nueva Vizcaya to Nuevo León, Texas, and Nuevo Santander insured that it would play an important commercial role after these provinces were settled. Furthermore, annual fairs in September encouraged trade, as they did in Acapulco and Jalapa. Merchants from other parts of New Spain came to sell cloth, wine, and olive oil from Spain; silk, porcelain, and perfume from Asia; and products from other regions of the viceroyalty. In exchange, Coahuiltecans offered the wheat and *serapes* of Saltillo, wine from Parras, wool and skins from Nuevo León and Coahuila, and beef on the hoof for the subsistence of miners in other sectors of the viceroyalty.[58]

Great public holidays were celebrated with fiestas, such as the annual fair and another in honor of Santo Cristo de la Capilla, a patron saint whose celebration occurred in Saltillo every August 6. Bullfights, horse races, cockfights, and traditional dances performed mostly by the Tlaxcaltecan Indians marked these occasions. Santa Cristo de la Capilla was a wooden religious image, originally purchased by a Basque at the fair in Jalapa in 1607 and brought to Saltillo. The settlers there built a parish church with a transept on its north side to house the patron saint; there the figure remained until 1762, when it was transferred to a new chapel.[59] This image and the concept of a patron saint for a civil community are reminiscent of New Mexico's *La Conquistadora*, described in Chapter 6.

Frontier society in Coahuila throughout the period of Spanish occupation and settlement was dominated by the agricultural and commercial nature of its people. Most of them were native born. They lived in a region where they were forced to work for themselves and to improvise on their own with very little outside assistance and control. Living in sparsely populated urban centers and scattered *haciendas*, they faced daily problems of survival against diseases such as smallpox, frequent incursions against them by marauding Indians, and climatic variations that could easily imperil their crops. They developed a fondness for controlling their own affairs and were little disturbed during the independence period by the uprisings taking place elsewhere in New Spain. Except for the capture of Father Hidalgo, Coahuila experienced little activity toward the establishment of independence until presented with a *fait accompli* when Agustín de Iturbide took over Mexico in 1821. On July 4 of that year, Coahuila proclaimed its loyalty to the new Mexican nation.[60] Until that time the large landholders, including the Sánchez Navarro family, had maintained political control of the province on behalf of the royalist cause.[61]

Nuevo Reino de León was settled earlier than its neighboring province of Coahuila, if we overlook the region around Saltillo and Parras, originally part of Nueva Vizcaya. Herbert E. Bolton correctly observed that Nuevo León was "the oldest of the provinces of the northeastern frontier."[62] Furthermore, its initial motivation for settlement—both mining interest and the search for Indian slaves—and its occupation from the Río Pánuco area provide contrasts to nearby Coahuila.

The first settlements of Nuevo León proved to be only temporary communities, ending in disaster for the province's founder and first governor, Luis de Carbajal y de la Cueva. After a preliminary entry into the region north of the Río Pánuco, Carbajal obtained a royal *capitulación* (contract) on June 14, 1579, authorizing him to explore, pacify, and populate an enormous region in the form of a square measuring two hundred leagues on each side. This region north of the Río Pánuco was named Nuevo Reino de León and Carbajal appointed its governor and captain general, with two *encomiendas* (grants of Indians, for labor) assigned him. According to the agreement, he was to recruit two hundred persons in Spain and other parts of New Spain to accompany him.[63]

Five years elapsed before Carbajal undertook the actual occupation of his assigned province. Recruitment was slow as efforts were made to assemble a strong force because the region was inhabited by many wild Indian nations. By 1584, Carbajal had enlisted over one hundred soldier-settlers, mostly in central New Spain and the Tampico region; these he combined with ten or twelve *vecinos* and their families from Saltillo.[64] With this force he entered Nuevo León and before the end of 1584 founded its first civil communities at León (now Cerralvo) and San Luis (present Monterrey), the latter being designated both a *villa* and capital of the province.[65] However, the search for silver and slaves contributed to the collapse of these early settlements. One detracted from the agricultural development of the province; the other began a terrible race war between Indians and Spaniards.[66] Toward the end of the decade, Carbajal, who was of Portuguese Jewish extraction, was arrested, charged with heresy as a "new Christian," and condemned by the Inquisition.[67] As its founder perished, the province of Nuevo León seemed destined for complete abandonment in the last few years of the sixteenth century.

Fortunately, Captain Diego de Montemayor, a resident of Saltillo, was appointed lieutenant governor and captain general of Nuevo León. He brought settlers from his region and collected the remnants of Carbajal's initial colonists; with this group he founded the city of Nuestra Señora de Monterrey on September 20, 1596.[68] The first permanent civil settlement in Nuevo León, Monterrey was established on the site of San Luis, not León, as is occasionally alleged.[69] It was named for the viceroy of New Spain, Don Gaspar de Zuñiga y Acevedo, Conde de Monterrey, and the city's limits were roughly described as extending fifteen leagues in all directions from the central plaza.[70]

Most of Nuevo León's population was concentrated in and around Monterrey for the next thirty years; no new civil settlement was made until Martín de Zavala became governor in 1625. He was instructed to found two new *villas* within four years, one with forty married settlers and another with twenty,[71] a provision he only partially complied with because of problems he encountered in pacifying resisting Indian nations. Within the next thirty-eight years he granted *encomiendas* to deserving livestock raisers, distributed lands, operated silver mines, and founded two new civil settlements. The first, San Gregorio de Cerralvo, was established on September 4, 1626, on the site of the depopulated *villa* of León, originally founded in 1584 by Carbajal.[72] Only one mulatto and his family had survived there from the time of the original settlement.[73] Eleven years later, on August 13, 1637, Zavala founded the *villa* of San Juan Bautista de Cadereita,[74] a second civil community as specified in his contract.

In the early eighteenth century the number of civil settlements increased with the founding of a new *villa* at San Felipe de Linares and other smaller communities. Linares was established on January 29, 1712, primarily to thwart Indian invasions of Nuevo León. It was elevated to the status of a *ciudad* in 1777.[75] By 1740 the governor of the province reported that there were three *villas* (Linares, Cerralvo, and Cadereita), the *ciudad* and capital of Monterrey, and nineteen other smaller establishments where Spaniards, mestizos, mulattoes, and pacified Indians resided.[76] Nicolás de Lafora noted in his visit of 1767 that Nuevo León had its capital, four *villas* (the fourth being La Punta de Lampazos, a new town having both some Cuervo Indians and forty families of civilized people), four mining towns, and "several" *haciendas*.[77]

In 1810 the province had two *ciudades* (Monterrey and Linares), four *villas*, sixteen *pueblos*, four mining districts, and twenty-three *haciendas*.[78] Miguel Ramos de Arizpe, reporting to the Spanish Cortes in 1811, observed that Nuevo León had two cities, five *villas* three mining districts, three villages, and eight valley settlements.[79] It is obvious from these designations that mining was uncertain and communities were undergoing changes in nomenclature. From its intitial civil settlement at Nuestra Señora de Monterrey in 1596, Nuevo León had by the last decade of Spanish administration added twenty other communities, including one *ciudad*, five *villas*, and fourteen smaller places.

The settlers themselves had greatly increased in number, particularly in the latter half of the eighteenth century and the first two decades of the nineteenth. In its early years Nuevo León was not only greatly underpopulated but in real danger of abandonment. Carbajal had brought between one hundred and fifty and two hundred persons with him in the early 1580s,[80] but there were hardly any of them left when Diego de Montemayor established Monterrey in 1596. He brought with him from Saltillo a total of forty people—nine married men, nine married women, three men without families, one Indian named Domingo Manuel, fourteen boys, and four girls.[81] Until a *villa* was established in Cerralvo in 1626, most of the province's settlers lived near Monterrey, and there were only a handful of them. Mota y Escobar reported in the early 1600s that Monterrey was only a "small place" (*lugarcito*) of Spaniards, there being only twenty *vecinos* in all,[82] or perhaps about one hundred persons.

Figures for the population of the province are more detailed after 1740. In that year Governor Joseph Fernández de Jáuregui Urrutía listed the settlements along with their population statistics, separating Spaniards, mestizos, mulattoes, and pacified Indians. He showed a total of 1,426 persons living in the province, all but 360 of whom were Spaniards and mixed bloods. By that time Monterrey had a population of 232; Cadereita, 101; Cerralvo, 96 (including 13 soldiers); and Linares, 41 (including seven Indians).[83] Twenty years later, in

1760, the bishop of Guadalajara reported that Nuevo León had 3,287 families, comprising 20,523 persons, or 6.24 persons per family, the largest such ratio in the provinces he observed.[84] Nicolás de Lafora noted in 1767 that there were 3,050 Spanish, mestizo, and mulatto families in the entire province,[85] or approximately eighteen thousand people in all. The city and eight *haciendas* of Monterrey alone had five hundred families, including a company of three officers, one sergeant, and twenty-two soldiers.[86]

The first census of the province, completed in 1803 by Governor Simón de Herrera y Leyva, showed a total population of 43,739,[87] a figure remarkably close to that of 43,681 reported in 1810. Of this total, for the latter year, 27,412 were considered Spaniards; 13,838, mixed bloods; and 2,431, Indians.[88] It is interesting to note that of the total inhabitants in the province during 1810, ninety-four per cent were Spaniards and mixed bloods. It is possible that Nuevo León had a population of fifty thousand when Spain relinquished the province in 1821.

From the earliest occupation of Nuevo León, it is evident that most of the settlers came from the Río Pánuco region and the Saltillo district of what was then Nueva Vizcaya. Coahuila probably supplied some settlers by the latter half of the eighteenth century, but census reports do not always provide information on population origins. Class distinctions seem to have meant very little except for statistical purposes. That there were various racial mixtures, including large numbers of Negro derivation, is evident from the reports of officials, who separated mestizos and mulattoes until the early nineteenth century. Nor were Indians kept apart from Spaniards and mixed bloods. Governor Herrera's census of 1803 reported settlements composed of Spaniards and Indians living together, with the exception of two communities inhabited by Tlaxcaltecan Indians, who had immigrated probably from Coahuila.[89]

Settlers were employed in various pursuits, but farming, stock raising, and mining predominated. However, almost all the people were in a miserable state.[90] Soldiers were among the settlers; citizen militias were tried with little apparent success as early as the first decades of the eighteenth century.[91] The people, whatever their occupation, had to cut the wood and grass for their first homes and "had to maintain themselves."[92] Some became great landowners, but most worked for their own subsistence.

The lifestyle of the settlers was dominated by their work and by the nature of their agrarian economy. Land was allocated both in large tracts and in small plots—both garden and building sites—as it was in Coahuila. Diego de Montemayor designated plots for farming and livestock raising upon founding Monterrey. The *hacienda* system was established early in Nuevo León, as it was in the neighboring province of Coahuila. Some *haciendas* were quite large and their range of products was extensive. According to Nicolás de Lafora, that of Mamulique had a population of five hundred persons; on it were raised mules, cattle, and horses, in addition to the growing of corn and sugar cane.[93] By 1767 the province's principal crops were corn, beans, fruits, and sugar cane, but raising horses and cattle was considered the major industry. In 1811, Miguel Ramos de Arizpe reported that there were over ten thousand head of cattle, an equal number of horses, more than two hundred and forty thousand sheep, and six hundred thousand goats raised in the province.[94] Mining remained of secondary and only sporadic importance. Lafora noted that Nuevo León had only low-grade silver ores, the best being at El Vallecito, but most mines were either neglected or abandoned.[95]

Education and living conditions remained primitive throughout the colonial period. The first public schools were not established until 1803, and then only in Monterrey. On July 4 of that year two schools opened—one for boys, taught by Pedro Crisólogo de Melo, and another for girls, instructed by his sister, Doña Josefa. Both schools were conducted in the house of José Manuel Sánchez Navarro. Instruction was gratuitous and obligatory; books were furnished free of charge to those students who could not afford them.[96] Although some homes, such as that of Sánchez Navarro, were large enough to accommodate these two schools, the fact is that most of the houses throughout the province were simple, small, and crudely constructed. The *jacal* (hut) of grass and palisaded sticks or logs seems to have been the basic structure from the beginning of settlement throughout the colonial period. The absence of adobe, especially in the early years, is characteristic of building in Nuevo León.[97]

Living on this remote frontier, the settlers of Nuevo León experienced many everyday problems that led to periods of decline and occasionally threatened abandonment of the province. Communications and transportation were crude at best. Except for contacts with Coahuila and with Texas after its settlement in the eighteenth century, there was little contact with the rest of New Spain. Not until 1762 did Monterrey have regular monthly mail service with Mexico City, using soldiers as postal couriers.[98] Smallpox epidemics, such as the one in 1646 that killed over five hundred whites and Indians,[99] were a constant threat. So, too, were floods, which caused the communities of Monterrey and Cadereita to be moved in 1612 and 1763, respectively, to new locations.[100] Furthermore, there were chronic conflicts of jurisdiction with Nueva Vizcaya which hindered progress in Nuevo León.[101]

Finally, there was the ever-present problem of Indian attack. From the outset of Spanish occupation there was trouble between the settlers and the wild Indians of the region. Slave-hunting expeditions as early as the 1580s were followed by harsh treatment of natives and their forced resettlement into *congregaciones* (Indian villages) by Governor Martín de Zavala. As a result, settlers experienced nearly two centuries of warfare, and many of the later civil communities were established expressly to defend the province against Indian incursions. Not until the last decades of the eighteenth century did this conflict abate.[102]

With all these problems in addition to their daily work, it is no wonder that settlers had little if any time for diversions. Yet there were some. On December 12, 1748, for example, the people of Nuevo León began an annual celebration of the cult of the Virgin of Guadalupe, an occasion marked by vespers, a sermon, lighting of wax candles, processions, and public festivities.[103] It is also probable that other celebrations in honor of saints and religious holidays were held, in addition to the usual preoccupation with gambling, horse racing, and cockfighting so apparent elsewhere on the frontier.

Nuevo León, like its neighboring province of Coahuila, was essentially an agrarian and pastoral frontier. Its settlers were mostly *paisanos*, but they accomplished the permanent occupation and gradual development of the province over the course of two and one-quarter centuries of continuous settlement. Their presence not only furnished a nucleus of Spaniards and mixed bloods in the development of the present population but also served as a source of colonists for the later settlement of northern Coahuila, Texas, and Nuevo Santander.

2. Texas

Spaniards explored Texas relatively early, but colonized it late. About the time Hernán Cortés began the conquest of México, Alonso de Pineda saw the Texas coastline as part of his lengthy Caribbean voyage. Scarcely more than a decade later Alvar Núñez Cabeza de Vaca and his companions began a long trek across southern Texas. Other explorations followed over the course of a century and a half. A missionary venture in East Texas in the late 1600s failed, and actual colonization of the region did not take place until the period from 1716 to 1731. Thus, Texas was one of the last provinces on the northern frontier occupied by Spanish settlers. It was, however, the second of four provinces within the present limits of the southwestern United States occupied by Spain, being preceded only by New Mexico.

The province of Texas—or Nueva Filipinas, as it was often called by Spaniards—was nowhere near the geographical equivalent of the present state. The Spanish province extended roughly from the Coahuilan boundary along the Río Medina and the Nuevo Santander line at the Río Nueces in southern Texas to the Sabine River in eastern Texas and the Red River in the north. These irregular boundaries meant that the Spanish province was approximately one-half the size of the present state. It did not include the settlements of the Paso del Norte region belonging to New Mexico, or those of the lower Río Grande which belonged to Nuevo Santander for the entire colonial period.

Spanish civilian settlers were concentrated at three points in Texas throughout the century of Spain's occupation. Béxar, present San Antonio, was the focal point, where the largest number of settlers lived. Its civilian settlement dates formally from the official establishment of the *villa* of San Fernando de Béxar in 1731, but some colonists had already occupied the place thirteen years earlier. Other settlers collected at La Bahía del Espíritu Santo (near present Goliad), and in the East Texas region the scattered Spanish population was ultimately concentrated at Nacogdoches after its founding in 1779.

It should be emphasized that each of these centers of civilian settlement was in close association with the other institutions of the Spanish frontier, particularly the mission, presidio, and *rancho*. Béxar was a good example of a mixed community, consisting of a *villa*, presidio, and ultimately five missions, of which San Antonio de Valero (the Alamo) and San José y San Miguel de

Aguayo were the most famous. La Bahía too consisted of a mission, presidio, and congregated settlers nearby. East Texas had its presidio at Los Adaes in the early years, along with the unsuccessful Franciscan missions, but civilian settlement was scattered. Cattle ranches were also prevalent in Texas, although there were no *haciendas,* as there were in nearby Coahuila and Nuevo León. They contributed greatly to the spread of Spanish people, institutions, and culture.

Pineda's contact along the Texas coastline in 1519 was followed by various expeditions touching wildly diversified parts of the province. Cabeza de Vaca, Esteban (the Moorish slave who may have been a Negro, and therefore the first of his race to enter the region), and their two companions moved gradually across southern Texas from 1530 to 1536. Francisco Vásquez de Coronado crossed the Panhandle of West Texas in the early 1540s, while the survivors of Hernando de Soto's expedition, led by Luis de Moscoso, evidently entered East Texas at about the same time. However, in 1685, the region was still a *tierra despoblada* (unpopulated land).[1]

Spain's permanent occupation of Texas took place largely because of her fear that the French intended to colonize the region.[2] It is true that Franciscan missionaries, such as Fray Damián Masanet and Francisco Hidalgo, promoted the settlement of eastern Texas primarily to convert the Tejas Indians. Presidial soldiers were dispatched to protect the missionaries and civilian settlers; the colonists themselves were sent largely to consolidate Spain's control over the region, to raise crops and livestock to supply the nearby presidios, and to insure the continued occupation of the province. It is unlikely, however, that missionaries, soldiers, or settlers would have been there at all had Spain not been concerned with the threat of French occupation, especially from Louisiana prior to its cession to Spain in the Treaty of San Ildefonso in 1762. Later, Great Britain and the United States were the major threats.

Therefore, like Alta California in a later period, Texas was settled principally as a defensive measure. The proposed colony of Robert Cavalier, sieur de la Salle, on the Texas coast caused a flurry of activity among Spanish authorities, who finally ordered Alonso de León, the governor of the newly established province of Coahuila, to find the French colony and arrest its inhabitants. La Salle landed at Matagorda Bay in February, 1685, and established a primitive settlement at Fort Saint Louis on Garcitas Creek near present Vanderbilt, Texas, but his colony failed and La Salle was killed by his own men in a mutiny two years later.[3] Alonso de León led four expeditions from Monclova, Coahuila, in an attempt to locate this settlement, and fear of another such community led immediately to the establishment of the first Spaniards in the eastern part of Texas.

The initial effort to colonize Texas was a combined military-clerical venture in the period from 1690 to 1693. Governor Alonso de León and Fray Damián Masanet, a Franciscan from the Apostolic College of Querétaro, in 1690 led an expedition of over one hundred soldiers and six missionaries to East Texas, where they established the first mission at San Francisco de los Tejas near the present town of Weches.[4] It and other such crude missions failed to prosper. By 1693, they were in desperate straits. Father Masanet reported widespread hunger, sickness, and crop losses because of too much rain one year and not enough the following one. The Indians were decimated by a measles epidemic and they resisted conversion to Christian doctrine as well as baptism, saying that they had "another God."[5] Furthermore, he noted, the soldiers violated the Indian women and set a bad example for the neophytes to follow.[6] As a result, the Indians refused to come to the missions and further failed to provide the food supplies upon which the missionaries and presidials depended. Since there were no Spanish settlers in East Texas to raise crops, and since efforts to bring in two hundred Spaniards and Tlaxcaltecan Indians never got beyond the proposal stage,[7] Father Masanet urged reluctantly that the missions be abandoned. This request was approved, and on October 25, 1693, the missions were set afire and all the Spanish soldiers and missionaries returned to New Spain.[8] At this point, Texas was considered *"la tierra . . . tan mala que nadie la querría"* (the land [that was] so bad that nobody would want it).[9]

Three major colonizing expeditions in the period from 1716 to 1721 brought about the permanent occupation of Texas by the Spaniards. Renewed French expansionist activities in the Louisiana country and trade with the Indians of the Great Plains attracted the interest of Spanish officials in the reoccupation of Texas. Fray Francisco Hidalgo also was particularly interested in re-establishing the missions among the Tejas Indians of East Texas. Finally, an independent French trader named Louis Juchereau de Saint Denis traveled to Coahuila to promote the occupation of East Texas so that he might enjoy a monopoly over the province's early trade. In Monclova he met the governor, Domingo Ramón, and later married his daughter before undertaking the venture into Texas.

Governor Ramón and Saint Denis led an expedition of seventy-five persons, recruited in Saltillo and Monclova, into Texas by way of the mission San Juan Bautista on the Río Grande, from which they departed on April 27, 1716. In addition to the governor, who was also captain of the expedition, there were twenty-five mounted soldiers who had come to settle the country permanently. Three Frenchmen, including Saint Denis and his new wife, María Ramón, accompanied the expedition. Fray Francisco Hidalgo and eight other Franciscans also eventually joined the other members of this enterprise. Eight of the soldiers were married and brought families with them; their wives were the first women to colonize Texas. In addition to the eight married women, there were two boys, a small girl, a Negro named Juan Concepción, two mule drivers, ten helpers to control the stock and cart the freight of the expedition, and five Indians who served as guides and drivers of carts.[10]

The Ramón-Saint Denis expedition, seventy-five strong, reached East Texas and founded the mission of Nuestro Padre San Francisco de los Tejas on July 3, 1716. It was located just to the east of the Neches River, only a few miles north of the mission site of 1690. By the end of the year 1716, Spanish Texas consisted of a cluster of six missions and a small presidio on the Neches River,[11] but no other settlement existed anywhere in the entire province.

Having now established themselves hundreds of miles from the nearest Spanish settlement, at San Juan Bautista, these early soldier-settlers were in a precarious isolated position. The Marqués de Valero, viceroy of New Spain, therefore decided to establish a permanent settlement on the San Antonio River to serve as a halfway station between the East Texas settlements and San Juan Bautista. He appointed Martín de Alarcón governor of Coahuila on December 22, 1716, and entrusted him with the organization and leadership of a new expedition to Texas. Alarcón paid a token fee of 137 pesos for this appointment, but the royal treasury supplied him with 28,150 pesos plus an annual salary of 2,500 pesos (limited to one year only). According to his contract, he was to recruit fifty soldiers, who were to be paid 400 pesos each; an engineer, who would be paid 450 pesos; and a mason, blacksmith, and carpenter, each of whom would receive 400 pesos. Finally, Alarcón was to be paid 4,000 pesos outright to purchase supplies and necessary equipment for the Texas settlements.[12]

Governor Alarcón proceeded to Monclova, where he took charge of the government of Coahuila and began recruiting for the expedition. By September, 1717, he had enlisted thirty-five soldiers, including six with their families, a carpenter, and a mason. He received his final instructions in March of the following year, and on April 9, 1718, crossed the Río Grande with a total of seventy-two persons, including seven families. These were the first families of the San Antonio settlement, not the Canary Islanders, as is often stated. In addition, the Alarcón expedition had 548 horses, 6 droves of mules, and cattle, sheep, goats, and chickens to provide the first livestock for the province.[13]

The settlers reached the banks of the San Antonio River on April 25 and established their first mission at San Antonio de Valero (later called the Alamo), somewhat east of the river, on May 1, 1718. On May 5 these same people began work on a log fortification named San Antonio de Béxar, probably using "Béxar" after the district of that name in the province of Salamanca, Spain. It was, however, west of the San Antonio River, between it and San Pedro Creek, three-fourths of a league, or about two miles, from the mission. Although not yet officially designated a *villa*, this settlement was the original civil establishment of the San Antonio area.[14] Alarcón's expedition leading to the founding of a mission and presidio at San Antonio de Béxar ranks with the later expedition of the second Marqués de San Miguel de Aguayo in consolidating Spanish control over Texas.[15] It appears that the same Marqués de

Aguayo played a role in the Alarcón expedition by sending horses and cattle from his *haciendas* near Saltillo to the settlers.[16]

To counter the French threat from the newly established port of New Orleans and French expansion westward beyond the Mississippi River, Spain ordered the Marqués de San Miguel de Aguayo to lead an expedition to Texas to solidify Spanish control over the eastern part of the province. He was appointed governor of the province of Texas, or Nueva Filipinas; his expedition was supported in part by royal funds and in part from his own financial resources. Taking five hundred men along with some four thousand horses, six hundred head of cattle, nine hundred sheep, and eight hundred mules (largely to carry supplies), the marqués reached East Texas in late July, 1721, and in September began the construction of a presidio named Nuestra Señora del Pilar de los Adaes. It had a garrison of one hundred men, including twenty-eight with their families, and was located only some eighteen miles from the French post at Natchitoches. Los Adaes was the first capital of Texas and remained so until all Spaniards left East Texas in 1773 to move back to San Antonio, where the governor had actually resided since 1735.[17]

The Marqués de San Miguel de Aguayo not only founded the presidio of Los Adaes but re-established missions in East Texas. In the San Antonio area he moved the presidio to a stronger position, founded two missions, and left a garrison of fifty-three men to defend the region. In March, 1722, he established a presidio of ninety men and a mission at La Bahía del Espíritu Santo, thereafter moved twice but always located in the vicinity of the lower San Antonio River.[18] In all, on his departure, the marqués left ten missions, four presidios instead of the former two, and a total of two hundred and sixty-eight soldiers in the province. Indeed, it was this expedition more than any other that firmly established Spanish authority in Texas.[19]

At the conclusion of this colonizing expedition, the marqués recommended that civilian settlers be recruited elsewhere and moved to Texas to consolidate Spanish control over the province. He asked that two hundred families be obtained from Galicia, the Canary Islands, or perhaps Havana, and an equal number of Tlaxcaltecan Indians be recruited to occupy Spanish Texas in support of its presidios and missions. This suggestion was long debated and delayed by authorities in Spain; finally in 1729 the Council of the Indies and the king ordered that families be sent from the Canary Islands to establish the initial formal civil settlement in Texas.[20]

On March 27, 1730, the first ten families of *isleños* (islanders) left Santa Cruz, Tenerife, in the Canary Islands, and traveled via Havana, Cuba, to Vera Cruz, where they arrived on June 30. There were fifty-nine men, women, and children in this group, but two died in Vera Cruz and one child perished on the road to Cuautitlán, where the remainder arrived in August.[21] Because of marriages since their arrival, there were fifteen families, with a total of fifty-six persons, when the party straggled into Saltillo, exhausted, on January 29, 1731. There the viceroy supplied them eighty-six horses, seventy-seven mules, sixteen yokes of oxen, sixteen metates (grinding stones), and a plow, ax, and hoe for each family.[22] The expedition proceeded northward, reaching San Juan Bautista on the Río Grande, where one child died, and finally arrived at Béxar on March 9, 1731.[23]

These fifty-five civilian settlers formed the nucleus of the new community known as Villa de San Fernando de Béxar, but they were *not* the first settlers of the San Antonio area. Governor Alarcón's expedition of 1718 had originally established colonists in the district and there may have been as many as two hundred people living in the environs of the missions and presidio when the *isleños* arrived in 1731.[24]

The viceroy of New Spain, the Marqués de Casafuerte, on November 28, 1730, had earlier established the conditions and privileges under which the Villa de San Fernando was founded. Members of the fifteen families and their legitimate descendants were declared *hijos dalgo* (*hidalgos*, or landed nobles), with all honors pertaining to the title and to the knights of Castile. The governor was instructed to select the first officials of the settlement, who would then, in turn, appoint two *alcaldes ordinarios* (municipal officials) in this "first civil settlement in the province of Texas."[25] Before the departure from Cuautit-lán, a royal official had mustered the families, listing the members of each, their birthplaces, ages, material possessions, and items furnished them by the crown for their subsistence en route to and after arrival at Béxar. Clothing, tools, arms, horses, and an allotment of thirty pesos (four *reales* per diem for a period of sixty days) were provided from royal sources.[26]

Upon the arrival of these fifteen families and four unmarried males[27] in San Antonio de Béxar about eleven o'clock in the morning of March 9, 1731, the captain of the presidio mustered the *isleños* and inventoried their possessions. There were 115 horses left of the original 146 furnished them at various places on their journey, some being exhausted and abandoned along the route. All of the families were lodged in the "comfortable houses of the presidio" until they could build their own homes, an arrangement which, according to the presidial captain, imposed hardship upon the soldiers already there.[28] Thus, from the beginning a feeling of hostility arose between the original settlers of the *villa* and the new arrivals from the Canary Islands.

By 1731, then, there were families of Canary Islanders combined with the earlier soldier-settlers in the civil community of San Fernando de Béxar; nearby was the presidio of San Antonio de Béxar, along with the five missions, four of which were administered by the Franciscan College of Querétaro and one by the Franciscan College of Zacatecas.[29] These settlements and the presidial-missionary establishments of La Bahía and East Texas constituted the only points of Spanish occupation in the province of Texas.

Although there were presidial and missionary settlements in Texas in the half century after the founding of San Fernando de Béxar, they were usually of a temporary nature and involved civilian settlers only as members of soldiers' families or as an adjunct to the principal community. An example of this type of settlement was the mission for Apaches founded at San Sabá (near present Menard) in 1757 to 1758; more than two hundred women and children of presidial families lived there, but none remained by the latter 1760s.[30] Another important mission, presidio, and adjacent civil establishment was located at San Juan Bautista, founded originally as a mission in 1699 and supplemented by a presidio in 1701. However, it was attached to Coahuila for administrative purposes, not Texas. It did serve as a gateway to Spanish Texas and was on the main line of communications from Coahuila to San Antonio and East Texas.[31] Father Juan Agustín de Morfi, chaplain for the new *comandante-general* of the Provincias Internas del Norte, Teodoro de Croix, visited the settlement of San Juan Bautista in December, 1777. He reported that it was a dirty little village where some eight hundred indolent people lived in squalor raising sheep, cattle, goats, oxen, mares, mules, burros, horses, swine, and not nearly enough crops to support themselves.[32] Six years after Mexico established her independence from Spain in 1821, this settlement was renamed Villa de Guerrero.[33] A third establishment was made in 1756 on the Trinity River, where Spaniards temporarily built a presidio and sent missionaries among the Orcoquisac Indians, but a projected civil community of Canary Islanders and Tlaxcaltecan Indians never materialized there. When the Marqués de Rubí visited the presidio in 1767 as part of his general inspection of the military conditions on the northern frontier, he considered it "useless" and it was suppressed by the Royal Regulations of 1772.[34]

Of greater importance to any study of civil settlements on the Texas frontier is the succession of events in East Texas leading to the founding of the *pueblo* of Nacogdoches in 1779. By the early 1770s, Spanish settlers in that region lived in widely scattered communities and throughout the countryside in the general vicinty of the Franciscan missions and the presidio of Los Adaes. Spain's acquisition of the Louisiana country from France in 1762, her preoccupation with Indian troubles elsewhere in the interior, and the general reorganization of the frontier led to the official decision to abandon East Texas. The Marqués de Rubí found only about thirty Spanish families living on scattered ranches near Los Adaes in 1767, and he regarded this frontier as one of Spain's "imaginary possessions."[35]

As a result of these impressions, the Royal Regulations of 1772 included a provision for the removal of all settlers in East Texas to San Antonio. The *comandante-inspector*, Hugo Oconor, was instructed to carry out this provision, but the governor, Barón de Ripperdá, generally opposed removal. Nevertheless, he complied with the orders of his superiors. He personally went to Los Adaes, where he reported prosperity and a population of more than five hundred people—Spanish, French, Indian, Negro, and all sorts of mixtures. Using one Antonio Gil Ybarbo, owner of a stock ranch near the Sabine River, as an intermediary, Governor Ripperdá instructed the people to be ready to march within five days to Béxar. Most of the inhabitants did not want to go, and they asked for an extension of time, a request which Ripperdá granted. It was reported that thirty-five persons fled to the woods when the march finally began on June 25, 1773, and others had to be driven from their homes to join the entourage. Unprepared for such a long journey, the people abandoned their stock and corn fields. Suffering was severe. Some refugees became too ill to travel, others dropped out, many proceeded on foot because of the scarcity of riding animals, some sold their rosaries to obtain food, and all of them ran into flooding rivers en route. The number of deaths might have been higher had not Governor Ripperdá previously arranged to have some supplies delivered at the Brazos River. One hundred sixty-seven families of Adaesanos reached Béxar on September 26, after an ordeal of three months, but thirty people died within the first three months after their arrival.[36]

Once in San Antonio, these new settlers were not pleased with their new home. They were allowed to choose dwelling sites from the vacant lands surrounding the *villa* of San Fernando de Béxar, but most refused to do so. Instead, some seventy-six families, consisting of two hundred and two persons, presented a petition to the governor only eight days after their arrival asking permission to return to East Texas. They made the excuse that they did not want to infringe upon the rights of the citizens already at Béxar and that furthermore they were already bankrupt and could not dig the necessary irrigation ditch to begin farming. They agreed, however, to bear the expenses incurred in a return to their homeland. Gil Ybarbo, their accepted leader, wanted to be near his ranch. Fortunately, their request was received by a sympathetic governor. Ripperdá wanted them to return to East Texas, where they could strengthen the defense of his province from the new menace of advancing British settlement.[37] He endorsed their petition, and the viceroy of New Spain approved it over the objections of Oconor. Arrangements were left to Governor Ripperdá.[38]

Back to East Texas trudged a happier group of colonists in the fall of 1774. Some seventy families, led by Gil Ybarbo and an escort of soldiers from the presidio of San Antonio, blazed a trail to the new settlement of Nuestra Señora del Pilar de Bucareli on the right bank of the Trinity River. Gil Ybarbo, captain of the newly organized militia and chief justice of the *pueblo*, supplied settlers with some of his own tools, oxen, and mules to get them started again. He brought nails and other ironwork from the abandoned presidio of Los Adaes and officially established Bucareli in September, 1774. The town was laid out with a plaza, and wooden houses or huts (*jacales*) were erected around it. A wooden stockade enclosed the settlement. One year later the community had many *jacales*, twenty homes of hewn wood, a wooden church, a guardhouse, and stocks in the center of the plaza. Although there were 347 people in the settlement by 1777, it did not survive. Crop failures, floods, a smallpox epidemic, contraband trade with foreigners and Indians, and especially the frequent incursions of the warlike Comanches brought about the abandonment of Bucareli. Between January 1 and April 30, 1779, some five hundred people moved from it to found the *pueblo* of Nacogdoches.[39] *Comandante-general* Teodoro de Croix approved their move in October, 1779, and appointed Gil Ybarbo as lieutenant-governor of the province of Texas at an annual salary of five hundred pesos.[40]

This episode has been given extended treatment here for many reasons. First, it shows the civil origins of the permanent settlement of Spaniards and other *gente de razón* at Nacogdoches in eastern Texas. Second, it illustrates the establishment of another civil community in Spanish Texas to supplement the one at Béxar and the collection of settlers already near the mission and presidio of La Bahía. Third, both Bucareli and Nacogdoches were true civil settlements, having nothing to do with missions and presidios. Finally, these communities clearly demonstrate that the local populace did have some voice in frontier New Spain in proposing and carrying out the establishment of settlements. It should be noted that the colonists in East Texas actually moved to Nacogdoches *before* they obtained royal approval. This was an unusual circumstance on the frontier, but it indicates that such a practice was at least possible.

The necessity of establishing civilian settlers in frontier regions such as Texas was realized by such viceroys as the Marqués de Altamira, who wrote in 1752 that civil settlement was a necessary complement to the mission and the presidio. He emphasized that confusion of administration and failure of colonies

will be true two hundred years hence unless there be established there *settlements of Spaniards and civilized people to protect, restrain, and make respectable the barbarous Indians* who may be newly congregated, providing them a living example of civilized life, application to labor, and to the faith. Without this they will always retain their original primitiveness, inherited for many centuries, as happens in the missions of the Río Grande, of [eastern] Texas, and all the rest where there are no Spanish settlements, for the Indians there, after having been congregated fifty years or more, return to the woods at will.[41]

Interestingly enough, it did not take large numbers of settlers to hold the frontier against marauding Indians and foreign threats. Spanish Texas was indeed a "remote and dangerous frontier, huge in area, vague in definition, and, to the end, meager in development."[42] Its population remained concentrated at three points: San Antonio, or San Fernando de Béxar, La Bahía, and Nacogdoches, the last having little social cohesion or stability because of the presence of so many refugees, adventurers, and drifters from foreign soil.[43]

Domingo Ramón's initial seventy-five persons and Alarcón's seventy-two were the only settlers, save for a few missionaries, by 1720 in the entire province of Texas. The Marqués de San Miguel de Aguayo not only strengthened the defenses of the province in the next two years but brought with him hundreds of permanent settlers who gave the Spaniards some strength in numbers in the early years. By the time the Canary Island colonists—fifty-five in all—reached San Antonio, there were already a couple of hundred persons residing there, and there was perhaps an equal number at La Bahía. With some Spaniards in East Texas, it is estimated that there may have been five hundred settlers in the province by 1731.

Fortunately, as the century progressed these early vague estimates can be improved upon by the careful observations of visitors and the compilation of the first census returns. Perhaps the first reasonably accurate figures were made available on the occasion of Father Morfi's visit to Texas. On November 6, 1777, Governor Ripperdá had completed a census which revealed that there were 3,103 Spaniards, mixed bloods, and peacefully settled Indians in the entire province of Texas. Of this total, there were 1,141 men, 902 women, 1,040 children of both sexes, and 20 slaves. Furthermore, there were 636 married men (nearly fifty-six per cent of the total males) along with 114 widowers.[44]

The total population evidently declined between 1777 and 1784, perhaps because of widespread Indian raids on the settlements. By the latter date there were 2,828 Spaniards, mixed bloods, and peaceful Indians (only 615 in all) at all locations in the province, an increase of only 9 persons over the figures for the previous year. The population of 1784 included 965 men, 820 women, 1,003 children, and 40 slaves. Of the 965 men, 673 (nearly seventy per cent) were married and 63 were widowers. Of the 820 women, 673 (about eighty-two per cent) were married, 84 were widows, and 63 were living alone.[45] Eight years later the census of 1792 showed a total of 2,992 people living in the single *villa*, two *pueblos*, three secularized parish districts, seven missions, eleven *ranchos*, and two *estancias* of the province. There were no chartered cities and no *haciendas* in Texas,[46] unless the two *estancias* might be so considered. Soon afterward, in January, 1793, the government began suppressing the missions, and all of them were ordered secularized by Pedro de Nava after April 10, 1794. The process was completed, except for the mission at Refugio, by 1821.[47]

Nineteenth century figures reveal an increase in the population of Texas, but not nearly so rapid an expansion as occurred in other provinces. The official census for December 31, 1804, showed 3,980 people in the entire province, an increase of nearly a thousand in the past dozen years. There were in 1804 exactly 782 married men, 789 married women, 150 widowers, 171 widows, 491 bachelors, 165 spinsters, 742 boys, and 680 girls.[48] Governor Manuel María de Salcedo y Quiroga reported in 1809 that there were 1,033 soldiers along with 3,122 settlers in the six jurisdictional regions of the province, for a total of 4,155 persons in all.[49] By the end of the Spanish period, although exact figures are lacking, it may be assumed that Texas contained approximately 4,500 people in its civil communities, about 3,500 of whom were actual settlers, a meager figure, especially when compared to the provinces of Coahuila, Nuevo León, New Mexico, Nueva Vizcaya, Sonora, and Sinaloa.[50]

Community growth is also reflected in the census reports and observations of visitors between 1777 and 1820. Morfi reported 2,060 people at the Real Presidio de Béxar and the Villa de San Fernando in 1777, with 696 at the Real Presidio del Espíritu Santo and 347 at the Nuevo Pueblo de Bucareli.[51] Thus, at that time nearly two-thirds of the Spanish-speaking people in Texas lived in the San Antonio area. After the founding of Nacogdoches in 1779, the growth of the three major settlements may be followed in general by referring to Table 1.[52]

Table 1

Population of Texas Settlements

Year	San Antonio	La Bahía	Nacogdoches
1783	1,248	454	349
1784	1,224	496	399
1793	. . .	. . .	538
1804	1,998	924	810
1807	2,000 (est.)	. . .	500 (est.)
1809	1,700	405	655
1820	1,814	600 (est.)	. . .

Most of the original settlers of Texas emigrated from the nearby frontier provinces. The Ramón, Alarcón, and Marqués de Aguayo expeditions were recruited largely in the Saltillo and Monclova regions of Coahuila. Following the first generation, there was little outside supply of settlers save for the Canary Islanders who came to San Fernando de Béxar and the increasing foreign population in East Texas. Most of the population growth in the latter half of the eighteenth century and the first two decades of the nineteenth may be attributed to natural increase, although there was a small trickle of immigrants from other provinces. The founding of Nacogdoches in 1779 is a good example. Most of its settlers were originally from East Texas, but had migrated from there to San Fernando de Béxar and Bucareli in the preceding years.

A detailed list of the troops and settlers at La Bahía in 1780 provides an excellent study of the origins and some of the characteristics of the population. Individuals are listed by name in this seven-page document, along with their class, origin, age, occupation, marital status, number of children, servants in each family, armament, and material possessions. Of the sixty-seven soldiers listed, twenty-three were originally from Monterrey, Nuevo León, ten from

Presidio of Nuestra Señora de Loreto at La Bahía del Espíritu Santo, Texas, established in the eighteenth century. Note the stone construction, the small window, and the presidial chapel. *Courtesy University of Texas Archives.*

Coahuila (particularly Saltillo, Parras, and Monclova), and one each from Querétaro and Chihuahua—that is thirty-five, or fifty-two per cent of the total, were from outside Texas. Twenty-nine were from within the province—nineteen from La Bahía, four from Los Adaes, and two listed from the province in general—while three were from unidentifiable locations. Of the one hundred and one men and women listed among the civilian settlers congregated near the presidio, fifty-one came from Coahuila and Nuevo León (sixteen and thirty-five from Coahuila and Nuevo León (sixteen and thirty-five, respectively), thirty-eight from within the province of Texas (twenty-four from La Bahía, eight from Béxar, and six from Los Adaes), eight from places outside of the northeastern region (one each from Querétaro, Parral, Guadalajara, San Luis Potosí, Chihuahua, the Canary Islands, Louisiana, and even Paris, France), and four from unidentifiable places. Thus, only about thirty-eight per cent of the civilian population at La Bahía originated within Texas, but eighty-eight per cent of the total came from the three provinces of Coahuila, Nuevo León, and Texas.[53]

A similar list of 308 families for the *villa* of San Fernando de Béxar in 1792 shows the specific origins of 198 *vecinos*. Of this total, 127 (sixty-four per cent) originated in Texas—110 in the *villa* and presidio of Béxar, 14 at the abandoned presidio of Los Adaes, 2 at La Bahía, and 1 in the province at large. Twenty-five family heads came from Coahuila, six from Nuevo Léon, and five from Nuevo Santander. Thirty-two had migrated from other points in New Spain (including four from Mexico City, three from Tlaxcala, and two from New Mexico), Central America (Guatemala had one settler), Louisiana (one each from New Orleans and Natchitoches), Europe (Cádiz, Castile, France, and Corsica), and Africa (two).[54]

Of unusual interest in the study of civilian settlers in frontier New Spain is the presence of Canary Islanders at San Antonio, and many foreigners in East Texas during the early nineteenth century. Frenchmen and Louisianans are noted in the above census figures for La Bahía and San Fernando de Béxar before the turn of the century. Nacogdoches censuses were taken on occasion solely for the purpose of learning how many foreign residents inhabited the community. Two such reports were made in 1796. The first, dated June 30, 1796, lists twelve foreign residents—one from New England, two from Virginia, four from Philadelphia, one from Italy, one from Flanders, two from Ireland, and one whose origin is not specified. Six of these people were laborers; two, merchants; two, carpenters; and one each was a blacksmith and a tailor. One of these foreign residents had lived in Nacogdoches more than twelve years, another ten, a third over four, and a fourth more than three years, but the rest had been there from one to six months.[55] The second report, dated December 31, 1796, listed only Frenchmen, twenty-two of them in all, largely from Canada, Natchitoches, and New Orleans. Most of them were traders among the Indians and one had lived in East Texas for the past twenty-eight years. Others were tanners, laborers, and carpenters.[56] It is evident from these reports that there were thirty-four foreign nationals living in Nacogdoches by 1796, representing more than six per cent of the total population of the community.

In general, Spanish society in frontier Texas was class-oriented in name only. For purposes of official records and census reports individuals were listed by *calidad* (class). However, distinctions between classes remained more theoretical than actual. Vague differences between classes grew more obscure with the passing of each generation. There was little class rivalry, except in San Fernando de Béxar between the Canary Island settlers and the original inhabitants, which continued among their descendants.

Fray Juan Agustín de Morfi noted the presence of "classes" in Texas as indicated by the Ripperdá census of 1777. There were at that time in the province some 3,103 people, of whom 957 were listed as Spaniards, 871 as Indians, 111 as mestizos, 669 as *colores quebrados* (broken colors), and 20 as slaves.[57] Three years later the census for La Bahía showed 67 soldiers, all "Spaniards," although their birthplaces were given as New Spain in every case. In addition, there were 101 persons listed as settlers there, of whom 40 were Spaniards; 52, mulattoes; 6, mestizos; and 3, *lobas* (female castes).[58] Of the 2,828 people counted in the census of 1784, 1,595 were listed as Spaniards; 615, Indians; 180, mestizos; 398, of *color quebrado*; and 40, slaves.[59] Nacogdoches reported a total of 538 people in January, 1793, of whom 255 were Spaniards; 124, Indians; 74, mestizos; 69, of *color quebrado*; and 16, Negroes.[60] In the previous year the census for the entire province of Texas had shown a population of 2,992 persons—1,166 Spaniards, 816 Indians, 179 mestizos, 415 mulattoes, 34 Negroes, 367 men and women of other castes, and 15 *"europeos"* (Europeans).[61]

With this statistical information on hand, it is possible to offer some tentative observations about Spanish society in Texas. There were very few Europeans—from Spain or France or the possessions of both—at any time, and they were not called *peninsulares* or *gachupines* as elsewhere in the viceroyalty of New Spain. The largest single group of settlers was that composed of *españoles*, who were not really Spaniards, but those of Spanish descent born in the New World. They comprised from thirty-one to fifty-six per cent of the total population, depending upon the census used and the uncertainties associated with exact determination of classes, but averaging about forty-two per cent of the total population. Peaceful Indians comprised from twenty-two to twenty-eight per cent of the population, averaging about twenty-six per cent at the end of the eighteenth century. This means that all mixed bloods, or castes, amounted to an average of approximately thirty-two per cent of the total population. Spaniards and mixed bloods, those usually considered to be the *gente de razón*, thus constituted over seventy per cent of the people in Spanish Texas. "Mestizos" in this province evidently meant those mixed bloods having a decided European appearance. There were relatively few of them in contrast to the *colores quebrados*, who were evidently of a darker color and were perhaps a mixture of Indian and Negro, thereby breaking the color line, or *limpieza de sangre* (purity of blood). As the Spanish colonial period came to a close, however, the term *color quebrado* seems to have faded from use. Negroes and mixed bloods were both present in frontier Texas, as were slaves, but the latter term does not imply that all slaves were of Negro descent. Slavery was an occupational status, not racial. A person of any race might be a slave.[62]

San Fernando de Béxar experienced a class rivalry after the arrival in 1731 of the Canary Islanders, who received a royal subsidy, land allotments, tools, clothing, and arms, and were given rights of self-government within the community. Proud of their titles as *hidalgos*, these people became an exclusive group who considered themselves the "first settlers" of the *villa*. They immediately offended the settlers were were already living around San Antonio.

Although the Canary Islanders were in reality mostly *labradores* (small farmers), who seldom could read and write, they had an exaggerated idea of their own importance. Within the first decade of their residence at San Fernando they showed their desire to have others, particularly mission Indians, work for them, especially as farmers. As a result, they became embroiled in heated controversies with soldiers, missionaries, and other settlers of their community on such issues as Indian labor, land allotments, irrigation rights, debts, preservation of crops, and pasturage of horses and cattle.[63] Nor was the situation greatly improved a generation later when in 1771 the Canary Island descendants petitioned Governor Ripperdá to exempt them from hauling stones and wood in their carts for the construction of presidial buildings on the pretext that they now needed to grow crops or starve. Ripperdá refused their request, ordering them to obey his decree that all settlers would participate or go to prison and pay a fine for disobedience. However, he allowed the dissidents to plant their crops first and haul building materials later.[64] What developed in San Fernando de Béxar then was an unusual class structure for frontier New Spain, with five groups of people: the Canary Islanders, the other settlers (*agregados*), soldiers, missionaries, and Christianized Indians.[65]

Most Spanish settlers in Texas were small farmers, day laborers, and merchants. The Baron de Ripperdá's census of 1777 used by Morfi reported that there were 332 labradores (small farmers) out of a total of 1,141 men in the province, or nearly thirty per cent. In addition, there were 62 day laborers, 185 servants, 12 merchants, 98 artisans, and 237 without a specified occupation.[66] La Bahía's 101 heads of households in 1780 included 22 *labradores*, 17 day laborers, 4 tailors, 4 mule drivers, 3 servants, 2 carpenters, 2 blacksmiths, a miner, and a notary.[67] Farmers, day laborers, masons, and other artisans were all present in the province for the census of 1792, along with seven merchants, one miner, two students, and two "barbers and bleeders," but no lawyers, doctors, or surgeons. San Fernando de Béxar was dominated by small farmers and day laborers, but nineteen artisans were also present—tailors, shoemakers, and blacksmiths, primarily—along with two students.[68]

Little change in these occupations occurred in the early nineteenth century, except for the diversification in types of work. Family listings for the *villa* of San Fernando in 1804 were still dominated by small farmers, day laborers, and servants, along with thirteen slaves (eight of whom were Negroes), twelve shoemakers, six blacksmiths, five traders or merchants, four tailors, four carpenters, two seamstresses, two notary publics, and one each of the following: silversmith, hatmaker, whipmaker, mason, sacristan, singer, and soldier.[69] By January 1, 1820, only eighteen months before Texas achieved its independence from Spain, a census for Béxar gave the occupations of 259 people as 110 small farmers, 108 day laborers, 33 artisans, 3 merchants, a retired military officer, a curate, an employee of the Royal Treasury, a scribe, and a schoolmaster. Among the artisans listed there were fourteen shoemakers, six blacksmiths, four tailors, four carpenters, four silversmiths, and two masons.[70]

The Spanish-speaking people of Texas were essentially hard-working, individually employed, agrarian-oriented individuals. They had to earn a living, mostly in farming and ranching, just to stay alive on this remote frontier. However, many pursued particular skills for which they had been trained; few were really professionals. Royal officials, military officers, missionaries, priests, and an occasional schoolmaster comprised the only true professionals of frontier Texas in Spanish times.

Because of conditions encountered on the Texas frontier, Spanish settlers became mostly stockmen and small farmers. In fact, cattle became the major source of wealth in the province.[71] According to one of the foremost experts on the cattle-raising industry, Spanish ranching "became the basic feature of economic development in Texas."[72]

Domingo Ramón brought sixty-four oxen, five hundred horses and mules, and over one thousand sheep and goats with his expedition. The Marqués de Aguayo added some four hundred sheep and three hundred cattle in 1721, bringing them from Coahuila and Nuevo León.[73] Franciscan missions also became centers of the livestock industry. La Bahía's mission of Espíritu Santo had three thousand head of cattle in 1758, four thousand the following year, and sixteen thousand by 1768.[74] Private ranchers acquired most of this livestock after secularization of the missions began in 1794. Canary Islanders in San Fernando de Béxar and Spanish inhabitants of Nacogdoches were both active in stockraising, an occupation that was regularized by *Comandante-general* Teodoro de Croix when brand registers (*libros de marcas*) were begun and all unbranded stock was declared the property of the king.[75] By 1800 there were three ranching centers in what is today the state of Texas: Nacogdoches (mostly horses), the San Antonio River area (both horses and cattle), and the lower Río Grande Valley (then part of the province of Nuevo Santander, but a significant region for the raising of cattle as well as horses).[76]

Land was allocated to individuals according to its intended use. Spanish authorities provided settlers with *solares* (town lots), *labores* (approximately 177 acres) for farming, and *caballerías* (about one hundred acres), also for agricultural purposes. Larger stockraising grants included the *sitio de ganado mayor*, frequently called a square league, approximately 4,336 acres, but usually generalized as 4,428 acres, for large animals; the *sitio de ganado menor*, approximately 1,920 acres, for sheep and goats; and the *sitio de criadero de ganado mayor*, a cattle-breeding ranch of approximately 1,084 acres. Usually the grants were made to individuals upon application and payment of a fee.[77] An *hacienda* was officially five *sitios*, but none existed in Texas, where the *rancho*, or large stockfarm as applied in Texas, dominated the scene. At the end of the eighteenth century Governor Manuel Muñoz reported that there were forty-five *ranchos* in the province; owners of five in the San Fernando de Béxar region are listed together with their families, servants, and possessions in an 1810 census.[78]

The Texan use of the term *rancho* indicated a frontier institution that supplemented the civil settlement in spreading Spanish culture. The ranching industry brought saddles, lariats, the roundup, or *rodeo*, cattle drives, sports, branding practices, stockmen's associations, and price controls, in addition to the animals themselves, to the frontier, affecting both the society and economy. Furthermore, it provided a means of using the semiarid plains where normal agriculture was difficult; supplied beasts of burden, food, wool, leather, and tallow to the Spanish presidios, missions, and civil settlements; stimulated commerce between Texas on the one hand and Coahuila and Louisiana on the other; provided recreation for the people; and contributed to an attitude of independence, scorn for authority, and individualism.[79]

Although agriculture was practiced in Texas, its development varied greatly from one community to the next, and its overall progress was not nearly so spectacular as it was in the Saltillo-Parras region of Coahuila or the Río Grande Valley of New Mexico. Irrigation was employed in the San Antonio settlements, using the waters of the San Antonio River and San Pedro Creek. Normal agriculture could be carried on near Los Adaes and, later, Nacogdoches, although failure of early corn crops and periodic floods caused the settlers to rely on the nearby French settlements for food supplies before 1741. La Bahía raised very little of anything before its last move in 1749; as late as 1803 there was little raising of crops there, the presidial company preferring to obtain its grain from Béxar. Corn, beans, and peppers were planted by Indians at the mission of San Antonio de Valero, and evidently at other missions nearby. The citizens of San Fernando de Béxar planted corn, but not in great quantity, according to the governor of Texas in his report of 1803. In addition, they grew beans, chile peppers, and some sugar cane. Pumpkins and melons were also grown locally.[80] However, agricultural production was generally at a subsistence level for Texas' sparse population and never rivaled the livestock industry in importance. This caused occasional severe shortages of food, particularly corn, especially during the early years of settlement.[81]

Transportation and communications within the province and with other frontier regions were at all times marked primitive. Trails formed the essential transportation network of Spanish Texas, with two long roads traversing the province. One (the *Camino Real*, or King's Highway) ran from San Juan Bautista on the Río Grande to San Antonio and finally to Nacogdoches, with a connecting link at San Antonio for La Bahía. Another ran from Laredo, after its founding in 1755, to La Bahía, then veered northeastward and intersected the *Camino Real* at the Trinity River. Oxen, mules, horses, and crude carts (*carretas*) provided the only means of transportation throughout the colonial period. Although beamed bridges were built by mission Indians across the San Antonio River as early as 1736, the many rivers remained major obstacles to commercial development in the province. This was undoubtedly one of the reasons why Governor Salcedo recommended the opening of a port at Matagorda Bay.[82]

One notable development in the field of communications was the establishment of a regular mail service at the end of the eighteenth century. Part of *Comandante-general* Teodoro de Croix's over-all plan for regularizing the mail service on the whole northern frontier, the Texas postal establishment served to tie the province closer to the rest of the provinces. Effective March 1, 1779, post offices were set up at La Bahía, Bucareli, San Antonio de Béxar, and the *villa* of San Fernando. Although administered by the Royal Exchequer in Mexico City, presidial officers were charged with the security, distribution, receipt, and inspection of mail and completion of related forms in their jurisdictions. Soldiers usually carried the mail within the province and between Texas and Coahuila. Each presidio had its own distinctive seal, stamp, and pouch. That this system continued and became an important revenue-producing function is indicated by the increased funds received by the post office at Béxar in the years from 1804 to 1808.[83]

Social life and the everyday life style of the Spanish settlers in Texas during the colonial period were influenced by the extreme isolation of the province, the sparse population, the presence of Indian and foreign threats, and the need for improvisation because of restrictions. The setttler's life revolved about his work and his family. Although the opportunities for him to obtain an education or to enjoy recreational activities were limited, the fact is that both schools and diversions existed.

Only a few of the early settlers could read and write. This was particularly true of the fifty-five original colonists from the Canary Islands who settled the *villa* of San Fernando de Béxar. In the early years of Spanish occupation of Texas, missionaries, presidial officers, royal officials, and a few of the more affluent citizens had been educated beyond the reading the writing stage. Missionary schools were used exclusively for the education of Indian neophytes. Spanish residents never had an opportunity to obtain a higher education within the province of Texas; they had to go elsewhere in New Spain or perhaps to Europe to obtain it. However, it is evident that toward the end of the eighteenth century some improvement was made in the development of primary education in Texas.

The earliest record of a school in Texas appears to be an inference to one during a dispute between two Canary Islanders in San Fernando de Béxar. One Joseph Padrón asked the governor to call the "schoolmaster" to testify concerning the transgressions of his rival, Juan Leal Goras.[84] Beyond that passing reference there are no other records of this school or any other before 1789. In that year Don José Francisco de la Mata, a native of Saltillo who had resided in San Fernando for three years, presented a petition to the *cabildo* (town council) asking permission to open a school in the *villa*. He deplored the ignorance of the local youth, offered to teach them their letters as well as obedience to their parents and basic Christian doctrine, and urged that the *cabildo* and parish priest cooperate with him against the expected interference of the parents. Evidently fathers and mothers threatened him if he punished their children or arbitrarily removed their offspring from school. De la Mata offered his services at a modest charge of twelve *reales* (one peso, four *reales*) per pupil. The request was granted, but there are no records available concerning the administration of the school, and it would seem that the institution did not last long, if indeed it really ever began.[85]

Comandante-general Nemesio Salcedo y Salcedo (1802–1813) was primarily responsible for reviving interest of Texas officials in establishing schools early in the nineteenth century. He wrote to Governor Juan Bautista Elguezábal expressing his concern over the illiteracy of frontier people, urging that "schools of primary letters" be established to correct this deficiency, and instructing the governor to find someone who could read and write for employment as a teacher. The governor was further ordered to provide the teacher a house with at least one room to be used as a classroom and to pay the teacher, or schoolmaster, one-fourth of a peso per month for every boy enrolled. No girls were mentioned. José Francisco Ruiz became schoolmaster at San Fernando de Béxar, but he had to use his own residence as a schoolhouse. At La Bahía the presidial commander reported that his community's teacher of the past twenty-two years had just died, but a school was in operation there again by July, 1804. At Nacogdoches, the lieutenant governor observed that it was very difficult to establish a school there, since the population was so dispersed and boys were needed on the ranches to assist with the everyday work.[86] Evidently there was no school in that area as late as 1804.

That the *comandante-general* continued to show interest in public schooling is apparent from the scattered references for the period of his administration. Furthermore, over the course of the next decade the governors of Texas endeavored to promote primary education in the province. Nemesio Salcedo wrote on January 16, 1805, that he had received six pages of work written by children enrolled in the school at the presidio of La Bahía del Espíritu Santo.[87] In the same year it appears that Nacogdoches established a school, since one official there wrote the governor requesting that he be sent two dozen primers and an equal number of readers, half religious and half secular, so that his children could catch up on their work and the school could continue to exist.[88] A petition of 1809 from schoolmaster Francisco Barrera states that he was unable to support his family while working as a teacher; he, therefore, asked permission to supplement his work by becoming a public scribe, an entreaty that was granted. Padre Mariano Sosa, curate of Nacogdoches, reported to the governor on educational problems in East Texas in 1810. He pointed out that parents lacked education themselves and could not lay the proper foundations for their sons, thereby contributing to the moral degeneracy of the district. What was needed, according to Father Sosa, was a "public school of Christian education," where the younger generation could be helped only if fathers were compelled to send their children regularly to class. Father Sosa recommended that children attend the school already established by Manuel Bustamente, who worked only for compensation in land.[89]

After March 1, 1811, officials in Béxar expressed their intent to build a schoolhouse. They provided 855 pesos to Don Bicente Travieso to erect a suitable building, and he had spent all but 12 pesos of the funds by August 12, 1812. However, an inventory of the furnishings of the building revealed that there were no locks on the doors and windows, benches for the students had been obtained from an earlier schoolroom, and furniture was not only scarce but crude. The school was to have an enrollment of seventy students, five of whom should be able to attend free of charge. Otherwise students were divided into two groups according to the ability of parents to pay; those in one group would pay one peso per month, and the others would pay only four *reales*. The teacher would receive a monthly salary of thirty pesos, and all books and paper would be furnished. The *cabildo* announced that one of its members would personally inspect the institution every day.[90]

Governor Manuel de Salcedo issued detailed instructions for this school to Don Manuel de Yndo, a native of Castile and "teacher of the primary grades," on March 1, 1812, as the schoolmaster for San Fernando de Béxar. Yndo contracted to teach twenty-four children, not seventy, their primary letters and the Christian doctrine, particularly emphasizing reading, writing, and basic arithmetic. He was not to leave for a period of five years, and he was to exercise the greatest care and diligence and impose only moderate punishments on the children under his instruction. Seventeen residents of the community agreed to provide twenty pupils at a cost of fifty pesos each, the total of one thousand pesos to be paid to Yndo every February so that he could draw upon it to meet expenses throughout the year. The other four children were to be taught free of charge, their families undoubtedly being unable to pay the required fifty pesos for enrollment. If any pupil failed to progress normally, the schoolmaster was to notify his parents and arrange for a replacement. Yndo was also informed that the new schoolhouse, its tables and benches, the reading books, and the writing paper did not belong to him but to the parents who executed this agreement as a sort of corporation.[91]

As in all societies in any period of history, there were criminals, vagrants, and dissolute persons in Spanish Texas. Many laws were issued to regulate the lives of the citizenry, control the populace as a whole, and provide punishment for transgressions against society and the state. Father Sosa complained that the citizens of Nacogdoches were mostly dissolute characters without any morals whatsoever. Louisiana's proximity affected them because it "overflowed with libertines," and many residents of Texas refused to believe the words of priests as a consequence, preferring instead to follow the example of these foreigners. Furthermore, he reported, family members often slept together in the same bed, leading to all sorts of illicit relationships. "You may imagine," he told the governor, "what must be the consequences of such a manner of living." Women who needed food and clothes sold "their bodies for their support" while their men were away hunting. Soldiers of the presidial garrison were among the worst offenders, according to Father Sosa. They often procured the services of women of the town, having intercourse with laundresses and their daughters. This led to family rifts, encouraged mothers to become poor examples for their children, created a large population of bastards, encouraged virgins to take up prostitution, and caused ribaldry among the young men of the district. In short, Father Sosa noted, idleness, indebtedness, vice, and dishonesty prevailed over virtue and religion. As part of the solution for such a degenerate society, he recommended an educational system, as described earlier, and the restriction of soldiers to their barracks when they were not cultivating the soil or performing their military duties.[92]

Father Sosa's complaints may have been somewhat exaggerated as well as prejudiced by his own beliefs. Yet civil officials also remonstrated against the dissolute character of certain settlers. One of these complaints from La Bahía in 1805 stated:

Resident Damián Balenzuela came here from that presidio [San Antonio de Béxar] in pursuit of a married woman. [He is a] carousing inebriate, who, when drunk, goes before her husband, insulting him because the woman refuses his advances. This pursuit has been going on for several years, and he has even been exiled, but he [always] returns. He became jealous of a man whom he saw in the house and tried to whip him, but he was hurt instead by a blow of a club. It will be very accommodating of you to send him so far away that he will never come back.[93]

Although the large majority of the Spanish settlers did not behave in such a manner, authorities found it necessary to establish all sorts of regulations for major as well as minor matters. Antonio Gil Ybarbo, lieutenant governor of Texas and resident of Nacogdoches, wrote in 1783 a comprehensive fifty-four-paragraph criminal code for his district. Before outlining specific offenses and punishments, he pointed out that the intent of the code was to preserve order in the communities of East Texas and to protect the lives and property of its residents. With a sense of realism and understanding of human nature, Gil Ybarbo wrote that he considered it the "natural propensity of mankind to shake off the salutary yoke of the most sacred, just, and admirable laws."[94]

Thereafter he listed some of the most common offenses and the punishment for each. Any blasphemy using the name of God, the Virgin Mary, or the saints, and outrages against holy images were to be punished according to the laws of the kingdom. Death was the penalty prescribed for speaking in a derogatory manner about the king, his family, or the government. It was also the punishment for burning a house, any building, or crops; any murder or homicide; challenging or accepting a duel; rape; adultery and incest; and stealing cattle, horses, twelve or more sheep, or more than five hogs. Treacherous killing and acts of witchcraft called for being drawn and quartered, then hanged. Illicit intercourse or any act wherein a woman lived with a married man would bring expulsion from the community for one year and a fine of one silver peso for the first offense, double the punishment for the second offense, and triple, in addition to one hundred lashes, for the third such act. Men who consented to the prostitution of their wives were to be exposed in public, rubbed in honey, made to wear a fool's cap with a string of garlic and a pair of horns, lashed one hundred times, and sent to the galleys for a period of ten years—all this for the first offense, since the second one was assignment to the galleys for life. Some of the other offenses and punishments prescribed are specified in Table 2.

Table 2

Offenses and Punishments, Nacogdoches, Texas, 1783

Offense	Punishment
Using indecent language in public	One hundred lashes and expulsion for one year
Insulting parents	Punishment in an "exemplary manner"
Vagrancy and idleness	Sixty lashes and expulsion
For young men, causing scandals, lacking respect for parents, living in idleness, drinking, gambling, and having intercourse	Jail for twenty days and expulsion for one year
Drunkenness, quarreling, or fighting at public or private dances	Jail for eight days and a fine of ten pesos
Unauthorized meetings	Punishment as rioters
Violation of curfew after retreat sounded	Jail for eight days
Not removing soot from chimneys every fifteen days	Jail for twenty-four hours and a fine of four pesos
Selling liquor to Indians	Lose the liquor and fine of ten pesos

In addition, Gil Ybarbo provided a general statement prohibiting all loitering, gambling, quarreling, theft, and drunkenness.[95]

One can assume from such an extensive list of crimes and punishments that these offenses did occur in the province or there would have been no need to

issue such detailed regulations. Yet the restrictions went even further. Young
men under the age of twenty-five had to obtain parental consent before marry-
ing, any discharge of firearms resulted in one month's forced labor on public
projects, and igniting fireworks near the powder magazine was absolutely prohibited. Juveniles were not allowed to wander about in the streets, and Spanish-
speaking people were forbidden to live with Indians. Inciting disturbances at
any time was punished by arrest and one hundred lashes. No person could leave
his home or village without first obtaining a license, or passport, from the local
authorities, stating his day of departure, route, and destination. This passport
had to be presented to obtain lodging anywhere. Riders and muleteers were
charged two *reales* to hitch their beasts of burden in public places. All owners
of vehicles were required to register them with local authorities, from whom
they obtained a numbered license to be attached to the front of their vehicles.
Men and women could not ride on the same horse; galloping and racing on
the streets was unlawful; all privately owned lands were to be fenced; shouting
in or near communities was prohibited; public amusements were stictly regulated; and burning of trash was forbidden because the smoke was obnoxious
and might be taken as a signal to Indians.[96]

In addition to the problems of crime, Indian raids, and foreign encroachments, there was always the danger of disease leading to widespread epidemics.
One such scourge of smallpox and measles broke out among the missions in
1739; La Bahía had frequent problems with smallpox, including one great epidemic in 1779; and cholera broke out there in 1780, subsequently spreading to
the San Antonio area, where it killed an average of three people per day.[97]

To combat disease Spanish Texas had very little in the way of trained personnel or medical facilities. There were no civilian doctors or surgeons until after
1806. Up to that point settlers relied upon barbers, who were in demand for
their bleeding services, and upon quack remedies such as brown sugar, used
in the treatment of smallpox. The first and only hospital was established in the
deserted mission of San Antonio de Valero on January 1, 1806, where part of
the abandoned building was reconditioned at a cost of 350 pesos, and Doctor
Frederick Zerban, a New Orleans resident, was hired as physician and surgeon.
A weekly allowance of two *reales* was provided for the support of each patient,
the hospital having forty-two of them by September, 1806. Drugs were scarce,
stewards were underpaid, and people disliked Dr. Zerban because his medicines
were expensive and ineffectual and because they preferred a Spanish doctor.
San Antonio's first dentist arrived from Louisiana in the same year; he evidently was more popular, probably because he offered his patients free medicines. Continued deterioration of the hospital and lack of finances to support
it led to its abandonment in 1809.[98]

While the hospital was functioning, smallpox vaccine reached San Antonio,
and twelve children (six from the presidio and six from the *villa*) were treated

on April 1, 1806. Efforts were made also to improve sanitation; authorities ordered that streets be kept clean and that residents remove the bodies of dead animals from their properties immediately, covering the blood with dirt. No garbage was permitted around homes, so that spread of disease might be prevented.[99]

Living conditions in Spanish Texas were primitive in the early years, but improved somewhat with the passing of generations. Poverty prevailed at Los Adaes, for example, in 1734. The clothing of the men consisted of rags, blankets, and buffalo hides; women had so little to wear that many would not leave their huts. There were no shoes, hats, hose, or soap for the settlers, food was rationed, and the lieutenant governor even requested a pair of pants for himself. The stockade at the presidio fell apart, rains washed the earthworks away, and all the cannon were dismounted and unserviceable. In fact, the governor reported in 1737, the presidio looked more like a cattle pen than a military fortress.[100]

Homes were normally constructed at first of wood and sticks with a grass or straw roof. Called *jacales*, these huts often remained a major part of the Spanish settlements, although stone and to a lesser extent adobe came into use in the second half of the eighteenth century. La Bahía had stone buildings after its final move in 1749.[101] Fray Juan Agustín de Morfi described San Fernando de Béxar in the late 1770s as a "wretched village," with fifty-nine stone and adobe buildings and seventy-nine wooden houses, all poorly built and arranged at random. The streets were tortuous and filled with mud after every rainfall.[102] Lieutenant Zebulon Pike noted that the houses of San Antonio in 1807 mostly had mud (adobe) walls and thatched roofs.[103]

Recreation and diversions were few and far between. The most common form of entertainment was dancing, usually in the plazas of the villages or at private homes. No matter where it was held, the dance was generally called a *fandango*. Pike attended one during his June, 1807, visit to San Antonio. Governmental and religious authorities tolerated these dances so long as they had the proper authorization and were closely regulated; however, one governor reported that certain "insolences" were sung during the festivities. Horse racing was also popular, but it was banned on religious holidays after 1781. From the regulations issued to control criminal acts, it is apparent that gambling, card playing, and drinking were other diversions often employed by Spanish residents to relieve the monotony of hard work and the daily routine. Bells installed at the Franciscan missions were used to warn the citizenry of impending Indian raids; they were also rung in honor of royal births, state marriages, deaths of prominent citizens, and coronations, as well as for public celebrations and to sound curfew.[104]

Unlike most of the other frontier provinces of New Spain, Texas was a land of violence and civil war during the war for Mexican independence in the period

Native *jacal* of straw and wood at San Antonio, Texas. *Courtesy Denver Public Library Western Collection.*

from 1810 to 1821. Although this was partially due to its geographic location, it was mostly caused by the long-dreaded presence of foreigners, particularly during the last thirty years of Spanish administration in the province. Beginning with the horse-stealing expeditions of Philip Nolan, leading to his death in 1801, Texas experienced two decades of foreign filibustering and fighting. A revolt against Spanish authorities at San Antonio de Béxar in 1811 was suppressed by royalist governor Manuel de Salcedo. As a reward for the loyalty of its populace, *Comandante-general* Nemesio Salcedo officially elevated the *villa* of San Fernando to the status of *ciudad*. Thus San Antonio (or San Fernando, as the terms were often used interchangeably) became a major city on the frontier of New Spain, having equal civil status with Durango, Saltillo, and Monterrey. But the uncertainties and civil warfare did not end. In 1812 an envoy of the Mexican revolutionaries, Bernardo Gutiérrez de Lara, joined a recently resigned United States military officer, Lieutenant Augustus W. Magee, in a filibustering expedition into Texas from Louisiana. They took Béxar on April 1, 1813, executed Governor Salcedo, and issued a proclamation for the independence of the "State of Texas." Magee died, Gutiérrez de Lara proved an incompetent military officer and poor leader, and the rebellion was crushed by royalist troops led by General Joaquín de Arredondo after a battle at the Medina River on August 18, 1813. Six years later a filibustering venture from Natchez led by one James Long against the province was eventually crushed.[105] Texas was still in Spanish hands when Mexico established her independence in 1821, and it peacefully proclaimed its allegiance to the Mexican nation.

After slightly more than a century of permanent occupation by Spanish-speaking people, Texas began a new stage in its development with the achievement of Mexican independence. Sparsely populated throughout the colonial period, it had, nevertheless, grown from its original seventy-five settlers to approximately four thousand people by 1821. The large majority of these settlers was concentrated in three geographic regions: East Texas (Los Adaes, Bucareli, and Nacogdoches), La Bahía del Espíritu Santo, and the settlements located in the San Antonio area—five missions, a presidio, and a formal civil settlement at San Fernando de Béxar. Others lived on *ranchos*, developing the livestock industry as the leading economic activity of the entire province. Dependent largely upon its own resources after the first expeditions from Coahuila and the arrival of the Canary Island settlers, Texas experienced the long-term threat of various Indian raids and foreign penetration, factors that ultimately led to its instability during the independence period. Settled primarily to protect Spain's northeastern frontier against the French, it remained an isolated, neglected frontier. Yet, its hard-working people, forced to adapt to their environment, formed the nucleus of the Spanish-speaking people of present Texas and contributed greatly to its Spanish heritage.

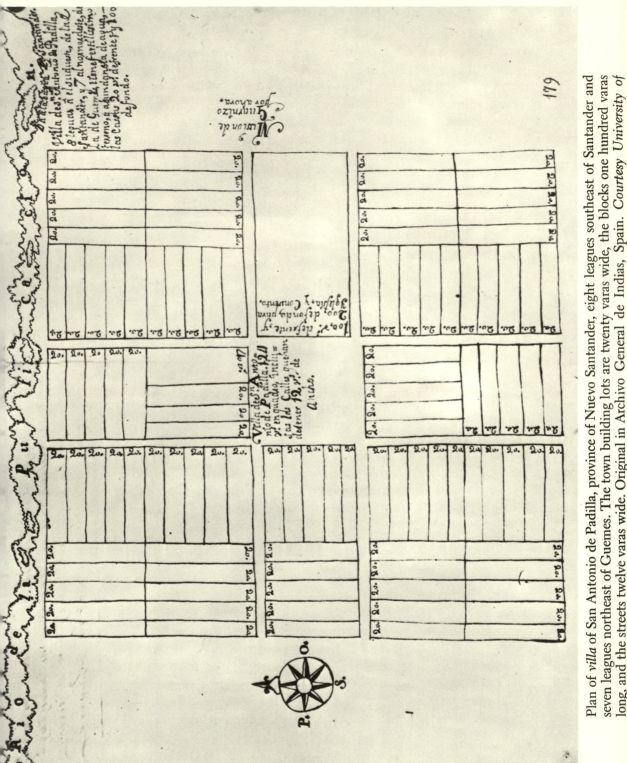

Plan of *villa* of San Antonio de Padilla, province of Nuevo Santander, eight leagues southeast of Santander and seven leagues northeast of Guemes. The town building lots are twenty varas wide, the blocks one hundred varas long, and the streets twelve varas wide. Original in Archivo General de Indias, Spain. *Courtesy University of*

3. Nuevo Santander
(Tamaulipas)

North of the Pánuco River, extending in a sweeping arc toward the northeast was a long expanse of terrain unoccupied, except for nomadic Indian tribes, for more than two centuries after the Spaniards arrived in the New World. Called the Seno Mexicano, it was not permanently settled until the middle of the eighteenth century. Although one of the last regions of northern New Spain to be occupied, it developed into an established colony with a large ranching industry before the beginning of the nineteenth century.

Nuevo Santander, or what is essentially the Mexican state of Tamaulipas today, became a province of New Spain in 1746, exactly thirty years after Domingo Ramón led Spanish settlers into eastern Texas. Initially colonized through the extensive planning, recruiting, equipping, and settling projects of José de Escandón over the course of a seven-year period, the province had two focal points of Spanish population in the last half of the eighteenth century: the interior and along the Lower Río Grande. In spite of the relative lateness of its occupation, Nuevo Santander grew to notable proportions, having more than thirty thousand people at the end of the colonial regime. Its numbers dwarfed those of nearby Texas and more nearly resembled the Spanish population of New Mexico. It also took on great importance as a major ranching area and stood as a bulwark against possible foreign encroachments along the coastline of New Spain.

Although two dozen settlements were made in the initial period from 1748 to 1755, many of these communities were later moved, and others were consolidated into single villages. Laredo and the *hacienda* of Dolores, although north of the Río Grande, were then part of Nuevo Santander, not Texas. Only Laredo proved to be permanent, tracing its origins to the few families of Spanish ranchers who settled there in 1755.

Royal authorities officially established the province of Nuevo Santander in September, 1746, appointing José de Escandón governor and authorizing him to colonize the region between the Pánuco River and Texas. The whole enterprise was undertaken to counter French influence from Louisiana, to halt Indian uprisings and raids sweeping out of the Nuevo Santander region into Nuevo León, Coahuila, and Texas, and finally to promote the Christianizing and civilizing of the natives. Escandón, who had been born in Soto la Marina,

Spain, but had spent most of his adult life in New Spain, mostly as a conquistador in the Sierra Gorda between Querétaro and the Pánuco River, led one hundred men from Nuevo León (Cerralvo, Linares, and Cadereita) along with others from Monclova, Coahuila, into the province in 1747. This reconnoitering expedition closely studied the land, the rivers, and prospective sites of settlement. Escandón emphasized the need for finding places where water was ample for men and animals, land was fertile enough to permit cultivation of crops, health would not be impaired, and settlers would not be hampered by boggy areas where floods might become a problem.[1]

Once he had returned from his first *entrada*, or reconnaissance expedition, Escandón recommended the establishment of fourteen communities. In his official report of October 26, 1747, he requested that five hundred families be recruited to settle these sites; soldiers of the first expedition were to be given priority and they were to be provided with lands for cultivation. Towns with plazas 124 *varas* square (about 345 feet on each side), public buildings, and a church were included in Escandón's original plans. Land was allotted to each settler for constructing a home, raising vegetables and grains, and pasturing livestock. In addition, each *vecino* was paid two hundred pesos and exempted from taxation for a period of ten years. With these generous provisions, some seven hundred families responded to the initial call, most of them coming from the nearby provinces of Nuevo León and Coahuila.[2]

With the dual role of lieutenant general of the colonizing expedition and governor of the new province, Escandón personally led 755 soldiers and nearly 2,515 colonists, along with their wagons, stock, and possessions, from Querétaro on December 2, 1748; twenty-three days later, on Christmas Day of 1748, he founded the village of Santa María de Llera with forty-four families, the first civil settlement in Nuevo Santander. A month later he established Güemes, a community some twenty miles east of the present Victoria, and subsequently founded the villages of Padilla and Jiménez before the end of February, 1749. Jiménez was founded while Escandón was proceeding northward to the Río Grande for the first time; it became the principal settlement of the province and was the first capital of Nuevo Santander, as well as the center of Escandón's own extensive landholdings.[3]

With settlers from Nuevo León he established the small community of Nuestra Señora de Santa Ana de Camargo on March 5, 1749, blessing a rude arbor as its church and speaking to its first colonists after they had built their *jacales* (huts). This settlement and that of Nuestra Señora de Guadalupe de Reynosa, founded nine days later with one Carlos Cantú appointed as its civil and military authority, were the first Spanish establishments in the Lower Río Grande Valley, both on the right bank. Escandón returned in 1750 with more colonists from Nuevo León and Coahuila, establishing them at the ranching community of Revilla (now Guerrero) in October. This settlement, incidentally, was the only one founded in this period without government support. Two years later on March 6, 1752, eighteen families, most of whom raised stock, established a community at Mier, and on May 17, 1755, the ranching community of Laredo was founded on the north bank of the Río Grande. These five settlements constituted the bulk of the Spanish population in the Lower Río Grande Valley from that time to the end of the colonial period.[4]

In all, Escandón planted twenty-three civil settlements in Nuevo Santander during the seven years from 1748 through 1755. His first colonizing expedition established a dozen such communities, with more than eight hundred families of settlers, in addition to some missions administered by the Franciscan College of Guadalupe de Zacatecas and ten squadrons of soldiers—all at a cost of ninety thousand pesos. The second colonizing venture, beginning in 1750, led to the founding of eleven more civil settlements during the next five years. By 1755, the twenty-three communities contained a total of 1,337 families and 144 soldiers, or 6,385 persons in all; there were also fifteen missions within the province. For all of this effort, Escandón bore approximately one-half of the expenses himself, the other half being supplied by the royal government.[5] Thus within seven years Nuevo Santander had a larger Spanish population than Texas ever achieved in over a century of occupation. Escandón's careful and detailed planning, his judicious selection of sites for communities, and his personal leadership accomplished the lasting settlement of Nuevo Santander.

Although scattered population figures exist for some communities in the province as early as 1750,[6] the first extensive statistics were compiled and reported by Escandón himself and by a royal inspector of Nuevo Santander named José Tienda de Cuervo. Escandón reported the presence of 1,337 families and 144 soldiers for a total of 6,385 persons in the entire province during 1755.[7] Tienda de Cuervo spent four months in 1757 as *juez inspector* (official inspector) of Nuevo Santander. Beginning on April 28, he surveyed existing conditions, compiled statistics, and examined the needs of the settlers.[8] He reported that there were already eight thousand people there, possessing eighty thousand head of cattle, horses, and mules, along with over three hundred thousand sheep.[9] He also listed the population of individual towns and ranching settlements along with generalized descriptions of communities. His observations are summarized in Table 3.[10]

Thus, Tienda de Cuervo's careful inspection revealed the fairly sizable Spanish-speaking population of the province as well as its wide dispersal; made reference to living conditions; emphasized the early importance of ranching; reflected two mining camps of rather limited production and population; further discussed the growth of such crops as maize, beans, pumpkins, and vegetables throughout the province; and finally pointed out that fish, salt, beef, mutton, hides, and tallow constituted the principal items of export.[11] Although his population figures for the entire province cannot be determined exactly because of his estimates and mixing of counts by families and persons, he did

Table 3

Population and Description of Settlements
in Nuevo Santander (1757)

Settlement	Population Description
Villa of Güemes	Nearly 400 people living in grass-covered huts.
Hoyos (today Hidalgo)	Some 575 people, including a few Tlax-caltecan Indians. Some stone houses, but mostly adobe huts.
Real del Borbón (now Villagrán)	Fourteen *haciendas* surrounding the mining community.
Villa de Aguayo (today Ciudad Victoria)	Slightly more than 400 people.
Llera	Had 71 families in "wretched" mud huts.
Altamira	On seacoast; had 356 inhabitants, mostly Negroes, mulattoes, and Huastec Indians.
Capital, Villa of Santander (today Jiménez)	Over 100 families totaling more than 450 people. Huts and a few adobe houses. Escandón's home made of stone and took up four-fifths of one side of block facing plaza.
Soto la Marina	Had 221 people, including 9 soldiers. Poverty-stricken, but some commerce in salt.
Reynosa	Had 289 inhabitants, mostly engaged in ranching.
Camargo	Largest settlement in the whole colony with 637 persons living in attractive adobe homes, well arranged in the town.
Mier	Had 39 families living in mud huts.
Revilla (today Guerrero)	Some 357 Spaniards, mestizos, and mulattoes.
Dolores	Ranch owned by José Vásquez Borrego, with 23 families of laborers living in huts.
Laredo	Ranching establishment of 85 people; owner was Captain Tomás Sánchez.
Real de los Infantes (today Bustamante)	Mining camp of 200 persons.

provide a detailed listing of population and livestock for the six settlements of the Lower Río Grande Valley in 1757, as shown in Table 4.[12]

Table 4

Numbers of People and Animals in Lower
Río Grande Valley Settlements (1757)

Settlement	Inhabitants	Livestock
Reynosa	290	17,261
Camargo	678	81,963
Mier	274	44,015
Revilla	357	51,008
Dolores	123	9,050
Laredo	85	10,211
Totals	1,807	213,508

An official report on the general status of Nuevo Santander in 1795 noted that the province contained 1 *ciudad* (Horcasitas), 25 *villas*, 3 *reales de minas* mining districts, 17 *haciendas*, 437 *ranchos*, and 8 missions. The total population of the province amounted to 30,450 *personas de razón* (reasonable, or civilized, people, meaning both whites and mixed bloods), 1,434 Christianized Indians, and 2,190 uncoverted Indians, called *Gentiles*. These people possessed a total of 799,874 head of livestock, including 111,777 cattle, 530,711 sheep and goats, 92,198 mares, 37,501 horses, 28,800 mules, and 8,621 burros. Some of the largest settlements were Santa Bárbara (2,147 people), Tula (2,103), Hoyos (1,884), San Carlos (1,346), and San Nicolás (1,313). The capital at Santander possessed a total of 806 people. Among the smallest communities were Croix (330) and Llera (334). Along the Lower Río Grande were Reynosa (1,191), Camargo (1,174), Mier (973), Revilla (1,079), and Laredo (636). In addition, the province had three companies of regular troops (222 men in all) and twenty-eight militia (2,660 men) for its defense.[13]

Although statistics are lacking for population figures at the end of Spain's administration in 1821, it is apparent that Nuevo Santander had already passed the thirty thousand mark as early as 1795. These figures may be somewhat misleading, since other districts may have been included in the total figures. However, Nuevo Santander itself had become an especially populous ranching frontier by the early nineteenth century and was in every way more heavily settled and more affluent than its neighboring province of Texas.

The *villa* of San Agustín de Laredo offers a particularly valuable case study in the expansion of the civilian population on this frontier. Although it was the last settlement established by Escandón, its location on the north bank of the Río Grande, its continuous occupation since 1755, and the nature of its early inhabitants seem to justify a more intensive analysis of its settlement, its people, their way of life, and its population growth in the Spanish period. Laredo was neither the largest nor the smallest of the civil communities in Nuevo Santander; it was, it would seem, a typical municipality.

Laredo's first four families, led by Tomás Sánchez de la Barrera y Gallardo, captain in charge, established themselves on May 15, 1755. In two years the population grew to eleven families and four bachelors, a total of eighty-five persons.[14] Captain Sánchez and his wife, Doña Catarina de Uribe, brought with them nine children and seven servants, the largest household listed.[15] By 1767, when Laredo was officially granted its charter as a *villa*, its population had reached two hundred.[16]

Twenty-two years later, in 1789, there were seven hundred Spaniards, mestizos, and mulattoes at Laredo.[17] The general report of 1795 showed a drop to 636 persons,[18] but an 1819 census, prepared only two years before the end of Spanish administration, revealed that Laredo consisted of the *villa* itself and forty-five independent *ranchos*, with a total population for the entire district of 1,418 persons.[19] Thus, this small ranching establishment of four families (perhaps twenty to twenty-five people) in 1755 grew to more than 1,400 inhabitants by 1819, making it larger than any settlement in Texas except San Antonio de Béxar.

Escandón recruited settlers originally at Querétaro, but Nuevo León and Coahuila furnished the overwhelming majority of the original residents. The Huastecan region south of the Río Pánuco also furnished some of the early inhabitants, and some European-born soldiers were among those who left Querétaro in late 1748 to establish the first communities. Cerralvo, Linares, and Cadereita in Nuevo León furnished one hundred men for the first colonizing expedition, and Monclova in Coahuila also supplied some settlers. The Saltillo area must have contributed the Tlaxcaltecan Indians reported by Tienda de Cuervo at Hoyos in 1757.[20] On this frontier, then, as on others in northern New Spain, most of the settlers came from nearby, earlier-established provinces, not from distant locations and certainly not in any number from Spain itself.

Class structures and distinctions seem to have been very hazy in Nuevo Santander from the beginning. Classes were not even reflected in the Tienda de Cuervo listing for Laredo in 1757. There was little, if any, rivalry reminiscent of that between *peninsulares* (Spaniards born on the Iberian Peninsula) and *criollos* in Mexico City, the older parts of New Spain, and other Spanish domains in the New World. [The only apparent record of the existence of classes on this frontier is in the listings of people for official reports and census returns.] One's class had nothing to do with the amount or location of the land he received, his occupation, or his status in the frontier settlements. In fact, census reports do not group people by class, but list them at random. The *gente de razón* consisted of Spaniards, including, as was the general practice all over the frontier, native-born people of Spanish descent; mestizos, and mulattoes. Civilized Indians, such as the Huastecs and Tlaxcaltecans on this frontier, were occasionally also counted as *gente de razón*. In the 1789 census report there were 334 Spaniards (47.7 per cent of the total population of 700), 188 mulattoes, and 178 mestizos. The 1819 census for Laredo reported no Europeans, 620 Spaniards (43.7 per cent of the total 1,418), and 798 Indians, mestizos, and other castes.[21]

The large majority of these settlers was occupied in raising cattle, other livestock, and crops. This was as true at the end of the period from 1748 to 1821 as it was at the beginning. Escandón planted ranching and farming settlements both in the central part of the province and in the Lower Río Grande Valley. Félix Calleja's general report of 1795 noted that most of the people were *pastores* (shepherds) and ranchers; only a few were full-time agricultural workers.[22] Laredo was settled exclusively by stockmen, and it remained so for its first dozen years. Tienda de Cuervo's inspection of 1757 revealed that corn, cane, and beans were grown by the settlers at Camargo in the river bottoms, and that the people living at Revilla raised their own foodstuffs. At all other settlements in the Lower Río Grande region, irrigation attempts had ended in failure and the raising of livestock had therefore become the principal occupation. Tienda de Cuervo, besides listing the numbers of livestock in 1757, reported on domestic animals; Laredo, for example, had a total of 201—166 horses, 20 jennies, 13 jacks, and 2 burros—among fifteen families.[23]

Soldiers, missionaries, royal officials, merchants, artisans, and servants made up the remainder of the male population of Nuevo Santander. A total of 2,882 troops, of whom only 222 were regulars, were present in the province in 1795. Franciscan missionaries came with the first settlers, but their numbers diminished in the early nineteenth century. A parish priest and two officials from the Royal Treasury appear in the Laredo census for 1819, along with fourteen soldiers and nine artisans. Two stonemasons, two carpenters, two tailors, and three shoemakers, all living in poverty and forced to find supplemental work, resided at Laredo that year. Ten years earlier the Laredo records had shown the presence of a merchant.[24]

Ranching dominated the Spanish way of life, both economically and socially, in Nuevo Santander. This does not mean that the prevailing system of land ownership was based upon large livestock ranches, although those of Escandón at Santa Ana, of Tomás Sánchez at Laredo, and particularly of José de Borrego at Dolores clearly reveal that each of these owners had many people working for him and that his holdings were indeed extensive. Borrego, in fact, was an absentee owner, living in Coahuila while twenty-three families performed the daily work at his *hacienda* north of the Río Grande.[25] The smaller *rancho*, or stock farm, however, was the predominant rural establishment in Nuevo

Santander, while the *villa* became the most numerous urban one in the seventy-two years of Spanish occupation.

With an economy based largely upon livestock raising and agricultural production, land allocation naturally became an important prerequisite in the settlement and growth of the province. From the beginning officials took extreme care to define the limits of land grants as well as a clearly established system for obtaining them, both within the communities and in the surrounding countryside. Difficulties arose from overlapping grants, resale and divisions of property, uncertain and changing natural boundaries, and conflicting claims arising not only among individuals but between settlements as well.

In the beginning, lands were not assigned or granted in severalty. Instead, large royal grants were made to the colonizer (Escandón), estimating two *sitios de ganado mayor* and six *caballerías* per family. Lands would then be apportioned by the colonizer to the settlers, with community captains receiving a double allocation. Colonists were usually exempted from royal taxation for ten years. This remained the prevailing land system in Nuevo Santander until the first private grants were made by royal officials after 1764.[26]

Don Juan Fernando de Palacio, a field marshal of the king's armies in New Spain, and Don José de Osorio y Llamas, an attorney, were commissioned in 1767 to visit the province of Nuevo Santander, primarily to distribute its lands and regularize the administration of the province. This general inspection resulted in the granting of land to private individuals in each community. Lands were allocated according to their intended use, some for grazing, some for agricultural purposes, and others for community use. Towns were officially surveyed, lots were laid out and distributed, and charters were granted to such settlements as Laredo, which on June 9, 1767, was officially incorporated as a *villa*. The commissioners revoked the previous grant of seventy-five *sitios* to José de Borrego, because the land had been intended for actual settlement, and this provision had not been carried out by the colonizer. The jurisdiction of Laredo was set as extending for six leagues (about sixteen miles) in all directions from its plaza. The plaza itself was surveyed to measure 80 by 100 *varas*, and streets (each 10 *varas* wide so that horses could pass freely) and town lots were laid out according to a precise system. Town lots were granted by the *alcalde mayor* (chief administrative official of the town), since a municipal form of government was being established to replace the military one. All colonists were required to build houses on their lots within two years of the original grant.[27]

The commissioners then specified that a standard lot would measure 20 *varas* across the front and 40 *varas* in depth. New settlers were to receive their allotments upon application to the *alcalde*, who would assign them vacant lands from the original grant. All settlers, however, were reminded that the land still belonged to the king, and that they were obligated to defend the settlement.

The householders were given the right to elect their municipal officials, by a simple plurality of votes.[28] Beginning on August 3, 1767, the commissioners laid out the towns of Mier, Camargo, and Reynosa, each having a standardized plaza and four-square-league jurisdiction.[29]

Adjoining agricultural and grazing lands were also surveyed and apportioned according to a system that prescribed their use for agricultural purposes or for pasture. The commissioners employed a system of measurement known as a *porción* (a lot, or portion), consisting of two *sitios de ganado mayor* for grazing and twelve *caballerías* for raising crops. Land on both sides of the Río Grande was included; upon application each settler was to receive at least one portion, with a river frontage of about nine-thirteenths of a mile and a depth of approximately eleven to fourteen miles. Double portions were provided for the founders of a settlement, specifically Tomás Sánchez at Laredo. At Laredo settlers were divided into three categories. Those who had resided six years or more in the colony were granted one portion each (two *sitios* and twelve *caballerías*); those who had lived in Laredo from two to six years were allotted two *sitios*, but only six *caballerías*; and, finally, the *agregados*, or recent group of settlers, who had arrived within the past two years were provided only two *sitios* and no land for agricultural purposes. Settlers were given their assigned lots, where some were already established, with the provisions that each must take possession within two months and erect suitable landmarks. Copies of deeds were given to the settlers as well as filed in the archives of Laredo.[30] Similar divisions of town lots and rural lands were made at Camargo and Reynosa.[31]

Unlike Texas, Nuevo Santander had some mining activity. Three *reales de minas* grew up in the latter half of the eighteenth century. The Real del Borbón (now Villagrán) and that of Infantes were both listed by Tienda de Cuervo in 1757. By 1795 they were in poor condition, apparently from bad administration. However, the mines at San Nicolás produced seven thousand *marcos* of silver (one *marco* being equivalent to about one-half pound) valued at seven pesos per *marco*, and eight hundred *quintales* (about eighty thousand pounds) of copper, produced at a cost of eight pesos per *quintal* and sold in Vera Cruz for eighteen pesos per *quintal*.[32] Yet this limited copper- and silver-mining industry never became the principal economic activity of the province or attracted many settlers. Compared to the mining activity of Nueva Vizcaya, it was insignificant.

Records of the community of San Agustín de Laredo are abundant for the period following its incorporation as a *villa* in 1767. Intensive study of one such community can give us an excellent understanding of Spanish-speaking society on the frontier and the characteristics of life in a civil municipality.

There is one document pertaining to an early primary school at Laredo. Santiago de Jesús Sánchez proclaimed on March 22, 1783, that farmers and ranchers of the Laredo jurisdiction were to send their children (presumably only boys) under the age of twelve to the new school within eight days after his order was issued. A fine of six pesos was set for those who failed to comply, and those heads of households who purposely concealed eligible children would be fined twenty-five pesos. Fines would be used to pay the teacher, Don Manuel de Aceves, who would be supervised by the parish priest. Each house-holder was instructed to consult with the schoolmaster to arrange for the number of children he might send to the school and to determine whether each child needed "to learn to read or only to pray."[33] Unfortunately, there are no further records for this or any other school at Laredo before Mexican independence was established.

The nearly constant effort by royal authorities to regulate the social life of the settlers tells us much about the customs and transgressions of the people of Laredo. Regulations were provided for even the most minute circumstances, indicating that the practice being outlawed or controlled was not unheard of.

For example, people were not free to enter and leave the *villa* at will. In fact, heads of households wishing to leave Laredo were required to present themselves before the chief magistrate, stating their business, destination, and length of intended absence. An official license, or passport, was required, whatever might be the purpose of their travel. Visitors to the *villa* were ordered to appear immediately before the chief magistrate to inform him of their intended destination and origins, routes by which they had come, and their business in the community. Residents of Laredo who received visitors were to inform this official of their presence or be subject to a fine. In 1779, a curfew was established at nine o'clock, at which time all persons were directed to go to their homes. A mounted soldier patrolled the streets, arresting violators, who were fined twelve pesos and jailed for fifteen days if they were members of the "upper class," or fined six pesos and placed in jail for one month if they were from the "lower class." Fines were used to defray the costs of constructing public buildings. Nearly a decade later the curfew regulation was reissued, but with the provision that violators and those without a proper passport would be put in jail for eight days.[34]

Apparently residents of Laredo had begun the custom of mixed bathing in the Río Grande by 1784. Because the practice was opposed by the parish priest of Laredo, was a bad example for the young children of the community, and was an offense against "Both Majesties," the chief justice issued detailed instructions for its prohibition in some instances and close regulation in others. Heads of families were instructed not to permit their daughters to bathe with any men, even if they were brothers. Married men might accompany their wives when bathing, but no other men could go with them. Women, otherwise, were to bathe at sunset and men only after the sounding of the Angelus. Violators were fined six pesos and put in jail for ten days.[35]

As early as 1781 authorities tried to regulate the introduction and sale of certain liquors. Neither *mescal* (liquor prepared from the agave cactus) nor a variation thereof called *Chinguirito* was to be made or sold by anyone, subject to a fine of fifty pesos and one month in jail for the first offense, and double the punishment for the second one. Nine years later a similar law was issued with the additional stipulation that the liquor should be emptied into the street. Santiago de Jesús Sánchez, chief justice of Laredo, and another official visited the home and business of one Alexandro Escalera, a former resident of Lampazos in Coahuila, who had moved to Laredo "to sell *aguardiente* (brandy) and *mescal* wine." Sánchez reported that he and his assistant poured the liquor out into the public plaza, placed Escalera in jail, and imposed the required fine.[36] Evidently prohibition and antiliquor laws were as difficult to enforce in the eighteenth century as in the twentieth.

Gambling was a major diversion among the settlers on this frontier. Royal and local officials took all sorts of measures to prohibit games of chance in public places and to regulate them in private homes. *Albures* (first draw at monte), *quinze* (fifteen in cards), *veinte y una* (twenty-one), *treinta* (thirty), and all other card games described as depending upon luck were prohibited, even in one's own home. Dice games, skittle, and bowling were also forbidden. In 1790 it was ordered that no one permit these games to be played in his house, since they corrupted families. A fine of six pesos was specified. Fines for violators as well as homeowners in a 1796 regulation ranged from fifty to one hundred pesos for the first offense, jail and exile more than ten leagues from the *villa* for the second offense, and presidial duty outside the province for a period ranging from two to five years for the third one. Artisans, tradesmen, teachers, officials, and day laborers were prohibited from playing even certain games not based on chance or luck during work hours, specified from six in the morning to noon and from two in the afternoon until after the sounding of the Angelus at night.[37]

Other regulations prevented the slaughter of beef cattle without a license from the chief magistrate and the carrying of firearms or other weapons except when residents were outside the *villa*. No parties were permitted to last later than nine or ten o'clock in the evening, and licenses had to be obtained to give them. Furthermore, residents were not to enter the Carrizo Indian village near Laredo without first securing a passport.[38] Apparently this last restriction was an effort to enforce the crown's policy of keeping settlers and pacified Indians apart, but more particularly to prevent unauthorized acquisition of Indian servants from among the 109 Carrizos present in 1788.[39] These Indians were evidently mistreated by settlers; some were placed in stocks or whipped by their owners, treatment that was absolutely prohibited by Captain Ramón Perea in the nineteenth century. He emphasized that any owners guilty of such ill treatment would be required to pay all back wages to their servants and release them immediately to find another job.[40]

Housing conditions in Laredo ranged from primitive *jacales* (brush or wooden huts) to homes of adobe and stone. In 1789 there were in Laredo nine stone houses, two adobes, and seventy-nine *jacales*, with fences and walls of stone, adobe, wooden stakes, and bullrushes.[41] Six years later Félix Calleja reported in his general survey of the province of Nuevo Santander that the cities and *villas* lacked jails, government buildings, inns, and all other public structures; he emphasized also that settlers' homes and principal public buildings were essentially *"xacales de paja"* (huts of straw).[42] Each resident of Laredo was instructed in 1790 to bring fifty large stones (large enough to be pulled by a rope from horseback) for the construction of a jail and other municipal buildings. Settlers or their servants were to contribute their labor for the erection of these buildings or pay a fine of twelve pesos.[43]

In 1814 José Antonio García Davila, chief magistrate of Laredo, prepared a list of thirty-eight residences, their owners, and an estimate of the value of each dwelling. The total worth of these houses was 20,850 pesos, individual amounts ranging from a high of 2,000 pesos each for two homes to a low of 100 pesos. Seven homes were listed at more than 1,000 pesos; eight, at between 500 and 1,000; and twenty-three at below 500.[44]

The material possessions of settlers in addition to their homes may be noted by a cursory analysis of goods listed in the wills of deceased persons. In 1771 Don Nicolás de Campos, of Laredo, listed a *jacal* with a roof of straw, a shotgun (*escopeta*) with its case, a sword, some silk stockings, a short undergarment, cloth trousers, a white undercoat, two large boxes with their keys, two pairs of scissors for shearing sheep, two large books and another of medium size, a picture of La Señora de Belén (the Virgin Mary) and another of Santa Bárbara, and nine hundred and ninety head of livestock—goats, sheep, mares, colts, mules, horses, cattle, and bulls.[45] Doña María Nicolasa Uriburu, a native of Nuevo León but living in Laredo in 1782, distributed her sheep and goats to her daughters and other designated persons. She left a large box to one of her daughters and a medium-sized one to another. Among her other possessions, she left a bed, two copper kettles, six plates, a dress of blue silk, one blouse, and her *jacal*, all to go to her immediate family.[46]

Faustino Ramírez left property valued at 767 pesos when he died in 1815, but his debts of 308 pesos reduced the value of his estate to 459 pesos. He left his home of one stone room and a surrounding mud wall, valued at 150 pesos, and one portion of land lying along the Río Grande and estimated at a value of 50 pesos. Listed among his possessions were eight mules at 25 pesos each, three work mules at 15 pesos apiece, one hundred goats at 4 *reales* a head, and four cows at 8 pesos each.[47] Four years earlier, José María Elizondo, a soldier of the militia company of Laredo, listed his stone house of one room, 200 head of cattle, 3,100 head of sheep and goats, and other livestock.[48] In the same year, 1811, Don Yldefonso García described his inheritance from his father-in-law, specifically itemizing a small house worth 150 pesos and 139 head of livestock, of which 100 were sheep.[49] The will of Doña Alexandra Sánchez, probated in

1815, listed among her possessions two small trunks, four sheets, a large silk shawl with green fringe, a rose-colored tunic, a used cotton coverlet (*colcha*), a religious image carved from wood (*bulto*), another colored silk shawl, cotton and silk stockings, some small boxes, three Talavera jars, a large crystal vase, various pieces of jewelry, handkerchiefs, three pillows, one pair of blue shoes, a rosary with a cross of gold, a silver medal of Nuestra Señora de Guadalupe, a religious image of San José with Jesús, and a large *jacal*. The total value of her estate was set at 526 pesos.[50]

These few selected wills give important information about the possessions of Spanish settlers in the Lower Río Grande Valley. The total value of the goods was not high in any instance. Houses were generally inexpensive, whether they were of stone or brush with straw roofs; most had only one room, and there is no indication that any of them was more than one story high. Furniture was notably absent from the wills, or at least scarce; few pieces other than trunks and boxes were listed. Clothing was not plentiful or pretentious. Large numbers and wide varieties of livestock constituted the principal material possessions of these settlers. Religious images were listed, as were books, although neither may be said to have been plentiful. Finally, in the one instance where land was conveyed, its over-all value was very low. All in all, it may be concluded that the people of Laredo had meager material possessions and very little personal wealth. Their subsistence economy and indebtedness to others showed them to be barely above poverty status.

Incessant attacks of Indians killed and wounded many of the settlers in Nuevo Santander's communities, especially in the first few decades. Indians also ran off large numbers of cattle and horses. This threat continued throughout the period of Spanish administration, particularly in the exposed settlements along the Lower Río Grande. In 1819 Laredo's census showed that thirty-seven of its nearby fifty-four ranchos had been abandoned because of the raids made by the "*naciones várbaras*" (wild, or savage, Indians).[51] In addition, there were the problems of isolation, limited communication with other settlements and provinces, and maintaining life from one day to the next in the face of epidemics, limited medical facilities and personnel, and natural disasters. Long droughts resulted in crop failures; when it did rain, in some years there were floods to drown the crops and demolish the poorly constructed homes. Malaria was reported,[52] and other diseases, especially small-pox, were always threatening these hardy frontier settlers.

The visit of one José María Sánchez, a draftsman on the Mexican Boundary Commission, to Laredo in 1828 provides a contemporary look at one of Nuevo Santander's *villas* just after the end of the colonial era. Sánchez was not impressed with Laredo; it was not, according to him, a prosperous settlement. It consisted of 2,054 people living in crude earthen houses with grass roofs, and it contained only two dusty plazas. The land was suitable chiefly for stockraising;

some corn, beans, and other crops were cultivated in the river bottoms, but no irrigation was practiced and supplies of food were extremely scarce. The people were robust, healthy, and largely white. Their diet consisted of corn and meat with little variety. Sánchez listed their principal occupations as raising cattle, freighting goods by muleback, farming, and military service. Many persons had visible lance and bullet wounds from their encounters with the Comanche Indians. Yet he deplored their leisurely lives, especially their carefree attitudes, fondness for dancing, and disinclination for work. The women, he observed, were attractive, but showed a tendency to pursue lives of luxury and leisure. They also had "rather loose ideas of morality," which caused many of them to have "shameful relations openly, especially with the officers, both because they are more numerous and spend their salary freely, and because they are more skillful in the art of seduction."[53]

Nuevo Santander, in summary, was settled by Spanish-speaking *paisanos* about the middle of the eighteenth century. They came from adjacent frontier provinces, were given royal financial aid, and were under the direction of royal authorities. From the beginning of occupation until the establishment of Mexican independence, these settlers were loyal to the king, government officials in New Spain, and their own local authorities. Even during the war for independence (1810 to 1821) their royalist leanings were preserved. Informed of the insurgency of Father Miguel de Hidalgo y Costilla and the later one of Father José María Morelos to the south, residents of Nuevo Santander refused to participate in either rebellion. Joseph Gonzáles, *alcalde* of Laredo, in fact issued a call on March 9, 1813, for all males to be ready to defend the community, prescribing the death penalty for anyone who dealt with traitors, insurgents, or Indians allied with revolts against royal authority.[54] This attitude was probably directed as much against the insurgencies and filibustering expeditions then prevalent in nearby Texas as it was against the better-known revolts in central Mexico.

The *paisanos* of Nuevo Santander effectively colonized an unpopulated region on the northeastern frontier of New Spain. They established Spain's claim to both banks of the Río Grande by right of actual occupation. Permanent civil communities were established, largely dominated by ranching and agrarian pursuits, but they were far more populous than similar settlements in Texas at any time. Furthermore, their economy and society were based upon private landholdings, family and community orientations, and considerable adaptation of the residents to their environment. These settlers were not great landowners or members of any aristocratic group. They were mostly small farmers and ranchers, artisans, day laborers, and occasionally merchants. Their society not only held this frontier for Spain, but established a Spanish-speaking nucleus of population for southern Texas and Tamaulipas. Their emphasis upon raising large numbers of livestock near the Río Grande became the basis of the huge Texas cattle industry that developed after the Civil War in the United States.

PART II
The North Central Frontier

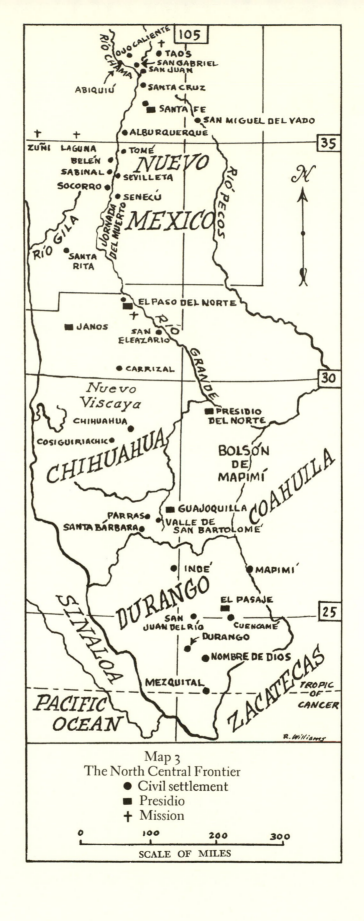

Map 3
The North Central Frontier
● Civil settlement
■ Presidio
✝ Mission

0   100   200   300

SCALE OF MILES

Introduction

Mexico's Central Plateau from Zacatecas to New Mexico was the most important frontier of New Spain during the colonial period. Nueva Vizcaya (New Biscay) and New Mexico were exactly what Herbert Eugene Bolton called this area, "the heart of the North."[1]

This central thrust of Spain's northern expansion led to the early settlement of an extensive region and the persistence of the frontier experience over a longer period of time than in any other region of North America, whether settled by Spanish, English, French, Dutch, or Swedish colonists. The civil settlement and frontier experience of Nueva Vizcaya covered a period of approximately two hundred and fifty years before Mexico achieved her independence from Spain in 1821.

Nueva Vizcaya was the keystone of the northern frontier. Its territorial limits were extended as exploration, discoveries, mining exploitation, and civilian settlements spread northward. From its first communities, in the modern state of Durango, the province expanded to include most of Chihuahua, Sinaloa, Sonora, and Coahuila. Not until 1734 was the combined province of Sinaloa and Sonora detached from Nueva Vizcaya. Chihuahua and Durango, the heart of the province, were a single entity until divided by the Mexican Republic in 1823. The community of Durango was probably the most important settlement in all the provinces considered in this book.

New Mexico was the earliest-settled Spanish borderland now located within the southwestern United States, and it was the most northerly region of the Spanish frontier until Alta California was occupied. Its territorial limits extended from a point south of present Ciudad Juárez indefinitely northward, eastward, and westward, with a nucleus of settlements on the Río Grande between El Paso del Norte and Taos. In the south the prosperous Paso del Norte region (present Ciudad Juárez and a district reaching southeastward along the Río Grande) was considered an integral part of New Mexico from the late seventeenth century to the early nineteenth. The history of this region, therefore, properly belongs to New Mexico in the Spanish colonial era rather than to the present state of Texas. Furthermore, *paisanos* lived in the entire region; they planted the roots of European culture along the Río Grande and established Spanish societal customs so thoroughly that some are still observed today.

81

The two provinces were alike in many ways. Both contained many Indians, ranging from highly developed, sedentary groups to nomadic peoples who spread havoc among the Spanish settlers at various times. Tarahumaras, Tobosos, Apaches, Comanches, Navajos, and Utes—all were in certain times and places a major threat to Spanish settlers. Warfare was endemic; it was perhaps more violent and more continuous on this frontier than on any other in northern New Spain. Yet missionary activities, largely those of the Franciscan order, were present in both Nueva Vizcaya and New Mexico from an early time. Presidios also played an important role in the gradual pacification of Indian nations and in the protection of settlers and missionaries. Civil communities where the number of civilian settlers exceeded that of other frontier districts became important frontier institutions in both provinces. At the beginning of the nineteenth century, New Mexico had more Spanish settlers than Texas, Alta California, and Pimería Alta combined. Nueva Vizcaya at the same time had a larger population of colonists than any other frontier province located south of the present international boundary. As a result of this long settlement experience, of the development of economic and social ties between Nueva Vizcaya and New Mexico, and of the relatively large population, Spain succeeded in planting a lasting Spanish culture on both sides of the Río Grande.

Two important differences between Nueva Vizcaya and New Mexico should be noted. Mining played an important role in the settlement and economic development of Nueva Vizcaya, whereas it had little to do with the permanent colonization of New Mexico. Agriculture was important to both provinces, but in New Mexico the absence of any other means of livelihood emphasized the importance of small farming, ranching, and pastoral pursuits to the settlers. Second, Spanish administration on the northern frontier tended to favor Nueva Vizcaya, not New Mexico. Durango was the center of political and church authority until well into the eighteenth century, when Chihuahua became increasingly important, especially after it became the capital of the Provincias Internas del Norte. Nueva Vizcaya, therefore, was the seat of Spanish authority on the entire northern frontier. On the other hand, the governor of New Mexico remained, like the governor of most Spanish frontier provinces, responsible and powerful only within the confines of his jurisdiction. Nor did New Mexico ever possess great political importance in the minds of Spanish officials; it was even considered for occasional abandonment but continued to exist, largely because the Spanish settlers were already there, many Indians had been converted to Christianity, and Spain needed it as a buffer against encroachments of unfriendly Indians and foreigners.

4. Nueva Vizcaya

The search for silver and the leadership of Francisco de Ibarra were principal factors in the occupation and settlement of Nueva Vizcaya. Following the discovery of silver bonanzas at Zacatecas in 1548, mining interest spread within a decade to the area north of that city. Before the end of the sixteenth century mining had become the principal impetus for the establishment of civilian settlers in the province of Nueva Vizcaya. Indeed, of the three mining regions—northwest coastal, basins and ranges on the eastern side of the Central Plateau, and eastern slopes of the Sierra Madre Occidental—the last lay almost entirely within the jurisdiction of Nueva Vizcaya, and it became the largest mining district of the entire northern region.[1] Yet agriculture and ranching prospered too, usually being introduced with the advance of the *reales de minas*, or mining districts,[2] primarily to supply the needs of the miners. This trend, established early in the history of Nueva Vizcaya, continued throughout most of the colonial experience there.

Francisco de Ibarra, nephew of the silver millionaire Diego de Ibarra of Zacatecas, became the most noted *conquistador*, explorer, and colonizer of the province he named "Nueva Vizcaya" after his home district in Spain. As governor and captain general of the new province, he explored the Central Plateau and the Pacific coastal regions, frequently crossing the Sierra Madre Occidental on his expeditions. He went on his first venture in 1554, at the age of sixteen, when Zacatecas was the most northerly settlement in the region.[3] When he died in 1575, before his thirty-sixth birthday, he left a legacy of lasting settlement from Durango and Nombre de Dios in the south to Sinaloa on the west and to Santa Bárbara, today in the southern part of the state of Chihuahua, on the north. His initiative, leadership, financial support, and organizational ability helped to secure Nueva Vizcaya for the crown.[4] He founded the province's first mine and *hacienda*, setting the pattern for its two industries—mining and raising livestock—during the colonial period; he encouraged the development of ranching and agriculture, as well as the evangelical projects of religious orders among the many Indian nations. "Under his hand Nueva Vizcaya was born and began to grow," although the number of Spanish-speaking colonists remained "pitifully small" for the first hundred years of its occupation.[5]

In 1558, only four years after his first expedition, Ibarra established the *real de minas* of San Martín. Thirty citizens, including one friar, came from Zacatecas and founded the settlement, primarily to work the mines.[6] Of greater importance, however, are his royal commission of July 24, 1562, and his founding of two permanent Spanish settlements, Durango and Nombre de Dios, in the following year. King Philip II in the royal *capitulación* of 1562 granted Ibarra the right to explore, conquer, and settle at his own expense the unknown region beyond San Martín. In return for his service to the crown, Ibarra was granted the titles of governor and captain general of Nueva Vizcaya for his lifetime and that of one descendant. He could award *encomiendas* of Indians to deserving members of his expeditions, and he had the authority to appoint lesser officials within his jurisdiction. In addition to these priviliges, he and his followers were exempted from payment of the *alcabala* for a period of twenty years, and Ibarra was required to pay only one-twentieth of the profits derived from the exploitation of precious metals instead of the usual *quinto real*, or one-fifth.[7]

Ibarra's principal exploratory and colonizing expedition left San Martín on January 24, 1563, and founded the communities of Nombre de Dios and Durango before the year was out. Thirteen *vecinos* established the settlement of Durango in November-December, 1563. Located in the fertile Guadiana River valley, its initial settlers were principally soldiers, led by Captain Alonso de Pacheco. They selected lots in the new community and the surrounding countryside and were furnished livestock, seed, and implements with which to begin their work. By 1569, Nombre de Dios and Durango were reported to contain thirty *vecinos* each, or perhaps a population of three hundred in all.[8]

Ibarra's town-founding activities did not end with these two settlements. In May or June, 1564, he directed the founding of San Juan de Sinaloa on the banks of the Fuerte River west of the mountains.[9] Three years later one of his followers, Rodrigo del Río, established a *real de minas* at Indé; before Ibarra's death in 1575 thirty Spanish families had also settled the mining district of Santa Bárbara, thus becoming the first colonists within the limits of the present state of Chihuahua. Others established the nearby farming and stock-raising district of San Bartolomé del Valle in the Río Florido valley. This collection of Spanish settlers was primarily intended to supply the mining community at Santa Bárbara with foodstuffs and other needed products.[10]

Nor were these settlements on the eastern slopes of the Sierra Madre Occidental the only sixteenth-century establishments in Nueva Vizcaya. The *villa* of Saltillo and the agricultural region near Parras were also settled in the mid-1570s by Spanish-speaking people; they were part of Nueva Vizcaya for administrative purposes until their transfer to Coahuila in 1787. Francisco de Urdiñola, energetic governor after Ibarra's death, arranged for the migration of four hundred Tlaxcaltecan Indians to the new settlement of San Esteban de

Nueva Tlaxcala, near Saltillo, in 1591. These early communities and later developments in northeastern Nueva Vizcaya are discussed more fully in the chapter on Coahuila and Nuevo León.[11]

The seventeenth century was a period of gradual expansion until the discovery of silver deposits near Parral. Durango remained the principal community, the capital of the province, and the only frontier civil establishment to be officially recognized as a *ciudad*, with all of its rights and privileges, after 1621. It was not only the seat of civil authority in the north but the principal clerical establishment, with the Bishopric of Durango having extensive administrative authority over the far-flung frontier regions of Sonora, Sinaloa, and New Mexico, as well as local authority.[12] Mota y Escobar described the city of Durango and its surrounding region in the first decade of the seventeenth century. He noted that it was already a *villa* of fifty Spanish *vecinos*, living principally in adobe houses. There were four principal streets running from east to west, with others from north to south. In addition to the *casas reales* (royal buildings), the town contained a parish church, a hospital, a stone mill for grinding wheat, and fifteen stores run by Spanish merchants where all sorts of Castilian, Chinese, and local clothing were available. Products were brought from Mexico City by cart for sale to miners, owners of large *estancias* (ranches and farms), and *vecinos*. The governor and captain general lived in Durango, according to Mota y Escobar, as did some eighty Negroes and mulattoes, who were slaves or free domestic servants for the *vecinos*. The people cultivated grapes and other fruits common to Castile in their gardens in addition to raising grain and livestock. To the south of the city there was a *pueblo* of pacified Chichimec Indians. However the principal fields, where wheat, corn, beef cattle, and other large animals were raised belonged to Spaniards. To the north and west were the principal mines. Although some were already abandoned, those near Cuencamé were prosperous, and about one hundred Spaniards lived there. At nearby San Juan del Río, Mota y Escobar reported a combined community of thirty Indian *vecinos* and thirteen or fourteen Spaniards raising fruits and producing wine.[13]

San José del Parral (now Hidalgo del Parral) was unquestionably the most important new civil settlement of the seventeenth century. The discovery of silver there probably occurred in 1629, and a mining rush evidently followed, because the *corregidor* (district official) of Zacatecas took great pains to prohibit the departure of his people from his jurisdiction the next year. Two bonanzas in the 1630s caused a mining rush to the new *real de minas*, the population reaching three hundred *vecinos* as early as 1632 and eight hundred by the end of the decade.[14] The Parral mines not only caused the growth of a new Spanish community but also stimulated the development of commerce, agriculture, and livestock raising throughout Nueva Vizcaya. "In a few years," according to the noted historian Francisco R. Almada, Parral "was converted

Overview of Chihuahua, Mexico, in the nineteenth century. *Courtesy Denver Public Library Western Collection.*

into the most important urban center of Nueva Vizcaya. . . ."[15] Although Durango remained the legal capital of the province, after 1667 most governors lived in Parral.[16] Within a year following the strike at a mine known as "La Negrita," San José del Parral had over three hundred miners, merchants, *hacendados* (owners of *haciendas*), clerics, slaves, adventurers, and drifters. Four hundred claims were filed in one year; the mines of Parral came to produce fifty thousand *marcos* of silver valued at nearly two hundred thousand pesos.[17] Indeed, Parral was known as the "principal place" in Nueva Vizcaya and produced the most income.[18]

Don Joseph Francisco Marín, the viceregal *visitador-general*, or inspector, of Nueva Vizcaya in 1693, left a comprehensive account of the province. He noted that the boundaries of Nueva Vizcaya began in the south about ten or twelve leagues below Durango, the capital, and extended northward to (but not including) the new settlements at Paso del Norte. Nueva Galicia, in the south, Sonora and Sinaloa to the west, and Nuevo León and Coahuila to the east roughly bounded the province. Durango remained the most important settlement, with Parral a close second.[19]

In addition to these two settlements there were new presidios founded to provide military protection on this distant frontier. At the beginning of the eighteenth century there were twelve presidios—six in Nueva Vizcaya, two in New Mexico, two in Nuevo León, and one each in Sonora and Coahuila—in the North Central frontier region. The total military force for all of these posts combined did not exceed 503 troops, each paid at the average annual salary of 540 pesos, although variations from one presidio to another existed and yearly changes occurred as well.[20]

Whereas Durango had been the principal community of the sixteenth century and Parral had rivaled it in the seventeenth century, Chihuahua was important in the eighteenth century. San Felipe el Real de Chihuahua grew to *villa* status from two small mining settlements, San Felipe and Santa Eulalia, founded in the first decade of the eighteenth century. By 1709, a number of Spanish-speaking people and their servants had come to live there; Governor Antonio de Deza y Ulloa authorized the founding of a district to be known as San Francisco de Cuellar on the site of the modern city of Chihuahua. On October 1, 1718, a viceregal decree elevated this civil settlement to *villa* status, specifying that its official name would be "Villa de San Felipe el Real de Chihuahua," the "Felipe" in honor of the first Bourbon monarch of Spain, Philip V.[21]

Other settlements of the eighteenth century included the new presidio of Santa María de las Caldas de Guajoquilla (now Ciudad Jiménez), with its surrounding civilian population, founded in 1753, and the new *pueblo* of Carrizal, established in 1758.[22] Originally designated a *paraje* (place), Carrizal was settled mostly by retired or invalid soldiers with their families. Forty-seven Spanish *vecinos*, mostly from the *villa* of El Paso del Norte and neighboring San Lorenzo, were selected to move southward from the Río Grande to form the initial complement of Carrizal.[23] It appears that fifty-two *vecinos* actually carried out the settlement, including forty-five married men, one widower, three widows, two bachelors, and one chaplain.[24] They established themselves, laid out the streets and plazas, and received house lots according to the plan depicted on page 89.[25]

The Spanish-speaking civilian population of Nueva Vizcaya grew in numbers and spread throughout the province over the course of two and one-half centuries. Expansion was gradual in the latter half of the sixteenth century, nearly stagnant except for redistribution in the seventeenth, and accelerated in the last one hundred years of Spanish administration, with both new settlements and population growth in the older communities. Dispersal to agricultural and

Chihuahua, Mexico, in the nineteenth century, showing the plaza, the orientation of streets with intersections at corners, the layout of blocks, and the arcade construction on one side of the plaza. *Courtesy Denver Public Library Western Collection.*

ranching lands from established towns also contributed to the population growth, as did the mixing of European, Indian, and Negro peoples. After the arrival of early settlers in Durango, there was little immigration, and that was from nearby provinces. In the eighteenth century the most notable population trend in the province was internal migration, from Durango to Chihuahua primarily.

The thirteen *vecinos* reported as founders of Durango in 1563 would seem to indicate about sixty-five persons in all.[26] Six years later, when the city and Nombre de Díos each had thirty *vecinos*, there were perhaps one hundred and fifty persons in each community, totaling about three hundred in the entire province.[27] With the continued expansion of civil communities northward, the

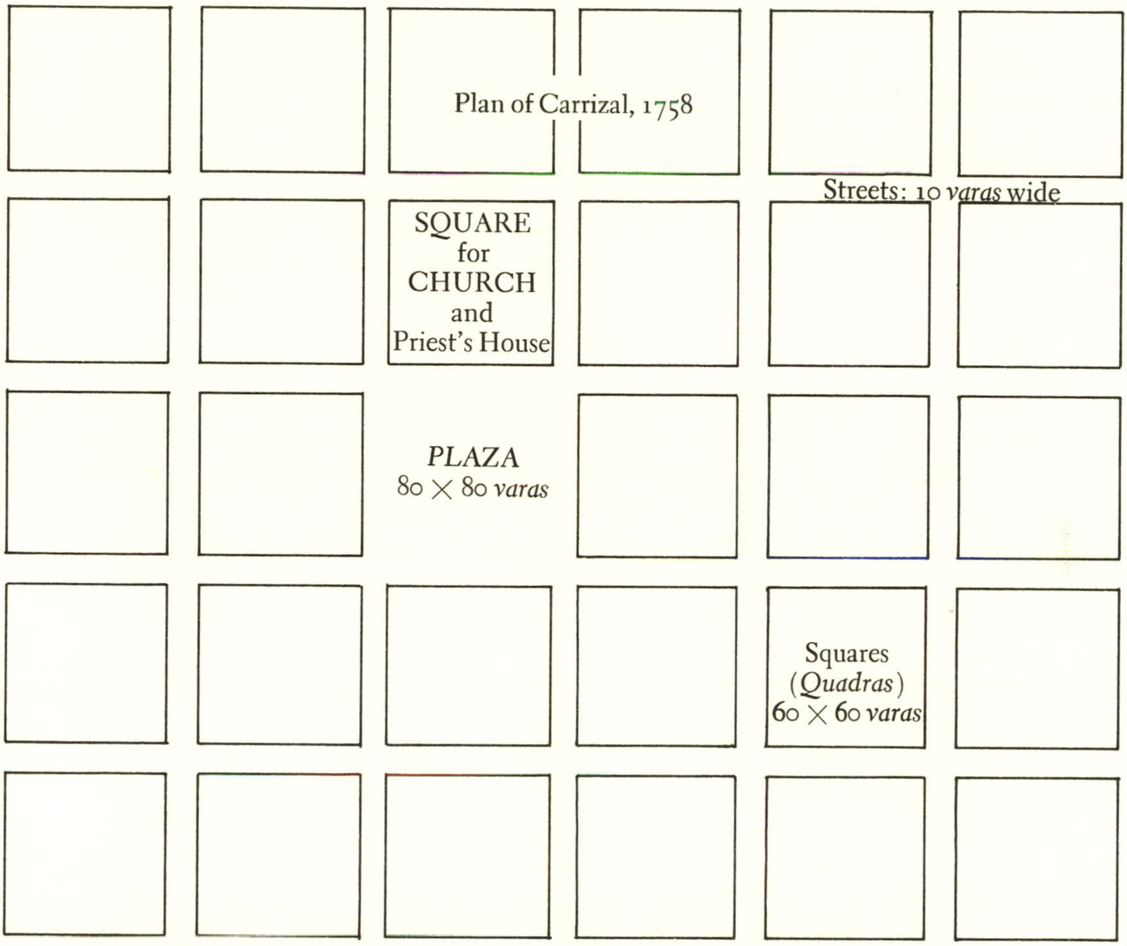

Plan of Carrizal, 1758

Streets: 10 *varas* wide

SQUARE
for
CHURCH
and
Priest's House

PLAZA
80 × 80 *varas*

Squares
(*Quadras*)
60 × 60 *varas*

Source: Indice, o descripción plano del pueblo, que se pretende hazer en el paraje llamado del Carrizal, Documentos de 1758, Juárez Archives, microcopy, Reel 42, Frame 061, University of Texas at El Paso Library

population increased gradually. Santa Bárbara, for example, the first Spanish establishment in the present state of Chihuahua, had thirty families, or perhaps one hundred and fifty persons in all, before the end of this initial period. In the first decade of the seventeenth century, Mota y Escobar noted that Santa Bárbara had some ten or twelve *vecinos*, who lived by farming, raising livestock, or merchandising; he added that there were other Spanish settlers in the farming community of Valle de San Bartolomé, seven leagues from Santa Bárbara, where there were large fields of wheat and corn and great quantities of live-stock.[28]

Governor and captain general of Nueva Vizcaya Francisco de Urdiñola (the younger, not the founder of the Tlaxcaltecan settlement near Saltillo) completed an extensive census of the province in 1604. *Alcaldes mayores* of the various jurisdictions prepared lists of the Spanish population in their areas, with the names of *vecinos*, their married status, and their trades, as well as details about wheat farms, mines, ranches, and ore-treatment plants owned by settlers. These lists were consolidated into one document of statistical information for each community and the province as a whole. According to the census, there were 472 *vecinos* in the province, or perhaps 2,300 people in all. Of the 472 *vecinos*, 233 were married, 198 were bachelors, 24 were widowers or widows, and 17 were of unspecified marital status. (Widows with their own households were considered *vecinos*, equal in status for census purposes to the male heads of families.) The settlers were scattered over twelve districts, five of which contained 324 *vecinos*, or 68.6 per cent of those in the province. Leading settlements in 1604 were Minas de Cuencamé (121 *vecinos*), Villa de Durango (80), Real de Santa Bárbara (51, including 29 at Valle de San Bartolomé), Valle de San Juan del Río (50), and Villa de Santiago de Saltillo (22). The remainder of the Spanish population was scattered in outlying settlements, in mining districts, on rural *haciendas* and *ranchos*.[29]

Although a new settlement was founded at Parral and occasional presidial establishments appeared in the seventeenth century, the population did not increase appreciably. *Visitador-general* Don Joseph Francisco Marín in 1693 estimated that there were not more than five hundred families in Nueva Vizcaya.[30] This would indicate that there were perhaps only 2,500 people in the province, reflecting very little variation from the figures of the first decade of the seventeenth century and an increase of approximately eight per cent in the course of nearly ninety years. The primary reasons for this slow rate of growth and underpopulation of the province, according to Marín, were the relative isolation of Nueva Vizcaya and the continued Indian depredations. Although none of the native tribes was considered large by itself, there were 159 separate Indian nations in Nueva Vizcaya. Pacification and conversion, interspersed with sporadic rebellions, among the Tepehuanes, Acaxees, Xiximes, Tarahumaras, Conchos, and Tobosos (a particularly wild people whom Marín described as having no permanent settlements and no planting or farming culture and as being prone to eat some of their captives while skinning others) had occupied the first three quarters of the century. Marín noted that there was still apostasy among these supposedly Christianized Indians, caused in part by knowledge of the Pueblo rebellion in New Mexico and in part by the Indians' natural desire to plunder and harass the Spanish population.[31]

To correct the "wretched state" created by Indian raids, sparse population, and an epidemic,[32] Marín recommended a general plan of action. First, a coordinated, full-scale war should be made against the hostile Indians. Second, the present five presidios should be retained and strengthened, and a sixth one added. Third, he urged settlement by soldiers and civilians to remedy its "depopulated" condition. Presidial soldiers, according to Marín, should be married men and should be encouraged to stay near their presidios, thus becoming permanent residents. They were to be given lands to cultivate as an incentive to staying. Civilian settlers, preferably those transported from Galicia in Spain or from the Canary Islands at royal expense, should be established in communities having sixty or seventy men. They were to be provided arquebuses, ammunition, horses, oxen, plows, and grains, and lands were to be divided equally among them. Furthermore, they should be exempt from paying tribute in return for their twin role as settlers and citizen militiamen.[33]

Eighteenth century statistics reveal a marked growth in the population of the province, especially during the second half of the period and in the southern portion of Nueva Vizcaya, where Apache incursions were seldom experienced by that time. It should be noted that the Comanche Indians appeared in New Mexico and on the Great Plains to the eastward about the first decade of the eighteenth century. With their superior horsemanship, efficient tribal organization, and more reliable supply of firearms from French traders, they became not only a serious menace to Spanish settlers in New Mexico but exerted a constant pressure on the eastern Apache nations, driving them southward into northern Nueva Vizcaya and Sonora. The former, roughly corresponding to the modern state of Chihuahua, bore the brunt of these Apache attacks, which lasted until the last decade of the eighteenth century and occurred intermittently thereafter. During the last century of Nueva Vizcaya's colonial experience the southern part of the province, corresponding approximately to the modern state of Durango, was largely a *"tierra de paz"* (pacified land), while the northern portion was still a *"tierra de guerra"* (land of warfare) and very much a frontier region.

About 1760, according to the population estimates of Bishop Pedro Tamarón y Romeral of Durango and Fray Francisco de San Buenaventura, Bishop of Guadalajara, there were approximately 117,200 people living in Nueva Vizcaya. From this figure we may subtract the 70,050 pacified Indians, to reach a total of 47,150 Spaniards and mixed bloods.[34] However, H. H. Bancroft's statistics are somewhat higher; he shows a total of approximately sixty thousand people of Spanish and mixed-blood heritage. Southern Nueva Vizcaya contained two-thirds of these people (forty-six thousand), nine thousand of them living in the vicinity of the capital city of Durango. The rest were scattered in thirty-six settlements around the province: two *villas*, one presidio, fourteen *reales de minas*, and many large *haciendas*.[35] Northern Nueva

Vizcaya had twenty-three thousand Spaniards and mixed bloods concentrated in sixteen settlements with their adjacent *haciendas* and *ranchos*. These included two *villas*, four *reales de minas*, and three presidios.[36] The four military presidios were undoubtedly Janos, Los Pilares, Guajoquilla, and El Pasaje.[37]

Some ideas about the people of this northern region and its communities can be obtained from reports by two contemporary observers. The first, Nicolás de Lafora, visited the Nueva Vizcayan frontier in 1767 as part of the general inspection conducted by the Marqués de Rubí. The second, Pedro Alonso O'Crouley, did not actually visit the province, but made extensive demographic studies from Mexico City in 1774. Lafora noted that the province was inhabited by Spaniards, mestizos, and mulattoes, mostly concentrated in the communities of Durango, Saltillo, Parras, Parral, Valle de San Bartolomé, six presidios, Chihuahua, and Cosiguiriachic, with others scattered throughout the countryside at numerous *haciendas*.[38] He emphasized the importance of such cities as Durango (also called Guadiana, after the river near by), with its population of 1,311 families of Spaniards, mestizos, and mulattoes, totaling 8,937 communicants; the *villa* of San Felipe el Real de Chihuahua, with its mixed population of some four hundred families, all in deplorable condition because the mines were not being worked as a result of the Apache threat; and Valle de San Bartolomé, a thriving settlement district of 4,751 Spaniards, mestizos, and mulattoes, who grew a wide variety of crops including good grapes, other fruits, maize, wheat, beans, and barley and made a little wine and brandy.[39] O'Crouley reported in 1774 a total population of 558,525 for the Bishopric of Durango, including 50,775 Spaniards, 203,100 mixed bloods, and 304, 650 Indians.[40] Of course, the bishopric included much more than simply the province of Nueva Vizcaya, but the figures do give an idea of the population of northern New Spain in a period when O'Crouley noted the total population of the viceroyalty as being 7,112,270.[41] According to his estimates, the city of Durango had 3,500 Spanish and mixed-blood families; the Real de Chihuahua, also 3,500; Villa de Parras, 500; Saltillo, 60; Valle de San Bartolomé, 300; the Real del Parral, 300; and the Real de Sombrerete, 500.[42] These figures and those for civil settlements within the bishopric in Sinaloa, Sonora, and New Mexico all seem somewhat high, perhaps because O'Crouley estimated the population on the basis of religious records and did not consult governmental reports.

Population estimates and reported figures for the period 1780–1821 reflected a total of more than one hundred thousand people in Nueva Vizcaya, in spite of Indian depredations, epidemics, and other calamities. Teodoro de Croix, first *comandante-general* of the Provincias Internas del Norte, estimated in 1780 that the five provinces under his jurisdiction had a total of 228,000 Spaniards, mixed bloods, and Christianized Indians. Whereas Coahuila had eight thousand people and Texas half that many, Nueva Vizcaya had "*más de* 100,000" (more than one hundred thousand).[43] He noted that the city of

Durango had 6,460 inhabitants (more than the whole province of Texas) and that there were 12,800 residents in its immediate jurisdiction, or *alcaldía*.[44]

Twenty-six such *alcaldías* were shown in the census of 1780, executed as instructed in the royal order of 1776.[45] In addition to Durango, there were twenty *haciendas* and some eight thousand people in the *alcaldía* of Nombre de Dios (2,300 in the *villa* and its immediate environs); 8,650 people in the jurisdiction of Saltillo (5,200 of them in the *villa* and the neighboring Tlaxcal-tecan settlement of San Esteban de Tlaxcala), where there were also forty-nine *ranchos* and *haciendas*; 7,300 residents in the twin *poblaciones* (towns) of Papasquiaro and Mezquital; 1,400 people at the old mines of Santa Bárbara in southern Chihuahua, now a secondary settlement to the agricultural com-munity of San Bartolomé, with its six thousand inhabitants; 1,700 persons at Mapimí; only 540 in the *alcaldía* called Gallo; and unreported numbers for the scattered livestock-raising *haciendas* in the vicinity of Parras and Cuencamé.[46] Even the twenty-two-year-old community of Carrizal showed a population of 168 persons, in spite of a recent epidemic.[47]

The 1788 census indicated a population of 124,151 in the northern part of Nueva Vizcaya alone. Chihuahua, Parral, San Felipe, Cosiguiriachic, and Valle de los Olivos each had more than five thousand people, whereas Santa Bárbara contained only 1,186.[48] Since the population for the Intendencia of Durango, including all categories except unconverted Indians (Gentiles), was estimated at about one hundred and twenty thousand in the last decade of the eighteenth century,[49] the total for the province of Nueva Vizcaya must have been approximately two hundred and forty-five thousand at the beginning of the nineteenth century.

Lieutenant Zebulon Montgomery Pike, United States Army, and members of his expedition visited Chihuahua involuntarily in the spring of 1807 at the request of *Comandante-general* Nemesio Salcedo and under escort of troops from New Mexico, following their capture in the San Luis Valley near present La Jara, Colorado. The party entered the province on March 23, 1807, from El Paso del Norte, was at Carrizal on the twenty-seventh, and remained in the *villa* of San Felipe el Real de Chihuahua from the second to the twenty-eighth of April.[50] Pike was a keen observer of Chihuahua's population, climate, top-ography, military dispositions, mining operations, social customs, women, and scorpions. He estimated the population of the province [Chihuahua alone or Durango, too?] at two hundred thousand—three-twentieths, Spaniards from Europe; five-twentieths, Creoles; five-twentieths, mixed bloods; and seven-twentieths, Indians. Durango, which he erroneously cited as having been founded in 1550, had forty thousand people, he thought, but he never came anywhere near the city or its jurisdiction. Chihuahua, according to Pike, was the second city of the province, the residence of the *comandante-general*, and had a population of seven thousand.[51]

Mexico achieved her independence from Spain in September, 1821, and two years later the federalist congress of the new republic, after expelling Emperor Agustín de Iturbide, separated Nueva Vizcaya into the individual states of Chihuahua and Durango, thus ending after nearly three centuries the most important and most populous province of New Spain's northern frontier. The official population of the new state of Chihuahua in 1823 was given as 112,694.[52] Assuming that Durango retained its estimated one hundred and twenty thousand people of the 1790s, the total number of residents in Nueva Vizcaya at the end of the colonial period must have approached two hundred and fifty thousand, a remarkable increase from the original thirteen *vecinos* or approximately sixty-five persons, who settled the community of Durango in 1563. In fact, Colonel Juan Camargo of the Royal Corps of Engineers reported in 1815 that the Intendency of Nueva Vizcaya, or Durango, contained a total of 190,564 persons scattered throughout the region in 190 towns, 142 *haciendas*, 304 *ranchos*, 34 missions, and 7 presidios.[53]

Who were these settlers? Where did they come from? What did they do in Nueva Vizcaya? As we have seen, questions can be partially answered by census returns and other official reports. Durango, Parral, Chihuahua, and Santa Bárbara–San Bartolomé were the most significant focal points of Spanish settlement on this frontier throughout the colonial era. Population statistics have been given earlier that depict the growth (decline in the case of Santa Bárbara) of these communities. Yet to understand their real composition, the character of the civilian settlers, and the day-to-day lives of these people, one can study the surviving manuscripts of at least one of these communities, San José del Parral. The Archivo de Hidalgo del Parral, 1631–1821, contains census reports and other documents for Parral, as well as Santa Bárbara and San Bartolomé, covering the last half of the seventeenth century and most of the eighteenth.

One census of 1788 for the *real de minas* of Parral and its jurisdiction gives the origins of some of the residents. Of 105 persons listed by name, slightly more than one-half (54) were native to Parral. The next largest number, fifteen, came from Chihuahua. Four came from Durango, two from the Valle de San Bartolomé, two from San Juan del Río, and one each from Santa Bárbara, Parras, Conchos, and Cosiguiriachic. All these communities were within the boundaries of Nueva Vizcaya. Therefore, a total of eighty-one Spaniards and mixed bloods (seventy-six per cent of the number listed in the census) originated within the province itself. Thirteen more citizens came from other mining camps north of Mexico City, including Zacatecas, Fresnillo, Guanajuato, and Aguascalientes. One man came from the province of México, seat of the viceregal capital, one migrated southward from New Mexico, and another was reported as being from "*tierra caliente*," a hot, humid region, which today would be identified as the eastern coast of Mexico. Eight people (less than eight per cent of the total) were from Spain—three from the Archbishopric of Burgos, one from the Archbishopric of Sevilla, one from the Bishopric of Calorra, and one each from Santander, Castile, and Vizcaya.[54] It would appear that these individuals were principally clerical officials, civil administrators, and merchants.

If we may consider this a typical case (and Parral was one of Nueva Vizcaya's foremost civilian settlements), migration within the province is an obvious fact of life. In Nueva Vizcaya, as in other frontier provinces, countless examples illustrate that the term "Spaniard" was used for all people of white blood born in the New World or to those practicing a Spanish way of life and showing no indication of Indian or Negro ancestry. Perhaps it is synonomous with the "Creole," used elsewhere in New Spain and throughout the rest of colonial Latin America, but which was never in general use on the northern frontier. In this census, for example, the *vecinos* numbered sixty-seven and sixty-eight are reported as Spaniards, but simultaneously as natives of Chihuahua. Mixed bloods listed under varying name designations, such as *coyotes*, free mestizos, and mulattoes, indicate the advanced state of the process described by Luis Navarro García as *mestización*, or mixing of the races.[55] Indeed, according to one specialist on Nueva Vizcaya's history, miscegenation "was more pronounced in the northern mines than in those of the south and central parts of Mexico."[56] Negroes were listed in the census of 1788 (family number fifteen, for example), and there were many mulattoes and "free mulattoes" in the population of Parral, as was the case elsewhere. Indians also lived in Spanish communities, as reflected in family number twenty-eight, where an Indian *vecino* employed as a miner is counted with the rest of the population.[57]

Parral is only one of many frontier communities where by the eighteenth century racial leveling and the process of *mestización*, a vehicle of acculturation, were both in evidence. Conditions on the frontier tended to erase differences between whites and mixed bloods. Although separate counts were taken in statistical data, it became common to classify people according to two generic categories: "*indios*" and "*no indios*" (Indians and non-Indians). Other classifications were "*españoles*," "*españoles y mixtos*," and, more frequently, the single heading "*gente de razón*," civilized people whether they might be Spaniard, Indian, Negro, or any mixture thereof. Actual Spaniards were often described by the term "*europeo*," an all-inclusive word which might be applied not only to Spaniards but to anyone who originated overseas.[58]

These Spanish-speaking people who settled the numerous small urban centers in Nueva Vizcaya implanted the social order, ideas, customs, and civilization of Spain in the New World. These frontier civilian settlers of New Spain created a society which was largely, but not entirely, dedicated to agricultural and pastoral pursuits.[59]

A close look at the occupations of the settlers reveals a wide variety of types

of employment in Nueva Vizcaya. A census of the *real de minas* at Santa
Bárbara in 1649 begins with an entry for one Diego Galiano, a "miner and
farmer" (*labrador*); the second entry is a merchant (*mercader*). Sixty *vecinos*
are listed, some holding two jobs, as indicated in the Galiano example above.
Eleven were miners, a surprising mere eighteen per cent of the total; four were
overseers (*mayordomos*); three, merchants; two, servants; and two, muleteers
(*arrieros*). The remainder included one farmer, a blacksmith, carpenter, cart
driver, mine guard, assayer of metals, and two keepers of the royal metals boxes,
presumably for collecting the *quinto real* due the king.[60]

Some one hundred and forty-nine occupations are listed for *vecinos* residing
in Parral at the time of the 1768 census. Twenty-eight (again about eighteen
per cent) are listed as miners, but another thirty-three were laborers in the
mines. Thus, there were sixty-one people (about forty-two per cent of the
employed population) working directly with mining. However, there were also
fifteen merchants and many artisans—two silversmiths, nine shoemakers, three
blacksmiths, thirteen tailors, two masons, seven carpenters, two barbers, six
mule drivers, and five cigarsellers—in the community. Four factory workers,
four farmers, one *ranchero*, a beef agent, and even two professional people—
one a surgeon and another a teacher named Don Gabriel Ruíz—were also listed
in this census.[61] Twenty years later a census showed that sixty-three per cent
(65 of 103 *vecinos* in the sample) of employed men in Parral was engaged in
mining. Carpenters, shoemakers, tailors, bakers (four of them), muleteers, and
merchants were still present, as was a parish priest, one subdelegate of the
intendencia, a druggist, and two surgeons, but no teacher appeared in the list of
occupations for this year.[62] One of the most difficult jobs on the entire northern
frontier was that of the *tenatero*, the ore carrier at a mine. *Tenateros* were
usually Indians or Negroes, some free and some slaves, who carried the ore in
225- to 350-pound sacks up rickety ladders a distance of 200 to 400 feet from
the bottom of the crude hole called a mine to the surface. Their only light was
provided by a tallow candle, and their load was always carried in rawhide bags,
usually supported solely by a strap across the forehead.[63]

These statistics and observations can be misleading, however, because they
reflect only the jobs held by people in two *reales de minas*. Agricultural settlements, such as that of Valle de San Bartolomé, accounted for a larger share of
the population than did individual mining districts by the latter half of the
eighteenth century. Thirty *haciendas* and four *ranchos* were inspected and
individually listed for the San Bartolomé Valley in 1707, although population
figures are not given and persons residing on each *hacienda* are not named.[64]
Farming and raising livestock joined mining as the principal occupations of
Spanish settlers in Nueva Vizcaya. In fact, the Spanish farmer was an integral
part of all mining districts, each being comprised of closely grouped mining
communities, farmlands, and stock-raising areas. Mining discoveries, indeed,

brought a lively development of agriculture and stock raising, both of which were necessary to support the miners. The mining community, stock ranch, and farm, therefore, became interdependent. Ranches raised cattle, sheep, and mules, supplying by contract to the mines not only meat but hides for ore sacks and water bags, tallow for candles, and other needed products. Farms largely met the needs of foodstuffs for the miners, although some grains and fruits were imported from other provinces. San Bartolomé was always a major livestock-raising area for the mines of Nueva Vizcaya.[65]

Although stock raising prospered from the beginning, the most important economic activity of the province was mining. Francisco de Urdiñola's census of 1604 for the province (Parral and Chihuahua were not yet settled, it will be remembered) showed that mining was the leading occupation, commerce was second, and farming and stock raising were third. About one-tenth of the people were listed as *vagabundos*, without occupation or jobless, but there were also some craftsmen—six carpenters, two charcoal burners, twelve tailors, five shoemakers, four blacksmiths, six bakers, and twenty-eight muleteers and cart drivers. Evidently there was a mining engineer (living at Indé), a surgeon, a cask maker, an *encomendero*, a protector of Indians, and a teacher within Nueva Vizcaya as early as 1604. Stock-raising *estancias*, fifty-four farms ("*Labores de pan y maíz*"), seventy mines, and seven wheat mills were noted by this census.[66]

Although Nueva Vizcaya was primarily a mining and ranching frontier, agriculture also was practiced, corn and wheat being the principal crops, although some grapes, fruits, and vegetables were grown. Artisans and professional people were present on this frontier from its earliest settlement. Furthermore, except for the dispersed portion of the settlers on *haciendas* and *ranchos*, most Spanish-speaking people in Nueva Vizcaya lived in an urban environment.

Land distribution meant a great deal to the miner, *hacendado, ranchero,* and *labrador* (small farmer) of Nueva Vizcaya. Francisco de Ibarra, as governor of the province and therefore official representative of the king, had begun by supplying prospective farmers and ranchers seeds, agricultural implements, and livestock. Settlers were then required to build houses, plant crops, and begin raising livestock within an established period of time. Corn became the principal crop, but wheat, cotton, and maguey were also grown. Once improvements had been made upon the land granted to him, the settler could obtain final title to it after four years of continuous residence.[67] In northern Nueva Vizcaya, or the modern state of Chihuahua, as in other frontier provinces, land could be claimed by a community or by settlers if it could be proved that it was neither populated nor used by Indians or other Spaniards. Possession was taken by standing on the property, throwing stones, scratching the earth, and beginning the tasks of settlement, all in the presence of witnesses.[68]

Latifundismo, the system of large land ownership, usually by a few persons, was present in Nueva Vizcaya, as it was in nearby Sinaloa, Sonora, and Coahuila. This system of private enterprise contributed to the growth of the livestock industry throughout the province. It also supplemented the small town and agricultural lots granted to farmers in civil settlements. *Haciendas* grew up in the Valle de San Bartolomé, near the *real de minas* of San José del Parral, and in the vicinity of both the communities of Durango and Chihuahua. All *haciendas* were not the same size. The legal measurement for a grant of land intended for the raising of bulls, cows, horses, and mules was set at 1,755 hectares, whereas that for raising goats and sheep was only 875 hectares.[69] These were not standard figures applied to every *hacienda*, the measurements of which continued to vary by country and region in the twentieth century. One source maintains that the standard measurement of an *hacienda* is 25,000 by 5,000 *varas*, or 21,684.97 acres,[70] considerably larger than that described above. The generally accepted minimum limit for an *hacienda* is today only 2,500 acres.

Many individuals became great *hacendados* in Nueva Vizcaya during the seventeenth and eighteenth centuries. As such they became politically, economically, and socially powerful figures, usually as *patrones*, or great landlords and protectors, of their districts. By the 1660s Don Valerio Cortés del Rey raised approximately forty-two thousand head of cattle and sheep along the Río Conchos for direct sale to the nearest slaughterhouse, at Parral.[71] Earlier, but in another region, Francisco de Urdiñola had become not only a wealthy mine owner but one of the largest landowners ever to live in Nueva Vizcaya. At the time of his death in 1618, he possessed 1,876 *sitios de ganado mayor* (approximately 4,428 acres each) for a total estate of over eight million acres.[72] The Marqués de San Miguel de Aguayo owned property extending over three provinces in northeastern New Spain by the last decade of the eighteenth century.[73] His great wealth and political prestige allowed him to undertake the consolidation of settlement in Texas in 1721, putting that province on its feet permanently after so many earlier precarious ventures. Although his holdings were originally in the province of Nueva Vizcaya, they are more properly treated in relation to Coahuila's history, for most of his land was located there after the annexation of Saltillo by Coahuila in 1787.

There were thirty *haciendas* and four *ranchos* in the Valle de San Bartolomé alone as early as 1707.[74] Don José Saens Moreno, a "Spaniard" originally from the Valle de San Bartolomé, possessed an *hacienda* named Santa Rosa near Parral in 1788. A widower seventy-four years old, he lived with his family, including a sister eighty-one years of age, a granddaughter of thirty-nine, a maiden of twenty-one, an orphaned boy aged eighteen, and five female Indians aged seventy, forty, thirty-eight, fifteen, and fourteen respectively. In addition to the *hacendado* and his family, there were 538 people in ninety family groups living on his *hacienda*. Indians, mestizos, and mulattoes, they originated largely in Parral, Conchos, and San Miguel el Grande. The *hacienda* also included two nearby *ranchos*, one with three families comprising seventeen persons, and another with four families or sixteen people.[75] The same source reveals not only the great landholding, wealth, and prestige of *hacendados* but also reflects the considerable number of Spaniards and mixed-blood people residing on such *haciendas*, a significant portion of the civil population on the northern frontier in addition to that in the communities.

Grants of land to settlers necessarily entailed certain responsibilities on their part. Not only did they have to live on the land, cultivate it, and stock it with animals, but they were required to be ready to defend it and the province in times of crisis. Indian uprisings constituted the greatest threat to the province, requiring periodic musters of available manpower together with animals, weapons, and equipment. As early as the mid-seventeenth century there were decrees and muster lists pertaining to the readiness of *vecinos* for the defense of Parral and Santa Bárbara against native uprisings.[76] All male residents of Parral from twenty to fifty years of age were required to pass muster and be in readiness from Maundy Thursday through Easter Sunday in 1666. Failure to do so resulted in a fine of twelve pesos.[77] Because the Indians disturbed the peace in the region around Parral in 1672, a similar order was issued at that time; *vecinos* were listed "*con todas armas*" (with all their arms), or deficiencies were noted on the muster list.[78]

Spaniards, mestizos, mulattoes and other mixed bloods were shown on muster lists in 1707 for the communities of Cosiguiriachic, Parral, Parras, Durango, San Juan del Río, and San Francisco del Oro. Although most possessed some arms and equipment, such as arquebuses, swords, *cueras* (leather jackets), *adargas* (bullhide shields), powder, balls, pikes, and lances, as well as horses (an average of two to six per man), many had no arms whatsoever and not a single horse.[79] The *villa* of Santa Bárbara in 1731 mustered eighty men to combat Indian depredations on its nearby roads. Nine captains and five individuals, titled simply "*El S.ᵒʳ*," along with thirty-one soldiers passed inspection with all their arms, consisting largely of *escopetas* (firelock guns), lances, *adargas*, and horses in varying numbers. Of the remaining thirty-five men listed, eleven had no equipment, and four even failed to appear.[80]

In general, civilian settlers in Nueva Vizcaya had little or no formal education, but schools were established periodically at least as early as the mid-eighteenth century. Some educational facilities may have been present in isolated locations as early as 1604, when a teacher was included in the Urdiñola census for the community of San Antonio de Padua. Evidently in 1742 a school was established in San Felipe el Real de Chihuahua, where the *ayuntamiento* (town council) granted a Parral resident named Santiago Pardiñas the right to open one for "paid male students." This school seems to have ceased operation in 1744 despite the Conde de Fuenclara, viceroy of New Spain, authorizing the establishment of "*escuelas de primeras letras*" (primary schools) in all towns of the viceroyalty. Parral had a school teacher ("*maestro de escuela*") in 1768, and Professor Miguel Mayor Rico, originally from Sevilla, Spain, died in 1790 after fifteen continuous years directing a school in Chihuahua. *Comandante-general* Nemesio Salcedo personally donated nearly two thousand pesos and influenced others to contribute toward the re-establishment of a school in Chihuahua in 1808. It was led by Profesora Eleuteria Carrasco,[81] who was probably the first woman to become a teacher on the northern frontier of New Spain.

An interesting document drawn up by the *ayuntamiento* of San José del Parral describes the founding of a "public school" in the period 1809–1811. Because of the notable neglect of education for the children of their community and because heads of families pretended not to understand the importance of educating their sons and domestic servants, the eight members of the *ayuntamiento* decided to establish a school. Its purpose was to teach children to read, write, count, and understand the Christian doctrine. The *ayuntamiento* ordered heads of families to send their sons to this school and to pay the teacher for the enrollment of their offspring. Poor families and orphan boys were also provided for through the assessment of those *vecinos* who were capable of supporting the school and its teacher. Don Rafael de Estrella, a resident of Parral, applied for the job as schoolmaster. Since he apparently knew how to run such a school, the *ayuntamiento* approved his request, appointed him to the job, and assigned him an annual salary of three hundred pesos, payable in increments of twenty-five pesos per month. He could not leave until he had complied with the terms of his contract, and members of the *ayuntamiento* were permitted to visit the school, making changes as they saw fit. In March, 1811, Estrella applied for release from his position as schoolmaster; the *ayuntamiento* approved his request and selected another resident, Don José Agustín Yndajauregui, because of his experience as a teacher "for some years," and on May 21, 1811, he evidently replaced Estrella as schoolmaster.[82] However, the record abruptly ends, and there is no evidence that the school either continued or was dissolved in the last decade of Spanish administration over Parral.

There were some literate individuals with extensive collections of books in Nueva Vizcaya, as there were on other frontiers. A Basque merchant named Joaquín de Amézqueta settled in the province during the latter half of the eighteenth century. He served both as an entrepreneur and commander of the military garrison at Guajoquilla until his death in 1800, when a list of books in his personal library showed thirty-eight tiles. These included a dictionary, two sets of military regulations, some religious works, historical titles comprising one-third of the total and including Alonso de Ercilla's famous epic poem entitled *La Araucana*, and Alvaro Alonso Barba's *Arte de los metales*. Cervantes was represented in this collection by *La Galatea*, *Viaje al Parnaso*, and *Novelas ejemplares*, but strangely not by *Don Quixote*. Eighteenth century works included three by Pedro Rodríguez, Conde de Campomanes in Spain, promoting the adoption of a rational approach to the solution of the empire's economic problems, and the *Establecimiento de las naciones europeas*, a work based on the Abbé Raynal's history and supposedly on the list of censored books in 1779. Thus, it is evident that in Nueva Vizcaya there were people who could read, that they did have books, that the ideas of the Enlightenment did reach the remotest frontiers as well as the larger civilized centers of Latin America, and that the traditional view that censorship kept books away from colonials is in error.[83]

Settlers frequently experienced health problems on the frontier, yet there were few medical facilities and doctors to help solve them. Indian depredations, floods, droughts, and famines were only a few of the hazards, which often resulted in crippling wounds, severe illnesses, death, and even some epidemics. Smallpox was a constant threat. To combat wounds inflicted in battle, illnesses, and epidemics, there were only a few doctors at scattered points along the frontier, and medical facilities, if they existed at all, were confined mostly to the larger communities. Evidently only one surgeon resided in the province of Nueva Vizcaya in 1604. He must have been fully occupied when a smallpox epidemic killed four hundred people four years later and a flood, followed by a severe drought and famine, hit one region in 1612–1613. Parral counted a surgeon among its people in 1768, probably a professional doctor assigned to the presidial garrison, as was usually the practice on the frontier. Twenty years later, in 1788, there were two surgeons and even one apothecary in the same community. The only records of the existence of hospitals in Nueva Vizcaya in colonial times pertain to one authorized and built after 1681 in Parral and another noted by Zebulon Pike at Chihuahua in 1807.[84]

Toward the end of the colonial era, efforts were made and significant steps taken in Nueva Vizcaya to overcome the threat of smallpox. Here, as on other frontiers, the newly developed practice of vaccination was employed, mostly for the youth of the province. *Comandante-general* Salcedo ordered vaccination throughout the province in accordance with the royal instructions. Under the supervision of Dr. Jaime Gurza of the military hospital, six children were vaccinated in Chihuahua every eight days. Once the vaccination took effect, the vaccine was transmitted to others from arm to arm. In this way approximately two thousand people were made immune to the dreaded scourge of smallpox over a period of twelve years.[85]

Transportation and communications, although considered primitive by modern standards, did at least exist. Two roads connected Durango with Parral by 1693, one passing through Cuencamé and the other proceeding more directly, although it was more exposed to Indian attacks. Bridges over rivers were less of a problem in Nueva Vizcaya than in Sinaloa, Sonora, and the northeastern provinces, largely because the province seldom experienced rainfall from September through June and rivers were not the major obstacles they were elsewhere. Nevertheless, Parral had so many that it was sometimes called the "City of Bridges."[86]

Of utmost importance in the development of intra- and interprovincial communications was the creation of an efficient mail service for the entire northern frontier, which centered in Nueva Vizcaya. The office of postmaster for New Spain had been established as early as 1580, when Viceroy Martín Enríquez de Almanza had granted the delivery of mail as a private concession (*merced*) to one Alonso de Olivares, but the service was not incorporated under direct governmental control until 1765, when the crown terminated the privileges of the private contractor. At that time new instructions were issued for the postal service of New Spain, establishing fees for each type of mail. Letters weighing up to one-half ounce cost a fee of two *reales*; those weighing three-quarters ounce to one ounce (called "*cartas dobles*") were four *reales*; those of one and one-half ounces were six *reales*; and a parcel of letters (*pliego*) weighing two ounces or more cost eight *reales*, or one peso. The rate for bulky packages was four *reales* per ounce.[87] Naturally, these high rates did not encourage the exchange of letters among settlers who worked hard for their subsistence and who had limited or no education, frequently being unable to write even their own names.

Comandante-general Teodoro de Croix created the first well-regulated monthly mail service for the entire frontier of New Spain in 1779. The route ran from Bahía del Espíritu Santo in Texas through San Antonio, Riogrande, Monclova, Saltillo, Parras, Chihuahua, San Miguel de Horcasitas, and Valle de Sonora to the terminal point of Arizpe, Sonora, Croix's first capital of the Provincias Internas del Norte. Connections at various points provided for monthly mail service with El Paso del Norte, New Mexico, Janos, and the presidios of Sonora, as well as those to the south.[88] Seventy soldiers—fifty-four from the presidial companies along the frontier and sixteen from the *compañías volantes* (mobile companies)—along with sixteen Indians and six *vecinos* from the *reales de minas* of La Santísima Trinidad and San Antonio de la Huerta in Sonora were employed to carry the mails.[89] Two soldiers, militiamen, Indians, or *vecinos* operated as a team to carry the mail; an escort of one corporal and six soldiers was provided the carriers in the dangerous, Indian-infested portion of the route between San Antonio and Riogrande.[90] The journey took about one month from one end of the route to the other. Mail for Durango was left at the Hacienda de la Zarca on the ninth of each month; on the thirteenth the carriers reached Chihuahua, where letters from San Sabá, Paso del Norte, San Eleazario, Carrizal, Janos, and New Mexico were supposed to be waiting.[91] Each presidio had its own special mail bag and seal, in addition to padlocks and small rods used to secure the bags.[92]

Within one year, Croix's mail system not only improved communications

The central marketplace in Chihuahua, Mexico, during the nineteenth century. Note the use of burros and the crude *carreta* for transportation. *Courtesy Denver Public Library Western Collection.*

on the frontier but was a financial success as well. It transmitted all sorts of mail, including that pertaining to military, governmental, legal, and financial matters. In addition, it contributed to the growth of commerce and the interchange of correspondence among the officials, merchants, and educated people of the northern provinces. Finally, it cost 7,231 *reales de plata* in its first year, but took in 11,195 *reales* in the same period, thus showing a profit of 3,964 *reales*.[93]

Perhaps one of the best descriptions of a Nueva Vizcayan community and its citizens was provided by Lieutenant Zebulon Pike. During his visit to Chihuahua from March 23 to April 28, 1807, he made many observations on the climate, living conditions, and nature of society there. Pike noted, as many visitors do now, the dryness of the air, a factor which produced such static electricity that flying sparks were observed every morning when his men removed their blankets. He emphasized the importance of silver mines in the vicinity of the *villa* of Chihuahua, noting also that there were many huge furnaces in the area which produced large volumes of smoke on every day except Sunday. Cinders in piles ten to fifteen feet high surrounded the city itself.[94]

The *villa* of Chihuahua, which according to Pike had a population of some seven thousand, was built in the form of an "oblong square" [rectangle?]. On the southern extremity there was a large church, while a "superb" hospital was located on its western side. The public square was situated in the center of the community and was surrounded by the principal church, a building for the royal treasury, a town hall or government building, and shops belonging to the wealthiest merchants. In addition, Chihuahua had a military "academy" at Santo Domingo and a large aqueduct about a mile south of the town. Pike was impressed with the "public walk" on the south side of the settlement. Formed by three rows of trees where the foliage nearly formed a canopy overhead, it had circular seats at the end of each walk. Here the men and women strolled, flirted, conversed, played the guitar, and sang songs until a patrol of soldiers regularly enforced a nine o'clock evening curfew, stopping every person found outside his home thereafter and examining him.[95]

The community of San Felipe el Real de Chihuahua had been established on the grid pattern so evident in most Spanish towns in America, around a plaza, as Pike had noted. Outside the original settlement, the town grew in helter-skelter fashion, with narrow streets conforming largely to topography. Most houses were of one story, built of adobe bricks, with rooms added to the original structure as family size increased. Fronts of houses were flush with the street, and the entire structure was plastered and painted white or some pastel color. Finer homes had two stories, with iron grillwork and shutters on the windows. All home life seemed to revolve about the inner patio. Both houses and streets lacked sanitation facilities. The plaza was the focal point for public gatherings, such as those for mass, weddings, christenings, funerals, business transactions, arrivals, departures, and especially fiestas.[96] It is apparent from Pike's observations that the public promenade was also a social center for community activities.

According to Lieutenant Pike, the hospitality, generosity, and sobriety of the people of Chihuahua were their most notable characteristics, and he thought they exceeded such traits of any other nation. He thought, however, that the inhabitants were lacking in national energy, patriotism, and independence of soul, although they were a brave and proud people. The women intrigued him. They had black hair and eyes and fine teeth, but generally did not have attractive figures. They dressed in short jackets and petticoats, high-heeled shoes, and usually wore a silk wrapper over the entire dress, bringing it up to their faces in the presence of men. They wore nothing on their heads or in their hair.[97] The young army officer was indeed impressed with the ladies of Chihuahua, noting that they possessed a "beauty of eye in a superior degree," and adding that he found two of them quite distinguished in learning, being everywhere considered the equals of men who visited their homes to discuss national problems and philosophical concepts of the age.[98] Lower-class men dressed in broad-brimmed hats, short jackets, large waistcoats, short trousers always open at the knee, and a kind of leather boot or legging bound around the leg and gartered thereon. Their boots were described as being of soft, pliable leather and were not of any distinguishing color. Both men and women were very proud of their fine hair, and they displayed it for all to see. People seemed to dress in the cities, according to Pike, after the fashions they had heard about from Europe or the United States.[99]

The settlers Pike met were "temperate" in their eating and drinking habits, although excessive drinking and outright drunkenness were frequent complaints of other observers before him. Early in the morning people began the day with a cup of chocolate and some cake. At twelve noon there was a major meal, consisting of meat, fowl, or fish, accompanied by confections, an elegant dessert, many glasses of wine, and a few songs. Thereafter all, be they rich or poor, retired for a siesta lasting from two to four in the afternoon. Windows and doors were closed, and the streets were deserted. At four everyone rose, washed, and dressed for the evening's entertainment, usually dining lightly on wine, water, and candied sugar about eleven o'clock at night.[100]

Pike's observations are apparently limited to the officials and merchants who entertained him, for the everyday settlers of the community and those in the rest of the province had a different diet. Spaniards were heavy meat eaters, particularly in a province where the raising of livestock was such an important part of the economy. Corn was also a basic part of the diet of the citizens of Nueva Vizcaya, especially since the farms surrounding San Bartolomé were so productive. *Pozole* (a stew made from meat, hominy, and chile peppers) was a popular food among miners and other settlers. Wheat was cultivated at a few points by irrigating, but corn was grown without resort to irrigation. Beans, chile, native squash (*calabaza*), watermelons, grapes, other fruits and some vegetables were grown in civil settlements as well as rural areas. Imported items included luxury products such as sugar, chocolate, citrus fruits, rice, tobacco, and particularly wine from the two centers of its production in northern New Spain, Parras, and Paso del Norte. *Aguardiente* (brandy) and *mescal* (native liquor) were also imported, as were woolen and cotton goods, along with household items and metalware. Goods were sold either in public markets (*alhondigas*) or in stores.[101]

Amusements included music, singing, dancing, and gambling. Ladies frequently played the guitar in their homes, where they sat cross-legged on the floor or reclined on sofas. They sang also on the public promenade, in French, Italian, or Spanish, the listeners usually joining them in the chorus, according to Pike's experience in Chihuahua. He also witnessed a *fandango* on Sunday, April 19, and described it as a lively, gay dance in which body gestures, snapping fingers, and occasional meeting of men and women in a "stretched embrace" all played a role. The richer class preferred the minuet, accompanied by the guitar, violin, and singers. Gambling, strictly prohibited by law, nevertheless abounded. Cards, billiards, horse racing, and cockfighting were the principal pastimes; indeed, Pike found money and horses the principal topics of conversation throughout his visit.[102]

Another popular diversion throughout the province, perhaps more so than in any other frontier region, was bullfighting, especially at Parral, although Chihuahua, too, held *corridas* during its great fair in December. *Fiestas de toros* (bullfights) were evidently held as early as 1649 in Parral, where the *ayuntamiento* granted licenses to individuals sponsoring the event and otherwise endeavored to regulate such celebrations. By 1803 a nine-day period was set aside during the first week in January for bullfights in the plaza. An order regulating the event was posted for all citizens to read.[103]

As on all frontiers, crime was a constant problem. The Parral Archives contain many documents relating to petty as well as major crimes in both the seventeenth and eighteenth century. Robbery, rape, vagabondage, murder, gambling, selling liquor to Indians, bad treatment of Indians, adultery, and witchcraft are only some of the specific transgressions for which persons were tried in Parral. Opening public stores without a license, absenting oneself from the province without official permission, and selling *"vinos mezclados"* (mixed or watered wines) were civil offenses. Selling *"vino mescal"* (local liquor made from maguey plant) at a price higher than that officially set by the government's regulations and bringing Indians from New Mexico to the *real* of Parral also got one into trouble with the law.[104]

Punishments for criminal acts included exile from the province for various periods of time, jail sentences, public whippings, hanging, execution by firing squad, and confinement to the stocks. Fines were assessed for most minor violations of the law. In Chihuahua fines were meted out for swearing and drawing caricatures of the holy images. Heavy penalties were prescribed for carrying knives or pistols. Public whippings were specified for fighting in the streets or cattle rustling. Drunkenness, a common problem on the frontier, had a peculiar punishment prescribed in Chihuahua. There all persons found drunk were to be dressed in a tunic and red beret, lashed twenty-five times, forced to drink water until ill, and then placed on public display in the plaza for a period of three hours.[105]

Probably the most famous criminal trial held in Chihuahua, or indeed in the entire province, was that of Father Miguel de Hidalgo y Costilla, in 1811. Captured near Saltillo in the province of Coahuila, the noted parish priest of Dolores, instigator of the Mexican struggle for independence, was chained and marched to Chihuahua, the seat of government for the Provincias Internas del Norte. He and his colleagues were confined to the military hospital until tried, first by clerical officials and then by a civil tribunal appointed by the *comandante-general*. Father Hidalgo was defrocked, and shot on July 30, 1811, just four years after Pike had visited the settlement and only a decade before Spain lost control of all her frontier provinces. The heads of Father Hidalgo, Ignacio Allende, and Juan Aldama were cut off by an Indian, packed in salt, and shipped to Guanajuato for display on the corners of the public granary which Hidalgo's hordes had stormed slightly less than a year earlier. The bodies of the rebels were buried at Chihuahua, but disinterred after Mexican independence and reburied more appropriately in Mexico City.[106]

Nueva Vizcaya was throughout the colonial period of major importance to the viceroyalty of New Spain. Although its silver mines did not produce wealth comparable to that of Zacatecas, Guanajuato, and Pachuca, its production was large enough and lasted over such a long period of time that the crown showed considerable interest in the region. It was the wealthiest of all the frontier provinces in precious metals mined. Politically, it was the center of royal administration in the north, even more so with the creation of the Comandancia General de las Provincias Internas del Norte in 1776. Except for one short period under Croix when the capital was situated at Arizpe in Sonora, Durango and Chihuahua were the major cities and administrative centers of the northern frontier.

The Spanish population of Nueva Vizcaya was larger than that in any other frontier region. Durango, Parral, and Chihuahua were the largest communities. Indeed, all of Texas, Alta California, Baja California, and Pimería Alta combined did not have a population equal to that of Durango and Chihuahua together. Nueva Vizcaya had civilian settlers throughout the province. Although they came from many backgrounds, they established on this frontier, as on others, a fairly homogeneous Spanish-speaking society. In spite of their accepted classification as Spaniards, most were born in New Spain. On the frontier they mixed with or accepted into their communities large numbers of pacified Indians. Negroes, too, were present in larger numbers than has previously been thought; they were an integral part of the frontier population. Life on the frontier, as we have seen, tended to erase class differences and prejudices so pronounced in the older regions of the viceroyalty. *Mestización* of the Mexican population began in Nueva Vizcaya, as it did elsewhere, with the first arrival of Spanish colonists. The *gente de razón* on this frontier might include true Iberians, native-born persons of European heritage (called Creoles in other regions), Indians, Negroes, and all sorts of mixtures, including *colores quebrados*, so long as they lived in an established community and practiced what was essentially a derivative of Spanish culture. Finally, it is apparent that these people developed a notable spirit of independence and self-interest, presuming themselves to be their own interpreters of the law. They resented harsh treatment, especially from outsiders; inspector Joseph Francisco Marín recommended in 1693 that they be treated with tact and gentleness by all who tried to govern them.[107]

Nueva Vizcaya was the heartland of the northern frontier, the first to be inhabited by Spanish settlers on the Central Plateau and the source of civilian settlers in other provinces such as Coahuila, Sonora, and Nuevo León. It was closely interrelated with the history of New Mexico, its immediate neighbor to the north. In fact, the boundary line between the provinces came to be set at the ruins of the deserted *hacienda* of Ojo Caliente, five leagues below Carrizal.[108] Nueva Vizcaya served a longer period as a frontier province than perhaps any other region save for Sinaloa. Gradually settlers progressed northward, establishing newer communities which formed the frontier as the southern half of the province became more stabilized and much more heavily populated. The civil settlement and its residents contributed to the well-being of mining districts, served as the nucleus of permanent colonization, and attracted such an influx of settlers that two new states could be created out of this vast frontier when the Mexican nation embarked upon its own historical experience. As Professor Lawrence Kinnaird has noted, the "towns marked a more permanent frontier advance than missions or presidios."[109] In Nueva Vizcaya, it might be added, they were also more permanent than the famous mining districts and their productive wealth.

5. New Mexico
Settlements and Settlers

For almost two centuries New Mexico was the northernmost frontier of New Spain. Explored early, colonized early, and yet a remote, exposed, and isolated frontier late in the Spanish colonial period, it was similar to an island outpost. In the interior of North America the Spanish advance never penetrated farther northward.

Exploration of the New Mexico region really began with the venture of Francisco Vásquez de Coronado from 1540 to 1542; it continued with the journeys of Fray Agustín Rodríguez and Francisco Sánchez Chamuscado, followed by that of Antonio de Espejo in the early 1580s. These explorations were necessary preliminaries to permanent occupation, serving to acquaint Spaniards with the region, especially with the natives of the Río Grande Valley, and providing a motive for carrying out the colonization of New Mexico, at least along the banks of the Río Grande.

The first civil settlement in New Mexico was a fiasco from beginning to end. Gaspar Castaño de Sosa, formerly a resident of Saltillo and later *alcalde mayor* (chief magistrate) of San Luis (now Monterrey) in Nuevo León, had become governor of that province following the unfortunate chain of events that unseated its founder, Luis de Carbajal. Castaño de Sosa organized and personally led an unauthorized expedition to colonize New Mexico from 1590 to 1591. Presumably in search of new mines to revive the spirits of the people and the financial depression of his own province, Castaño de Sosa's expedition violated the Spanish colonization laws of 1573 requiring the viceroy to issue licenses to colonizers. Castaño, without bothering to obtain such a license, simply started out on his own with 160 to 170 men on July 27, 1590, from Almadén (Monclova), in Coahuila. He took along a supply of corn, wheat, and cattle for slaughter, and at least ten carts. The caravan marched up the Pecos River, reached the Indian pueblo of Pecos on December 31, and subsequently arrived near Santo Domingo Pueblo. However, the expedition did not found any permanent settlement, and Castaño was arrested in the spring of 1591 by Captain Juan de Morlete, who had been sent by Viceroy Luis de Velasco to find and return Castaño and his settlers to their homes in Nuevo León and Coahuila.[1] Thus ended the first effort to colonize New Mexico, predestined to fail because it took place without prior royal approval.

Juan de Oñate led the first official colonizing expedition to New Mexico in 1598. A native of Zacatecas and descendant of the multimillionaire silver king, Cristóbal de Oñate, he had proposed to carry out the occupation of New Mexico on behalf of the crown. For this enterprise he promised to recruit two hundred men, fully equipped at his expense. He pledged further to provide firearms, lances, shields, flour, corn, jerked beef, seed for sowing wheat, 3,000 sheep, 1,000 rams ,1,000 goats, 1,000 cattle, 100 black cattle, and 150 colts and 150 mares, in addition to the tools needed to begin work after arrival in the new land. The king agreed to furnish three cannon, thirty quintals of powder, one hundred of lead, and six thousand pesos as a loan from the royal treasury to support Oñate. Once he had obtained the royal authorization to conduct the settlers to New Mexico, Oñate began recruiting colonists in Zacatecas and, later, in Santa Bárbara and Valle de San Bartolomé, both in Nueva Vizcaya. By January, 1597, he had enlisted a total of 205 men, largely natives of Spain, central New Spain, the frontier regions near Zacatecas, and what is today southern Chihuahua. Delays, generally caused by contested authority and lengthy inspections, had reduced Oñate's expedition to only 129 men when the royal inspector, Juan de Frías Salazar, completed his inspection and muster of soldiers and settlers on January 8, 1598.[2]

Oñate led these soldier-settlers, many with their families, together with carts, livestock, and equipment, northward via El Paso del Norte (not settled then) and along the Río Grande to its junction with the Río Chama. There, in July, 1598, he and his advance party founded the first Spanish settlement on the east bank of the Río Grande, naming it San Juan de los Caballeros. The main body reached the settlement on August 18, but before the year was out all had moved to the site of the Tewa Indian pueblo of Yuque Yunque, on the Río Chama where it joined the Río Grande. There were four hundred houses at the site for the Spaniards to use in the community of San Gabriel de los Españoles. It remained the single Spanish settlement and capital of New Mexico in spite of the dissatisfactions of the colonists and near desertion of the colony in the first decade of the seventeenth century. In 1610, the new governor of New Mexico, Pedro de Peralta, founded the *villa* of Santa Fé and moved the remaining colonists from San Gabriel to become its original settlers.[3]

New Mexico in the seventeenth century down to the time of the Pueblo revolt of 1680 contained scattered missionary establishments, no formal presidios, and the one civil settlement at Santa Fé. In addition, Spanish-speaking people were dispersed at various points along the Río Grande from Taos to below the site of Alburquerque.[4] These were largely clusters of farming or small ranching families rather than formal organized communities. There were perhaps seven hundred and fifty Spaniards, mestizos, and converted Indians living in Santa Fé by 1630, and approximately twenty-nine hundred in the entire province by August, 1680, when the Pueblo Indian uprising began. The ma-

Santa Fé, New Mexico, showing the plaza, irrigation ditch, and adobe construction in the latter half of the nineteenth century. The Sangre de Cristo Mountains are in the background. *Courtesy Denver Public Library Western Collection.*

jority of the settlers lived in the Río Abajo region (present-day Bernalillo southward) and around the capital at Santa Fé. Some soldiers were also present in
the *villa*, and thirty-two missionaries lived among the Indian pueblos in the
province. After 21 of them and 380 settlers had been killed in the uprising,
Governor Antonio de Otermín and Lieutenant Governor Alonso García collected respectively fifteen hundred and a thousand settlers at separate locations and retreated independently to El Paso del Norte. There, in a muster
conducted after some people had already deserted for Nueva Vizcaya, only
1,946 people were officially listed as survivors of New Mexico's first colonization period.[5]

These settlers—Spaniards, mestizos, and friendly Pueblo Indians—insured
the continued occupation of settlements in the Paso del Norte region. However, they were not the first Spanish settlers there. Three Franciscan missions
had been founded there for the conversion of the peaceful Mansos Indians.
The first was the mission of Nuestra Señora de Guadalupe, founded by Fray
García de San Francisco y Zúñiga about one-half league (one and one-half
miles) from the Río Grande on its right bank on December 8, 1659. A
temporary building of adobe bricks and straw was erected there, but the present
structure was begun in April, 1662, and completed in 1668, celebrating the
occasion of its dedication to the Virgin of Guadalupe by a special mass attended by four hundred celebrants.[6]

Spanish settlers appear to have occupied the lands adjoining the missions
soon after Nuestra Señora de Guadalupe del Paso was established. Before 1680
there were enough colonists in the settlement to warrant the appointment of
an *alcalde mayor*. The first recorded marriage of a Spaniard occurred on November 29, 1678, when Francisco de Archuleta and Doña Bernardina Baca
were united in wedlock. Thirty-one Spaniards are also listed in the baptismal
and burial records for Guadalupe del Paso before 1680. Therefore, it is evident
that the nucleus of a Spanish civil community existed at El Paso del Norte
before the arrival of the refugees in the early fall of 1680.[7]

It is undeniable, however, that the flood of nearly two thousand people from
New Mexico gave El Paso its first real population problem and necessitated
relocation, dispersal, and organization of the civilian settlers in that district.
Men, women, children, servants, and 317 Christianized Indians from the
pueblos of Isleta, Sevilleta, Alamillo, Socorro, and Senecú (all Piro and Tiwa
pueblos) passed muster with a total of only 471 horses in their possession, most
of which were unfit for use, at La Salineta campground, four leagues north of
El Paso, where the refugees camped from September 18 to October 9, 1680.
Temporary huts were erected, but Governor Otermín established a more
permanent community on the site of the *real* of San Lorenzo, probably before
February 11, 1682. Nine locations—six Indian missions and three Spanish
settlements—were occupied below the mission of Guadalupe del Paso during

the first few years after the arrival of the settlers from New Mexico.[8] The three Spanish communities, all founded by 1682, were San Pedro de Alcántara, El Santísimo Sacramento, and Real de San Lorenzo, at distances of two, four, and six leagues, respectively, downriver from Guadalupe del Paso. Each family constructed its own house of "sticks and branches," called a *jacal*.[9] Governor Otermín tried desperately to halt the wholesale desertions that began as soon as he and the retreating colonists reached El Paso. He permitted the old and the ill to depart, authorized others to search for food, but established the death penalty for any unauthorized departures. He was so upset with his many problems and untenable position that he wrote, "For the love of God and Saint Anthony, as soon as you arrive in Mexico, do everything you possibly can to get me out of here."[10]

Fortunately, a *junta general* (general meeting of officials) convened by the viceroy approved the establishment of a presidio at El Paso, to consist of fifty soldiers enlisted in Zacatecas at a promised annual salary of 315 pesos each. A new governor was sent to replace Otermín, and he selected in 1683 a site for the new presidio between the mission and the Real de San Lorenzo. In addition, the Spanish settlements in the district were collectively elevated to *villa* status. Since the governor brought with him only twenty of the authorized fifty soldiers, he had to enlist others from itinerants in the Paso del Norte region and from Otermín's veterans. Within the next year missions and civil settlements were reorganized by Fray Nicolás López to insure that Indians—Piros, Sumas, Tiwas, Tompiros, and Janos—did not become mixed in the same communities with Spanish settlers.[11]

With all the stresses and problems created by the arrival of the new settlers and soldiers, it is no wonder that the formerly peaceful Mansos Indians rebelled in 1684. Generally restless from the time of Otermín's arrival with the refugees in 1680, the Mansos were encouraged by nearby Apaches to resist, to return to their old way of life, and to make common cause with them against the hated Spaniards. The rebellion began on March 14, 1684, and ended the following year. It emphasized the need for more compact Spanish settlement for purposes of defense. Thus, the communities of El Paso del Norte were consolidated. The presidio was moved to Guadalupe del Paso, near the ford over the river, where a community of Spaniards and peaceful Indians was established nearby. Spanish settlers did not take kindly to this move, for they preferred to remain in their scattered hamlets spread over the Río Grande Valley. In spite of all efforts to concentrate them into one settlement, they remained in five locations throughout this period and in the century thereafter. Their villages consisted of Guadalupe del Paso (now Ciudad Juárez) with its mission, presidio, and civil community, San Lorenzo (one to two leagues below Guadalupe), Senecú (two leagues from Guadalupe), Isleta (three leagues from the mission), and finally Nuestra Señora del Socorro (five leagues, or about twelve miles, downriver from El Paso's first mission). All five were mixed communities of Spaniards and Christianized Indians, in spite of the royal policy of keeping them separated.[12]

Yet the people of El Paso suffered greatly, and the population continued to decline as some fled to Parral, Casas Grandes, and other Nueva Vizcayan points. Not only was there the menace of the Apaches and Mansos in the winter of 1684 to 1685, but there were acute shortages of food and clothing. Droughts, limited irrigation potential, and Indian depredations destroyed crops, forcing many to eat wild herbs. Some reportedly would not go to mass because they claimed that they did not have enough clothes to cover their nakedness.[13] Between 1681 and 1685, Nueva Vizcaya contested the fact that the Paso del Norte settlements belonged to New Mexico, claiming that her jurisdiction extended to the Río Grande; since the settlements were on the south bank of the river they were, therefore, within Nueva Vizcaya's domain. Royal authorities, however, denied this claim and ordered that El Paso be considered a portion of New Mexico, a decision which was confirmed in 1685.[14]

All this time the population dwindled. A muster roll of November 11, 1684, showed a total of 1,030 persons in the entire district, with 488 of them at Guadalupe del Paso, 354 at Real de San Lorenzo, and only 188 at Isleta.[15] Thus, the total had dropped 916 persons between 1680 and 1684. When Diego de Vargas reached the *villa* in 1691, he found about one thousand persons there, presidial soldiers without swords and *cueras* (leather jackets), and only 132 horses in the entire community.[16] Within a decade, then, the number of Spanish refugees who had arrived at El Paso del Norte in 1680 had shrunk to about half.

Still, with these meager resources and by enlisting soldiers and colonists elsewhere in New Spain, Vargas was able to effect the reconquest and reoccupation of New Mexico. To re-establish Spanish authority and to prevent another revolt, he proposed to establish a presidio of one hundred solders and a *villa* of five hundred colonists. King Carlos II approved his request and provided forty thousand pesos from royal funds to purchase seed, livestock, tools, carts, and other necessities. After a preliminary reconnoitering expedition in 1692, Vargas began recruiting and equipping his expedition for the reoccupation. By October, 1693, he could count one hundred soldiers, some seventy families, and eighteen friars in his company. In addition, he had about nine hundred head of cattle, more than two thousand horses, one thousand mules, and a large group of Indian allies he had recruited to accompany him. Before the year was over they had reoccupied Santa Fé, after a heated engagement when the Tanos Indians would not voluntarily vacate the site.[17]

Just as Santa Fé became an established *villa* and presidio in late 1693, once again the center of Spanish settlement in New Mexico, it also became the source of colonists for the province's third *villa* in the present Española Valley

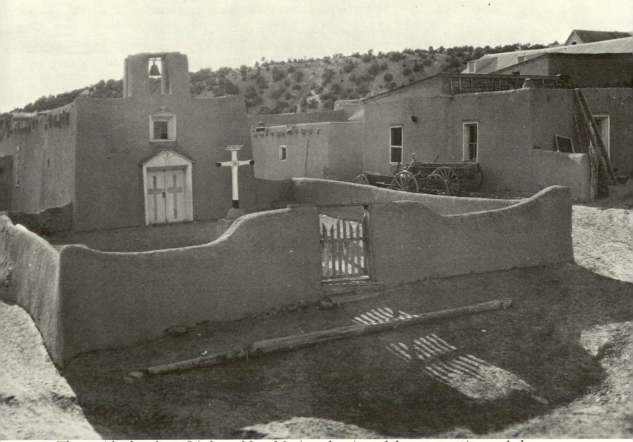

The parish church at Córdova, New Mexico, showing adobe construction and the use of *vigas* to support the roof. Photographed by Harmon Parkhurst about 1930. *Courtesy Mr. and Mrs. T. R. Waring and Major and Mrs. Edmund B. Stewart.*

north of the capital. La Villa Nueva de Santa Cruz de Españoles Mexicanos del Rey Nuestro Carlos Segundo—Santa Cruz, or La Cañada, as it came to be known—was founded by Governor Vargas in 1695 with settlers from Santa Fé. Forty-four families left the capital at nine o'clock in the morning on April 21, 1695, evidently recruited from sixty families of *"españoles mexicanos"* residing there. Arriving at the site of the pueblo of San Lázaro, Governor Vargas took possession in the name of the king, appointed an *alcalde mayor*, and established a civil-military government; the settlers took oaths to be loyal vassals of their monarch and to defend to the death their new community. On April 23, Vargas began dividing the lands among the *vecinos*, and the foundations were laid for the building of a chapel. Lands were apportioned to the settlers on the basis of being able to sow half a *fanega* of corn on each plot. Governor Vargas then visited the Indian pueblos of San Cristóbal and Jémez to encourage their cooperation with the new civil community.[18]

On May 9, 1695, forty-four families recruited by Juan Páez de Hurtado in Zacatecas and Sombrerete arrived in Santa Fé. They were mustered in the plaza and assigned to the homes vacated by the settlers who had gone to Santa Cruz de la Cañada.[19] By September 25, only four months after the initial occupation of Santa Cruz, the settlers calling themselves *"los mexicanos pobladores"* executed a request that they be paid three hundred pesos annually for each family as a type of subsistence until they could sow and harvest crops to sustain themselves.[20]

A fourth *villa*, Alburquerque, was founded in 1706 by Governor Francisco Cuervo y Váldes. Between January and June of that year (the actual document indicating the date and conditions of the grant has been lost or destroyed, if indeed it ever existed), the "Villa de Alburquerque" was established near the Río Grande where there was good soil, pasturage, and timber, as well as a plentiful supply of water. The community was founded in accordance with the instructions set forth in Book IV, Title VII of the *Recopilación de leyes de los reynos de las indias*, and Alburquerque's initial 35 families, or 252 persons in all, were placed in possession of their lands by the governor's agent Juan de Ulibarrí.[21]

These were the only *villas* founded in New Mexico during the colonial period. Atrisco, a small village near Alburquerque and a part of its jurisdiction, was founded as early as 1703;[22] Galisteo was settled by 150 families of Christianized Tanos Indians in 1706, about one and one-half miles from the present town. Most of its inhabitants moved to Santo Domingo, however, after 1794, when repeated Indian raids and a smallpox epidemic decimated its population.[23] Neither settlement ever attained the status of a *villa*.

Toward the end of the eighteenth century, as the Indian menace declined in northern New Mexico, Spanish settlers began to expand westward, northward, and eastward, occasionally encroaching upon lands and settlements already inhabited by Indians. Settlements of *genízaros* (Indians of nomadic tribes who after capture or ransom became an integral part of Spanish society) were made at Abiquiú, Sabinal, and San Miguel del Vado. Spaniards and mixed bloods settled near Laguna and Zuñi pueblos,[24] reoccupied small communities such as Ojo Caliente, and spread out in numerous smaller settlements in the northern part of the province. San Miguel del Vado, east of the Sangre de Cristo Mountains, was originally settled in 1794 as a frontier outpost against Apache raids. Laid out as a "defensible unit," it had a plaza surrounded by adobe houses and a church apparently built before 1807. Its first citizens were *genízaros*, who farmed and fought. After 1799 they were joined by mestizos and other *genízaros* from Belén and the Río Abajo region who were searching for good farming land. Some Pueblo Indians from Nambé and a few pacified Comanches even came to live in the settlement.

Although the census of 1827 for this community came six years after Spain had relinquished its control over New Mexico, it is close enough to the Spanish colonial period and important enough to merit attention here. There were 2,893 people living at this village, and 714 of them had listed occupations. A general summary of these occupations and the marital status of the entire population is indicated in Table 5.[25]

Table 5
Occupations and Marital Status of
Residents of San Miguel del Vado (1827)

Occupations		Marital Status	
Farmers	401	Male children, unmarried	709
Craftsmen	93	Female children, unmarried	799
Day laborers	217	Men, married	634
Merchants	2	Women, married	634
Schoolteachers	1	Widowers	53
		Widows	64
Total	714	Total	2,893

At this point perhaps one should pause and summarize the types of Spanish settlements in New Mexico during the eighteenth century. New Mexican settlers, as noted, tended to disperse to rural areas—isolated small farms, ranches, and hamlets principally situated along the Río Grande. Loose collections of these establishments made up the "communities" of the province. Even the four *villas*—Santa Fé, Alburquerque, Santa Cruz de la Cañada, and El Paso del Norte—each consisted of many smaller communities. Unlike Nueva Vizcaya, New Mexico never had a fully recognized city, such as Durango. However, in addition to the four *villas* the province did have many *poblaciones*, villages of loosely grouped *ranchos* or "plazas" of a few Spanish households usually near farming lands or orchards. The *rancho* in New Mexico was more of a small agricultural plot, a farm, than a subsistence-level livestock-raising unit, as it was, for example, in Texas. "Plazas" in New Mexico came to mean very small settlements or country villages, built around a plaza. Some of them were primarily agricultural, but others such as Ojo Caliente and Torreones were defensive in nature.[26]

The term *"pueblo"* never seems to have been used to designate a Spanish town in New Mexico, in contrast to the practice on other frontiers in northern

Ruins of the parish church at Talpa, New Mexico. Photographed about 1930 by Harmon Parkhurst. *Courtesy Mr. and Mrs. T. R. Waring and Major and Mrs. Edmund B. Stewart.*

New Spain. This was so, apparently, because from the beginning Indian communities along the Río Grande and westward were known as *pueblos*, and their inhabitants were named by the Spaniards Pueblo Indians. Spanish communities, usually fronting along an irrigation ditch or stream and extending inland to the semiarid rangeland of higher altitudes, were generally known in New Mexico as *villas, poblaciones, ranchos*, and plazas. In fact, the settlers' desire to live near their fields resulted in scattered settlements ,conflicting with the Spanish government's desire to concentrate its people at a few major points for defensive purposes.[27]

A Mexican *carreta* in the nineteenth century, employing oxen for drawing power. *Courtesy Denver Public Library Western Collection.*

Spanish settlers in New Mexico grew in numbers gradually after the foundation of Santa Fé in 1610 until there were approximately 2,900 persons in the province by 1680. Juan de Oñate originally brought 129 male heads of households from Nueva Vizcaya in 1598, when the first civil settlement was founded in New Mexico. This probably meant that there were between six and seven hundred people in the colonizing expedition. It is evident that the number of settlers dwindled between 1598 and 1610, because of death and desertion, without appreciable replenishment but increased thereafter. France V. Scholes has estimated that the total population of Spaniards in New Mexico during the seventeenth century did not exceed 2,500 persons. However, there must have been nearly 2,900 people in 1680 if there were 21 missionaries and 380 settlers killed in the Pueblo revolt, along with 2,500 refugees.[28] At any rate, the population of Spaniards and mixed bloods was small in comparison to the later eighteenth century figures, which showed ten times this number. However, New Mexico's seventeenth century population after eight decades of settlement was about equal to that of Spanish Texas or Alta California after each had been permanently occupied for a comparable period of time.

By comparison, in the seventeenth century the number of settlers in the Paso del Norte region was very small until the arrival of the refugees in 1680.

Between 1659 and 1680 there were perhaps a few hundred civilian settlers living in the vicinity of the mission of Guadalupe del Paso. With the addition of 1,946 refugee colonists as well as their Indian allies, El Paso del Norte became a true civil settlement of considerable importance on the frontier of New Spain. Mission, presidio, and civil community—these were the elements of Spanish civilization in this area. Although people began deserting the colony almost at once, it survived to provide a nucleus for the growth of the community during the eighteenth century.

Although Spanish officials occasionally made efforts to concentrate settlers and Christianized Indians in a few communities, the people resisted. The population increased and dispersed, mainly downriver from the pass itself. As a result, Spanish and Indian settlers lived in mixed communities on both banks of the Río Grande, extending over a distance of twenty-five to thirty miles southeastward from the mission of Guadalupe del Paso.

Fray Miguel de Menchero, a *visitador* for the entire province of New Mexico in 1744, noted in his report that there were 613 families of Spaniards and Indians living in ten communities and a 40-man presidio at El Paso. They were distributed throughout the jurisdiction as indicated in Table 6.[29]

Table 6
Population of El Paso Communities
(1744)

Settlement	Spanish Families	Indian Families	Total Families
Mission of Nuestra Señora de Guadalupe del Paso	180 (plus 40 presidial soldiers)	40	220
San Lorenzo	12	50 (Sumas)	62
San Antonio Senecú	5	70	75
San Antonio de la Ysleta		90	90
Nuestra Señora del Socorro	6	60	66
Nuestra Señora de las Calvas y Hacienda El Capitán		60	60
Ranches of Ojo Caliente y El Carrizal	20 (mixed with Indians)		20
Hacienda de la Ranchería	20	"some"	20
Totals	243	370	613

Although these figures are only approximations, and Fray Menchero often resorted to vague wordings to describe the size of communities, they do show the relative sizes of the Paso del Norte settlements, the scattered nature of the communities, the relative numbers of Spaniards and Christianized Indians living there, and the mixed quality of the population. The mission of Nuestra Señora de Guadalupe, its accompanying presidio, and the nearby civil establishment formed the largest concentration of Spanish settlers in the entire jurisdiction. Some 180 of the 243 listed Spanish and mixed-blood families lived there, with other civilian settlers residing at San Lorenzo, Senecú, Socorro, and two new ranching communities, El Capitán and Hacienda de la Ranchería, twenty miles downriver from El Paso del Norte.[30] The total number of people, although never so stated in the Menchero report, probably exceeded three thousand. This would indicate that the population had trebled since the last decade of the seventeenth century. About one-third to one-half of the people at El Paso del Norte were Spaniards or mixed bloods.

That the population of this jurisdiction increased notably in the last half of the eighteenth century is apparent from an examination of census reports and observations of official visitors for that period. Nicolás de Lafora noted in 1767 that El Paso del Norte had a total of five thousand persons, its settlements lying on both banks of the Río Grande and extending seven leagues (about eighteen miles) along the river. Guadalupe del Paso was the largest single settlement, being inhabited by Spaniards, mestizos, mulattoes, Indians of the Tiwa and Piro nations, and some *genízaros*. In addition, it had a presidial company consisting of three officers, one sergeant, and forty-six soldiers.[31] A resident of Paso del Norte in 1773 described the jurisdiction as consisting of a settlement on the south bank of the Río Grande (Guadalupe del Paso) along with its five missions—Guadalupe, containing Spaniards, Indians of the Manso, Piro, and Pima [?] nations, now thoroughly mixed into one society; San Lorenzo el Real with its Suma Indians; Isleta with its Christianized Indians, some white people, and many soldiers who were described as "not at all industrious and inclined to marauding, which they call foraging . . ."; and Socorro, a community of Apaches ransomed from the warlike Comanches,[32] thus meriting the name of *genízaros*.

Fray Juan Agustín de Morfi described eleven *poblaciones* of 4,827 persons (3,387 Spaniards and 1,440 Indians) at El Paso del Norte in his report written in 1782. He noted that, although four of the settlements had been established for Spaniards and seven for Indians, the two groups were in reality now combined in these communities. Piros, Mansos, and Janos Indians lived with some Spaniards at "El Paso del Río del Norte"; Sumas did likewise at San Lorenzo el Real, originally founded as a *villa* by Spaniards; Piros lived at Senecú; Tiwas and Spanish *vecinos* made up the population of Ysleta (Isleta); and both Piros and Sumas were mixed with Spaniards in the community of Socorro.[33]

Census returns for the period from 1784 to 1805 were frequent and detailed. They reveal the concentration of Spanish settlers primarily at El Paso del Norte, but their continued presence in other communities downriver from that principal point is also apparent. The total population and its increase in the Paso del Norte region is reflected in Table 7.[34]

Table 7
Population of El Paso del Norte, 1784 to 1805

Year	Total Population	Year	Total Population
1784	4,101	1800	6,136
1787	4,122	1802	5,827
1789	5,310	1804	6,190
1790	5,244	1805	6,209

The figures do not show a continuous growth from one year to the next. Errors in addition, omissions of certain settlements, and differences of standards being used affect the census results and could account for the slight decreases that occur in some years. However, the trend is toward a population increase over the course of the twenty years considered—an increase, in fact, of about fifty per cent. There were more people in the Paso del Norte settlements by this time than there were in the whole of Texas, in Baja and Alta California combined, or in the Pimería Alta region of Sonora. Furthermore, by 1804, there were seven times as many Spanish settlers in these communities as there were Indians.[35]

The entire province of New Mexico reflected an even more dramatic population increase during the eighteenth century. Diego de Vargas brought one hundred soldiers and seventy families northward with him for the reconquest and resettlement of New Mexico beginning in 1693. By December 31, 1817, only four years before Mexico established her independence from Spain, there were 36,579 people in New Mexico. This included both those of European and Indian descent, residing in five major jurisdictions, but no longer included the Paso del Norte settlements. Subtracting the 8,788 Pueblo Indians of the Keres and Zuñi linguistic groups, there were 27,791 Spanish-speaking people living in the vicinities of Santa Fé, La Cañada, Taos, Abiquiú, Alburquerque, and Belén.[36] This gives some idea of how populous New Mexico really was in relation to the rest of the provinces on New Spain's northern frontier, especially those now located within the boundaries of the United States.

Fray Miguel de Menchero also visited the settlements of New Mexico above El Paso del Norte in 1744. In his lengthy report he noted the presence of 505 Spanish families, or approximately twenty-five hundred persons, not counting the Paso del Norte region or Pueblo Indian settlements at Zuñi and Isleta. The number of Spaniards, mestizos, and Christianized Indians living in New Mexican communities is given for 1744 in Table 8.[37]

These figures did not include the Indian pueblos, or other settlements of Indians (except for Abiquiú perhaps), nor were the missions of New Mexico reflected in Menchero's statistics. A new *pueblo* of *genízaros* was specifically excluded from these figures. At Tomé, south of Alburquerque, there were forty families of these Indians in a community founded perhaps in 1740; they practiced agriculture, had erected a church, and were frequently employed as allies of the Spaniards and Pueblo Indians to fight the Comanches.[38] In addition, Menchero estimated that there were 1,535 Pueblo Indians living at twenty separate communities, with Taos and Zuñi being the farthest points in the north and west, respectively, occupied by Christianized people. He further noted the presence of a Jicarilla Apache mission, reportedly established in 1733 some five leagues from Taos, and observed that there were some Comanches living at Pecos Pueblo and a Navajo woman who resided at Zía Pueblo.[39]

Table 8

Population of New Mexico Settlements

(1744)

Settlement	Families	Settlement	Families
Villa of Santa Fé	120	*Rancho* of Embudo	8
Villa of Santa Cruz de la Cañada	100 ("a little more")	*Ranchos* de Taos (four of them)	10
Rancho de Chama and Río del Oso	11	*Ranchos* de las Bocas	12
		Ranchos of Bernalillo	10
Puesto of Santa Rosa Abiquiú	20	*Ranchos* of Alameda	8
Puesto and *ranchos* Jocaliente (Ojo Caliente)	16	*Villa* de Alburquerque and *aldea* of Atrisco	100 ("a little more")
Hacienda and *ranchos* of Nuestra Señora de la Soledad	40	*Población* of Nuestra Señora de la Concepción	50
		Total	505 families

It is apparent from this report that there were more than two thousand families in the Spanish and Indian settlements of New Mexico by 1744, totaling around ten thousand people in all. One out of every four persons was a Spaniard or a mestizo of some type. As expected, Santa Fé, La Cañada, and Alburquerque, the three *villas* were the largest settlements. Together they contained more than sixty per cent of the Spanish population beyond El Paso del Norte. Santa Fé had very few Indian residents, mainly "because they do not want to live with the Spaniards."[40] Finally, it should be noted that some members of Plains Indian nations—Comanches and Jicarilla Apaches—and an occasional Navajo had moved into the Spanish communities at this early date, thus beginning the process of mixing with the people of European heritage in the formation of New Mexico's Spanish-American, or Hispano, society.

Eight years later, in 1752, Governor Tomás Vélez Cachupín's census of New

Mexico's sixteen settlements of *"gente de razón"* reflected a total of 3,402 persons in 676 families, not counting the inhabitants at El Paso del Norte (although they too were included in the governor's over-all totals for the province). Almost half of these people were at Santa Fé, La Cañada, and Alburquerque, but a close examination shows that Spaniards had spread out to communities near Indian pueblos and had established new settlements. Table 9 shows the communities inhabited by *"gente de razón,"* with population figures for this 1752 census.[41]

Table 9
Population of New Mexico Settlements
(1752)

Settlement	Population
Villa and capital of Santa Fé	605
Cañada of Cochití	37
Villa of Santa Cruz de la Cañada	556
Partido (district) of Chimayó	355
Partido of the pueblo of Quemado	139
Partido of La Soledad	140
Partido of El Embudo	45
Partido of Chama	242
Partido of Abiquiú	73
Partido of Pojoaque	183
Vecinos of Taos	74
Partido of Santa Bárbara de Pecuries	77
Villa of Alburquerque	476
Partido of Belén	65
Partido of Fonclara	255
Partido of Bernalillo	80
Total	3,402

The census showed a total of 4,448 people (no Indians included) in the province of New Mexico when the 1,046 settlers of El Paso del Norte were added.[42] Therefore, slightly more than seventy-five per cent of the *gente de razón* lived in the area along the Río Grande and Río Chama from Taos and Chama in the north to Belén and the vicinity of modern Socorro in the south; just under twenty-five per cent lived in the Paso del Norte region.

Bishop Pedro Tamarón y Romeral visited New Mexico in 1760 and made an extensive report concerning the inhabitants, their occupations, and the status of religious activity within the province. He noted that El Paso del Norte was the "gateway of the interior of New Mexico." It had 354 families totaling 2,479 Spaniards and "Europeanized" citizens (mixed bloods and Indians); Alburquerque had 270 families comprising 1,814 persons; Santa Fé was composed of 379 families of 1,285 people; and the *villa* of Santa Cruz de la Cañada had 241 families with 1,515 persons.[43] Thus, there were 1,244 families made up of a total of 7,093 persons, or an average of nearly six persons per family, in these four communities alone.

Nicolás de Lafora pointed out seven years later, in 1767, that the whole province of New Mexico contained 9,580 Spaniards and mixed bloods apportioned among 1,487 families. In addition, there were 2,703 families of Indians amounting to 10,524 people in the same region; therefore, the over-all population of the province, according to Lafora, was 20,104. Santa Fé had a population of 2,324 persons, made up of 80 families of soldiers, 274 Spanish households, and 89 families from various Indian nations. Seventy Spanish families made up the population of the *villa* at Alburquerque.[44]

Fray Francisco Atanasio Domínguez noted in 1776 that the Spanish population of New Mexico had continued to increase since the visits of Bishop Tamarón and Nicolás de Lafora. He also made extensive notes about both the Spanish and Pueblo Indian communities. He emphasized the fact that the Paso del Norte district consisted of a Spanish *villa* and four Indian *pueblos* spread out over a distance of ten or twelve leagues (twenty-five to thirty miles); the interior New Mexico region consisted of three Spanish *villas* and twenty-two Indian villages on both sides of the Río Grande spread out over a distance of forty leagues (one hundred miles).[45] The Santa Fé jurisdiction, according to Fray Domínguez, had a total of 387 families with 2,014 persons within its boundaries, but only the governor, his family of 6, and 229 Spanish families lived in the *villa* itself. In addition, there were 42 families of *genízaros* with a total of 174 persons living in the *villa*, where they worked for the Spaniards.[46] At La Cañada there were a number of scattered *ranchos* and *"haciendas."* Settlements at Chimayó contained 71 families with 367 persons; the *villa* of Santa Cruz, 125 families with 680 people; Quemado, 52 families of 220 inhabitants; and Las Truchas, 26 families with 122 residents in all. The total for this district was 274 families with 1,389 people.[47] The *villa* of Alburquerque was still the largest for its district, counting 157 families of 763 persons. Settlements at Alameda, Valencia, Tomé, Atrisco, and Corrales brought the total for this region to 453 families having 2,416 members.[48] Domínguez reported 7,550 people living in the Río Arriba (upriver) region and 10,794 in the Río Abajo (downriver, or lower river) district, for a total of 18,344 inhabitants in the province of New Mexico.[49] This total must have included Pueblo Indians and *genízaros*, because the entire Spanish population for these three jurisdictions was only 5,819 persons, an increase of 2,417 since 1752.

Fray Juan Agustín de Morfi and Governor Fernando de la Concha conducted thorough inspections of the New Mexican settlements, both Spanish and Pueblo Indian, and wrote out their findings during the 1780s. Neither, unfortunately, bothered to total the population of the province, but both provided extensive information on the nature of each community and its people. Morfi noted that New Mexico was composed of eight *alcaldías mayores* (administrative districts supervised by chief magistrates)—Santa Fé, Santa Cruz de la Cañada, Taos, Queres, San Carlos de Alameda (or Sandía), Alburquerque, Laguna, and Zuñi—in addition to the *"pueblo"* and missions of El Paso del Norte. Spanish families, according to him, resided at some twenty settlements and numerous outlying *ranchos*, many of which were in the vicinity of Isleta and Alburquerque, where he described the people as being spread all over the valley. Santa Fé still had the largest single number of people, with 1,915 residents, while Santa Cruz de la Cañada showed 1,821 people in all its communities. The *villa* of Alburquerque, according to Morfi, had 381 families. Some settlements, such as Tesuque, Isleta, Laguna, and Taos, contained both Pueblo Indians and Spanish *vecinos*.[50] However, Morfi's figures do not provide an accurate estimate of New Mexico's population, since he often indicated only numbers of families, made approximations, and frequently mixed numbers of people and families, thereby making no effort to standardize or equate the two separate systems of counting inhabitants.

Governor Fernando de la Concha personally conducted a general inspection of New Mexican communities in 1789. After publishing an official notification to the citizens of the various jurisdictions,[51] he evidently visited every Spanish and Indian community in the province, excluding those at El Paso del Norte. His journey took him from Taos to Senecú in the period between September 11 and December 9, 1789. He completed a census for each village, with notations on its arms and preparations for defense; furthermore, he listened to complaints, endeavored to resolve problems, and made observations concerning both religious and civil matters. However, he failed to separate Indian and Spanish residents at pueblos such as Taos, Laguna, and Tesuque, thus preventing us from arriving at an accurate count of New Mexico's Spanish settlers. Yet, he did provide figures of total settlers and communities, as shown in Table 10.[52]

Table 10
Population of New Mexico Settlements
(1789)

Settlement	Population
Las Trampas de Taos	308
Las Trampas de Picurís, Embudo, Truchas, and Quemado	956
Santo Tomás de Abiquiú (not counting 160 *genízaros*)	992
Pueblo of San Juan de los Caballeros	1,838
Villa of Santa Cruz de la Cañada	1,301
Pojoaque and Cundiyó	459
Pueblo of San Buenaventura de Cochití	426
Pueblo of San Diego de Jémez	118

Table 10 (*continued*).

Settlement	Population
Pueblo of Nuestra Señora de Dolores de Sandía	730
Villa of San Felipe Neri de Alburquerque	1,347
Pueblo of San Agustín de Isleta	576
Plaza of Belén	2,030
Villa of Santa Fe	2,901
Total	13,982

This total population of Indians and Spanish-speaking people probably should be increased to approximately fifteen thousand to account for those settlers living in omitted communities (such as Acoma, Laguna, and Zuñi). Nevertheless, it represents an appreciable increase over the Domínguez figures for 1776. When Governor Concha added the 4,782 people from the Paso del Norte settlements (which he did not visit), it can be seen that New Mexico's population approached twenty thousand by 1789.

The province's most detailed, accurate census was that of 1790. It does contain occasional errors of duplication, omission in numbers of families listed, and simple mathematical mistakes, but in general it provides what is perhaps the best listing of families by community in any frontier region at a given time. Not only does it supply listings of heads of families by name, but family members, ages, origins of some, servants, and occupations. In addition, the total population, as well as the numbers of men, women, boys, and girls, is shown for each community and for the province as a whole. Finally, it should be noted that the census was taken in the very same year that far away to the eastward the first census of the United States was being completed.[53]

According to the 1790 census, New Mexico had a total population of 30,953, including all men, women, and children listed for Spanish and Pueblo Indian settlements. Subtracting the 5,244 residents of the Paso del Norte region, we find 25,709 persons living in New Mexico proper. Of this total, 18,587 people lived in the vicinty of the three *villas*—Santa Fé (3,733), Alburquerque (5,959), and La Cañada (8,895)—with the remainder in the Queres, Laguna, and Zuñi jurisdictions. The census also shows a total of 20,289 "Spaniards" and "*castas*" (mixed bloods) including the Paso del Norte settlements.[54] It is apparent that some Indians by that time, as in earlier years, lived in Spanish-speaking communities and that, in turn, Spaniards had come to reside in the vicinity of Pueblo Indian villages, no matter what the royal regulations were concerning the segregation of the two races. The figures for this census closely resemble those compiled by Governor Concha the preceding year.

It should be noted that the numbers of inhabitants at both Alburquerque and La Cañada in 1790 surpassed those at the capital of Santa Fé for the first time. The Alburquerque jurisdiction included six plazas of the *villa* itself, with a total of 248 families listed, and twenty-five outlying plazas, along with one Indian pueblo, San Agustín de Isleta, where 103 Indian and 8 Spanish families were individually listed. Other settlements in the Alburquerque district included San Antonio, Atrisco, Valencia, San Fernando de las Silvas, Tomé, San Ysidro de Paxarito, Los Padillas, San Antonio de los Lentes, Los Cháves (six plazas alone), Belén (three plazas), San Antonio de los Trujillos de Belén, Nuestra Señora del Pilar de Belén, and San Antonio del Sabinal.[55] This dispersal of Spaniards into many rural communities surrounding a central *villa* was a typical settlement pattern in New Mexico.

During the last decade of the eighteenth century and the first one of the nineteenth, the population of New Mexico continued to expand and to spread out from the central area along the Río Grande. In 1793 the province had 34,201 people, with 29,041 of them in New Mexico proper and 5,160 at El Paso. Santa Fé (4,346), La Cañada (10,185), and Alburquerque (6,255) combined had a total of 20,786 people, or an increase of 2,199 since 1790. The entire province counted 22,851 Spaniards and mixed bloods along with 11,350 Indians.[56] In 1800 the total population was 33,490, including the Paso del Norte region, a slight drop from the figures for 1793. Of this total, 24,492 were listed as Spaniards and mixed bloods, while 8,998 were reported as Indians. The number of Spaniards, castes, and Indians by jurisdiction within the province is given in Table 11.[57]

Table 11
Population of New Mexican Settlements
(1800)

Settlements/Jurisdictions	Spaniards/Castes	Indians
Santa Fé and vicinity	4,003	314
Santa Cruz de la Cañada and vicinity	7,452	1,079
Taos and Picurís	1,349	782
Jémez, Zía, Santa Ana	458	1,166
Zuñi	7	2,716
Alburquerque, Isleta, *genízaro* communities	4,423	603
Alameda, Sandía, San Felipe, Santo Domingo, Cochití	1,489	1,513
Paso del Norte, San Lorenzo el Real, Senecú, Ysleta, Socorro	5,311	825
Totals	24,492	8,998

Lieutenant Zebulon Montgomery Pike was in New Mexico from the first to the twenty-first of March, 1807, after his capture near present La Jara, Colorado, and before he was sent to Chihuahua by his captors. He estimated that the population of New Mexico was about thirty thousand, not including the Paso del Norte settlements.[58] Pike described Santa Fé, which he reached on

March 3, as a village three streets wide, about a mile long, looking like a "fleet of flat-bottomed boats . . . descending the Ohio River."[59] He estimated the population to be about 4,500.[60] Fray Josef Benito Pereyra reported three years later, in 1810, that the total population of New Mexico (no longer including El Paso) was 36,016, with 26,926 being Spaniards and castes and 9,090 being Indians. According to his figures, there were 4,962 people living in Santa Fé, 2,402 in La Cañada, 2,441 in San Juan de los Caballeros, 2,143 in Abiquiú, 2,125 in Belén, 2,590 in Isleta, and 2,625 in the *villa* of Alburquerque.[61]

Fortunately, New Mexico had a detailed census report completed on December 31, 1817, thus providing us with statistical information and observations on New Mexican society only four years short of the end of Spanish control over the province. This census contains a fairly accurate estimate of the total population, a listing of the principal sites occupied by Spaniards, and a reasonable idea of how many Spanish-speaking people there were in New Mexico. There were 36,579 people in the province, of whom 27,157 were Spaniards and mixed bloods, together with 9,422 Indians at the pueblos, in the settlements, and at *genízaro* communities. The *villa* and presidio of Santa Fé along with the surrounding settlements numbered 6,728 people; the *villa* of La Cañada and its vicinity counted 12,903; and the *villa* of Alburquerque with its environs had 8,160.[62] Of importance is the fact that the number of Spanish settlers in any one of these three jurisdictions at the close of the Spanish period outnumbered the total population of Texas, Pimería Alta, Baja California, or Alta California. New Mexico had indeed become one of the most populous of the provinces on New Spain's northern frontier.

In summary, it should be noted that over two centuries of Spanish occupation had brought about the establishment of many civil communities in New Mexico, along with a dispersal of people from four principal centers, an increase in population, and a mixing of Spanish and Indian people. Juan de Oñate had originally brought 129 families of perhaps six hunderd settlers in all to establish San Juan de los Caballeros and San Gabriel in 1598. The Spanish population increased slowly, reaching almost 2,900 inhabitants by 1680, when the Pueblo revolt occurred. Although there were no settlers in New Mexico proper for the next thirteen years, one thousand people hung on at El Paso del Norte, becoming the nucleus of a civil community which reached more than six thousand in the early nineteenth century. Diego de Vargas brought one hundred soldiers and seventy families with him in his expedition of 1693 for the reconquest and resettlement of interior New Mexico. By 1752 there were 3,402 Spaniards and mixed bloods there, and twenty-five years later the number had nearly doubled. It more than doubled again between 1776 and 1789 and passed the twenty-thousand mark in the decade of the 1790s. Thereafter, the number of Spaniards and mixed bloods continued to grow, reaching a total of 27,157 in 1817, a figure more than forty-five times that of the original estimated colonists.

Spanish settlers in New Mexico came initially from both the Old World and the New. Oñate and his 129 families included fifty-four *vecinos* from identifiable places in Spain (41.5 per cent of the total), including such cities as Madrid, Sevilla, Jérez de la Frontera, Barcelona, Córdoba, and Santiago de Compostela, along with the provinces of Castile, Aragón, Galicia, and Andalucía. Thirty-nine *vecinos* (thirty per cent of the total) came from New Spain —fourteen from the captital of the viceroyalty in México, comprising the largest single group, eight from Zacatecas, four from Sombrerete, three from Puebla, three from Guadalajara, two from Pánuco, and one each from various other communities extending as far south as Oaxaca. Finally, there were thirty-seven *vecinos* (28.5 per cent of the total) from unspecified places, unidentifiable locations, or other parts of Europe and America. Seven Portuguese settlers accompanied Oñate, this being in the period when the Spanish and Portuguese crowns were united under Philip II. Furthermore, there was one settler from the island of Tenerife in the Canary Islands, another from Havana, and, surprisingly, even a Greek settler named appropriately Juan Griego.[63]

Therefore, it is likely that some of the settlers who reoccupied New Mexico with Diego de Vargas in 1693 may have been descended from true Spanish blood, an allegation often heard among Hispano residents of the Río Grande area today. However, such a conclusion could be very misleading if allowed to stand alone. Once in New Mexico, these colonists were not supported or reinforced by any sustained immigration over the years. Instead, they intermarried with various other groups and had children who were not full-blooded Spaniards but retained the identification *españoles*. Real Spaniards became a decided minority, and most of the people—perhaps more than eighty per cent and possibly as high as ninety per cent—were natives of New Mexico or other points in New Spain. A considerable number of mixed bloods existed among the original colonists,[64] and this element of the population tended to swell as the process of *mestizaje* (intermixture) advanced with each generation. Many different racial mixtures were evident in the census returns, indicating the ever-decreasing European nature of the population and its ever-increasing mixed character.

Two censuses in the latter part of the eighteenth century clearly show that the overwhelming majority of the people came from within the province of New Mexico. Of 796 families listed in the 1788 census for Paso del Norte communities, the head of the family was a *"natural del Paso"* in 718 cases, or 90.3 per cent of the total. The others included very few *"europeos"*; they were mostly people migrating from nearby provinces and communities, such as Chihuahua (twenty-two *vecinos*), New Mexico (fourteen), Valle de San Bartolomé (eleven), Janos (nine), and Carrizal (six).[65] In the 1790 census for New Mexico only sixty-eight people are cited as natives of some other jurisdiction from the one in which they were reported. Twenty-two of these people came from the Paso del Norte jurisdiction, ten from Chihuahua, nineteen from other points within New Mexico, six from Mexico City, five from other locations on the northern frontier, four from central New Spain, and only two from outside the viceroyalty.[66]

It is evident from these figures that the frontier Spanish population of New Mexico did include some people who were indeed Spaniards. However, with the passing of time and lack of migration from Spain, the province was forced to rely upon its own human resources or those of nearby frontier provinces. Friendly Tlaxcaltecan Indians from central New Spain may have settled in the *barrio* (ward or district) of Analco on the southern bank of the Rito de Santa Fé within the limits of the capital itself. If so, they came in ones and twos, for there was never a planned program to colonize New Mexico with Tlaxcaltecans, as there was in Coahuila, for example. Some "Mexican" Indians retreated with the Spaniards to El Paso in 1680, and a few evidently returned with Diego de Vargas to resettle Analco before it was overrun by *genízaros* in the eighteenth century.[67] It can be noted, nevertheless, that in spite of Spanish restrictions on people moving from one settlement to another, the necessity of obtaining licenses, or passports, to travel, and strong attachments of families to particular geographic locations, there was some migration within the northern provinces and especially in New Mexico itself. There was a dispersal of people over the Río Grande Valley at first, then away from it to Abiquiú, Laguna, San Miguel del Vado, and the mountain communities of the Sangre de Cristo range.

Societal differentiations among residents of New Mexico existed mostly in official records and census reports. There was, in reality, little difference between or animosity among the classes; certainly there was no intense rivalry similar to that between *peninsulares* and Creoles so evident in other parts of New Spain and elsewhere in Latin America. Governors of New Mexico were usually Spaniards, and the early settlers in the Oñate colony contained a sizable number of European-born persons. With the passing of generations, however, the Spaniards (frequently called "*europeos*)" became the exception rather than the rule. New Mexicans had been isolated so long from the rest of New Spain that there was little if any difference between Spaniards and Creoles. Both groups held local military and civil offices in New Mexico,[68] and census listings, although they usually gave the origin of the individual, did not bother to list the groups separately.

Spanish frontier society in New Mexico was increasingly flexible both within the societal order and in the acceptance of new races and mixtures into the community. Individuals advanced easily from one class to another by intermarriage or adoption of the way of life practiced by the Spanish settlers. By the eighteenth century most settlers were, in reality, a military and pastoral people, *paisanos* of the country itself, not convicts or peons, a popular misconception, working on the *haciendas* of large absentee landowners. They did not come to New Mexico seeking religious liberty or civil freedoms, but often because they might receive the title of *"hidalgo"* if they stayed[69] and frequently because they were granted land, building lots, subsidies, and farming implements to begin life anew on this frontier. Indeed, some mixed bloods, or castes, did achieve high military rank within the frontier system; some became *alcaldes mayores* and members of the Cabildo of Santa Fé. As early as the seventeenth century there did seem to develop a local aristocracy based upon family ties, service to the crown, and material possessions. A few families who had served the crown faithfully in the province advanced to *hidalgo* status.[70]

The presence of so many castes and the acceptance of Indians into the Spanish community were also distinguishing features of society in New Mexico, in contrast to the central portion of New Spain. Mixtures were generally designated by the terms *"casta," "color quebrado,"* and *mestizo*, depending largely upon local use. Complicating the exact identification of these people was the fact that such localisms as *"coyote"* and *"lobo"* were also applied to mixed bloods. In general, the social system grew and went through changes as the colonial era progressed. By the end of the eighteenth century census reports showed only two basic entries for each community—"Spaniards and castes" and "Indians." Pueblo Indians, Comanches, Apaches, Navajos, Utes, and members of various other nations simply described as *"genízaros"* lived in Spanish communities and were readily accepted into the general society. They even married Spaniards and castes and practiced some of the same occupations as those of the settlers. Furthermore, there were Negroes and many mulattoes in the civil communities, both in New Mexico proper and in the Paso del Norte settlements.[71]

The extended family was the basis of society in New Mexico. Census reports in the period from 1790 to 1817 are based upon individual family listings within each community. Heads of families might be either men or women, married or single persons, widows and widowers. The large majority was made up of males, who were listed first with other family members and their relationship specified thereafter. A typical entry named the nuclear family first— head of family, spouse, and children (broken down by sons and daughters)— followed by relatives, servants, and others adopted into that family. Some examples typical of hundreds in the Alburquerque census for 1790 are:[72]

1. Juachín López, Esp.[1], sembr.[r], de 47 a.[s], C.[do] con Feliciana Jaramillo, Mest.[a], de 35 a.[s], un hijo varon de 8 a.[s], una hija de 5 a.[s] (Juachín López, Spaniard, farmer, 47 years old, married to Feliciana Jaramillo, Mestiza, 35 years old, one legitimate son 8 years old, one daughter 5 years old.)
2. Comm.[e] Juan Cand.[a], Esp.[1], Texedor, de 53 a.[s], C.[do] con Bárbara García, Esp.[la], de 50 a.[s], un hijo varon de 23 a.[s], dos hijas, una de 14 a.[s], otra de 11 a.[s], Dos sobrinos varones Esp.[les], uno de 17 a.[s], otro de 14 a.[s], un huerfano *coyote* de 23 a.[s],

una Yndia sirv.^{ta} de 26 a.^s, tres hijos varones, uno de 11 a.^s, otro de 7 a.^s, otro de 4 a.^s, una huerfana Esp.^{la} de 4 a.^s (Comandante Juan Candalaria, Spaniard, weaver, 53 years old, married to Bárbara García, Spaniard, 50 years old, one legitimate son 23 years old, two daughters—one 14 years old and the other 11 years old. Two male nephews, Spaniards, one 17 years old and the other 14 years old. One male orphan, *coyote*, 23 years old. A female Indian servant 26 years old. Her three legitimate sons—one 11 years old, another 7 years old, another 4 years old. A female orphan, Spaniard, 4 years old.)

The first family noted above contained only four persons, while the second had thirteen, including five in the nuclear family. In general, Spanish families tended to be large. Marriages evidently occurred frequently in the teens, and child-bearing often started when the wife was fifteen to eighteen years of age. Widows, widowers, and orphans, although also listed separately, were often integrated into extended family listings. Mothers-in-law, nieces, nephews, brothers, sisters, and other relatives were usually included as a part of the family itself. Of particular interest is the fact that where financially and socially possible whole families of Indians, widows, and orphans were freely accepted into the families of the *paisanos*.

Spanish settlers in New Mexico throughout the colonial period were employed principally in agriculture, stock raising, a variety of skilled trades, and some rudimentary forms of commerce. El Paso del Norte's census of 1784 contains specific information on the occupations of 484 heads of families. Of this total, 439 (90.5 per cent) were employed as *labradores*, or farmers. Six others were engaged in commerce, while there were also six tailors, five carpenters, two masons or builders, and six blacksmiths and silversmiths, for a total of twenty-seven people engaged as artisans. Professional people were few —only the lieutenant governor, a minister, a notary, and one scribe represent this class.[73]

In general, hard-working, individually employed small farmers and artisans comprised the majority of the Spanish-speaking residents of New Mexico. The garrisons of soldiers stationed at Santa Fé and El Paso del Norte plus the Franciscan missionaries in the province did not amount to more than ten per cent of the total Spanish population. It is evident that individuals generally worked for themselves except for those employed as servants, an occupation that might include Spaniards as well as Indians and castes. Spanish settlers in New Mexico neither endeavored to avoid work nor depended upon the labor of Indians, characteristics so frequently cited by advocates of the Black Legend to prove that Spaniards were not the true, hard-working colonists the English were.

Five occupations—farming, weaving, day labor, stock raising, and the trades —dominated the 1,658 jobs listed for heads of families at Santa Fé, Alburquerque, Santa Cruz de la Cañada, and Alameda in 1790. Farmers constituted the majority (927, or 55.8 per cent of the total), with the largest proportion (67.2 per cent) in Santa Cruz. Day laborers (219, or 13.2 per cent of the total) constituted the next largest group, while individuals associated with weaving— *cardadores* (carders), *hilanderos* (spinners), and *tejedores* (weavers)—occupied third place (216, or 13 per cent of the total, with a heavy concentration of 177 people in the Alburquerque region). Surprisingly, there were a great many artisans living in New Mexico and fewer persons associated with stock raising than might be expected. Indeed, stock raising accounted for only 113 persons (6.8 per cent), whereas 111 people (6.7 per cent) were employed as artisans. There were forty carpenters, thirty-three shoemakers, fourteen tailors, fifteen blacksmiths, six masons or builders, and three silversmiths scattered in the civil settlements of the province.[74] Other occupations included those of Indian interpreters residing in both the Indian pueblos and Spanish settlements, schoolmasters, merchants, hunters, and muleteers.[75] Dual employment as soldiers and farmers is evident at Alameda, while family adherence to a particular occupation, such as that of the Rendón family in Santa Fé to tailoring, may be noted.[76] Some people are listed as "without occupation," vagabonds, absent from the province, or with no indicated occupation because of blindness, advanced age, infirmity, or simple omission.

There was no single race or class employed exclusively as servants. Voluntary and involuntary servitude existed, mostly in the form of domestic servants for families who could afford to employ them. The 1790 census shows 248 people employed in New Mexico as servants (called *"sirvientes"* in the Río Abajo region and *"criados"* in the Río Arriba settlements), with 97.6 per cent of them at Alburquerque (111 people), Santa Fé (96), and Santa Cruz de la Cañada (35). Of the total number of servants, 136 (54.8 per cent) were Indians, 24 (9.7 per cent) were Spaniards, 81 (32.7 per cent) were castes, and seven were of unspecified classes. Although not all Indian servants were listed by tribe, it is apparent that many were of Apache derivation while others were Utes, Comanches, Navajos, Kiowas, and Hopis. Finally, by sex, it may be noted that most servants (60.5 per cent) were females, of various ages.[77]

Obviously, manual labor was an accepted way of life among the Spanish settlers of New Mexico. Farmers, artisans, day laborers, weavers, and a few professionals largely made up the colonial society of New Mexico. Although stock raising was present, it was not so important in the province as it would become in a later era when Indian depredations had diminished and the population had dispersed into areas away from the comparatively densely settled Río Grande Valley. Of importance, however, is the changing nature of colonial society in New Mexico with the passing of time. Growing numbers of people, mixing of races, and a blurring of class differences contributed to the emergence of a society that reflected frontier conditions and was anything but static.

To understand the nature of that society, it is necessary to look at the life style of the settlers. In the following chapter we will examine colonial customs, educational and medical developments, problems faced by the settlers, their achievements, and their diversions.

6. New Mexico
Life Style of the Paisanos

Life in seventeenth century New Mexico was characterized by a certain rough-ness, absence of luxuries, hard work on the part of individual settlers, and lack of education. Only a few people had attended any type of formal school prior to coming to New Mexico; once there, the only available schools were in the missions, and these were restricted mostly to Indian neophytes. Muster rolls of men capable of bearing arms revealed that many could not even sign their names; women, too, were unable to sign official depositions and legal docu-ments. Most of the people lived and died in New Mexico, isolated from the rest of the world in thought and practice, for they seldom had opportunities to learn to read, to exchange ideas with those outside the province, and to travel to other frontier provinces.[1] Men spent their time primarily in farming, raising livestock, and participating in military campaigns against the frequent Indian incursions; women managed the home, reared the children, and in large part supervised and directed the everyday family activities. Life was a con-tinuous round of eking out a living from one day to the next, a pattern that seems more monotonous to people today than it did at that time. There were few diversions other than gambling, gossip among friends, local games and dances, and occasional scandals.

Perhaps the greatest continual source of conversation, apprehensiveness, and "entertainment" was the seventeenth century struggle between clerical and civil officials over Indian control and employment, mission discipline, con-flicting economic interests, interference of the clergy in secular matters, and the question of ecclesiastical immunity. Leaders of both the church and the state were responsible for causing crises to arise and to continue, sometimes reaching fever pitch in the period before 1680. As a result, the nonaboriginal community became divided, provincial authority was weakened, and insubordi-nation among the populace was unconsciously encouraged. Indians became demoralized; they tended to return to their former idolatry and developed a spirit of rebellion in the latter half of the seventeenth century, a danger sign pointing toward the Pueblo revolt of 1680.[2]

Pueblo Indians were given in *encomienda*, that is granted to Spaniards for their care, supervision, and labor in return for individual services to the crown. Thirty-five *encomiendas* apparently were made in the seventeenth century, mostly for defensive purposes, since the royal government could not defend the region effectively and there was no presidio in New Mexico until after the Pueblo revolt. *Encomenderos* were permitted to collect tributes in the form of labor, grain crops, or cotton cloth from their Indians, and were obligated to participate with their arms, horses, and Indian subjects in the defense of the realm from the marauding Apaches.[3] Juan de Oñate had been given the early right to establish *encomiendas* for three generations descending from those who assisted him in the occupation of New Mexico. After the Spaniards were expelled in 1680 and the reconquest began in 1693, these initial *encomiendas* were lost and never recovered.[4] Diego de Vargas petitioned for, received, and had validated an *encomienda* exclusively for his use following the reconquest. According to the terms of his contractual agreement with the royal authorities, Indians were to pay him tribute in produce—blankets, buffalo hides, buckskins, and corn—but he took no steps to make the grant operative before his death at Bernalillo in 1704, and his heirs never received a single peso's worth of goods from the *encomienda*.[5]

There were no *encomiendas* in eighteenth century New Mexico, or for the rest of the Spanish colonial period, for that matter. Yet, the agricultural/pastoral society of Spanish-speaking people in the province faced many difficult problems and did a great deal to overcome them.

Important developments in secular education occurred toward the end of the eighteenth century and continued into the nineteenth. Prior to these, formal education had been confined primarily to the instruction of Franciscan missionaries. However, census reports for 1790 reflect the presence of *"maestros de escuela"* at Santa Fé and Alburquerque, although there is no other record pertaining to these schools.

Comandante-General Nemesio Salcedo in 1803 seems to have initiated in New Mexico, as he did elsewhere on the northern frontier, the first real government interest in *"escuelas de primeras letras"* (primary schools). He proposed that they be founded and maintained by contributions from settlers and presidial troops. Teachers were to be selected from men in the presidial garrisons or settlers who knew how to read and write. Parents whose sons attended the school were to pay the teacher two pesos per month for one son and five pesos for two. All males up to twelve years of age were required to attend school, and local officials were to override parental resistance. Teachers were to instruct pupils in Christian doctrine and the fundamentals of reading, writing, and simple arithmetic. Furthermore, each teacher was obligated to instruct the sons of the poor without charge, their expenses evidently being taken care of by the families which could afford to send their own children to school.[6]

Settlements in the Paso del Norte district had established schools for boys twelve to fifteen years of age by 1805. The *pueblo* of Socorro reported thirteen children and no Indians in its school, and their names are all listed in a school roll.[7] Socorro was only one of thirteen schools in the Paso del Norte region as of 1805. Nine schools existed in the *villa* of El Paso del Norte, with the other four located at San Lorenzo el Real, Senecú, Ysleta, and Socorro. The total enrollment was 856 children, but records indicate that of the 443 in the *villa* only 32 had learned to write and only 41 could read a book.[8] Fortunately, there is also an extensive summary of the Paso del Norte schools for 1806, listing *partidos* (districts) of the five major settlements in the jurisdiction, teachers, numbers of students, and those qualified to complete certain requirements, such as reading a letter, writing, reading a book, working in a primer, and saying prayers. There were 584 students in the five communities, 443 of them in the *villa* of El Paso del Norte itself. Thirteen teachers were listed by name, one for each school, but the report on their students reflects the widespread illiteracy of the frontier. Only 111 children knew how to write, 96 could read a book, and 31 could say their prayers.[9] In the following year, 1807, the number of students dropped to 460 in the same jurisdiction, with 356 of them at the *villa* of El Paso del Norte, where there were now only eight schools and three new teachers. A note explained that some children had left school after partially learning to write, and others had gone because they had reached an age where they had to help their parents support the family.[10]

Documentary evidence concerning the establishment and continuation of schools in other parts of New Mexico is scanty. The fact that they existed is evident from various census reports and letters making references to teachers, public schools, students, and materials used in classrooms. Teachers are included in the 1790 census rolls for Alburquerque and Santa Fé. In a letter of 1808 to the governor of New Mexico, *Comandante-General* Salcedo complimented him for taking measures to establish and encourage the growth of public schools. However, Pedro Bautista Pino deplored the lack of public schools in New Mexico in 1812, emphasizing the fact that they could be found elsewhere, but also noting that in New Mexico "primary letters" were provided for those children whose parents contributed to the support of the schoolteacher. Five political and religious tracts of a subversive nature were apparently being used in the primary schools of New Spain in 1816; they were banned from further use, and officials, including those in New Mexico, were ordered to collect any copies they might find and send them to Mexico City. Indians and Spanish settlers who could write were specifically listed by the governor of New Mexico in a letter to the audiencia of Guadalajara in 1820, thus indicating at least some primary education in the province at the end of the colonial period.[11]

Although primary education was apparently sporadic, restricted to a few male students, and obviously lacking in highly qualified instructors, it represented a positive step and was better than no education at all. No public schools or colleges existed in New Mexico before 1822; none were established until the Mexican period, and then only a few public schools appeared in the province.[12] Yet, learning was not be restricted solely to formal schools. Books, personal and church libraries, and even some early literature existed on this frontier, although no press was brought to New Mexico until the decade of the 1830s, well beyond the Spanish period. Only a few persons, particularly Franciscans and provincial governors, owned books, but it is evident that these books were frequently loaned to other literate people. Soldiers and some colonists also possessed books, many of a religious nature, but some secular works were present, as indicated in the inventories of Governors Bernardo López de Mendizábal (1659 to 1661), Diego de Peñalosa (1661 to 1664), and Diego de Vargas (died 1704). Vargas' library consisted of thirty-three books, including historical works on Kings Carlos I (Charles V of the Holy Roman Empire) and Philip IV; political tracts; many standard law treatises; six items on government, militias, and administrative matters in the Americas; a half-dozen devotional writings; and even one cookbook. Fray Domínguez inventoried 256 books at the library of Santo Domingo Pueblo (now lost) and in 1776 observed the teaching of Christian doctrine at various pueblo schools, where he found primarily religious and doctrinal works in mission libraries.[13]

There were, of course, no books published in New Mexico during the Spanish colonial period. Yet literature pertaining to the province originated as early as 1598 with the work of Captain Gaspar de Villagrá, a junior officer in Oñate's colonizing expedition. This soldier-poet chronicled the events of the first decade of European occupation and settlement in his lengthy history of New Mexico, published at Álcala de Henares, Spain, in 1610. His epic poem compares favorably with the letters of Hernán Cortés; the writings of Bernal Díaz del Castillo,[14] Pedro de Valdivia, and Pedro Cieza de León; and the well-known *La Araucana* of Alonso Ercilla in South America during the early period of Spanish-American literature, characterized by letters, reports, diaries, and epic historical works.

Medical practice in New Mexico remained in the rudimentary stage throughout the colonial era. Usually the settlers had to depend upon the surgeon assigned to the presidial garrisons if one happened to be in their vicinity. Otherwise they resorted to a wide variety of herbs, local remedies, and even Indian treatments for diseases and battle wounds. Evidently the greatest scourge threatening the province, the one promoting the greatest fear among the people, was the periodic outbreaks of smallpox. One of these occurred in the period from 1780 to 1781. Probably originating with the earlier epidemic at Mexico City in 1779 or carried to New Mexico by the Comanches, it struck Spanish population centers on the Río Grande and caused a great many fatalities in those communities and in the Pueblo Indian villages. In the late spring of 1780, thirty-one people succumbed in Alburquerque alone. But the epidemic was at its worst in January and February, 1781. Santa Fé lost one hundred and forty-two settlers and soldiers in those two months, when ten adults and five children were buried there on February 21 alone; fifteen adults and four children in Alburquerque died between January 9 and February 6. Neither Spaniards nor Indians had any way whatsoever of combating the dreaded disease.[15]

Edward Jenner published the results of his cowpox vaccination process in Europe in 1799. Five years later it was introduced into distant New Mexico with the support of the crown and the viceroy. The king in 1804 reported the discovery of the vaccine and its successful tests on the Canary Islands and in Puerto Rico and ordered that the vaccine be transmitted from arm to arm to the chief settlements of his vast domain. An official expedition was dispatched from Spain to introduce the vaccine in the Americas; it returned three years later, having succeeded beyond its expectations.[16]

Comandante-General Nemesio de Salcedo advised Governor Fernando de Chacón that the vaccine had been used successfully in Chihuahua by August 10, 1804. He ordered the governor of New Mexico to send surgeon Cristóbal Larrañaga with the annual caravan at the end of the year, bringing with him six or eight children, sons of the soldiers, so that they might be vaccinated and transmit the serum to others in New Mexico from one arm to the next. The cost of one and one-half *reales* for each vaccination was to be paid out of contributions from the principal families of the realm and money derived from the sale of gunpowder. In this way the vaccine reached the children of El Paso, Sevilleta, Sabinal, and Valverde by March, 1805. Surgeon Larrañaga reported on May 24, 1805, that he had vaccinated 257 children from the *"pueblo"* of El Paso del Norte northward through Alburquerque to Santa Fé. In five periods in the *villa* of Santa Fé, 150 children were vaccinated. The surgeon also reported that measles throughout the Río Grande Valley were a distracting factor and that parents were reluctant to bring their children to him for vaccination. By November 20, 1805, Larrañaga reported the vaccination of 3,610 children in New Mexico at a cost of one *real* per person. He believed the entire operation completed except for Zuñi, Laguna, Acoma, and Cebolleta in the west. Even the bishop of Durango issued an official statement urging the entire populace to have its children vaccinated in accordance with the royal will.[17]

Not only did the smallpox vaccination program have a successful beginning but it continued annually for the next decade. Instructions issued in 1808 and lists of children, including one of 152 names at La Cañada, show that it was maintained. Larrañaga reported in his log book covering the period from May 10 to September 6, 1815, that he had vaccinated 822 people, both parents and children, Spanish settlers and Pueblo Indians. Those vaccinated included 109 people from the *villa* and presidio of Santa Fé, but the largest numbers were at Santo Domingo and Cochití pueblos, where he vaccinated 185 and 172 respectively.[18] This ten-year effort to vaccinate the population of New Mexico unquestionably contributed to a decline in smallpox epidemics, improved longevity, and, therefore, the population increase during the last two decades of Spanish administration.

Economic life in New Mexico for Spanish settlers centered upon the raising of crops and stock and the development of a primitive commerce. Crops were raised largely for subsistence, not for export. Pedro Bautista Pino reported in 1812 that New Mexicans raised corn, wheat, vegetables, and cotton; they produced no manufactures other than cotton and woolen goods (blankets, quilts, *serapes*, coarse hose, tablecloths, and sackcloth), along with a few bridles and spurs. Fine wine, especially that from the vineyards established originally at El Paso del Norte by Fray García de San Francisco, was the only article that produced any appreciable revenue. It sold for one *real* per pint, and its quality made El Paso del Norte the rival of Parras in Coahuila in wine sales during the latter part of the eighteenth century. Tobacco was grown widely throughout the province and sold at four *reales* a pound, but no factory existed in New Mexico for the production of cigars and cigarettes. *Punche,* a type of native tobacco which grows well at altitudes approximating seven thousand feet, matured to a height of three to six feet and evidently was raised by both Spaniards and Pueblo Indians. Although viceregal orders of March, 1766, had prohibited its cultivation as a violation of the tobacco monopoly in New Spain, New Mexicans continued to grow it in isolated locations. The prohibition on it was difficult to enforce. Governor Pedro Fermín de Mendinueta considered the ban detrimental to the welfare of the people because they traded *punche* to the Comanche Indians for hides and dried buffalo meat and because it was grown primarily for local consumption. When the leaves of the plant had matured, they were dried in the shade, pulverized with the fingers into a powder, and kept in a miniature flask, called a *tabaquera*, with a wooden stopper attached by a leather thong. *Hojas,* or papers, usually inner leaves of corn husks cut into convenient squares, were carried with the *tabaquera*; each smoker "rolled his own."[19] Smoking was a common pastime for both men and women, a fact which shocked the early Anglo-American visitors to the province.

Livestock in New Mexico included horses, cattle, sheep, and goats. Horses became such a valuable commodity to the Indians of the Plains in the eighteenth century that they were frequently the chief article of trade and the object of depredations by the *indios bárbaros.* Whole herds were stolen from Spanish ranches; periodic shortages such as the one over all New Mexico in 1775 were met with requests for horses from other provinces for use in defending settled areas.[20]

Trade and commerce was rudimentary throughout the colonial period. Despite glowing reports and great hopes expressed by early missionaries, officers, and governors, New Mexico never amounted to much as a mining frontier in the Spanish period. Lack of capital, an absence of experienced miners, and lagging interest after failure to find any significant mines retarded the development of this industry. One exception existed in the southwestern corner of the province, where Lieutenant Colonel Manuel Carrasco discovered the important copper deposits of Santa Rita del Cobre in 1800. Four years later this region was producing copper for export to the rest of New Spain, especially to Mexico City, where it was used for coinage.[21]

Geographical isolation, lack of currency, and poor transportation hindered the development of commerce between New Mexico and other frontier provinces. In the latter part of the eighteenth century there was trade with Chihuahua. It was forty days' journey between the settled communities along the Río Grande in New Mexico and the city of Chihuahua, but annual trading caravans of five hundred or more persons assembled in late November near Sevilleta for the trek. Only a few individuals had the capital or means of transportation to undertake extensive trading ventures. These included Franciscan missionaries and royal governors, both of whom as early as the seventeenth century made use of the mission supply caravans from Nueva Vizcaya to import luxury items and sell them at handsome profits. Merchants set the value for commodities and developed near monopolies of commerce with Spanish communities and within them. They also sold goods at first directly to presidial soldiers, but later to their captains, who were sometimes as rapacious as the merchants themselves. In the early eighteenth century, Governor José Félix Martínez owned a store in Santa Fé, where he sold provisions to troops at marked-up prices and employed a former governor as his storekeeper.[22] All sorts of efforts were made to resolve the problem of presidial supply in the eighteenth century, including the letting of private contracts to merchants, and goods were imported from Jalapa, Puebla, México, Querétaro, and Michoacán, but the problem of inflated prices was never solved either for soldiers or civilians. Although prices would not seem high by modern standards, there was in fact little currency in the province to pay for products when they were available. Very few people, for example, paid their dues to a religious brotherhood in Santa Fé in 1818 with currency; instead, they used coarse woolen cloth, *punche*, chile peppers, fleece, squash, and other commodities to meet their obligations. No customhouse existed in New Mexico to control the importation of goods, but all imports and exports were taxed at Chihuahua.[23]

Two important trading fairs were taking place by 1776 at Taos and Abiquiú. Fray Domínguez pointed out that trading day at Taos was an annual occasion when great crowds milled about, reminding him of secondhand markets in Mexico City. Plains Indians, mostly Comanches, traded with New Mexicans at these fairs. They sold their buffalo hides, dried buffalo meat, Indian slaves, firearms, powder, tobacco, and hatchets to the colonists in return for knives, bridles, horses, clothing, and especially corn. Domínguez believed that the Comanches obtained many of their goods from the Jumanos, who in turn got

them from French traders on the Great Plains. According to the barter schedule, a buffalo hide was worth one knife; two hides bought a bridle; meat was
exchanged directly for corn; a girl slave of twelve to twenty years of age brought
two good horses and some trifles of clothing or saddle blankets; and male slaves
evidently were worth less. Usually the Spaniards fared better in the trading
bargains. At Abiquiú in late October or early November a similar fair was
the occasion of trade with the Ute Indians, to exchange Spanish horses for the
deerskins of the natives (one horse was worth fifteen to twenty skins). The
Utes also brought deer or buffalo meat and captive Indians, but no firearms to
sell, as the Comanches did. In return, they received, besides horses, knives, hard-
ware, and corn.[24]

Transportation and communications were difficult not only within the
province but with outside areas because of the long distances and crude equipment possessed by the settlers. Horses, mules, and primitive *carretas* (carts)
were the principal modes of transportation for Spanish settlers throughout the
colonial period. Oñate's colonizing expedition introduced domesticated stock,
including the horse, into New Mexico. Burros were also used by relatively poor
settlers for farm-to-market transport, and the mule was used both as a beast of
burden and as a draft animal, sharing this function with the ox. However, the
chief use of oxen was in drawing the locally manufactured, distinctive *carreta*.
This was a crude, two-wheeled vehicle made almost entirely of wood. The axle
was fashioned from pine logs and the other parts of the cart of cottonwood,
held together by wooden pegs and rawhide thongs. The bed of the *carreta* was
a rectangular block approximately four feet long, two and one-half feet wide,
and one foot thick hewn from a cottonwood trunk. A hole was drilled or burned
through this block, and a pine rod inserted as an axle. Wheels were fashioned
from split sections of tree trunks, held together by pegs in relatively circular
"rounds" about four feet in diameter, which were secured to the axle by wooden
pegs. A pole for a tongue was attached by rawhide thongs to the front of the
bed and posts were imbedded in the four corners of the body to complete the
carreta; oxen were yoked behind their horns to draw it. When in motion, the
vehicle careened forward, its wheels staggering, the entire body wobbling, and
the whole *carreta* screeching on its seldom sufficiently greased wheels.[25] Oñate
had brought wagons with him in 1598, and thereafter missionary caravans
(begun in 1610) consisted of thirty-two larger wagons organized into four sections, accompanied by an escort of soldiers and a herd of spare draft animals.
Bishop Tamarón reported the presence of carts in 1760, calling them
"*volantes.*"[26]

Roads were generally of packed or sandy natural soil; otherwise they were
unimproved. Throughout most of the eighteenth century there were no reported bridges over the Río Grande, although it is evident that foot bridges
were in use. Bishop Tamarón, not knowing how to swim, apprehensively noted

Site of Spanish settlement at San Gabriel de los Españoles in New Mexico from about 1599 to 1610 at the junction of the Río Grande and Río Chama. Photographed about 1930 by Harmon Parkhurst. *Courtesy Mr. and Mrs. T. R. Waring and Major and Mrs. Edmund B. Stewart.*

that he and all the people in his expedition as well as horses, mules, and one hundred sheep had to be ferried across the Río Grande at El Paso by a crudely constructed raft pulled by Indian swimmers. After 1791 bridges were built at San Felipe Pueblo, Belén, and El Paso del Norte. Sacks filled with heavy rocks were sunk in the Río Grande near Belén and oxen were used to haul wooden *vigas* (beams) to rest on them and form the bridge. Local labor was employed to build the bridge under the direction of the chief magistrate, but some people would not cooperate and were arrested. The bridge at San Felipe Pueblo had a simple bed of pine logs supported by eight caissons (wooden crates filled with stones, sand, and clay, then sunk in the river bed). Built by Indian labor, without handrails, it could not support wagons or carriages and apparently washed away before 1846. The most extensive bridge building occurred at El Paso from 1797 to 1816. After an initial failure, when the first bridge washed away in a flood before November, 1798, timbers were floated down the river from the Taos and Sabinal areas. Work was completed by October 15, 1800, on a bridge supported by eight caissons and with a bed of cross poles; it was over five hundred feet long and about seventeen feet wide. In spite of repairs made on it later, it too apparently washed away around 1815, because a new bridge was constructed in 1816.[27]

There were no inns or other public accommodations on the roads of colonial New Mexico. Wagons or mule trains usually stopped at points where water and wood were available. The caravans made forced marches over long desert stretches, as at the Jornada del Muerto, in southern New Mexico, but the journey from Santa Fé to Chihuahua still took from forty to fifty days. Nevertheless, it can be seen from these crude means of transportation that Spaniards adapted very well to their environment in New Mexico.[28] Innovations were necessary for them to maintain themselves in their isolated region.

Mail service depended upon a combination of wagon caravans, mule trains, and dispatch riders, with exchanges occurring at El Paso del Norte. Evidently there was a royal mail service by 1768 in New Spain, as we have seen in the chapter on Nueva Vizcaya, and punishments were set for anyone who broke open the mailbags. Teodoro de Croix's integrated mail service for the northern frontier after 1779 included a spur connection from El Paso to Santa Fé. Mail carriers usually were presidial soldiers from either end of this line.[29]

Between 1781 and 1819 efforts were made to instruct postal officials on the proper operation of their service, including protection of the mail, providing military escorts for royal mail, and regularizing the service by employment of proper officials and efficient collection of fees. Signatures, rubrics, and numbers of copies to be made of official correspondence were outlined in a royal order of 1781. Two years later, because of trouble with Indians, protective measures for escorts and instructions for travel at night were issued.[30] Detachments of troops, sometimes consisting of only two or three soldiers but at others comprising a formidable number, were assigned as escorts. Since the military had other functions, such as repairing bridges, accompanying criminals or other unwanted persons out of New Mexico, and performing guard duties at isolated locations, the mail-carrying responsibility was simply another task that weakened the actual strength of presidios. Apache Indian allies also served as mail carriers in the period from 1802 to 1804. To insure that all persons delivering the mail were recognized both in the settlements and on the roads, the *coman-*

dante-general ordered that they wear distinctive badges identifying them as "*correos conductores*" (mailmen); furthermore, they were not to be held up or otherwise delayed anywhere along their routes.[31] *Comandante-General* Jacobo Ugarte y Loyola was appointed to the position of *subdelegado de correos* (subdelegate of mails, or postmaster) as early as 1787, and a position of general superintendent of the mails was in existence at Mexico City by 1815. The standard cost of mailing a letter in frontier New Mexico in 1819 was three *reales*, as evidenced by letters sent from Santa Fé to San Eleazario.[32]

Since the basis for New Mexico's economic and social life was its agricultural/pastoral society, land was the principal measure of wealth. Two types of land grants, or *mercedes*, apparently were made in New Mexico: municipal concessions and private grants to farmers and stock raisers. Land originally belonged to the king, but was allotted by the viceroy, governor, or a designated representative for settlement or private grants. This system remained in effect throughout the colonial period and was even adopted by the Mexican Republic thereafter. Spanish custom defined the municipality as an urban area including its rural environs within the community, the granting of land by an act known as a *merced* became an important inducement to settlement and organization of frontier settlements. The grantee had to reside on the land and cultivate it for four years before it was actually confirmed in his possession. Under Spanish law, Indians such as the Pueblos were recognized as owners of the land they lived on and cultivated. Spaniards were not allowed to claim Indian lands or obtain grazing permits close enough to cause damage to Indian crops. This was the theory; in New Mexico there were Spanish encroachments on Indian lands both west and north of Santa Fé.

The governor of New Mexico was authorized to make land concessions to individuals who submitted a written petition and stated therein that the land was vacant public domain. He would then order the chief magistrate of the appropriate district to investigate the claim and to determine if there were conflicting interests. Indians and Spaniards were given the opportunity to protest; thereafter the magistrate presented his report, duly signed by two witnesses, to the governor, along with a sketch map of the proposed grant. If all was in order, the governor had a certificate of title drawn up and forwarded to the magistrate. The final ceremony took place on the site itself in the presence of two witnesses. The chief magistrate pointed out the boundaries to the grantee, who then threw rocks and tore up the grass while shouting "Long live the king" as an official sign of possession. When the settler had remained on the land and used it gainfully for four years, to obtain final title he filed a report that the terms had been met. During that period the grantee could not sell the land, nor could he obtain land elsewhere without relinquishing the first grant. After final title was confirmed he was free to sell his grant to whomever he wished.[33]

Making a community grant varied somewhat from the above procedure. A viceroy was authorized to give lands and house lots to those settling in frontier regions; he also had the final authority over the land in the name of the king. Land was granted to colonizers without reference to ownership of any minerals that might be discovered there subsequently. Viceroys generally passed on this authority to grant land to the governors responsible for the establishment of new communities. Instructions to Governor Pedro de Peralta emphasized the fact that the foundation of a new settlement, known then as "the *villa*," but soon to become Santa Fé, was to receive first priority when he arrived in New Mexico. He was ordered to see that local officials immediately marked for each resident two lots for a house and garden, two *suertes* (field lots) for a vegetable garden, and four *caballerías* (each 100 to 125 acres) for grazing animals. Residents were obliged to live on the land for a period of ten years continuously; if they left their grant for a three-month period, they would lose the land. Furthermore, the governor was warned not to allow anyone to move from one place to another without a permit.[34]

This last provision is an important one, because the Spanish population of New Mexico was not able to move at individual discretion. This was true in all of New Spain's northern provinces throughout the colonial period. Unlike frontier Anglo-Americans, Spaniards and mixed bloods were not free to leave their communities on business, for health reasons, to visit relatives or friends, or simply to start life anew in another location. To move at all, they were required to petition for and obtain an official government permit, which specified who they were, where they were going, for what purpose, and how long they intended to remain. Persons without authorized permits were arrested and prosecuted as criminals. In this way Spanish officials maintained some semblance of control over frontier regions, especially the civil settlements. Denying settlers the opportunity to travel freely intensified the isolation of a province such as New Mexico.[35]

Both community and individual land grants were thus made in New Mexico during its colonial period under Spain. The Alameda grant, partly in modern Bernalillo county, of the eighteenth century was made to settlers from Alburquerque in the name of the king. Settlers observed the customary ceremonies when they took possession of their grant, marking boundaries, throwing stones, pulling up weeds, and loudly proclaiming "Long live the King our Sovereign."[36]

Land and property transfers took place throughout the eighteenth century. In 1708 a parcel of land (amount not specified) near Alburquerque changed hands and was paid for in kind as follows:[37]

400 pesos in ewes at 2 pesos each
10 pesos in sheep at 2 pesos each
1 piece of linen at 12 *reales* per *vara*
1 mule at 30 pesos

> 1 fine scarlet skirt at 60 pesos
> 6 buck sheep at 4 pesos each; 24 pesos
> 60 fleeces of wool for 15 pesos
> 1 silk garment at 50 pesos
> 4 cows with calves at 25 pesos each for 100 pesos

This land sale also shows the nature of New Mexico's barter economy. Antonio de Salazar, resident of the *villa* of Santa Cruz in 1714, petitioned for and received vacant lands near the junction of the Río Grande and Río Chama; Francisca Antonia de Gijosa, widow of Antonio de Mora and resident of Santa Fé, in the following year petitioned for lands in the Taos valley formerly occupied by a deceased resident. She promised to settle on the land and was granted possession on June 16, 1715, providing she occupied it within six months.[38] A Spanish settler named Juan "Gutierres" from Bernalillo asked for a tract of land near present Placitas, then known as Las Huertas, in 1765, speaking for himself and eight families who wished to settle there. The petition was granted and officially dated three years later.[39]

All sorts of difficulties arose with this Spanish land system in New Mexico. As lands were subsequently sold or subdivided, boundaries became obscure. Family rivalries, claims of unscrupulous adventurers, falsehoods, questionable titles, encroachment on previously claimed lands, and costly as well as lengthy litigation further muddled the land picture. Finally, Spanish settlers frequently trespassed on Pueblo Indian lands, as at Laguna Pueblo, when the Baca and Pino families obtained grazing permits in 1769, creating the basis for a Spanish community at Cebolleta which by 1800 consisted of thirty families in a region formerly owned and cultivated by Pueblo Indians.[40]

Labor systems in New Mexico varied from self-employment to slavery. By far most of the Spanish settlers in the province were self-employed, usually as *labradores*, or *sembradores* (both were terms used to describe the small farmer). Of the remainder, many were day laborers, especially after the seventeenth century. The *encomienda* system was tried in the early colonial period, but it did not work satisfactorily and was allowed to die out. Nor did any standardized system replace it. Indians, Spaniards, and mixed bloods worked as domestics for other families, cared for herds and flocks, and were employed in weaving enterprises. Forced unpaid labor of Indians to sow crops, construct public buildings, and build bridges was reported from time to time. Slavery existed, but it was restricted to a small number of persons—Indians, Spaniards, or mixed bloods. Usually it was confined to only a few Indians who had been captured in battle or ransomed from Indian owners. In fact, *genízaros* were mostly non-Pueblo Indians who had been held in slavery by the Comanches and Utes and ransomed by Spaniards in trade with their enemies during the last half of the eighteenth century.[41]

Spanish colonists in New Mexico were true *paisanos*, country people in the sense that they lived off the land and close to it, not that they merely lived in rural areas. After the first few generations, most of them were native born residents who had become used to their isolated existence, hundreds of miles from El Paso del Norte and more hundreds from Chihuahua, Tucson, San Antonio de Béxar, and Alta California. Beset with constant threats of Indian attack until late in the eighteenth century, and then faced with foreign encroachments from the French, British, and finally the Anglos from the new republic known as the United States of America, they developed an individually oriented, defensive, self-sufficient agricultural society. Economic necessity required that they perform manual labor; they had to work or starve. They learned to improvise. When there were insufficient numbers of clergy to meet their needs, the *paisanos* created their own lay brotherhoods (*cofradías*), responsible for the conduct of religious services and related activies. When ceremonies and special celebrations of a religious nature were lacking, they developed their own, adopted patron saints such as La Conquistadora and the Virgin of Guadalupe, and began staging both secular and religious *fiestas* to commemorate Christmas, important family and religious days, and the arrival or departure of prominent persons. With little or no furniture, the *paisanos* began making their own, and in time there developed whole generations of fine wood carvers in New Mexico. Lacking any theater and music, New Mexicans staged their own forms of drama and made use of musical instruments for their festive occasions. Typical of their improvisation were *carretas*, the development of adobe architecture, paintings on buffalo hides or walls, and creation of a local folklore. Indeed, much of what they established can still be observed in parts of New Mexico today.

Sometime after 1776, in the absence of secular clergy for Spanish and *genízaro* villages, penitential confraternities (*cofradías*) were established to administer religious affairs. The Cofradía of Nuestro Padre Jesús Nazareño, with its two branches, the *Hermanos de Luz* and the *Hermanos de Sangre*, suddenly appeared in the so-called "secular period" from 1790 to 1850, particularly in the growing number of mountain communities and those of *genízaros*. Members of this lay brotherhood known as Penitentes, scourged themselves, carried heavy crosses, performed acts of penance, and occasionally tied one of their group to a cross. Reminiscent of practices in Medieval Europe, especially in the neighborhood of Seville, Spain, these ceremonies and specific practices may have been introduced into New Mexico by a Spanish settler or perhaps through a book carried to the frontier. In reality, what developed was a form of folk religion to meet the needs of the Spanish settlers. It was often condemned by the Catholic Church, because it disregarded proper authority, was a secret society, and adopted overly rigorous practices which cast an unfavorable light upon the church.[42]

Religious images and altars came to play an important role in the devotional

A *bulto* of the *carreta de la muerte* (death cart), Córdova, New Mexico, late nine-teenth century. The height of cart and figure, 49 inches; length of cart and tongue, 55 inches. Note the crude wheel and the wood and leather-tie construction of the cart. *Courtesy Taylor Museum, Colorado Springs Fine Arts Center.*

The ruins of San Miguel church in Santa Fé, New Mexico, before restoration. Note the use of adobe bricks in the construction and the graves in the courtyard. *Courtesy Denver Public Library Western Collection.*

life of New Mexicans. Since there were none to be had in trade except at ruinous costs and after long delays, New Mexico developed its own woodworkers. The colonists were already accomplished in shaping wood into beams, corbels, balustrades, railings, tables, chairs, chests, beds, *trasteros* (cupboards), and other house furnishings.[43] In the latter half of the eighteenth century professional *santeros*, carvers of religious images, appeared in New Mexico. They were in reality commercial artists, who sometimes traveled from one village to another with their burros. Often they carved images on the spot for sale to the local populace. There were two types of *santos* made by these woodcarvers: *bultos*, or statues carved in the round from cottonwood or pine, and *retablos*, or images painted on pine slabs for altar screens or on wall hangings. Realism, commemoration of a saint, preoccupation with death as in the grotesque "*carreta de la muerte*" (death cart), and crude features are the principal characteristics of these *santos*. Nails were never used in assembling a *bulto*, but use of wooden dowels and pins permitted the arms and legs to move,

The *retablo* of San Ysidro with angel, oxen, and corn in the background, 1788. The artist was Pedro Antonio Fresquis, who was born in Santa Cruz, New Mexico, in 1749 and died at Truchas in 1821. *Courtesy Taylor Museum, Colorado Springs Fine Arts Center.*

A *bulto* of Nuestra Señora de Guadalupe (Our Lady of Guadalupe), New Mexico, eighteenth century. Note the illuminating rays of light, hand-carved and inserted into the figure. *Courtesy Taylor Museum, Colorado Springs Fine Arts Center.*

or pieces of leather and cloth allowed for movements of the arms. The figures were painted with earth and vegetable colors in red, yellow and blue. Some of the *bultos* were elaborately dressed before their sale. The *santos* represent a unique folk art, a craft that arose to meet the needs of the *paisanos*, some of whom were *penitentes*. Examples of this intriguing artistic expression are on view in collections such as those of the Museum of New Mexico at Santa Fé and the Taylor Museum of the Fine Arts Center in Colorado Springs.[44]

Spanish-speaking *paisanos* of frontier New Mexico also developed other forms of artistic expression in the fields of painting, weaving, music, drama, and architecture. Evidently painting on tanned elk and buffalo hides began soon after resettlement, in the period from 1693 to 1696, and continued into the early eighteenth century. Juan de Archibeque, resident of Santa Fé until his death in the Villasur expedition of 1720, had thirty-one such painted skins listed in an inventory of his possessions. Alburquerque and Santa Fé were centers of the colonial weaving art and industry among Spanish settlers. Country-made, crude looms were owned by some colonists, who wove coarse woolen material called *yerga* in strips about two feet wide; lengths of this homespun material were sewed together to make blankets and carpets. Río Grande blankets known as *colchas*, with geometric patterns and bands of flowers woven from yarns colored with vegetable dyes, made colorful wall hangings. Master weaver Ygnacio Bazán and his brother Juan Bazán, both members of the weavers' guild in Santa Fé, were employed under contract in 1805 to teach their art to the youths of the community. They were paid eighteen *reales* a day for their services and as additional compensation received three horses with saddles and bridles, one musket, one saber, and two blunderbusses, as well as an initial payment of three hundred pesos. They worked from 1807 through 1809 on what was supposed to be a six-year contract, but the governor evidently excused them from the remainder of the term, since the brothers stated that they had taught their pupils all they knew about the art in the first few years.[45]

Spanish drama in New Mexico began with the Oñate colonizing expedition. Near El Paso del Norte on April 30, 1598, soldiers staged a play concerning the coming of Franciscans to New Mexico. Mansos Indians, for whom the play was written and presented, then asked to be baptized and received into the faith, according to Villagrá, who witnessed the occasion and later wrote about it in his epic work on the early settlement of the province. Other one- and two-act plays presented in New Mexico during the colonial period included *Las Posadas* (The Inns), relating the story of Mary and Joseph seeking shelter in Bethlehem; *Los Pastores* (The Shepherds), pertaining to the birth of Christ and the coming of the shepherds to Bethlehem; and *Los Tres Reyes Magos* (The Three Kings), relating the coming of the Magi to see and pay homage to the Christ child. All probably originated in Spain or other parts of New Spain. They were staged in New Mexico usually by Franciscan missionaries for the education and religious training of both Spaniards and Indians. Morality

A *bulto* of San Miguel (Saint Michael) slaying the devil, about 1800, from the church at San Miguel del Vado in New Mexico. *Courtesy Taylor Museum, Colorado Springs Fine Arts Center.*

A *retablo* of San José (Saint Joseph) with the Christ Child in a wooded scene. The inscription in the lower right corner bears the name Captain Don Salbador García de Noriega and the year 1783. *Courtesy Taylor Museum, Colorado Springs Fine Arts Center.*

plays, they were built around a single theme, the eternal struggle of good and evil, resulting in the victory of the former. *Las Posadas* and *Los Pastores* were presented before Christmas, while *Los Tres Reyes Magos* took place on or near Epiphany (January 6).[46]

Music consisted largely of religious *alabados*, or hymns of praise, ballads known as *romances tradicionales*, and popular local quatrains called *coplas populares*. Each mission established in the seventeenth century had its own Indian choir, accompanied by bells, clarions, trumpets, and even organs. *Alabados* of Spanish and New Mexican composition, usually in praise of the Blessed Sacrament, the Virgin, or the saints, were sung widely in Spanish and Indian communities. Traditional ballads of Spanish origin were preserved and sung by *cantores* (singers) from one generation to another, being orally transmitted. Folk tales, proverbs, and riddles were recited by *cantadores* to the accompaniment of guitar and violin. *Versos*, evidently a popular entertainment at almost all social gatherings during the eighteenth century, were verses composed around some proverbial saying, philosophy, idea, or feeling, consisting always of four short stanzas and sung by a *cantador*.[47] Music was played not only for church services, but for baptisms, weddings, and all special social occasions, both religious and secular.

Although there were no engineers in New Mexico during the colonial period, there were masons and Franciscan missionaries to plan and direct the construction of public buildings. Paisanos generally built their own homes, probably with the advice and assistance of their neighbors and the masons residing in most communities. Friars were left to their own devices as to the design, construction, and decoration of all churches and missions throughout the province.[48] There were no arches or domes used in New Mexico. All churches, government buildings, and even private homes (except in the mountain communities) were made of adobe bricks measuring ten by eighteen by five inches and weighing fifty to sixty pounds each, the load one man could conveniently handle. The Spanish brought the craft of forming bricks by using wooden molds, as well as the *horno*, or beehive-shaped oven, to New Mexico. Walls thirty to forty-eight inches thick were formed from these adobe bricks. The process was quite simple and made use of soil and climate conditions found in New Mexico. Clay was kneaded with one's bare feet or with a hoe into a mud paste; straw was then worked into the mud to act as a binder and to prevent cracking during drying. The mud was then formed into standard-sized bricks, using a wooden mold, and left to dry in the hot sun for a day or two. Stacks of these bricks were allowed to accumulate so that they could be used for whatever construction project might require them next. Beamed roofs were also introduced; the *vigas* or beams provided support and decoration across the ceiling; smaller sticks were laid crossways before adobe was applied to the flat roof. The size of a house was often described by the number of its beams.[49] Utility and a combination

A *bulto* of San Ysidro (patron saint of farmers) with angel and oxen. The artist was Fray Andrés García, who worked in New Mexico between 1750 and 1770. *Courtesy Taylor Museum, Colorado Springs Fine Arts Center.*

of Spanish and Pueblo Indian construction practices were the distinguishing features of Spanish building in New Mexico, another example of adaptation on the part of Spanish settlers to their environment.

As we have mentioned, the colonial home was generally made of adobe. It was built around a courtyard, or patio, in an ell shape or with rooms arranged in a single row. Usually, individual rooms opened onto the patio, but seldom, if ever, from one room to another. The family slept in a room which also doubled as a kitchen; every room had a corner fireplace, the only method of providing warmth in the winter. New rooms were added as the family grew or its needs changed; old ones were abandoned to become storage areas, chicken houses, pigpens, and finally dumps. Floors were of packed earth, although Pike noted the use of some brick by 1807, and they were sprinkled before regular sweepings. Doors were small, averaging about five feet in height, with sills raised off the ground. To pass through them a man of normal stature had to duck his head and step up. Windows were small, not numerous, set high in the wall, and were shuttered on the outside for security and protection against the cold. Furniture was simple and country-made for most of the people. *Paisanos* usually did not have beds, but slept on woolsacks or sheep pelts, each person wrapped in a blanket. Chairs were scarce, but stools and small low tables made of pine were widely used. Other furniture present in the home included the *trastero*, or cupboard, sometimes seven feet high, chests of many sizes, trinket boxes, and hanging shelves for *bultos*, candles, and paper flowers. Spanish majolica pottery, a ware made of soft paste with a lead-tin glaze, decorated by painting generally after firing, came to New Mexican homes probably from Puebla in central New Spain where the common blue-on-white decoration was also found. Spoons, ladles, scoops, and dippers in New Mexico were generally made of wood since, the province had a scarcity of iron. Bowls were also made of wood, but copper kettles, caldrons, and drinking mugs were used in frontier communities.[50] In summary, it can be noted that homes and furnishings were largely utilitarian, the colonists not being given to ostentatious display and unnecessary items.

There were many social occasions and opportunities for diversion at *fiestas* and special celebrations. Baptisms, marriages more people than simply those in the immediate family. Fray Domínguez noted that funerals seemed to be staged more for the living than for the dead, with special distinction falling on those persons in the procession who carried a large cross, burned incense, and conducted the elaborate mourning exercises. All along the route to the *camposanto* (cemetery) there were designated stops, or *pasos*, each with particular ceremonial acts; since each stop cost a certain amount, the number of stops was an indication of the wealth of the deceased.[51]

Saint's days divided the calendar into special festive seasons when the *paisanos* would celebrate with particular ceremonies, such as that of the patron saint for all farmers, San Isidro. On December 12 of every year the citizens of El Paso del Norte held an annual *fiesta* in honor of Nuestra Señora la Virgen Santíssima de Guadalupe (Our Lady of Guadalupe, patron saint of Mexico, for whom the first mission was named at El Paso). Annual permission to hold this ceremony was obtained from the governor, and a committee of citizens planned and supervised all the festivities. In Santa Fé, May 29 was the special *fiesta* set aside for Our Lady of Light, a title for the Blessed Virgin introduced into Mexico in 1732. In New Mexico, Governor Marín del Valle contributed to the building of a military chapel known as the Castrense, on the south side of the plaza across from the Palace of the Governors, in 1760 to 1761, and helped finance the beautiful *reredos* with a painting on it of Our Lady of Light. A *cofradía* supervised the annual celebration, including vespers, a mass, a sermon, and a procession in her honor. In addition, both men and women took an oath to defend the Immaculate Conception and encouraged veneration of Our Lady of Light.[52]

Widespread homage was paid to "Nuestra Señora del Rosario, La Conquistadora" Our Lady of the Rosary, La Conquistadora—a twenty-eight-inch statue evidently carved by an early *santero*, by the Spanish-speaking people of New Mexico. *Paisano* devotion to this image was a unifying factor in colonial society. A *cofradía* was evidently formed in the seventeenth century in its honor; both the statue and the brotherhood were mentioned as being at Real de San Lorenzo in the 1680s, after the retreat of Spanish settlers following the Pueblo revolt. The statue was brought back to Santa Fé in an enclosed wagon by Diego de Vargas in 1693, but popular legend now has it that La Conquistadora led the Spaniards into battle against the so-called heathens during the reconquest. An annual celebration complete with mass and processions was begun in her honor by the colonists of Santa Fé in 1712. A new confraternity was formed in 1770 to supervise the festival and promote the veneration of La Conquistadora, by then the patron saint of New Mexico.[53] The image itself still exists and is kept in the Cathedral of Santa Fé. It is undoubtedly the same one that was present at El Paso del Norte in the seventeenth century.

At Christmas the morality plays were performed for the public. Religious holidays usually began with the lighting of small bonfires (*luminarias*). Farolitos, small lanterns of burning candles set in sand inside paper bags and arranged in rows, were apparently introduced for the Christmas season during the late Spanish period. On May 29, 1760, Bishop Tamarón visited Pecos Pueblo, where he received a joyous reception and the natives performed feats of horsemanship in his honor. In September, an Indian carpenter of that pueblo named Agustín Guichí made himself some bishop's vestments and, accompanied by two assistants, rode a mule through the pueblo, where he was greeted by loud hurrahs. "Bishop Agustín" then scattered his blessings on the women, "confirmed" others, and held a huge banquet, all on the first day of his burlesque. On the second he said mass, distributed *tortillas* for the communion,

A *retablo* of Nuestra Señora de la Luz (Our Lady of Light) on a pine board. It was sent to New Mexico when Governor Marín del Valle built the *castrense* in Santa Fé. *Courtesy Taylor Museum, Colorado Springs Fine Arts Center.*

then held a dance for the remainder of that day and all of the next one. According to Bishop Tamarón, who was appalled by this lack of respect, the impersonator died on the fourth day, after he had been attacked by a bear.[54]

Secular celebrations also took place from time to time in New Mexico. Friars were warned in 1786 that they were to have nothing to do with *bailes*, or dances, because they were considered to have a bad influence on young people and were focal points for the vices of the settlers. That popular dances known as *fandangos* were still performed in the province in the early nineteenth century is noted by Pike, who saw one at Ojo Caliente on March 1, 1807.[55] Governor Joaquín Codallos y Rabal received a tumultuous welcome to New Mexico extending over a three-day span in January, 1748, when he arrived in Santa Fé. Bells pealed, a huge parade was held one afternoon, *luminarias* were lighted at night, troops fired volleys, formal oaths of allegiance were proclaimed, mass was celebrated, Indian dances were performed, and plays were staged before the ceremonies concluded with the loud acclamations of the crowd.[56] The arrival of distinguished visitors, then as now, obviously provided an excuse for a special public celebration.

José E. Espinosa has written that the Spanish-speaking people of New Mexico "were frontiersmen, with all the moral virtues and weaknesses, all the practical gifts and intellectual shortcomings of any group living on the fringes of civilization."[57] The high degree of illiteracy, extreme isolation of the province, ever-present threat of Indian attack, and moral laxity on the part of some Spanish officials quite naturally led to superstition, alleged cases of witchcraft, and exaggeration of all sorts of events in the public imagination. Governor Juan Manso de Contreras had an illicit love affair with an officer's wife, resulting in the birth of an illegitimate child; Governor López de Mendizábal used his office for extensive personal gain, engaging in business operations and merchant practices from the very beginning of his administration.

Fray Esteban de Perea became the New Mexico agent for the Holy Office of the Inquisition as early as 1630, primarily because of the heated civil-religious conflict. He spent most of the next nine years investigating problems dealing with bigamy, superstition, and especially alleged witchcraft. Here the presence of Indians influenced the Spaniards directly. Many of the early seventeenth century soldier-settlers were evidently unfaithful to their wives, who then sought love potions from their Indians servants to win back their wayward husbands. Herbs, powders, pastes of herbs and corn to be applied to the body during intercourse, fried or mashed worms cooked in gruel (*atole*), and wine were only some of the potions used. Peyote was resorted to for bewitched people so that they might have visions. Beatriz de los Angeles, a Mexican Indian, and her daughter were denounced for sorcery, inducing death, and bewitching people, particularly since the daughter possessed "the evil eye."[58] There was difficulty ascertaining the truth in these witchcraft cases, and they evidently continued to exist until the middle of the eighteenth century. Most of the alleged witches in the period from 1708 to 1732 were Pueblo Indians who gave native remedies to Spaniards and then were accused of having caused grave illnesses or death by poisoning. Other Indians were denounced for practicing idolatry, an understandable situation where the Christianized natives had been so recently converted and where others such as the unconverted, uncontrolled *indios bárbaros* were always present.[59]

Crimes in New Mexico ranged from the colonists' being idle, lewd, violent, and having poor morals[60] to the murder of Governor Luis de Rosas by a soldier named Nicolás Ortiz after the latter discovered his wife in the governor's bed.[61] Men and women were banished from the province for various reasons, including dereliction of duty in public office. One of the growing problems of the New Mexican frontier, as elsewhere, was the increasing number of vagabonds in the last two decades of the eighteenth century and continuing until the end of the colonial era. Authorities at all levels issued a series of regulations to control this menace by requiring all people when away from their homes or communities to carry a properly issued passport. Fugitive Indians and colonists apparently masqueraded as Apaches in 1783, committing robberies, murder, and other atrocities. All persons were ordered to carry an authorized passport, or license, thereafter; violators were to be prosecuted as vagabonds and imprisoned immediately. If the violator were an Indian, he would be given twenty lashes for his first offense, forty for the second, and one year at hard labor on public works for the third. Spaniards and all castes who failed to have a proper passport were to receive two months in prison for the first violation, four months for the second, and either ten years of service in a frontier presidio or two years in a royal factory for the third.[62] These repeated orders and regulations from 1783 to 1791, and even thereafter, are indicative of the continuing lawlessness and the concern of governmental officials with the growing problem of controlling the populace.

Ralph Emerson Twitchell, prominent historian of New Mexico, once wrote, "As to the social habits and customs of the people, there is nothing worth recording."[63] This popularly accepted image of the Spanish settlers in the colonial era has persisted among all but a few who have turned to the intensive study of the *paisanos* and their ways of life. The work of these few serious researchers has revealed much about this frontier civilization, but scarcely any effort has been made to depict the culture as a whole, and much remains to be done to understand completely the character of everyday society in colonial New Mexico. Recently a prominent geographer, D. W. Meinig, emphasized that the spread of Spanish colonists is "a little-known event of major importance. . . ."[64] Unfortunately, only a few historians have taken note of the Spanish civilian settlers, while most have concentrated on soldiers, missionaries, and government officials. Yet, the fact remains that these settlers founded the present urban centers of El Paso, Alburquerque, Santa Fe, and Española-Santa Cruz.

The paisanos of New Mexico developed a distinctive society that was a mixture of Spanish and Indian cultures. It will be helpful perhaps to review some of the steps in this development.

First, Spanish-speaking settlers entered New Mexico early and established a frontier society over a century before this occurred in Texas, Pimería Alta, or Alta California. In fact, they arrived before parts of Sonora, Nueva Vizcaya (especially present Chihuahua), and Nuevo Santander were settled.

Second, settlement was concentrated in northern New Mexico and at El Paso del Norte, nearly two hundred and seventy uninhabited miles apart. The two regions were united loosely as the province of New Mexico throughout most of the colonial era.

Third, within these two areas of settlement, *paisanos* tended to disperse into rural communities and small family-oriented settlements along the Río Grande. One concentration covered a two-hundred-mile stretch from Taos to Socorro in northern New Mexico, a region subdivided into the Río Arriba and Río Abajo districts, with the boundary just north of Bernalillo. Another concentration ran southeast from the mission and villa at El Paso del Norte, stretching twenty-five to thirty miles from one end of the settlements to the other. As Roland Dickey succinctly states, "Like the Pueblo Indian and the Iberian, the New Mexican was a farmer who lived in a village."[65]

Fourth, New Mexico's original settlers came partly from Europe, but particularly from other frontier provinces north of Mexico City. This frontier experience undoubtedly aided the settlers when they reached distant New Mexico. With new generations, New Mexico's population gradually became native-born. Indians of many nations were assimilated into Spanish frontier society; Negroes and mulattoes were present in New Mexico as elsewhere on the frontier. All sorts of combinations occurred, and these mixtures were considered part of the "civilized people" on the frontier.

Fifth, class differences came to mean very little in New Mexico, and there was little hostility of one class for another. The fusion of classes may have been one of the reasons why New Mexicans did not actively seek independence from Spain in the period from 1810 to 1821, when New Spain was in a state of turmoil.

Sixth, small in numbers at the beginning of settlement in 1598, New Mexico's Spanish population grew enormously, surpassing twenty-seven thousand people in a total population of thirty-six thousand by the end of the colonial era. The major increase in the last century was due to three factors: the declining Indian threats, as Comanches, Navajos, Utes, and some Apaches sought peace; the introduction of cowpox vaccine to combat smallpox epidemics, thereby increasing the lifespan of the settlers; and the maturing of large numbers of children of the generation extending from 1790 to 1821. There was little immigration after the first generation.

Seventh, El Paso del Norte was principally settled by refugees from northern New Mexico, although a colony of Spanish-speaking people existed there before 1680. This large influx of settlers influenced the survival, growth, and societal customs of the settlements in the Paso del Norte region. Dispersal along the Río Grande, resistance to outside authority, a farming and grazing economy, village orientation, and intermingling with Indians were only a few of the characteristics shared by settlers at El Paso with those of the rest of New Mexico.

Eighth, New Mexicans established a true settlement society with lasting institutions, often the product of innovation and adaptation to their environment.

Ninth, *paisanos* were a hard-working lot. They initially received land, tools, seeds, stock, and some financial assistance from the viceroy and the governor. Economic necessity forced them to perform manual labor. They were principally small farmers, weavers, day laborers, and artisans, not professional soldiers, missionaries, or rich *patrones*, as they have been sometimes depicted.[66]

Tenth, in colonial New Mexico the extended family was the basis of society and of the economic system. Families were large, including children, in-laws, relatives, orphans, and servants. The family was always treated as a unit by Spanish officials.

Eleventh, society was not static in New Mexico; it changed continuously from its early closely controlled, semiaristocratic nature under the *encomenderos* to the individualistic, folk-oriented culture of the latter half of the eighteenth century. Flexibility was evident as people moved up and down the social scale, intermarried, changed their economic status, and brought about a general fusion of the class structure into what was basically only two groups by the end of the colonial era—Indians and non-Indians.

Finally, Spanish settlers established a self-contained agrarian society in New Mexico. They fed themselves, worked for themselves, overcame a variety of local problems with inventiveness, and transmitted their religion, language, courtesy, love of politics, methods of transportation, foods, community orientation, attachment to family and birthplace, and self-reliance to the generations that followed them.[67]

Life in this isolated rural folk society of New Mexico occasionally has been depicted as monotonous.[68] Such a conclusion springs from a comparison with modern life in the United States. *Paisanos* did not live monotonously by their own standards. They led eventful lives in which each day was a struggle for existence. It is perhaps true that their work was drudgery, but they did have diversions and special occasions to break the routine of everyday life, just as people do today. They developed an ever-changing frontier society that has left many legacies for the present inhabitants of the Upper Río Grande Valley.

PART III
The Northwestern Frontier

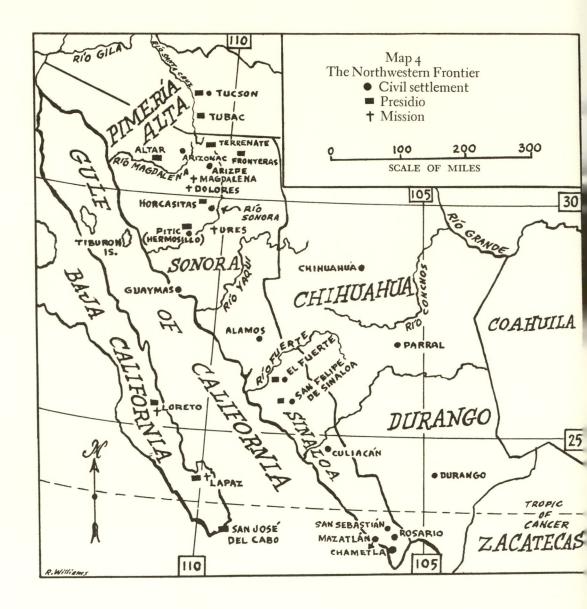

Map 4
The Northwestern Frontier
● Civil settlement
■ Presidio
† Mission

0   100   200   300
SCALE OF MILES

RÍO GILA
RÍO SANTA CRUZ
PIMERÍA ALTA
● TUCSON
■ TUBAC
RÍO MAGDALENA
ALTAR ■
■ TERRENATE
ARIZONAC ■ FRONTERAS
† ARIZPE
† MAGDALENA
† DOLORES
GULF
HORCASITAS ■ ● ↙ RÍO SONORA
PITIC (HERMOSILLO) ■ ● † URES
TIBURON IS.
SONORA
BAJA CALIFORNIA
OF
GUAYMAS ●
RÍO YAQUI
ALAMOS ●
CALIFORNIA
RÍO FUERTE
EL FUERTE ■ ●
SAN FELIPE DE SINALOA ■ ●
SINALOA
† LORETO
CHIHUAHUA ●
CHIHUAHUA
RÍO CONCHOS
RÍO GRANDE
COAHUILA
● PARRAL
DURANGO
N
† LA PAZ ■
CULIACÁN ●
● DURANGO
■ SAN JOSÉ DEL CABO
TROPIC OF CANCER
SAN SEBASTIÁN ●
MAZATLÁN ● ● ROSARIO
CHAMETLA ●
ZACATECAS

110
105
30
25

R. Williams

Introduction

One of the oldest frontiers in New Spain and in all of Spanish America was located on the western coast in the narrow, river-crossed strip between the Sierra Madre Occidental and the Gulf of California. From the founding of Culiacán, Sinaloa, in 1531, to the creation of the presidio at Tucson in 1776, portions of the northwestern frontier remained sparsely settled and comparatively little developed; other sections, particularly in Sinaloa, had advanced well beyond the frontier stage by the time Mexico became independent from Spain in 1821.

Today this region comprises the states of Sinaloa, Sonora, and part of Arizona. Throughout most of the colonial period the entire jurisdiction belonged to the province of Nueva Vizcaya, although in the last century of Spain's domination it became the combined province of Sinaloa and Sonora. There were various subregions, with hazy ever-changing boundaries, which were frontier areas at differing times. Beginning in the south, the area known as Culiacán originally extended from the Chiametla (today Chametla) district in the far south to the Río Sinaloa in the north. Between that river and the Río Mayo the district of Sinaloa proper existed; above it, extending to the Río Yaqui, was the region known as Ostimuri. Finally, extending indefinitely northward beyond the Yaqui was the area called Sonora, with its own subregion known as Pimería Alta (present northern Sonora and southern Arizona below the Gila River), named for the Pima Indians of that region. By the eighteenth century the entire continental district west of the mountains was known as "Sinaloa and Sonora," with the dividing line arbitrarily established in the vicinity of the Río Yaqui. Pimería Alta, although always a part of Sonora in the Spanish era, constituted an important frontier of New Spain, because it represented the northernmost advance of Spanish settlement in this region and contributed to the Spanish heritage of present Arizona.

Mission stations and presidios were the principal Spanish settlements here. Indeed, without the reports of Jesuit missionaries and presidial officers there would be very little record of Spanish activity on this remote frontier. Yet civilian settlers did live here in *villas*, *pueblos*, and especially *reales de minas* (mining communities and districts). Usually they came to support missionary or presidial establishments, around which the civil communities developed.

Scattered *reales de minas* and *ranchos* sometimes existed only temporarily; with exhaustion of mines and land, settlers frequently moved elsewhere.

This thrust of Spanish civil settlement progressed gradually northward, usually under governmental authorization and direction. Sinaloan communities were founded after the third decade of the sixteenth century and before the middle of the seventeenth. Sonora's growth as a permanently occupied frontier occurred largely during the last half of the seventeenth century and all of the eighteenth. Pimería Alta became a settlement frontier largely in the eighteenth century. By then, especially in the latter half of the period, Sinaloa could no longer be considered a frontier because of its density of population, the reduction or near elimination of Indian threats, secularization of its missions, and establishment of regular Spanish institutions.

Isolation, however, remained a major characteristic of most of this frontier region. Mining, livestock raising, and agriculture were the principal activities of the civilian settlers here. Spanish colonists established *villas* at San Miguel de Culiacán, San Sebastián de Chametla, San Felipe y Santiago de Sinaloa, and Fuerte de Montesclaros within what is today the state of Sinaloa. All became centers for *pobladores* (settlers), as did Mazatlán and the mining communities in the Rosario district of the southern part of the province. The *villa* of Pitic (later called Hermosillo) in Sonora and other centers such as Arizonac, Ures, Horcasitas, and Arizpe became important islands of civil settlement in eighteenth century Sonora. During the latter half of that century presidial establishments at Tubac and San Agustín de Tucson were founded in Pimería Alta, and civilian settlers came to reside nearby. These two Spanish settlements were not only among the last to be founded, but remained among the most remote communities on this frontier until the end of Spanish administration.

7. Sinaloa

Nuño de Guzmán founded the first civil settlement in Sinaloa at San Miguel de Culiacán in 1531. He began the permanent colonization of this frontier as part of his continuing struggle with Hernán Cortés, the conqueror of the Aztecs. Desiring to win fame, power, and wealth as his predecessor had done, Guzmán's expedition of five hundred Spanish soldiers and ten thousand Tlaxcaltecan and Aztecan Indian allies passed through Michoacán and Jalisco to Sinaloa. He established the *villa* with sixty to one hundred soldiers as the first *pobladores*; to each settler he gave land, cattle, and swine. Although the community moved twice thereafter, it endured and became an important administrative and agricultural center. Civilian residents eventually came to join the early soldier-settlers, and within the first decade of its existence Culiacán had a regular Spanish local government under the supervision of an *alcalde*.[1]

Three other *villas* and at least one small *pueblo* were founded in Sinaloa during the next century. In the mining region of the southern part of the province, three settlements were closely associated—the *villa* of San Sebastián de Chametla, the major mining community of Rosario, and the small Indian *pueblo* of Chametla. North of Culiacán, after numerous unsuccessful efforts to plant a settlement at San Juan de Sinaloa, Spaniards founded San Felipe y Santiago de Sinaloa, probably in 1585. Although there were only five settlers there a short time afterward, the community endured and was reinforced when a presidio was established in the next decade, with twenty-five men in its garrison by 1596. The community came to have *villa* status in the eighteenth century, as did El Fuerte (known as Fuerte de Montesclaros when it was founded on the south bank of the Río Fuerte in 1610). Sometime before 1633 a small pueblo also was founded at San Juan de Mazatlán on the Gulf of California.[2]

Together, these four *villas*—San Miguel de Culiacán, San Sebastián de Chametla, San Felipe y Santiago de Sinaloa, and El Fuerte—and the small towns such as Mazatlán comprised the nucleus of Spanish settlement in the province throughout the colonial era. There were scattered *reales de minas*, *ranchos*, and even some *haciendas*, but most of them were not occupied permanently. Of the ten jurisdictions reported in the census of Sonora in 1783, six were in Sinaloa, including the Real del Rosario, San Juan Bautista de Maloya, San Joseph de Copala, San Miguel de Culiacán, Sinaloa, and El Fuerte. Within this region were ten gold mines and forty-eight silver mines, most of which were south of Culiacán.[3]

The population of Sinaloa did not increase markedly until the latter half of the seventeenth century, when Indian uprisings had been overcome and the frontier had pushed northward into Sonora. By then the southern half of Sinaloa was no longer a real frontier; a century later, by 1763, the whole area to the Río Yaqui had been consolidated, undergoing such a transition and adjustment to Spanish occupation that it could not be considered a frontier province.[4] Sonora was the frontier of northwestern New Spain by that time.

At the turn of the seventeenth century there were perhaps 60 *vecinos*, accounting for possibly as many as 250 to 300 people, in all of Sinaloa and no Spaniards at all in Sonora, where Jesuit missionary work among the Indians of the river valleys had begun just nine years earlier. Considering heads of households, spouses, children, and other family members, these 250 to 300 people represented an increase over the original 60 to 100 soldier-settlers who occupied Culiacán in 1531. Furthermore, at least two other Spanish-speaking centers had been established by that time. There were more than thirty *vecinos* located at San Felipe de Sinaloa, twelve to fifteen at San Sebastián de Chametla, and thirty, controlling two thousand Indians, at Culiacán. Some of these early settlers, probably those residing in Culiacán, were Aztecan and Tlaxcaltecan Indians, brought in both by Nuño de Guzmán and other leaders, such as Francisco de Ibarra.[5] These were the only Spanish settlements in the province that seemed in 1600 to have any prospect of surviving.[6]

Population statistics and evaluations of Sinaloa and Sonora in the remainder of the Spanish period are not as complete and frequent as they are in other regions of the northern frontier. Census returns are scarce, even for the latter part of the eighteenth century, when they were at their fullest for Alta California, Texas, and New Mexico. Yet, an occasional census report and the observations of clerical, administrative, and military officials give some idea of the growth of the Spanish population in Sinaloa and Sonora.

Alonso Mota y Escobar reported about 1605 that there were eight or ten Spanish *vecinos* at Chametla, twenty at San Sebastián, thirty in the *villa* of Culiacán, and twenty-one soldiers at the presidio of San Felipe y Santiago de Sinaloa. With these fifty-eight to sixty Spanish *vecinos* and twenty-one soldiers were their families.[7] Thus, there were perhaps as many as four hundred Spanish residents in the whole province by that year. In 1640 it had between eighty and one hundred *vecinos*,[8] amounting to a total Spanish population of perhaps four to five hundred. Settlements at El Fuerte and Mazatlán had been made, thus adding to the dispersal of the population in the seventeenth century. By 1678 Sinaloa had some six hundred Spanish and mixed-blood families,[9] perhaps three thousand people in all. A century later, about the end of the Jesuit era, there were some thirty-two thousand Spanish colonists in fifty or more settlements—*villas*, presidios, and *reales de minas*. Six thousand Indians had been congregated in over forty native settlements in the south, while there were reportedly twenty-five thousand Indians living in villages under the supervision of Jesuit missionaries.[10] About 1760, San Felipe de Sinaloa had a Spanish population of 3,500; El Fuerte, 1,886; Rosario, 2,459; San Sebastián, 2,500; Culiacán, 2,216; and Mazatlán, 996. The 13,557 Spanish residents of these six settlements amounted to nearly one-half of the total population of *gente de razón* on this entire frontier.[11]

Perhaps the most accurate estimate of the Spanish population of this area may be derived from the extensive figures reported for Sonora and Sinaloa, in 1783. According to the statistics compiled by the Caballero de Croix, there were 87,644 people in the province, of which 41,567 were living in the six jurisdictions within Sinaloa, 25,036 in Ostimuri, and 21,041 in Sonora proper. Thus, over forty-six per cent of the total resided in Sinaloa. The Real del Rosario showed a total population of 5,627; San Juan Bautista de Maloya, 1,750; San Joseph de Copala, 8,371; San Miguel de Culiacán, 10, 490; Sinaloa, 9,178; and El Fuerte, 6,151. These figures included all members of colonist families and 388 slaves (235 of whom were in Culiacán alone) throughout the province.[12] Although these numbers reflect population in jurisdictions, not specific communities, it is evident that Sinaloa possessed a Spanish population exceeding that of any other frontier province except Nueva Vizcaya by the end of the eighteenth century. Furthermore, these statistics reflect the concentration of Spanish people at Culiacán, Sinaloa, and El Fuerte, as well as the relatively insignificant number of slaves, less than one per cent of the total population. The dispersal of colonists throughout Sinaloa is also indicated by this census, which listed 5 *villas*, 56 *pueblos*, 6 missions, 10 *reales de minas*, 15 *haciendas*, 311 *ranchos*, and no presidios within these six jurisdictions.[13]

Although figures for the over-all population of Sinaloa at the turn of the nineteenth century are lacking, it is apparent that the above settlements, with the possible exception of San Sebastián de Chametla, continued to grow. According to Alexander von Humboldt's figures, Rosario had reached a population of seven thousand by 1800; three years later San Miguel de Culiacán had jumped to 13,800, San Felipe de Sinaloa had 12,000, and the *villa* of Montesclaros (El Fuerte) had 10,100.[14] Thus, there were more residents in these four settlements alone than there had been in the entire province of Sinaloa less than a half century earlier. Since the area had apparently become stabilized by this time and Indian threats had been nearly eliminated, the population tended to grow more rapidly.

Population growth evidently continued in the nineteenth century, although figures are scarce. According to one report in 1815, there were 123,854 residents in the combined province of Sonora and Sinaloa. Of this total, there were 55,042 adults in Sinaloa, including 52,100 people of all ages in its principal settlements.[15] Sinaloa and Sonora separated peacefully from Spain in 1821, declaring their allegiance to the Mexican empire of Agustín de Iturbide. Nine years later, when the provinces were divided, the population of Sinaloa was estimated at one hundred thousand,[16] or more than three times the figure given for the combined province only seventy years earlier.

There is little evidence of class distinctions and rivalries on this frontier. Mota y Escobar indicates the existence of only four or five sons of *conquistadores* at Culiacán in 1605. The census of 1783 gives the number of persons in each of four categories: Spaniards (here as elsewhere on the frontier meaning native-born people of Spanish heritage), Indians, mixed bloods (mestizos), and those of *"color quebrado"* (broken color). Of the total 41,567 people in the province, 39,593 are so categorized. There were 24,592 people of Spanish or mixed blood (10,908 Spaniards, only 2,139 considered as mestizos, and 11,545 as *"colores quebrados"*). The remaining 15,001 were tabulated as Indians, with heaviest concentrations in the jurisdictions of Culiacán, San Felipe de Sinaloa, and El Fuerte.[17] From these figures it may be noted that the Spanish interpretation of the term "mestizo" was a highly restrictive one, those mixed bloods of Indian and Negro appearance being combined under the classification of *"color quebrado."*

Most of the immigrants to Sinaloa were soldiers, miners, stockraisers, or small farmers. Soldier-settlers established Culiacán, San Felipe de Sinaloa, and El Fuerte. Since land, cattle, and swine were distributed to them, it may be concluded that small farming and ranching were the principal occupations of these early colonists. Some Aztecan and Tlaxcaltecan Indian allies were settled in Spanish communities, particularly at Culiacán.[18] A few Portuguese people had come to reside in Sinaloa by 1606, four being reported in various settlements, including one at San Felipe de Sinaloa, which also had three residents from Genoa, Italy.[19] It should be remembered that during the period from 1580 to 1640 Portugal and Spain were united, and official Spanish policy permitted the migration of Portuguese to Spanish America. Some reached the northern frontier of New Spain at San Felipe de Sinaloa and apparently at Parral in Nueva Vizcaya somewhat later. Because of experience with the African slave trade, Portuguese became agents for the sale of small numbers of Negro slaves in frontier districts. This, in fact, may have contributed to the growth of the Negro and mulatto population in Sinaloa, particularly in the southern part of the province. There the most prosperous silver mine, the Tajo near Rosario, required heavy labor, and the nearby *pueblo* of Chametla reported some mulattoes in its population by 1745. Mazatlán listed mostly mulattoes as residents by that time, and the *villa* of Culiacán had mulattoes among its inhabitants, probably because of their usefulness in the extensive sugar cane industry.[20]

Sinaloa evidently had civilian settlers who pursued a variety of occupations. *Reales de minas* abounded, but they seemed to be occupied only temporarily, except for the Rosario district. Eight of the ten *reales de minas* the province had in 1783 were in the region south of Culiacán; forty-nine of the fifty-six gold and silver mines were in that area. Mining, however, was a very unstable industry, and the over-all output in Sinaloa was never equal to that of the more prominent mining communities in Nueva Vizcaya on the Central Plateau east of the mountains. Francisco de Urdiñola reported six owners of mines at San Sebastián in 1604. In addition, he observed that there were two merchants, one priest, one mine foreman, some gunsmiths, and an *alcalde mayor* in the same jurisdiction. About the same time, Mota y Escobar indicated that the eight or ten Spaniards residing at nearby Chametla were engaged in trade, including the sale of fish, oysters, and shrimp to the Indians. At Culiacán there were a few *encomenderos*, but most of the *vecinos* were merchants, importing clothes from Castile and China or retailing wines, olives, fine linens, and agricultural products brought from Mexico. Some worked in the fisheries; others mined salt for use in the patio process in the extraction of silver from its ores.[21] Some residents, as we have seen, were slaves in the employ of Spanish settlers.

Several *haciendas* producing corn, sugar, and stock were reported in 1745 north of the *villa* of El Fuerte, and the residents of Mazatlán seemed to have existed by raising corn and fishing.[22] Spanish settlers were operating fifteen *haciendas* in the province by 1783, all located in the area southward from Culiacán; in addition, they maintained three hundred and eleven *ranchos* scattered throughout the province. Settlers raised other crops to supplement their staple of corn; pumpkins, fruits, cotton, and sugar cane were also reported. The sugar cane industry was concentrated near Culiacán, where there were thirty-four sugar mills in 1783. The livestock industry included cattle, oxen, sheep, horses, mares, mules, swine, goats, and burros. In its early days this industry was not nearly so prosperous in Sinaloa as it was in other provinces, perhaps because the Jesuit livestock industry was so extensive, with more than one hundred thousand head of cattle on ranches associated with mission stations by 1638. Yet, by the end of the eighteenth century there were 80,010 head of cattle, 10,431 horses, 9,949 mules, 5,241 yoke of oxen, only 1,645 sheep, 996 burros, and 285 swine scattered over six jurisdictions of the province.[23] In general, it may be noted that agriculture was not nearly so well developed in the area from Rosario to San Felipe de Sinaloa as it was in other frontier regions.[24]

Living conditions in Spanish communities were necessarily simple, although the condition of settlements and homes improved with the passage of time. Mota y Escobar noted that the *villa* of Culiacán had a great plaza and wide streets; all of its buildings were low structures made of adobe. Other than churches, in 1783 the province of Sinaloa counted 3,008 dwellings in its six jurisdictions. Of this number 1,916 were built of sticks and straw, 1,059 of adobe, and only 33 of stone.[25] This indicates both the building materials in use and the gradual improvement from the early sticks and straw through adobe and finally to the permanency of stone dwellings. It also reflects the comparative economic status of the homeowners.

In general, life in Sinaloa for Spanish settlers was simple and primarily concerned with eking out a day-to-day existence. Christianity was well established among the Indians by the mid-seventeenth century as far north as the *villa* of San Felipe de Sinaloa. Settlers faced many problems, and there were differences of opinion regarding their character. Some officials complained that the early *"gente de razón"* would not work hard in the humid *"tierra caliente"* (hot lands) of Sinaloa and that the people tended to migrate to a few districts and to the mountains, where they did little or nothing but raise a few crops and hunt. Floods evidently destroyed towns and houses from time to time, since most of the dwellings were of perishable materials and the province was crossed by rivers that sometimes flooded. Food shortages and occasional famines were also noted.[26] The near-poverty level of miners, livestock raisers, and farmers alike undoubtedly contributed to periods of economic depression and a growing problem of unemployment. Petty crimes, lack of educational and cultural development, and stagnation of the economy were all among the major problems experienced by the middle of the eighteenth century. Coupled with the population increase thereafter, it is no wonder that Spanish officials encouraged colonists in Sinaloa to migrate to Sonora and recruited them as settlers for the permanent occupation of Alta California.

8. Sonora

Beyond the Yaqui River was Sonora. Spanish occupation of this remote region did not begin until the early seventeenth century. First to come were missionaries, soldiers, and miners. Civil settlements soon followed; so many communities were established in the latter half of the eighteenth century that Sonora possessed a sizable civilian population by the end of the colonial period.

The continued threat of Indian depredations and periodic serious uprisings among the Seri, Yaqui, and Pima Indians plagued the advance of the frontier northward beyond Sinaloa. In the latter half of the eighteenth century Apache raids created a major threat to the continued occupation of Spanish communities in Sonora. Gradually pushed southward and westward by the Comanches, Apache bands raided frequently deep into Nueva Vizcaya and Sonora, taking foodstuffs, livestock, and slaves from among the Christianized Indians and the scattered, ill-defended Spanish communities. As a result, Sonora never developed beyond frontier status during the Spanish era, unlike its neighbor Sinaloa. (It should be remembered that Sonora and Sinaloa first belonged to the province of Nueva Vizcaya. After 1734 they were one province until 1830, nine years after Mexico became independent.)

The twin forces of the military and the church spearheaded the exploration and colonization of Sonora early in the seventeenth century. Military campaigns of Diego Martínez de Hurdaide against the *indios bárbaros* paved the way northward from one river valley to another. The Jesuits also entered the region, establishing twenty-eight missions serving seventy-two Indian villages with a total population of forty thousand by 1678. About the same time the district had approximately five hundred Spaniards and mestizos, most of whom were engaged in mining at scattered *reales de minas* as far north as the Sonora River valley.[1]

Some settlements were founded during the first half of the seventeenth century. These included San José de Guaymas (1617), Arizpe (1644), Bavispe and Bacerac (1644 to 1646), and Fronteras (1645). Others followed before the end of the century, including Magdalena (1689), Caborca (1692), and Altar (1694).[2] However, most communities were really presidios and *reducciones* (Jesuit missions for converting Indians). Many ranches, towns, and mining settlements appeared in the southern and central parts of Sonora in

177

the two decades before 1710, when the frontier line halted temporarily near the Altar River.[3]

Mining and military activities stimulated the settlement of Sonora. Although silver was discovered early in the seventeenth century, deposits proved superficial and were soon exhausted at any one location. This resulted in the establishment of temporary mining camps by Spaniards and mestizos, to sudden booms in one region or another, and ultimately in the abandonment of numerous settlements and subsequent migration of residents to new areas. Soldier-settlers were a major ingredient in the early population. By 1684 there were 186 armed men in six districts of Sonora, as shown by a series of musters. There were sixty-two at Bacanuchi, eleven at Nacatobari, twenty-nine in the valley of Santa Ana Tepachi, twelve in the valley of Tenricachi, and thirty-six each in the *reales* of San Juan Bautista and San Miguel de Horcasitas.[4] Most of these men were not royal soldiers, but merchants, miners, and other settlers (only about a dozen in all) who presented themselves with their arms and horses for military service.[5] The only true civilian settlers seem to have been the twelve Spaniards brought from New Mexico by Don Pedro de Perea before 1640.[6]

After Sonora, Sinaloa, and the two Californias were separated from Nueva Vizcaya in 1734 and Sinaloa was combined with Sonora as one administrative unit, there seems to have been considerable growth and development in Sonora. In the eighty-seven-year period before the end of the colonial period in 1821, more civilian centers of population appeared, and some degree of community regularization occurred. No one factor brought about this development, but again missionary, mining, and military activities were chiefly responsible for settlement of the region. New communities of Spaniards and meztizos grew up adjacent to missions, presidios, and *reales de minas*, such as those at Horcasitas, Alamos, Fronteras, Arizonac, Arizpe, and Pitic (now Hermosillo).

In 1735 the northern part of Sonora depended mainly on the presidio at Santa Rosa Corodeguachi to protect settlers and miners from Indian raids, although the presidio of Janos in Nueva Vizcaya cooperated in times of crisis. Southern Sonora depended on the presidio at San Felipe de Sinaloa in emergencies.[7]

A mining boom at Arizonac in northern Sonora (in the region known as Pimería Alta) in the years from 1736 to 1741 caused a sudden growth of population in that area and accented the need for more effective Spanish military control. In many ways this boom was typical of the temporary nature of mining activity throughout the region during the colonial period. A Yaqui Indian reportedly revealed the presence of silver ores in northern Sonora just south of the present Arizona-Sonora Border. This discovery in 1736 led almost immediately to a rush of Spanish miners to the vicinity of what became known as the Real de Arizonac. The Bolas de Plata mine, named for the huge balls, or pieces, of silver found on or near the surface, caused a flurry of activity and excitement. Military and political leadership in the region was furnished by Juan Bautista de Anza, father of the presidial officer who later commanded the garrison at Tubac and Tucson. The elder Anza lost his life in a campaign against marauding Apaches in 1739, but he had already proven to be an outstanding frontier administrator. The Arizonac boom led to the establishment and strengthening of presidios at Terrenate and Fronteras and to an increase in population in northern Sonora, causing alarm among the Yaqui and later the Pima Indians, thereby leading to the strengthening of the garrison at San Miguel de Horcasitas. This military force was subsequently moved to nearby Pitic, which became the present city of Hermosillo, capital of the state of Sonora.[8] Finally it should be noted that, although this mining boom ended in 1741, the Real de Arizonac contributed its name to the state of Arizona.

The silver boom at Arizonac, the uprising of the Yaqui Indians in the region between the Yaqui and Fuerte rivers in 1740, and continued difficulties with the Seri Indians seriously affected the permanent occupation of Sonora by Spanish-speaking people.[9] As a result, a new presidio was founded at Pitic from 1741 to 1742; by 1745 it was reported to have a garrison of fifty men, while the presidio at Fronteras reported fifty-one.[10] Evidently the presidio at Pitic did not last, for it had to be reestablished forty years later. In 1748 José Rafael Rodríguez Gallardo, a *visitador general* (general inspector) reported that there were no *reales* or civil settlements having more than ten permanent families in the province. According to Rodríguez, the people of Sonora were scattered all over the district. San Juan was nominally the capital, but San Miguel de Horcasitas seemed to be the administrative center of Sonora and was at least entitled to be called a *"vecindario formal,"* or formal establishment.[11]

This same situation evidently existed in the 1760s when Bishop Pedro Tamarón y Romeral visited the Sonoran frontier and Father Juan Nentuig is thought to have written the *Rudo Ensayo*. Although the bishop reported on conditions in both Sinaloa and Sonora, he noted that southern Sonora was almost as peaceful at that time as Sinaloa. Spaniards and mixed bloods were concentrated at the mining communities of Alamos, where there were 3,400 people, Bayorca (1,004), Río Chico (1,400), Trinidad de Plata (715), and Soyopa, or San Antonio de la Huerta (300).[12] Thus the total population of southern Sonora amounted to 6,819 people in six principal settlements. In contrast to this pacified, settled, and consolidated district, northern Sonora was a true frontier, with Indian threats, Jesuit missions, and presidios at Fronteras (population of 484), Terrenate, Tubac, and Altar. Bishop Tamarón concluded that there 348 whites and mixed bloods at scattered mining camps, and another 1,117 at the presidios, in addition to the 4,223 Indians in the Jesuit *reducciones*.[13] In summary, then, there were 1,465 Spanish-speaking people in the north; when combined with Sonora's southern region, the total population of *gente de razón* was 8,284. Most were missionaries or soldiers and miners, some with families; others were civilian settlers who had come to the frontier to raise crops and livestock or to accompany soldiers and miners.

The author of the *Rudo Ensayo* noted in 1763 that very few places outside the missions were occupied by Spanish settlers. He described five small *reales de minas*, none of which was prosperous, the presidios of Fronteras (founded in 1690), Terrenate (1742), Tubac (1752), and Altar (1753 to 1754), and occasional Spanish ranches near mining communities. He concluded that conditions in Sonora were in a sorry state, with hardly ten places occupied by Spaniards and more than eighty ranches or farms destroyed in Apache and Seri depredations.[14] His summary of Sonora reflected a depressing picture of civil and clerical settlements alike. According to Father Nentuig, there were on November 27, 1762, only 22 mining settlements and Spanish towns (including 5 presidios); 48 uninhabited settlements, most of which were abandoned mining communities; 2 inhabited ranches and farms; 126 uninhabited ranches and farms; 2 parishes (one at San Juan Bautista de Sonora, now San Miguel de Horcasitas, and the other at Nuestra Señora del Rosario del Nacosari); and only three secular clergymen.[15]

Nicolás de Lafora also visited this region in the 1760s as part of the general inspection of the frontier made by the Marqués de Rubí. Lafora noted that Sonora contained in late 1766 only the Villa de San Miguel de Horcasitas, three mining towns, three small *pueblos*, and the presidio of San Ignacio de Tubac in Pimería Alta in addition to the presidios of Sonora proper. He noted that the presidio of Horcasitas was just a "small and insignificant place," consisting of a garrison of fifty-one officers and men, with their families, plus sixty civilians and many Indian families living nearby. This settlement was the capital of the province and the residence of the governor.[16] It is apparent that by 1766 Horcasitas was both a presidio and a civil settlement, thus illustrating the close interrelationship that existed on the northern frontier between the two.

During the last half century of Spanish sovereignty the civilian population increased in numbers and seemed concentrated at scattered locations, such as Alamos, Horcasitas, Arizpe, and Pitic. When Juan Bautista de Anza (the son) recruited settlers in Sinaloa and Sonora for his overland trek to Alta California in the mid-1770s, he included people from Culiacán in Sinaloa; from Ures, Alamos, and San Miguel de Horcasitas in Sonora proper; and from Tubac in Pimería Alta.[17]

The census of 1783 compiled by the Caballero de Croix contains information on communities, people, types of homes, mining establishments, crops, and livestock. According to this report, there were in Sonora two *villas*, fifty *pueblos*, twenty *reales de minas*, twenty-nine missions, six presidios, nine *haciendas*, and sixty-seven *ranchos*. These settlements were under four district headings; Cosala, Alamos, Ostimuri, and Sonora. There were 25,036 people in Ostimuri and 21,041 in Sonora, making a total of 46,077 for what is today the state of Sonora. Alamos reported a population of 7,837 in this census of 1783.[18] Twenty years later it had nine thousand people. San Miguel de Horcasitas, a *villa* and a presidio, had thirty-eight adobe houses in 1778; it remained the capital of Sonora until Arizpe replaced it temporarily under *Comandante-General* Teodoro de Croix of the Provincias Internas del Norte. Arizpe itself had 118 adobe houses and 1,534 people, including 1,020 Christianized Indians, probably Opatas, in 1778;[19] well situated in the middle of the region and in the vicinity of good farming lands, it grew in importance. It had evolved evidently from a simple Indian village on the west bank of the Río Gondra and had a badly constructed irrigation ditch bringing water to the *villa* from the river. The community had a *plaza mayor* (central plaza) with a church and residence for the priest on its south side. The village was built on two levels, with a large cultivated plot and a gristmill on the lower level. A good climate, absence of diseases, and high yield rates for wheat, corn, and beans also favored the location of Arizpe.[20]

Of importance not only for Sonora but for the entire frontier of New Spain was the founding of the *villa* of Pitic during the 1780s. This community is a splendid illustration of the extensive planning that characterized the founding of civil settlements in America, as well as an excellent example of the Spanish policy of combining civil and military settlements. The Villa de San Pedro de la Conquista del Pitic was officially established in 1783. Extensive instructions drawn up by engineer Don Manuel Mascaró but not approved by royal authorities until 1789 were issued for the founding and organization of Pitic (and of future civil settlements on the northern frontier). Article Three of the Plan of Pitic provided that the presidio at San Miguel de Horcasitas was to be moved to Pitic to protect the new town. The site of the *villa* and presidio was the same as that of an abandoned military establishment of the 1740s. It was intended that the plan serve as a model for future communities in Alta California, Texas, and other northern provinces. The provisions pertaining to the frontier as a whole were discussed in the Introduction. For Sonora, however, a few of the most important instructions should be emphasized. First, the combined civil-military nature of the *villa* is a feature observed in other Spanish frontier communities, such as Santa Fé in New Mexico and San Antonio de Béxar in Texas. This practice cannot be overlooked in any study of civil communities in frontier New Spain. Second, it should be noted that both civil and criminal jurisdiction over the settlement remained clearly in the hands of the captain or commandant of the presidio. Third, a governor was appointed to administer and develop the new settlement, apportioning lands and building lots, designating water rights, and following all royal instructions. Fourth, the *villa* was granted four leagues of land, either in square or rectangular form, to be measured, marked, and distributed to the original settlers. Additional land (an *ejido*) was provided for the settlers to share in common, primarily for use as pasture and as a source of wood and water. Lands distributed to individual families had to be occupied and improved over the course of four years, at the end of which time settlers were confirmed in their ownership and could sell their land if desired. Finally, the Plan of Pitic provided that a pueblo of Seri Indians was to be included within the *villa's* jurisdiction, subject to its laws and sharing in the privileges of its citizens as well as having the right to elect its own *alcaldes* and *regidores* (representatives in the *cabildo* or town council).[21]

Some idea of the approximate costs of establishing new civil communities in Sonora may be gathered from a 1778 document describing the anticipated costs for a *"población de españoles"* composed of fifty families, estimated to have five persons per family, all of whom would be transported to the new settlement and maintained at royal expense for a period of one year. Authorities estimated that the total cost of such a settlement would be 22,745 pesos, 6 *reales*, and 8 *granos*. An itemized list of these expenses follows:[22]

	pesos	reales	granos
Transport (on the basis of 200 beasts of burden, tents, saddles, and one-half *real* per league)	3,750		
Fifty days on the road at six *reales* per day sustenance	1,875		
100 horses to be given two each at destination at 8 pesos each	800		
200 mares at 20 *reales*	500		
50 jackasses at 5 pesos	250		
50 burros *maestros* at 10 pesos	500		
50 burras at 5 pesos	250		
100 cows at 8 pesos	800		
50 bulls at 3 pesos	150		
50 yokes of oxen at 17 pesos	850		
50 plows at 4 pesos	200		
50 axes at 20 *reales*	125		
50 adzes at 3 pesos	150		
50 hoes at 12 *reales*	75		
50 pickaxes at 3 pesos	150		
50 sickles at 2 pesos	100		
50 chisels at 1 peso	50		
50 *barreras* (medium cupboards) at 4 *reales*	25		
50 iron bars of 18 pounds weight at 6 *reales* per pound	675		
50 *fanegas* (1 fanega = 2.5 bushels) of corn for sowing at 4 pesos per *fanega*	200		
100 *fanegas* of wheat at 2 pesos	200		
16 *fanegas* and 8 *almudes* (half a *fanega*) of *miniestras* (provisions, general ingredients, or greens for daily consumption) at 4 pesos per *fanega*	66	5	4
650 *fanegas* of corn and wheat for a year's ration of 3 *almudes* per week at 3 pesos per *fanega*	1,950		

1300 *arrobas* (1 *arroba* = 25 pounds) of dried beef at ½ *arroba* per week at 12 *reales*	1,950		
216 *fanegas,* 8 *almudes* of *miniestras* at one *almud* per week and at 4 pesos per *fanega*	866	5	4
182½ *arrobas* of lard at 4 ounces daily at 5 *reales* per *arroba*	912	4	
25 *cargas* (loads of two *fanegas* each) of salt at 5 pesos each	125		
Allowance of 7 pesos monthly for each family for one year	4,200		
Expenses of commissioner to conduct the families and buy the provisions needed, sending the bills with their justification	1,000		
Totals	22,745	6	8

This singular document is of great importance in understanding royal policy toward civilian settlers on the northern frontier of New Spain. Also, it provides details on what settlers should be furnished and indicates how they were to exist on this remote frontier. Authorities expected to supply each family animals, seed, and tools necessary to begin farming in a small way. They provided animals for transportation, tents for use en route, per diem payments on the trail, and a year's salary after the settlers had arrived. Each *poblador*, or settler who was head of a family, could expect to be furnished two horses, four mares, two cows, one jackass, one male burro, one female burro, one bull, and one yoke of oxen. Seed to begin farming—primarily wheat and corn—was received from the commissioner designated to supervise the founding of the community (at a salary of one thousand pesos). Salt, wheat, corn, dried beef, and *miniestras*, or general provisions and greens, were provided the commissioner at fixed rates for distribution to all settlers and their families. Finally, farming tools such as plows, sickles, and hoes and building implements such as axes, chisels, and adzes were supplied to each family. These government-provided livestock, seed, and tools served as inducements to help colonize the Sonora frontier, bringing civilian settlers to regions that would have remained uninhabited perhaps for the rest of the colonial era. This colonization policy whereby royal authorities furnished so much to assist the settlers is in marked contrast to that of Great Britain and, later, the United States toward the pioneers who pushed the frontier westward in the region north of New Spain.

Population estimates for Sonora reveal a slow growth in the seventeenth century and a more rapid increase in the last seventy years of Spanish sovereignty, as well as the continued existence of a frontier society, quite unlike the experience of Sinaloa at the same time. However, Sonora in the last century of Spanish administration had two distinct centers of European settlement. Southern Sonora, including Alamos and various *reales de minas*, resembled the consolidated, pacified region of Sinaloa, whereas northern Sonora, including the settlements of the Sonora River valley, remained a frontier region. From the early seventeenth century arrival of two hundred Spaniards—mostly soldiers, missionaries, and miners—the population of Sonora increased to approximately six hundred by the end of the century. By 1760 there were 8,234 Spaniards and mixed bloods in the Sonoron region, three-fourths of whom were located in the southern district. When civilized Indians were added, the total population of *gente de razón* may have been as high as thirty-two thousand. With the growth of new civil and administrative centers at Arizpe, Pitic, and San Miguel de Horcasitas in the latter half of the century, the population increased further. By 1783 there were 46,077 people in the Alamos and Ostimuri regions. In the early ninteenth century Sonora reported a population of 135,385, including 38,640 Spaniards, 35,766 mixed bloods, and 60,855 village-dwelling Christianized Indians. Beyond Arizpe to the northward, however, were only a few Europeans, in scattered settlements of the Pimería Alta.[23] This sum may be somewhat high, in view of the fact that Sonora had only about one hundred thousand people in all when it was made a separate state in 1830; however, it is evident that the total number living in Sonora more than doubled in the period from 1783 to 1830.

Spaniards in Sonora did not comprise a homogeneous society. As in Sinaloa there were three basic classifications of people. First, there were the "Spaniards," which often included the mixed bloods and all others of European heritage as "*gente de razón.*" Census figures for 1783 show this grouping broken down into Spaniards, mestizos, Indians, and persons of "broken color." Second, there were the Christianized, settled Indians, who were organized into pueblos and curacies. Finally, there were the missionary Indians, originally established at missions and governed solely by the Jesuits. These latter two groupings seem to have been combined with the rest of the settled population after the expulsion of the Jesuits in 1767. *Encomiendas* of Indians granted to deserving Spaniards for labor and tribute as a reward for services to the crown, although important in central New Spain and Nueva Vizcaya, were of little or no significance in Sinaloa and Sonora.[24]

By the mid-eighteenth century society had become more complex, and struggles existed within the Spanish community. Miners and missionaries competed for control over the pacified Indians. Discord existed between the governor and the Jesuits, with colonists supporting both sides. Some Indians submitted to the control of ecclesiastical officials, others to governors and *pobladores*, while still others were hoping to take advantage of the internal divisions among the Spaniards to establish their own independent status.[25] Settlers in some *reales de minas* protested to the viceroy, alleging that the Jesuits oppressed the Indians under their jurisdiction, requiring that they sow crops that would produce a cash value of two or three thousand pesos a year, and otherwise deprived them of their liberty. With such productive capacity on the part of the Indians, it is no wonder that the Spanish *vecinos* wanted to acquire Indian labor for themselves rather than for the Jesuit communities.[26]

Yet, Jesuits contributed in many ways to frontier history, especially in leaving detailed descriptions of the people and their customs in the eighteenth century. These informative reports reflected conditions not only among the Indians under Jesuit control but in the Spanish communities as well. Father Ignaz A. Pfefferkorn provided one example of this detailed description of Sonora in the period from 1756 to 1767, including information on both the Indians and the nature of Spanish society, the occupations, dress, foods, and disposition of the settlers, and the prevalent customs of Spanish-speaking colonists.[27]

Father Pfefferkorn emphasized that most of the people in the Spanish community were of mixed descent. According to him, only the governor, officers of the presidial garrisons, and a few merchants near the *reales* could legitimately be called Spaniards, tracing their origins to families of pure Spanish blood. The mixtures bore various names, but basically comprised four categories: *coyotes*, elsewhere called mestizos, the offspring of European and Indian parents, who were described as being not so brown as the Indians of Sonora but having more intelligence, stability, enterprise, and liveliness than the natives; mulattoes, as elsewhere derived from a Spanish father and Negro mother, who had dark skins and in general were not considered trustworthy; *lobos*, who came from a mulatto parent on one side and a Negro [Indian?] on the other; and *castizos*, who resulted from the mating of a Spaniard and a *coyote*. *Lobos* were considered by Father Pfefferkorn to be the ugliest of all settlers, being of black and brown colors tainted with a yellow hue. Fiery, crafty, and of evil dispositions, they and the mulattoes were regarded with contempt by the other groups, and the term *lobo* was considered insulting. There were very few *castizos* in Sonora, and they looked and acted so much like Spaniards that they could not be clearly identified. In fact, children descended from *castizos* and Spaniards were considered "real Spaniards," with all of the rights and privileges of that category. In addition to these mixed bloods, Father Pfefferkorn stated that there were Creoles, born in America of Spanish heritage, but in reality he thought they were mostly rabble.[28]

Most of the population was employed either in agriculture or in mining. Some lived on large estates, cultivating fields and raising livestock, until the depredations of the Apaches and the Seris destroyed their properties. Thereafter they established small farms near the Spanish garrisons and also sought food from the nearby missions. The rest of the Spaniards, including some who were Sonoran-born, lived in *reales de minas* where they were almost without any religion whatsoever.[29]

Miners evidently were the most notable residents of Sonora in Father Pfefferkorn's estimation, for he considered mining the "motivating force of all economic activity."[30] Upon the success of the miners, their bonanzas, really depended the permanent colonization of Sonora, especially the profits derived by the merchants and the cattle-raisers of the region.[31] In 1770 there were five gold mines and six silver mines operating, including one at Cananea discovered in 1762, where some lead was also produced. Mine owners, miners, and other Spaniards lived at the *reales de minas*, where royal officials were stationed ostensibly to keep order. Merchants supplied necessities at a "rich profit" to residents of mining districts in Sonora. By 1783, the census of the Caballero de Croix showed a total of thirteen gold mines and one hundred silver mines in twenty mining districts in Sonora, Ostimuri, and Alamos. Actually, all the gold mines and eighty-five of the silver mines were in the northernmost section of Sonora proper, thus indicating the over-all importance of the region.[32] The most productive mining regions on the northwestern frontier were located in the extreme south of Sinaloa and the far north of Sonora.

Save for some of the wealthier Spaniards, most colonists dressed poorly. Men wore short jackets of red cloth reaching barely below the hips and with small copper or silver buttons in the front that were for decoration only since the coat was worn open. Under it was another jacket of blue cloth with long sleeves. Complementing these garments were durable red or blue trousers. Wealthier people trimmed their suits with silver borders. Men wore round, stiff hats trimmed with silver piping. Their mantles were blue with fine red material for decoration in front; they were worn in church or on journeys, but not for everyday functions. Shoes did not have enclosed toes, but consisted of several one-inch-wide strips with spaces between, somewhat like a modern sandal. Sonora stockings were footless, ending at the heel, and were made of cotton; over them men wore leggings of deerskin instead of boots. Generally, men tied their hair close to their heads or braided it in a long plait, although those who considered themselves Spaniards shaved their heads and covered them with fine muslin caps trimmed with lace. Males were very conscious of position and were ambitious to improve their status, prestige, and social classification, according to Pfefferkorn. Many arbitrarily assumed the title Don, signifying a noble origin, but in truth they were of a farming or artisan heritage. Although they frequently were heavily in debt, often lacked linen goods, and rarely had more than two shirts to their names, they always tried to put on a grand appearance.[33]

Women wore long pleated skirts and a shirtwaist garment closed at the neck by a collar. For special occasions the shirtwaist was elaborately embroidered on the sleeves, collar, and upper part with silk, gold, and silver thread. A jacket might be worn. On feast days more elaborate versions of silk, gold, and silver color appeared with gowns of a similar nature. Women, like men, displayed an intense desire for prestige and position, in addition to their natural womanly trait of highlighting their beauty to the utmost. All braided their hair as the men did, and the wealthier women wore a silk ribbon embroidered with gold and silver in their hair. Every female wore a *rebozo*, or scarf, which was also a status symbol; silk ones distinguished the wealthier women from more common females, whose *rebozos* were cotton.[34] Opata Indians wove cotton for clothing, using crude looms. However, except for *rebozos*, men's drawers, and women's petticoats, the last two of which were hidden, Spaniards generally would not wear cotton clothing; they preferred linen as a symbol of heritage and class distinction.[35]

Spanish colonists generally lived in simple homes with few furnishings, except for wealthier people and officials. Houses were constructed of sun-dried or baked adobe bricks and generally contained only two or three rooms. According to the census of 1783, there were 1,843 homes of sticks and straw, 1,167 of adobe, and only 78 of stone in the entire region. It is notable however, that Sonora proper, not counting Alamos and Ostimuri, contained no homes of straw and sticks, only five of stone, and all the remainder of adobe. Thus it may be concluded that stone and wood were scarce in Sonora. Furnishings were few and not ostentatious. A clothes chest, benches or logs for seats, some earthen pots and plates, and a few utensils were found in most homes. Beds were of raw oxhide covered by a woolen blanket or a man's mantle. A bundle of rolled-up cloths made up the pillow. Beds served for sleeping at night and as all-purpose tables by day.[36]

Foods of the colonists included corn, dried beef, mutton, chicken, beans, lentils, vegetables, and pumpkins. Wealthier families usually ate chicken, mutton, and other, more refined dishes, but most people had a plainer diet. They did not eat rats and snakes as the Indians did. In addition to wheat and corn, they had beans, vegetables, and lentils, because these were the crops best adapted to the river valleys of Sonora. One observer noted, however, that sweet potatoes, carrots, radishes, lettuce, and garden vegetables could be raised if only the Spaniards and Indians would work harder.[37] No sugar cane appears to have been raised in Sonora. Livestock raising was a major industry in Sonora, much more important than it was in Sinaloa. Cattle led in number, although horses and mules were also raised in quantity, making Sonora an important supplier of animals for transportation throughout the northern frontier. However, a constant menace faced by those raising livestock was the frequent Apache or Seri raids; one of the principal objectives of these attacks was to steal horses and mules. Sheep raising was not nearly so extensive in Sonora as it was elsewhere in New Spain; scarcely anyone had more than three thousand head, and these apparently were kept only in the vicinity of the settlements, where they did not fare too well. Although there were very few swine, goats and numerous cats existed, and one observer noted that there were so many dogs in the province that "another country could be populated from their number without a shortage being noticeable."[38]

Sonora's colonists showed a fondness for brandy, chocolate, cinnamon, sugar,

and especially chile peppers. Corn was eaten in many forms, including *posole,*
atole, and *tortillas. Posole* was in wide use among both Spaniards and Indians.
It was (and still is) made by boiling corn until the kernels burst and became
soft; it was eaten, kernels and all, in this mushy form. *Atole* was served at break-
fast when one could not afford chocolate. Corn was first boiled, then the pith
was pressed from the kernels, strained through a copper sieve, ground, and
emptied into a pot, where it was combined with water and boiled into a por-
ridge. Some Spaniards added cinnamon and sugar, while others added chocolate
instead of plain water in the final cooking phase. *Tortillas,* or corn cakes, were
eaten instead of bread. Mexican-born Spaniards particularly relished them,
bringing them in a napkin to all meals, but evidently foreign-born persons had
to develop a taste for them.[39]

Chile peppers were grown abundantly in Sonora and were in wide use to
flavor meats and lenten dishes. Father Pfefferkorn pointed out that the people
were fonder of chile than of garden lettuce; they made a chile pepper sauce
which was used on everything they ate.[40] He observed, as many have since, that
this sauce was exceptionally hot to the taste:

No dish is more agreeable to an American, but to a foreigner it is intolerable,
especially at first, because of the monotonous hotness of the peppers. The constant
use of this hot sauce is at first an unbelievable hardship for the European. He must
be content with either dry bread or burn his tongue and gums, as I did when, after
a difficult fifteen hour journey, I tried for the first time to still my hunger with such
a dish. After the first mouthful the tears started to come. I could not say a word and
believed I had hell-fire in my mouth. However, one becomes accustomed to it after
frequent bold victories, so that with time the dish becomes tolerable and finally
more agreeable.[41]

In general, Father Pfefferkorn found the people of Sonora more gentle, kindly, and charitable than were the Spanish-born *gachupines.* Women greeted
strangers warmly and nourished the sick with love and great care.[42] However,
the learned Jesuit believed that Spaniards had a "real genius" for idleness. None
would undertake a journey of any length on foot. Even when loafing, they rode
horses from one house to another. According to Father Pfefferkorn, the only
occupation the colonists had any talent for and really seemed to like was raising
livestock, a pursuit at which they were untiring as well as hardened to the saddle;
they therefore made expert cavalrymen for military service.[43]

To keep clean in a region where soap was expensive and scarce, colonists
crushed the stalks of the soapberry tree, which yielded a white, milky substance
that foamed like soap. There was a drawback, however; shirts had to be rinsed
in fresh water or severe body itching resulted when the garment was worn.[44]

There were no doctors or surgeons in the province as late as the 1760s. Smallpox was the major health hazard dreaded by all, but more Indians than Spaniards died from it. One observer noted in the later years of the Jesuit presence

in Sonora that fatal cases were rare and that people of all origins (Spaniards, Mexicans, Germans, and mixed bloods) lived to a comparatively advanced age. Several colonists even passed the century mark.[45]

Sonorans were fond of smoking, both as a means to drive off poisonous reptiles and as a pastime. The Indians planted a native tobacco, called *"matt,"* the leaves of which were dried in the sun, crushed, and smoked by everyone— Spanish men, women, and even children ten to twelve years old. They did not use pipes, but smoked *cigarros,* crude cigarettes made with paper wrappers one inch wide and the length of a finger; this paper was filled with crushed tobacco and rolled, as was the practice in New Mexico. Also, many smoked *puros,* whole tobacco leaves rolled up without any paper and thus resembling a modern cigar. Both *cigarros* and *puros* were stocked and sold by shopkeepers. Everyone carried his own makings, consisting of cut tobacco, finished *cigarros,* flint and steel, and a cotton wick which ignited easily. Most colonists carried these in paper or tin boxes, but the richer people had special containers decorated with gold or silver and sometimes set with precious stones. *Cigarros* were customarily offered to a guest in one's home after chocolate had been served. It was a special honor, impolite to refuse, if a woman lighted a *cigarro,* touched it to her lips, took the first puff, and then handed it to her guest.[46]

Everyday life in Sonora during the eighteenth century would be considered dangerous and dreary by modern standards. There was a certain monotony in the daily struggle for survival, and contacts with other provincial and viceregal settlements were rare. Yet, here as on other frontiers the settlers held *fiestas* in honor of saints, and on the occasion of religious holidays, weddings, baptisms, funerals, and the arrival or departure of prominent visitors. Dancing and drinking were important parts of the festivity. Friends assembled for these special occasions, held a great feast, and then followed it with demure, modest, restrained, yet gay dances involving the general public. Usually a man or woman danced alone at first; when he or she completed the dance, which involved intricate foot movements, a second dance was initiated by the other "partner." This routine allowed all to dance in turn, although merry singing frequently interrupted the performance. Brandy was served during each dance and chocolate at the conclusion.[47]

Sonora—at least the northern part—remained a frontier until the end of the Spanish administration in North America. Missionaries, miners, and soldiers brought the rudiments of European civilization to the region, and other colonists came in considerable numbers before the end of the eighteenth century. They settled near military and missionary establishments and mines at first, but created their own centers, such as those at San Miguel de Horcasitas, Arizpe, and Pitic, in the latter half of the century. Many of the people came to support the mining industry, and since mining was such a temporary venture in Sonora, as noted in the example of the Arizonac boom and bust, this made life in any particular location precarious. In addition to this uncertainty, settlers faced the ever-present danger of Indian uprising or attack, floods, disease, and long periods of famine resulting from crop failure.

Yet with all these dangers and other internal problems, Spanish colonists remained permanently in Sonora. Their numbers, in fact, increased in the last fifty years of Spanish administration, and they contributed in many ways to the formation of the present state of Sonora. They brought farming and the livestock industry to another frontier of New Spain, establishing in Sonora an important cattle, horse, and mule-raising industry. Although agriculture was not as well developed, it was practiced, and the crops introduced became the basis for later agricultural development. The settlers also brought the rudiments of Spanish society, including Christianity, town life, land distribution systems, celebrations of special occasions, family orientation, and early organizational patterns for administration under the *alcalde* and *cabildo* system. Furthermore, they supplied colonists who were experienced in frontier living for settlement ventures in the province of Alta California toward the end of the eighteenth century. *Pobladores* of the Sonoran frontier had to work—they had to build their own homes, largely of adobe, and they were forced to farm or raise livestock to support themselves where no one else was available to do the work. Many of the customs begun in this era, the building practices, the foods, and the reliance on government support of new settlements conditioned Spanish society on this frontier and established characteristics still observed in the twentieth century.

Above all, it should be noted that these settlers held the Sonoran frontier for Spain by right of occupation, not by discovery and exploration alone. Their advance reached its most northerly point, a district of Sonora known as Pimería Alta, in the latter half of the eighteenth century. Properly speaking, Pimería Alta was not a separate administrative unit at any time. It was a subregion or district of the combined province of Sonora and Sinaloa from 1734 until the end of the Spanish regime in 1821. After 1786 it belonged administratively to the intendency of Sonora.

The name is derived from that of the Pima Indians, the major Indian group in the area when the Spaniards arrived. The region's boundaries in colonial times ran from the Altar River of Sonora in the south to the Gila River of the present state of Arizona in the north. Today the international boundary between the United States and Mexico splits this district into northern Sonora and the southern third of Arizona.

A special emphasis is placed on Pimería Alta for a number of reasons. First, it had great importance to Spain as an eighteenth century frontier located strategically between New Mexico and Alta California. Second, it served as a significant supplier of colonists in the settlement of Alta California after 1774 and remained an important way station en route there by land until the Yuma

Indians closed the land route along the Colorado River after 1781. Third, it was the farthermost Spanish colonization venture on the northwestern frontier. Finally, it made the present state of Arizona a Spanish borderland almost a century before the Anglo-American frontier opened. When citizens of the United States spread westward into this region following the war with Mexico, they found a Mexican population that originated in the Spanish settlement of Pimería Alta.

Numerous expeditions crossed the region before it was finally settled. Fray Marcos de Niza, Francisco Vásquez de Coronado, and Antonio de Espejo all entered what is today the state of Arizona during the sixteenth century, but it was the untiring efforts of Father Eusebio Francisco Kino in the twenty-four years from 1687 to 1711 that first familiarized Europeans with the region and later promoted its settlement. His missionary activities among the Pimas resulted in the first permanent religious communities, including Dolores, Magdalena, Caborca, and Sonoita in present Sonora and San Xavier del Bac near present Tucson, Arizona. The noted Jesuit missionary did more than convert Indians. He explored and mapped the entire district as far as the Colorado River and Baja California. He straightened out the geography of the region for future Spanish ventures and clarified the relationship between Baja California as a peninsula and the rest of the mainland. He taught the Pimas to raise livestock and crops, and they learned the rudiments of European civilization from him. The Pimas came to settle near his missions, were baptized, learned to pray, chanted hymns, recited the Christian doctrine, and openly practiced the outward forms of the new religion. Furthermore, they learned to build houses and churches, to fashion doors and windows, to cultivate wheat and corn, and to develop their artistic qualities, becoming artisans in their own right as carpenters, weavers, and blacksmiths.[48]

Neither Kino's work nor the mining boom at Arizonac from 1736 to 1741 brought immediate colonization of Pimería Alta. The founding of presidios at Terrenate, Altar, Tubac, and, later, Tucson did. Soldiers and their families were the first colonists of the region; civilian settlers followed, establishing themselves near those frontier posts. Spanish people came to settle two locations in what is today Arizona: San Ignacio de Tubac and San Agustín del Tucson. Although others temporarily occupied villages near the junction of the Colorado and Gila rivers, those settlements were more properly associated with the colonization and development of Alta California, even though today the sites are within the boundaries of Arizona. However, they were abandoned after the Yuma Indian uprising in 1781.

San Ignacio de Tubac was established as a presidio on the west bank of the Santa Cruz River on March 7, 1752, as a direct result of the Pima revolt the previous year, which had resulted in the deaths of one hundred Spanish settlers in Sonora, especially Pimería Alta. Fifty soldiers under the command of Cap-

Tubac, Arizona, in the latter half of the nineteenth century, showing the adobe-brick method of construction. *Courtesy Denver Public Library Western Collection.*

tain Tomás de Beldarraín constituted the garrison. Around this post the first Spanish settlement of present Arizona grew. By 1757 the presidio and *pueblo* of Tubac counted 411 people. After 1759, under Captain Juan Bautista de Anza, it was Pimería Alta's principal settlement until the presidial force was transferred to Tucson in 1776. Although it subsequently declined, it was occupied by a few families until the end of the colonial era.[49]

After 1776 the presidio and *pueblo* of San Agustín del Tucson became the major Spanish community in Pimería Alta. Although a small agricultural and mining settlement may have existed at Tucson as early as 1735,[50] there is no official record to substantiate that claim. By 1772 it was described as a *visita*, or temporary outlying settlement without a resident missionary or priest, of San Xavier del Bac, with a small group of resident Indians.[51] The *Reglamento de 1772*, a Spanish order for the general relocation of presidios and consolidation of frontier defenses along the lines recommended by the Marqués de Rubí and Nicolás de Lafora, directed that the Tubac presidio be moved down the Santa Cruz River to the site of a Pima-Sobaipuri Indian village called Tucson, to protect the new overland route to Alta California. Colonel Hugo O'Conor carried out the fifty-mile transfer of the garrison in the summer or autumn of 1776. A new presidio was built on the east bank of the river and named San Agustín del Tucson. It was used by Anza during the winter of 1775–76 and to defend the mission Indians congregated at San Xavier del Bac.[52] In 1778 this presidio had a garrison of seventy-seven soldiers, commanded by Captain Pedro Allande y Saabedra,[53] as well as families and other colonists who must have accompanied them from Tubac.

The Spanish population of Pimería Alta remained sparse throughout the colonial period, although it grew slowly in the three decades from 1791 to 1821. From the fifty men in the initial garrison at Tubac in 1752, the population increased to 411 (both military and civilian) within five years.[54] By 1769 there were 2,018 converted Indians and 178 *gente de razón* (Spanish and mixed bloods), along with soldiers and their families, in all of Pimería Alta.[55] A settlement law of 1791 encouraged the emigration of families from other frontiers, setting aside four square leagues at each presidio for allotment to settlers, so that a permanent Spanish community might be established. Both Tubac and Tucson evidently grew in population under this plan.[56] José de Zúñiga, presidial captain at Tucson in 1804, reported that there were thirty-seven civilians, more than two hundred Indians, four thousand cattle, twenty-six hundred sheep, and twelve hundred horses located at the presidio and its adjacent *pueblo*. In addition, there were a few settlers at Tubac, along with one thousand head of cattle.[57] These figures did not include the presidial soldiers and their families or the company of Pima Indian allies stationed as a garrison force at Tubac. By 1819 there were sixty-two Spanish settlers in addition to the soldiers and their families at Tucson, along with fifty-six hundred head of cattle.[58]

Some authorities have estimated that when Mexico achieved its independence, Pimería Alta may have contained some two thousand Spaniards, mixed bloods, missionaries, and presidial soldiers within that portion that is today Arizona.[59] In view of the small numbers in the region in 1819, this estimate seems high. Unfortunately, there are no census returns at the end of Spanish administration, and therefore figures are conjectural. If there were sixty-two colonists, or heads of families, in 1819, this would account for approximately three hundred people. A garrison of fifty troops with their families and a few missionaries would amount to about two hundred and fifty people. The total would therefore be in the vicinity of five hundred and fifty people at the very most, and it may have been considerably fewer. Thus Pimería Alta, or at least the portion in the present state of Arizona, was among the least populous of the northern frontier regions. It ranked with Baja California in having the fewest civilian settlers, but it must be remembered that it was only a part of Sonora, not a separate province. Even though there were few settlers, they brought a lasting society to that distant, often forgotten frontier.

Unlike Sonora, Sinaloa, and Nueva Vizcaya, Pimería Alta's few early settlers were not miners. The early Arizonac boom had faded by the time Spaniards and mixed bloods came from the southern provinces to stay. Mining was an attraction to colonists, but they found very little reward in that occupation.

Livestock raising and agriculture were the principal pursuits of the civilian settlers in Tubac and Tucson. Subsistence farming centered on crops such as corn, wheat, beans, chick-peas (*garbanzos*), and lentils.[60] Cattle, sheep, and horses comprised most of the livestock raised in the district.

Tubac and Tucson were both founded, in general, according to procedures specified in the *Recopilación de leyes de los reynos de las indias* with four square leagues being granted to each settlement; house and planting lots were assigned to each settler from within that grant. In 1789, for example, one Torbio de Otero asked the presidial commander for a grant of a house lot and farming lands. The allotment was made, subject to the condition that he make full use of the assigned lands.[61] Stock-raising grants in the San Pedro, Santa Cruz, and Sonoita river valleys were made in the period from 1790 to 1820, subject to the conditions that the owners erect markers on the boundaries of their grants and that the land would revert to the public domain if it should be abandoned within three years from the date of the grant.[62]

Tucson was essentially a walled city after 1776, with scattered buildings outside the post. The presidio was built of adobe bricks in a square, with walls 10 to 12 feet high and 750 feet on each side. Soldiers' quarters occupied the south wall, stables the north, and civilian houses the eastern and western sides. There were various buildings randomly situated within the enclosure, including a store or saloon owned by Juan Burruel. A single gate permitted access to the *pueblo* outside the walls, where there were at least three stores among the scattered adobe buildings of the village.[63]

Apparently the civilian settlers and presidial families at Tucson were a dissolute lot. When the Apache menace had subsided in the 1790s, Spanish officials urged some of the Western Apaches to settle near the presidio. However, they had to be kept apart from the colonists, who were reported to be corrupting the Indians with their card playing, gambling, dancing, blasphemies and obscenities, prostitution, and heavy drinking.[64]

Although the pacification of most Apache bands permitted the development of agriculture and ranching in Pimería Alta, the region remained isolated from the rest of Sonora and New Spain. Efforts were made to open more direct and reliable communications between the garrisons at Tubac and Tucson on the one hand and Alta California and New Mexico on the other. Fray Francisco Garcés, Padre Silvestre Vélez de Escalante, Padre Francisco Atanasio Domínguez, and Captain José de Zúñiga all pioneered new routes to connect Pimería Alta with other Spanish frontiers. Only in the period from 1774 to 1781 did it appear that regular commerce might develop between Pimería Alta and California. Juan Bautista de Anza's exploration of new routes south of the Gila River and his escort of settlers from Sinaloa, Sonora, and Tubac to the new communities in Alta California, as well as the establishment of two *pueblos* on the left bank of the Colorado River by 1780, all seemed to indicate prosperity and perhaps further settlement for the villages of Pimería Alta. The Yuma uprising of 1781 and the abandonment of the Colorado River communities severed this connection, thus affecting the future development of both Alta California and Pimería Alta for the remainder of the Spanish period. Settlers at Tucson and Tubac, as well as ranchers in the Santa Cruz Valley, were thereafter left to fend for themselves. The Pimería Alta colonists had no regular commerce with any outside area, including even the rest of Sonora, a fact which contributed to the self-sufficiency of their region, its slow growth of population from natural increase, and its continuance as a frontier of New Spain until the end of the colonial period.

Missionary activity of the Jesuits and later of the Franciscans introduced Pimería Alta as a possible location for Spanish settlement. The mining boom at Arizonac, although short-lived, attracted other settlers temporarily to this northernmost frontier of Sonora. Soldiers and their families were the first colonists at Tubac and Tucson. Small numbers of civilian settlers, including storekeepers, small farmers, and ranchers, finally came to occupy northern Pimería Alta. They became the nucleus of Arizona's earliest Spanish-speaking population.

PART IV
The Pacific Frontier

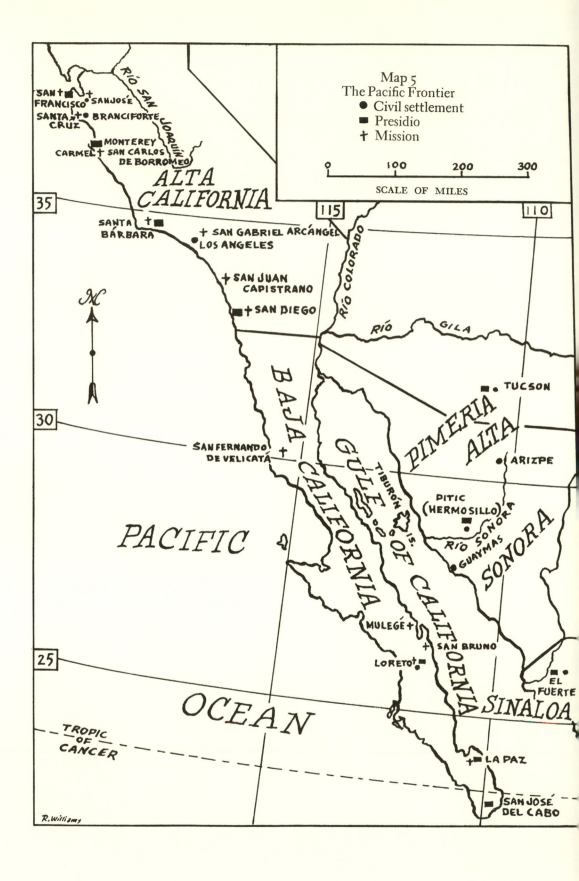

Map 5
The Pacific Frontier
● Civil settlement
■ Presidio
✝ Mission

SCALE OF MILES

0   100   200   300

SAN FRANCISCO
SAN JOSÉ
SANTA CRUZ
BRANCIFORTE
MONTEREY
CARMEL
SAN CARLOS DE BORROMEO
ALTA CALIFORNIA

35

SANTA BÁRBARA
SAN GABRIEL ARCÁNGEL
LOS ANGELES

SAN JUAN CAPISTRANO

SAN DIEGO

RÍO SAN JOAQUÍN

RÍO COLORADO

RÍO GILA

115

110

N

BAJA CALIFORNIA

GULF OF CALIFORNIA

TIBURÓN IS.

PIMERÍA ALTA

TUCSON

ARIZPE

30

SAN FERNANDO DE VELICATÁ

PITIC (HERMOSILLO)

RÍO SONORA
GUAYMAS

SONORA

PACIFIC

MULEGÉ

SAN BRUNO

LORETO

25

EL FUERTE

OCEAN

SINALOA

TROPIC OF CANCER

LA PAZ

SAN JOSÉ DEL CABO

R. Williams

Introduction

Spain's extreme northwestern frontier faced the Pacific Ocean. It included the Californias: Baja (Lower) California and Alta (Upper) California, which ultimately extended as far north as Nootka Sound on Vancouver Island in present British Columbia, where a temporary military post was established in the period from 1790 to 1795. The division between the two regions was a vague delineation between the Franciscan and Dominican mission areas in the latter part of the eighteenth century. Actually, the two were united as one political entity from the settlement of Alta California in 1769 until 1804, when a royal order separated them and provided governors for each province.

Geographical isolation, extreme hardships on the part of the settlers, irregular supply lines, and official neglect characterized the frontier in both Californias. They were mostly dependent upon Sinaloa and Sonora for settlers and supplies to maintain their precarious establishments. Both were originally colonized by establishment of missions and presidios. Yet, some civilian settlers migrated to each province. Historical research and published works have concentrated on experiences of missionaries, governors, and military officers, while neglecting the role of the civilian colonists and their achievements.

There were no civil settlements per se ever established in Baja California during the Spanish colonial period. However, families of soldiers assigned to the presidios at La Paz and Loreto, miners, and additional civilian inhabitants in missionary and presidial communities were present. Yet, the number of settlers in Baja California from the founding of Loreto in 1697 to the achievement of Mexican independence in 1821 was among the smallest of all the Spanish frontier districts on the North American continent.

In Alta California the situation was much the same for the first decade of its permanent occupation, but civil communities came into being in that province after 1777 with the founding of the *pueblo* of San José de Guadalupe. This region came to have three civil settlements thereafter. In addition to San José, there was another *pueblo* at La Reina de Los Angeles after 1781, and a struggling *villa* at Branciforte, near Santa Cruz mission, after 1797. Settlers also could be found in the vicinity of the presidios at Monterey, San Francisco, San Diego, and Santa Bárbara and at such missions as San Gabriel. In addition, many were owners of *ranchos* near both San José and Los Angeles. As a result, Alta California came to have a much larger civilian population than did Baja California.

199

9. Baja California

Baja California was not settled in an effective way until the end of the seventeenth century. Many attempts were made to promote occupation of the arid peninsula, but none resulted in permanent occupation. Hernán Cortés, the *conquistador* of México, initiated a colonization venture at La Paz, near the tip of the peninsula, but it had failed by 1536. Other settlements were begun from time to time, but they too failed,[1] largely because of poor leadership, inadequate planning, diverted interests, difficulty in supplying the colony, internal dissension, lack of motivation, and political bickering.

Perhaps the closest approach to permanent settlement of Baja California occurred in the period from 1683 to 1685 with the contract and colonization project of Isidro Atondo y Antillón, governor of Sonora. This earnest effort was undertaken primarily for missionary purposes. Father Eusebio Francisco Kino, later renowned for his work in Pimería Alta, was "convinced that it is God's decree that I should go to California" for the conquest and conversion of souls as well as the colonization of that remote province.[2] From April to July, 1683, a small missionary settlement called Nuestra Señora de Guadalupe was established at the site of La Paz. A little church, a fort, and miscellaneous other dwellings were constructed, and trade with the Indians and preliminary religious instruction began, but scarcity of supplies and native hostility forced abandonment on July 14, 1683.[3]

Governor Atondo and Father Kino tried again on the barren peninsula in October of the same year. This time they founded a colony at a site some fifty miles north of the previous site near the later location of Loreto. The new community was named San Bruno. Kino married some Christianized Indians who had accompanied their expedition from the mainland and baptized a dying Indian child, whom he considered the "first Californian who went to Heaven."[4] Provisions, horses, goats, and mules arrived from Sinaloa; a mission, fort, and other dwellings were built. The Spaniards planted melons, pumpkins, vines, pomegranates, and quince trees, but from the beginning lack of rainfall thwarted their agricultural efforts. Missionary work proceeded slowly. Only five Indians were baptized in the first fourteen months, and four of them died within a few hours after being given the sacrament. Father Kino reported that efforts were made to learn the Indian languages and that some of the natives could say their prayers partly in Spanish. He concluded that the Indians were impressed by the fact that the Spaniards had come to teach them.[5]

By the end of 1685, however, the colony of San Bruno had been abandoned, and all the Spaniards had returned to Sinaloa. Atondo's expeditions to the interior of the peninsula had discovered only more Indians and a good salt mine, not the wealth always hoped for by the Spaniards. Provisioning was difficult, rainfall was lacking, and financial assistance was inadequate; the viceroy therefore ordered that no new settlements be established.[6]

Nevertheless, this conscientious effort to colonize Baja California was important to the permanent occupation a decade later. It provided an initial contact between Spaniards and Indians, an introduction of the language, religion, and culture of the Europeans that could be used later to facilitate colonization by the Jesuits. It familiarized the missionaries with a new field of opportunity for the conversion of Indians to Christianity; furthermore, it opened a new area for possible colonization. Father Kino, although transferred later to Pimería Alta, never forgot this incompleted missionary field. He suggested its future pacification and encouraged the work of Father Juan María Salvatierra there in addition to the establishment of regular communication between the mainland and the peninsula in the first decade of the following century.[7]

Both the Jesuits and royal officials were responsible for the permanent occupation of Baja California after 1697. Fathers Kino and Salvatierra revived the idea of pacification and conversion; a royal license of February 5, 1697, granted the Jesuits complete authority over the peninsula if they would undertake the settlement and conversion at their own expense but in the name of the king. Contributions of devout individuals in Mexico for the establishment and maintenance of the missions, collectively known as the Pious Fund and later incorporated to keep them going, furnished financial support for the founding of Loreto mission in October, 1697, and for the creation of sixteen more such religious centers before the Jesuits were expelled from New Spain after 1767. Eighteen "Spaniards"—two *padres*, seven soldiers, five sailors, and four Christianized Indians—established the settlement at Loreto, to which were added more missions, presidios at San José del Cabo and Loreto, and even some primitive mining settlements during the eighteenth century. After the expulsion of the Jesuits in 1767, the Franciscans arrived on the peninsula and founded the mission of San Fernando de Velicatá. They, in turn, were replaced by the Dominicans in the next decade, and this order remained in control of all Baja California missions until the end of Spanish rule.[8]

Civilian settlers appeared sporadically in Baja California, but not in any organized, separately planned settlements. Miners from the mainland arrived to work in isolated districts after 1760, in spite of the opposition of missionaries, who considered them poachers in their exclusive domain and a bad influence on the Indians in their charge.[9] At least one *real de minas* was established at Santa Ana in 1768. Although the mines were reportedly exhausted four years later, a settlement of sorts with a predominantly non-Indian population survived. By the last decade of the eighteenth century this district had a population of some five hundred to seven hundred people, less than forty per cent of whom were Indians.[10] Another threat was the pearl fishers, usually employed by private individuals who obtained licenses from the king, but they did not establish permanent settlements or directly challenge missionary supremacy except for the seizure of native laborers.

José de Gálvez, general inspector of New Spain in the late 1760s, was the first Spanish official to consider seriously the possibility of bringing settlers to Baja California. In keeping with his general plans to effectively occupy the frontiers of New Spain, he insisted on establishing colonists throughout the peninsula to replace the missions. He selected Loreto as the site for one hundred families; most were to be induced to come from other missions and inhabited places on the peninsula. On August 12, 1768, he issued a decree to establish this settlement, simultaneously outlining regulations pertaining to it. Crown lands were to be separated from mission property and offered to Spaniards of "good character." Their only obligation was to make improvements on their allotments and to pay a small annual tax to the king. Loreto was planned as a combined Indian and Spanish town where the natives would be taught to raise crops and to go about their lives clothed instead of in their present state of nakedness. The first colonists were discharged or retired soldiers and sailors from the garrison at Loreto, and there were, according to Father Francisco Javier Clavigero, more than four hundred inhabitants there in 1768, including Indian neophytes, soldiers, sailors, and families. In the period from 1790 to 1800 the settlement's total population varied from four hundred and fifty to six hundred persons, more than half of whom were reported to be of Spanish and mixed blood.[11]

Between four hundred and eight hundred people of all categories and racial mixtures, not counting Indians, were reported for Baja California in 1800; the total population was estimated as about forty-five hundred.[12] Colonists included residents of Loreto; the *real* of Santa Ana; San Bernabé, a small settlement near Cape San Lucas established to provision the Manila galleon on its return voyage from the Philippines and the Marianas Islands; a second *real de minas* at San Antonio del Oro; and a small garrison of one sergeant and eight soldiers stationed at La Paz.[13]

Agriculture and livestock raising constituted the major pursuits of settlers, soldiers, and converted Indians alike. Wine, brandy, cotton, and fruits were produced, but there is little evidence that grain crops were raised in abundance. In fact, this was one of the principal factors limiting permanent Spanish colonization and development of the region. Livestock fared somewhat better. Between 1794 and 1801 the number of sheep grew from 2,486 to 7,255; cattle, from 1,666 to 5,454; and horses, from 472 to 1,109. Mules, burros, and hogs were also raised.[14] In all cases, however, the numbers were small and barely sufficient to support the local populace. A comparison to the numbers of animals raised in Sonora, Sinaloa, New Mexico, Nueva Vizcaya, Nuevo Santander, Coahuila, and even Pimería Alta will show how insignificant this industry was in Baja California. Indeed, this region would rank last in the numbers of each kind of livestock raised on the northern frontier.

Trade between the little settlements of Baja California and the other Spanish provinces was irregular and of an extremely limited nature. Obtaining provisions from the mainland depended on tenuous financial resources and sporadic arrivals of small vessels, usually from Sinaloa. San José del Cabo became a small presidial settlement after 1735 for the convenience of the Manila galleon, and a small but lively trade developed there in the latter part of the century.[15] Economic distress, however, and official neglect continued into the first decades of the nineteenth century. Furthermore, the tiny settlements were inadequately protected, as demonstrated just after the period of the Mexican War for Independence when Lord Cochrane sailed into San José del Cabo on February 17, 1822, to bombard and sack the town.[16]

Baja California remained a peripheral, much neglected frontier for the 124 years of Spanish occupation. Beset as the province was with problems of arid lands, inadequate and irregular rainfall, uncertainty of provisions, weak links to the mainland of New Spain, constant financial deficiencies, divided authority between missionaries of the Jesuit, Franciscan, and Dominican orders and military and royal officials, sporadic Indian rebellions and open hostility to the Europeans, and lack of any paying industry, the wonder is that it survived at all. Survive it did, although not prosperously. Originally the province had only a few missionaries and soldiers, but eventually it added miners and other civilian settlers and increased slowly in population. From the initial eighteen people, none of whom were women or children, who landed at Loreto in 1697, Baja California could count over six hundred *gente de razón* by the turn of the nineteenth century.

When Mexican independence was achieved in 1821, the peninsula was a separate province. However, it was still very much a frontier region, with no evidence of secular schools, little improvement in health and medicine, a crude transportation system with roads resembling mere trails, and no major achievements in the folk arts such as had occurred in New Mexico. Society had developed little beyond a two-class system of "Spaniards" and Indians. Everyone was principally concerned with eking out an existence, mainly by subsistence agriculture and raising livestock. Provincial isolation, lack of economic incentive, and official neglect were as marked then as they had been a century earlier. Yet, in spite of all these drawbacks, Spain had succeeded in planting permanent settlements here as elsewhere on the northern frontier. The Spanish settlers of Baja California made a most significant contribution in the occupation of Alta California after 1769.

10. Alta California

Although explored early, Alta California was colonized late. Bursts of enthusiasm and vigorous exploration were followed by years, sometimes decades and even centuries, of neglect. Juan Rodríguez Cabrillo and Bartolomé Ferrelo reached San Diego and the California coast as early as the years 1542–1543. Ferrelo probably sailed as far north as Cape Mendocino or the present California-Oregon boundary line. During the next two centuries various exploratory voyages took place, including that of Sebastián Vizcaíno, but no colonization was attempted.[1]

There were two principal motives behind the Spanish occupation in the period from 1769 to 1821. Religious conversion of the Indians was a major objective. Baja California was granted exclusively to the Jesuit order, Alta California to the Franciscans. Fear of foreign encroachment—originally, the Russian threat—was also an important factor in the decision to occupy Alta California.

Whereas *pobladores*, or colonists, in Baja California reached a total of approximately six hundred by the turn of the nineteenth century, there were more than three thousand in Alta California by the end of the Spanish regime in 1821. Furthermore, there were at least three planned, organized, and systematically settled Spanish civil communities in Alta California, in addition to the scattered population of *gente decente* at the various *ranchos*, presidios, and missions. This was in marked contrast to Baja California's lack of a planned civil settlement. The early presidial and missionary settlements of Alta California played an important role in the establishment of civil communities. They often served to provide the first residents for them, and retired military personnel with their families frequently helped swell the Spanish civilian population.

The first colonization of Alta California was the result of a four-pronged expedition, in 1769, planned by José de Gálvez and carried out by Gaspar de Portolá and Father Junípero Serra. This was wholly a military-clerical venture undertaken by two maritime and two land expeditions from Baja California, all of which were to be reunited at San Diego.

Each of the seagoing expeditions was composed of a single ship. The packet boat *San Carlos* sailed first on January 9, 1769, reaching San Diego on April

29 after a perilous voyage that took the lives of twenty-four men, chiefly from scurvy. Sixty-two people were on board at the outset—the ship's captain, a mate, a crew of twenty-three sailors, two boys, Lieutenant Pedro Fages, twenty-five Catalan soldiers who had formerly served in Sonora, an engineer-cosmographer named Miguel Costansó, a surgeon named Pedro Prat of the royal navy, two blacksmiths, four cooks, and a Franciscan chaplain. The packet *San Antonio* sailed on February 15, reaching San Diego first on April 11 with its complement of twenty-eight sailors, two chaplains, and "some" blacksmiths and carpenters.[2]

The two land divisions consisted of a detachment commanded by Captain Fernando de Rivera y Moncada and one led by the interim governor of the Californias, Gaspar de Portolá. Chaplain Father Juan Crespí of Majorca, cosmographer José Cañizares, twenty-five soldiers from the Loreto garrison, forty-two Christianized Indians, and three muleteers comprised the captain's force, which departed from San Fernando de Velicatá in Baja California and reached San Diego on May 14. Governor Portolá with the second overland contingent left Loreto on March 9, assembled his detachment just north of San Fernando de Velicatá, and reached San Diego on July 1. With the forty-seven-year-old Catalan went Father Serra, Sergeant José Francisco de Ortega, nine soldiers of the Loreto garrison, forty-four Christianized Indians, four muleteers, and two servants belonging to Father Serra.[3]

The sea and land expeditions brought a wide variety of provisions and equipment for the establishment and maintenance of the settlements planned. These included military supplies, religious effects, livestock and seed, tools and equipment, consumer goods, and gifts for the Indians. Although a summary of all this paraphernalia would be tedious, some of the equipment and provisions is of interest in emphasizing the fact that these people intended to stay in Alta California. Twenty-three bronze cannon, over seven hundred firearms, machetes, swords, powder, cartridges, and cannon balls dominated the military list; statues of saints, religious vessels, bells, ornaments, vestments, rugs, crucifixes, rosaries, and medals largely comprised the clerical inventory. In addition, 306 head of cattle, 262 horses and mules, hundreds of chickens, and six sheep were brought northward. Corn, beef, wheat, fish, chocolate, beans, sugar, figs, raisins, salt, red pepper, garlic, flour, bread, rice, chick-peas, water, cheese, and bran were listed in the inventory of foods and grains transported. Consumer goods and tools included handkerchiefs, clothing, tobacco, cigarettes, shoes, axes, knives, carpenter's tools, and plates. Finally, seven thousand pesos were provided to meet expenses.[4]

From this beginning came the first permanent settlements in Alta California. Over one hundred persons of Spanish blood made up these initial missionary-military expeditions, along with eighty-six Christianized Indians from the missions of Baja California. However, it must be remembered that many perished en route on the *San Carlos,* some deserted, others died on the overland journey or within a few months of their arrival, and sailors departed with their ships. These losses decreased markedly the number of colonizers remaining in Alta California. Probably there were no more than 80 people of Spanish blood among a total of perhaps 150 settlers by the end of the year.[5]

Spanish-speaking people established four basic types of settlements in Alta California during the half-century from 1769 to 1821.[6] Missions and presidios, founded earliest, remained in existence until the end of the Spanish regime. *Pueblos* and a *villa* comprised the civilian towns, established usually as support for the missions and presidios. The pueblos were founded about a decade after the initial occupation; the *villa* was not created until nearly a generation had passed. Finally, *ranchos* were granted to individuals after the middle 1780s. They were closely related to all other communities. Both towns and *ranchos* continued in existence until the end of the colonial period.

The first Spanish settlements in Alta California were San Diego and Monterey. By 1773 there were five missions—San Diego de Alcala, San Gabriel Arcangel, San Luis Obispo de Tolosa, San Antonio de Padua, and San Carlos de Borromeo—and a single presidio, located at Monterey. Nineteen Franciscans operated the missions and sixty soldiers comprised the military force. Only about twenty of them were stationed at the presidio, the rest being scattered among the missions as guards for the otherwise unprotected missionaries. The military and religious personnel, neophytes undergoing conversion at the missions, a few artisans in the pay of the government, and some servants made up the whole population of the frontier province. In the strict sense, these people were not colonists, nor were there as yet any women in Alta California. Furthermore, there were no civil settlements or privately owned *ranchos.*[7]

Twenty-seven years later, at the turn of the nineteenth century, there were eighteen missions, four presidios, three civil settlements, and a number of *ranchos.* The total number of *gente de razón* had increased to approximately eighteen hundred,[8] and this number had risen by the end of the Spanish period to about thirty-three hundred.[9]

The primary purpose of the mission establishments, or *reducciones,* as they were sometimes called, was to convert the natives to Christianity and to elevate them from barbarism to civilization, according to Spanish standards. Usually there were two Franciscan missionaries at each station, although occasionally one had to handle it alone. They were the spiritual, political, and economic masters of their settlements and served simultaneously as the direct agent of the king. Each mission included a small garrison. In theory no Spaniards other than the missionaries and the soldiers were supposed to reside there. The royal *hacienda* (treasury) provided salaries for the missionaries, but all else had to be secured through the operation of mission industries and individual gifts. Once in the mission, Indians could not legally leave it, and severe punishments

Plaza of the presidio of Monterey, Alta California, in the latter part of the eighteenth century. Note the soldier wearing a *cuera* (leather jacket), the straw roof of the presidial chapel, and the grilled windows in the quarters. *Courtesy Bancroft Library, University of California.*

were established to discourage desertion. Instruction in the catechism, vocabulary, and ceremonies was provided; services were frequent, and attendance was compulsory. Each missionary required the Indians to work, the goal being self-sufficiency for the community. Men planted, tended, and harvested crops; they also raised livestock, did carpentry, constructed buildings, dug irrigation ditches, built walls, and completed "public works." Women and children were engaged in spinning and weaving in addition to some of the small industries developed at the missions. Indians tanned hides, made shoes and parts for saddles, made tallow and soap, fashioned coarse pottery, and operated flour mills. According to Spanish law, missions were supposed to remain in existence for a period of ten years and then become secularized, but the Alta California missions, unlike those in Texas, did not progress to that second stage until well into the Mexican era.[10]

Presidios were essential to the expansion of the frontier in all of New Spain, and Alta California was no exception. According to one authority, "not a mission was founded without soldiers, and none existed without them."[11] Presidios were not only the political and social centers of Alta California but provided permanent settlers for the later civilian towns of the province. Monterey was

View of the presidio of Monterey, Alta California, at the time of the Malaspina visit, 1791. Note the straw or thatched roofs, the *carretas* (carts), and the livestock. *Courtesy Bancroft Library, University of California.*

always the most important presidio, but there were others at San Diego, San Francisco, and Santa Bárbara. Regional administration, military affairs, reception of visitors, outdoor sports, and social diversions (music, games, dancing, horsemanship, gambling, drinking, and prostitution) characterized life at the presidios. In fact, non-military activities came to dominate the presidios to such an extent that their original functions as military posts were either neglected or almost completely forgotten. Supplies from far-off San Blas were infrequently received and were often inadequate; pay was low and at times far in arrears; equipment was poorly maintained; soldiers were employed as farmers, laborers, livestock raisers, and mail couriers; and there was little contact with the rest of the world beyond Alta California. By the early nineteenth century the presidios had declined as military institutions. On one occasion it was reported that the garrison at San Francisco had to borrow powder from a visiting Russian ship to fire a salute to the visitors.[12] Yet, retired soldiers and their families, familiar with the way of life at the presidios, became a significant colonizing force at the two civilian *pueblos* and single *villa* established in Alta California during the period from 1777 to 1797.

The first colonists *per se* came to Alta California in 1775 and 1776 as members of two planned colonizing expeditions. They were brought to the province

View of the convent, church, and Indian huts of the mission of Carmel, near Monterey, Alta California, at the time of the Malaspina visit, 1791. The view from the interior shows the brick-and-straw construction of the buildings, *carretas*, and the dress of the Spaniards. *Courtesy Bancroft Library, University of California.*

by Captain Fernando de Rivera y Moncada and Captain Juan Bautista de Anza. Principally recruited in Sinaloa and Sonora, they came for two principal reasons: to reduce the number of poverty-stricken settlers in the older provinces of northwestern New Spain, and to solidify Spain's tenuous hold on Alta California by providing permanent residents who could raise crops and livestock in support of the presidios and missions.

Of the two colonizing expeditions, Anza's was the larger and more significant one, but Rivera's was the earlier. Having received lengthy instructions from the viceroy, Rivera recruited soldiers and settlers (mainly families of the soldiers) in distant Sinaloa. With fifty-one persons of all ages, he reached Loreto in Baja California in March, 1774, and brought them overland to Alta California. He was then ordered to relinquish his command and was transferred to the *real* of Pachuca.[13] Five years later he was back in Alta California, where he played an even more important role in the founding of the *pueblo* of Los Angeles.

Juan Bautista de Anza, the son of the early frontier officer of the same name, at the time of his colonizing enterprise (1774 to 1776) was commander of the presidio at Tubac in Pimería Alta. On an exploratory expedition to establish communications between his district and Alta California, he proved that an overland route was feasible. Use of this route would simplify the task of maintaining the distant Pacific province, decrease its isolation, and provide an alternative to the difficult practice of supplying Alta California by sea from San Blas.

In 1775, the very year that British colonists rose in rebellion against their mother country, Anza obtained royal permission to bring settlers to Alta California. He began assembling colonists in Culiacán, Sinaloa, most of them from that province with a few from Jalisco and Sonora. The families he recruited were generally quite large, having an average of four children, although two had nine children each. Most of the settlers were so poor that they had to be provided money and clothing to make any sort of move. Men were given garments of Puebla cotton with ribbons for their hats and hair. Women were given clothes also made in Puebla's textile *obrajes* (mills or factories), Brussels stockings, hats, *rebozos*, and ribbons. For defensive purposes leather jackets of seven thicknesses were worn and carbines, swords, and lances were carried.[14] Anza marched his contingent overland from Culiacán through Sonora to Tubac, a distance of more than six hundred miles, collecting additional settlers en route.

At Tubac, his home station, Anza added more settlers and conducted an inventory of people and equipment assembled for the journey westward. His muster of personnel listed 250 people in all: Anza as commander, the Franciscan chaplain Fray Pedro Font, Fathers Fray Francisco Garcés and Fray Tomás Eixarch, *alférez* Don José Joaquín Moraga, Sergeant Juan Pablo Grijalva, ten soldiers from the presidio at Tubac who were to return there when the expedition was completed, twenty-eight soldiers from the provinces of Sonora and Sinaloa who were to remain in Alta California, twenty-nine wives of soldiers and officers, one hundred and thirty-six additional family members of both sexes and all ages, fifteen muleteers, three cowboys, three servants for the fathers, four of Anza's servants, five interpreters, and a commissary.[15]

When the expedition began its march on October 23, 1775, there were 240 persons, 165 pack mules, 302 cattle, and 340 saddle animals.[16] The journey via the small Spanish settlement of San Agustín del Tucson (population, eight families) and along the Gila River to its junction with the Colorado River proceeded smoothly, and the force reached San Gabriel in the southern part of Alta California on January 4, 1776. After seventy-four days on the trail,

Drawing of presidio of San Francisco about the beginning of the nineteenth century. *Courtesy Bancroft Library, University of California.*

Anza arrived in the Pacific province with a total of 242 people, three children having been born along the way and one woman having died in childbirth the first night of the journey.[17]

The entire expedition is in marked contrast to the initial ventures into Alta California only six years earlier. Anza's intelligent leadership, his willingness to halt periodically to rest his people or await the birth of children, and his mixing of hard marches with periods of diversion contributed to the success of the expedition. For example, on December 17, 1775, after reuniting his three subdivisions, he permitted the settlers to hold a *fandango*—over the objections of the chaplain, Fray Pedro Font. Apparently the celebration lasted quite late, and Font reported that a "bold widow . . . sang some verses which were not at all nice, applauded and cheered by the crowd."[18] Her newly acquired male consort became angry and punished her severely, an act approved by the Franciscan chaplain but censured by Anza, who reprimanded the man for beating the woman.[19] A week later, on Christmas Eve, Anza ordered another halt while a child was born. Following the birth, he gave a pint of liquor to each of the soldiers, again over the opposition of Father Font, and permitted the settlers to sing and dance in celebration of the occasion.[20]

After a delay of over a month at San Gabriel, Anza and seventeen soldiers, together with their families, resumed the march northward to Monterey, reaching the capital of Alta California on March 10, 1776. There the people took up temporary residence in the presidio, described as a square of mud and log structures surrounding a central plaza. On one side was the house of the commander and a storehouse; on the opposite side was a small chapel and quarters for the soldiers; and on the two adjoining sides were huts for the families and other people living at the presidio.[21]

Although Anza's colonizing expedition was not purely a civil enterprise and he did not actually found any settlements himself, it is important for the many contributions it made to the occupation of Alta California by people who came to stay permanently and who helped in solidifying Spain's control over the remote province. First, it doubled the Spanish population of Alta California; almost overnight the numbers of *gente de razón* increased to three hundred or three hundred and fifty people. Second, the expedition introduced soldier-settlers along with their families into both southern and northern portions of the province, at San Gabriel and Monterey. Third, it furnished an impetus for the founding of other settlements, using some of the colonists brought by Anza as settlers of these new communities. The presidio of San Francisco, formally founded on September 17, 1776, by Lieutenant José Joaquín Moraga, and the *pueblo* of San José, established the following year, were settled by soldiers, families, and other colonists from the Anza expedition. Finally, it opened a trail from the mainland provinces of northwestern New Spain to Alta California, a route which in the next five years was used by more than three hundred additional settlers, including the original inhabitants of Los Angeles, before it was closed permanently by the Yuma Indian uprising.[22]

Within the two decades following the arrival of Anza's colonists, Spanish officials authorized, planned, and carried out the founding of three permanent civilian towns in Alta California—the *pueblos* of San José and Los Angeles, founded in 1777 and 1781, respectively, by Governor Felipe de Neve, and the *villa* of Branciforte, founded in 1797 by Governor Diego de Borica. Two small settlements were started on the left bank of the Colorado River in the fall of 1780 with settlers and laborers who had been brought overland from Sonora together with their livestock, but these communities were abandoned after the Yuma uprising in June, 1781.[23]

San José and Los Angeles were originally established to provide agricultural products to Spaniards living throughout Alta California, especially those near the presidios. Shipments of grain and other provisions from the port of San Blas were both expensive and uncertain. Governor Neve proposed as an alternative that civil communities be established to support the missions and presidios, thereby reducing, or perhaps eliminating, dependency other regions. He selected two sites, one in the south on the Río de Porciúncula and one in the north on the Río de Guadalupe.[24]

View of the Spanish establishment at San Francisco in the early nineteenth century. *Courtesy Bancroft Library, University of California.*

Viceroy Antonio María de Bucareli y Ursúa authorized Governor Neve to proceed with the proposed agricultural settlements. The governor designated nine presidial soldiers from Monterey and San Francisco, along with five *pobladores* (colonists) from Anza's original party, to be the founders of the first community. With their families, there were sixty-eight settlers in all. Lieutenant José Joaquín Moraga led this contingent to a spot on the east bank of the Río de Guadalupe, about three miles from Santa Clara mission, and on November 29, 1777, broke ground for the new settlement, San José de Guadalupe.[25]

Each settler received a plot of ground (*solar*) on which to build a house and a field (*suerte*) large enough to plant corn for a yield of about two bushels. In addition, each *vecino* was paid ten pesos a month and given daily rations for a period of three years. This was in reality a loan since the recipient was expected to repay the government out of his crops. In addition, each *poblador* was supplied with two cows, two oxen, two mares, two sheep, two goats, one mule, and necessary agricultural implements. The first census of people and animals at San José, in April, 1778, showed a total of sixty-eight persons, counting fifteen men, thirteen women, twenty-seven male children, and thirteen female children. Livestock included twenty-one horses, forty-five mares, twenty-one mules, twenty-nine oxen, thirty-seven head of cattle, eighteen calves, five burros, thirty-one sheep, thirty-one goats, and twelve swine.[26]

Before founding a second such agricultural community, in the south, Governor Neve issued extensive instructions on June 1, 1779, for the establishment, organization, and administration of all future presidios, missions, and *pueblos* in Alta California. Of the fifteen *títulos* (articles, or headings) contained in this regulation, only the fourteenth pertained primarily to the government and organization of civil settlements. In eighteen paragraphs, Governor Neve outlined in full the procedures that should be followed by civil communities. He specified that new *"pueblos de gente de razón"* (towns for civilized people) were to be established for the planting and cultivation of the ground, growth of livestock, and other branches of industry for the support of the presidios. Settlers with their families were encouraged to migrate from Sinaloa and Sonora by offering them grants of 120 pesos annually for the first two years and "rations" for three years thereafter. As at San José, authorities would provide each settler with mules, horses, mares, cattle, sheep, goats, and farming tools, as well as a lance, *escopeta* (firelock), *adarga* (bullhide oval shield), ax, and knife.[27]

Building lots and farming plots were to be designated by officials at each *pueblo*, and the town would be laid out with its plaza and streets corresponding to those provisions specified in the laws of the kingdom. Allotments to settlers were made in the name of the king and were granted in perpetuity to be passed on to descendents. Some building sites were set aside at the outset to provide for soldiers who could be expected to retire to the community.[28] Each agricultural lot was to be two hundred *varas* square,[29] or what was considered enough to raise one *fanega* of corn.[30] New settlers were declared exempt from paying tithes for a period of five years, but they were required to possess specified numbers of animals and to make property improvements during that time. It was also stated that under penalty of a fine of twenty pesos they could not sell animals among themselves or to any persons other than those at the presidios in this initial period. Finally, each settler had an obligation to maintain himself in a state of military preparedness, with two horses, saddles, firelock, and other arms, for the defense of his district or for provincial defense as directed by the governor.[31]

These detailed instructions were applied to the founding of Los Angeles in 1781. *Comandante-general* Teodoro de Croix authorized Governor Neve to establish a new *pueblo* on the banks of the Río de Porciúncula. The governor then sent Fernando de Rivera y Moncada to Arizpe to recruit settlers from both Sonora and Sinaloa. Originally there were to be twenty-four families, including a mason, a carpenter, and a blacksmith. Each family was to be paid ten pesos a month, together with an advance of livestock, clothing, seed, and farming implements, for which the settlers were to repay the government over the next five years. They were bound to remain in the new *pueblo* for a period of ten years.[32]

Rivera actually obtained fourteen families of settlers, only eleven of whom reached Loreto in Baja California. Escorted by seventeen soldiers, they proceeded overland via San Diego to San Gabriel mission, while Rivera and forty-two soldiers (thirty of whom had their families with them) marched northwestward across the mainland via the junction of the Colorado and Gila rivers, bringing with them a herd of 960 horses and mules.[33]

The settlers were at San Gabriel on August 18, 1781, and eight days later Governor Neve issued specific instructions for founding the *pueblo*. He specified that they select a slightly elevated site exposed to northern and southern winds and that all possible measures be taken to avoid the danger of floods. The plaza in the community was to be three hundred *varas* long by two hundred wide; it should be placed so that it faced eastward, on which side the church and government buildings would be erected. A proper location for a guardhouse should also be designated. He directed that four main streets should run from the mid-points of each side of the plaza, with two other streets running from each of its corners, which were to face the cardinal points of the compass so as not to expose the central part of the *pueblo* directly to the four winds. This orientation of the new community was in accordance with the provisions specified by the *Recopilación de leyes de los reynos de las indias*. Settlers would draw lots for the selection of house lots, which were to measure a standard twenty by thirty *varas*. Agricultural plots, marked by stakes and numbered so as to begin with the lowest numbers nearest to town, would then be distributed, each settler being entitled to four square leagues, with each plot measuring two hundred *varas* square. Finally, Neve instructed that a tract of land two hundred *varas* wide be left between the fields and the community itself to allow for future expansion. This was the *ejido*, or common land, possessed by the village as a whole and not available for original distribution.[34]

In accordance with these instructions, eleven families consisting of forty-four persons founded the *pueblo* of La Reina de los Angeles on September 4, 1781. The list of first settlers included twelve families, or forty-six persons, but Antonio Miranda Rodríguez and his wife were not in Alta California for this occasion. Only two of these original inhabitants claimed to be of Spanish blood, the remainder being of Negro, Indian, or mulatto origins.[35] Not one of them could read or write.[36]

After the founding of San José and Los Angeles by Governor Neve, no new *pueblos* were established, and there was no major immigration of settlers,[37] the land route having been closed by the Yumas in 1781. By 1790 San José had been moved to a higher location, after a wet winter and spring floods in 1778.[38]

It then had a population of about eighty people, including eight of the original *pobladores* and at least ten new settlers. The latter were retired soldiers from nearby presidios; they received no pay or rations from the government as the first settlers had.[39] Los Angeles in the same year was a community of twenty-nine adobe buildings surrounded by a wall of the same material. It had a total population of 109, new settlers having been gained by retirement of soldiers from the southern presidios.[40]

The third civil community, the *villa* of Branciforte founded in 1797, was established for different reasons than the two *pueblos* had been, and it was initially populated in part by people recruited from within Alta California. Fears of foreign encroachment and aggression on the west coast of North America revived Spain's interest in colonization during the viceregal administration of the Conde de Branciforte. Miguel Costansó, a noted engineer and military authority who had participated in the founding of early settlements in Alta California, was the person who gave impetus to the establishment of the *villa*. Aware of British colonial successes based on commercial development, he proposed a settlement in Alta California which would serve both as a center of industry and as a fortress. The new *villa* was to be colonized in part by soldier-settlers. Governor Diego de Borica of the Californias asked the viceroy to also send vigorous, robust country people from colder climates, especially carpenters, blacksmiths, masons, tailors, tanners, shoemakers, tilemakers, ship-wrights, and even a few sailors to settle the proposed *villa*.[41] From this list of artisans it may be noted that the governor went along with Costansó's suggestion to make out of the new community an industrial center.

After considerable deliberation and delay, a site was selected on the Río San Lorenzo across from the mission at Santa Cruz, and the new community was laid out according to the successful plan for the founding of Pitic in Sonora in the previous decade. Nine families were recruited in Guadalajara, evidently the dregs of society who were not wanted there. Seventeen so-called Spaniards in all, they included two farmers, two tailors, one carpenter, one miner, one merchant, one engraver, and one man with no occupation whatsoever. At a cost of 23,405 pesos they were supplied with tools, livestock, and other equipment; they reached Monterey on May 12, 1797. Under strict instructions from the governor prohibiting gambling, drunkenness, or concubinage in the new settlement, they were established at the *villa* in July, 1797.[42]

Although San José, Los Angeles, and Branciforte were the only true civil communities ever established in Alta California, other settlers did locate at presidios, at missions—San Gabriel, for example—and particularly on *ranchos*, which were privately owned and entirely separate from the civil settlements. Often, however, the owner's family would live in the nearby *pueblo*; therefore, one must include the *ranchos* as a part of the civil community during the Spanish period. When compared to the Mexican period, after 1821, the number of such holdings in the Spanish era was small.[43]

One grant for a *rancho* was made as early as 1775 to Manuel Butrón for land near Carmel, but most of these private holdings were established after 1784. In that year Governor Pedro Fages granted a *rancho* named "San Pedro," near the *pueblo* of Los Angeles, to Juan José Domínguez, and two others in the same vicinity, "San Rafael" and "Los Nietos," to José María Verdugo and Manuel Nieto, respectively. Thus began the pastoral era of Alta California, continuing with another grant in 1785, ten more in 1795, one in 1797, three in 1802, two in 1803, one in 1804, one in 1808, two in 1809, three in 1810, two in 1819, and three each in 1820 and 1821.[44]

Officials intended that *ranchos* should be granted primarily to disabled or retired military veterans. The grants were provisional; that is, title to the land was retained by the Spanish crown, although each owner received exclusive use of the land. It was specified that no person might have more than three *sitios*, or square leagues, of land,[45] and that it must be at least four leagues (about ten and one-half miles) from any presidio or *pueblo*. The grant could not encroach upon existing mission properties or lands, nor could it be near existing Indian *rancherías* (camps or temporary settlements). One stone house must be built upon the land, and at least two thousand head of cattle must be raised. A Californian who wished to become an owner of such property usually applied to the *alcalde*, or chief magistrate of his district. He and that official, along with two witnesses, personally measured the land by using a fifty-foot rope and marked the boundaries with stone piles. Other than the land itself, the *ranchero* received nothing from the government—no subsidy, no rations, and no livestock. He worked his grant at his own expense. Yet, the land and small herds of cattle were enough. Within a few years livestock on individual *ranchos* multiplied rapidly, ranging from fifteen hundred to two thousand horses and mules, two thousand to ten thousand head of cattle, and ten to twenty thousand sheep.[46]

The Spanish-speaking population of Alta California, referred to both as *gente de razón* and *gente decente* (both meaning civilized people), increased notably in the period from 1769 to 1821, but it never amounted to more than three thousand to thirty-five hundred people. Four years after the initial occupation, the total included only sixty-one soldiers, eleven Franciscan missionaries, and a few artisans, but no doctors, white laborers, or women. Six soldiers had married Indian women.[47] By 1779 there were five hundred persons of Spanish or mixed blood,[48] and the figure passed one thousand sometime between 1790 and 1800. By 1810 it was estimated at 2,130 persons, and ten years later at the end of the Spanish period there may have been 3,270 people in the province.[49] However, this number was about one-tenth of the population of New Mexico at the same time and an even smaller percentage of the figures for Nueva Vizcaya, Nuevo Santander, Sinaloa, and Sonora.

It should be noted that San José, Los Angeles, and Branciforte, although not necessarily prosperous, generally contained a large portion of the civilian set-

tlers. They each reflected some growth over the years, although that at Branciforte was insignificant. A comparison of the population figures for these three
settlements is given in Table 12.[50]

Table 12
Population of Civil Settlements in Alta California

Settlement	1777	1781	1790	1797	1800	1803	1810	1820
San José	68	..	78	..	170	...	110	240
Los Angeles	..	44	131	..	315	359	365	650
Branciforte	..	..	...	17	66	101	40	75

Residents in Alta California fell mainly into three groups: survivors or descendents of the original colonizers, those who retired from military service
at the nearby presidios, and immigrants recruited in Sonora and Sinaloa. After
the founding of Los Angeles in 1781, there was no major overland migration to
Alta California from the rest of New Spain. The original colonists emigrated
largely from the western and northwestern mainland provinces, principally
from Sinaloa, but with significant numbers from Sonora and a few from Jalisco;
hardly any came from Baja California.

These people have been described as a dissolute lot, largely of "worthless
character."[51] One official, commenting upon the character of the original
settlers of Branciforte recruited in Guadalajara, noted that their absence "for
a couple of centuries at a distance of a million leagues" would prove beneficial
to to the province of Jalisco and to the service of God and king.[52] In general,
most of these original settlers remained in the three civil communities, although a few migrated elsewhere, particularly in the case of the *villa* of Branciforte. Children of large families grew up and stayed in the *pueblos* of San José
and Los Angeles, and they, together with the retired soldiers and their families,
increased the population of these settlements.[53]

Convicts and orphans in limited numbers also were sent from New Spain
to Alta California. In 1791 three convicts were shipped to Monterey; twenty-
two more arrived in 1798. Nineteen orphans were sent from central New Spain
in 1800.[54] Neither convicts nor orphans were sent thereafter, and no official
measures were later taken by Spanish authorities to encourage immigration.[55]

The people of Alta California were divided into five major categories in
census reports. They were listed as Spaniards, Indians, mestizos, *colores quebrados*, and slaves.[56] "Spaniards" on this frontier, as on others of northern New
Spain, were principally those of white blood who claimed Spanish ancestry.
Only the governors, commanders of presidial establishments, and some of the
original soldier-settlers seem to have been natives of Spain. As for the mixed
bloods, including some people of Indian and Negro origins, there seems to
have been a differentiation between those who looked mostly white (mestizos)

and those who had an obvious color derivation (*colores quebrados*). However, together with the "Spaniards" they comprised the *gente decente* of the civil communities, although they were often looked down upon by the upper-class residents of the presidial settlements.[57] Otherwise, except for the official listing of the population in census returns, there seems to have been little class distinction or racial prejudice in the civil settlements of Alta California. What evolved was basically a two-class society consisting of *gente decente* on the one hand and Indians on the other.

Large families prevailed in Alta California as elsewhere. Anza's colonists in 1775–1776 averaged four children per family; two families had nine children each.[58] Fourteen families comprising sixty-eight persons, including forty children, settled San José in 1777.[59] Eleven *vecinos* and their households, totaling forty-four persons, established the *pueblo* of Los Angeles four years later.[60]

The civilian settlers in Alta California generally farmed, raised livestock, or practiced a trade. Agricultural products included wheat, corn, barley, chickpeas, and kidney beans. Fruit was apparently grown also in the *pueblo* of San José.[61] Irrigation by digging an *acequia madre*, or main ditch, was practiced in both Los Angeles and San José, using the waters of the Río de Porciúncula and Río de Guadalupe, respectively.[62]

Ranching and livestock raising became a principal occupation of the settlers. Each original pueblo grant provided for a distribution of riding animals as well as breeding stock. Together with the animals raised in great numbers on private *ranchos* and at missions, domestic livestock became the foundation of business enterprise in Alta California before 1821. Extracting tallow and tanning and selling hides were the main industries, although the hide trade did not really reach its peak until after Mexico gained independence. Horses, mules, cattle, sheep, pigs, and oxen abounded as early as 1791, when Alejandro Malaspina visited the province.[63] By 1800 there were 187,000 head of livestock, including 88,000 sheep, 74,000 cattle, 24,000 horses, and 1,000 mules.[64] Ten years later the total had almost doubled, reaching 337,388 head in all, comprising 121,988 cattle, 17,701 horses, 1,685 mules, and 197,014 sheep.[65] In fact, the increase was so rapid that it became necessary to kill surplus animals to prevent devastation of crops. Cattle were slaughtered at the San Francisco presidio as early as 1784, while surplus horses were killed after 1805 because they roamed over the San Joaquín Valley and other fields near established communities.[66] It is notable, too, that the numbers of cattle, sheep, horses, and mules far exceeded those in Baja California, an older region with a smaller civilian population and a climate less adaptable to the raising of crops and livestock.

As on other frontiers, Alta California had its share of artisans. Governor Pedro Fages encouraged the immigration of persons with various trades, primarily to instruct the Christianized Indians in their specialties. He asked specifically for carpenters, blacksmiths, armorers, masons, weavers, master mechanics, tanners, tailors, stonecutters, and potters; evidently Alta California received some twenty artisans before 1795, all under contracts supposedly of five years' duration and at an annual salary of 300 to 600 pesos.[67] Los Angeles in 1790 counted among its residents one mason, one tailor, two shoemakers, one blacksmith, and one master mechanic. Throughout the province in the same year there were two silversmiths, five miners, two master mechanics, five carpenters, three blacksmiths, six tailors, two masons, eight shoemakers, and one doctor.[68]

Mission industries also supplemented the work of the artisans and other colonists. By 1797 Indians were weaving woolen cloth and tanning hides. Carpentry and masonry were practiced by trained Indians at San Carlos, blacksmithing at San Francisco, tanning at Santa Clara, and flour-milling at both San Luis Obispo and Santa Cruz.[69]

Land was of primary concern to settlers engaged in agriculture and stock raising, since both San José and Los Angeles were established for the purpose of creating agricultural self-sufficiency in Alta California and reducing its dependency upon the trade from San Blas. The original grants to each of these *pueblos* provided not only for building lots but also fields and common lands. Authorities made provisional grants of one house lot, two tracts of land for cultivation, and two more for pasture and a loan of farming tools. Grants were confirmed to the original settlers in these communities after five years of occupancy and tangible improvements, in which period the settler could not sell or transfer any part of his allotment.[70]

Private grants of *rancho* properties to settlers were made largely to encourage the raising of livestock, and they were always situated beyond the *pueblos*, missions, and presidios. They were not to exceed three square leagues of land in all, and were worked completely at the owner's expense without salary, rations, or livestock provided by the government, as was the case with community grants.[71] Title to all land, however, remained in the hands of the crown, although this was more symbolic than actual in the case of both community and ranching grants.[72]

Historians and other authors often have described California's history in the Spanish era as the "Romantic Period," as though settlers led an idyllic, peaceful, orderly existence.[73] Life on this remote frontier was anything but ideal. It was a daily challenge, a matter of survival at first and subsistence in later years. Problems of all sorts beset the colonists, and the continued occupation of the region was occasionally in doubt. Lack of adequate transportation and communications facilities, primitive educational arrangements, hazards to health with little to combat them, a sparse population scattered over hundreds of square miles, and limited commercial opportunities inhibited the growth and development of Alta California. As was true on all the northern frontier of New Spain, citizens were faced with the necessity of hard, unrewarding work, in addition to long periods of neglect on the part of Spanish officials both in Mexico City and in Spain. Everyday life in the *pueblos* revolved around the often boring, arduous tasks of farming or raising livestock; the hard-working colonist was nothing like the romanticized stereotype of the suave, sophisticated gentleman farmer. If any California aristocracy existed, it was confined to the presidios or to the *ranchos*.[74] Spanish *pobladores* were a poor lot, practicing a subsistence economy, and settled in isolated settlements where there was neither frequent contact with the outside world nor opportunity to change either one's residence or occupation.

Although fashions changed over the years then as now, basic articles of clothing remained essentially the same. By the early nineteenth century men wore a dark-colored, broad-brimmed hat, a short jacket, sometimes a waistcoat, knee breeches, and white stockings, or perhaps trousers slashed below the knee. Deerskin leggings, shoes, a red sash, and a *serape* completed this ensemble. Women dressed in a loose-fitting, short-sleeved gown of silk, crepe, or calico, a bright-colored belt, satin or kid shoes, and always wore a *rebozo*, or shawl, indoors. In womanly fashion, they adorned their clothing with lace and themselves with necklaces and earrings, occasionally a high comb in the hair if married. They generally wore their hair in long braids before marriage and done up on top of the head afterwards.[75] These descriptions, however, pertain to the more affluent people of Alta California; the dress of the average colonist was much simpler.

Food for the *paisanos* consisted largely of beef, red beans, and *tortillas* or other corn products. Those of greater means added chocolate, milk, or coffee to the diet, but wine was not in wide use because of its high cost.[76] Prices of foods, judged by modern standards, were reasonable, but for simple folk eking out a day-to-day existence they must have been high. One dozen quail, for example, cost one-quarter of a peso (2 *reales*); jerked beef, about three cents a pound; fresh beef, only a penny; and eggs, twenty-four cents a dozen.[77] Alejandro Malaspina noted some food costs during his official visit on the coast of Alta California in 1791:

pound of cheese	one-half *real*
fanega of wheat	2 pesos
fanega of corn	1 peso, 4 *reales*
fanega of barley	1 peso
fanega of kidney beans	2 pesos, 4 *reales*
arroba of common flour	1 peso, 2 *reales*
arroba of prime flour	2 pesos
arroba of jerked beef	6 *reales*
arroba of fresh meat	2 *reales*
one chicken	1 *real*[78]

Prices were evidently regulated by law to establish uniformity, prevent unfair charges, and ensure that all Californians could purchase needed goods on the

A presidial soldier of Monterey at the time of the Malaspina visit to Alta California, 1791. Drawing by José Cardero. *Courtesy Bancroft Library, University of California.*

Wife of a presidial soldier of Monterey at the time of the Malaspina visit to Alta California in 1791. Drawing by José Cardero. *Courtesy Bancroft Library, University of California*.

local market. Authorities issued regulations periodically and had price lists posted in public places to prevent overcharging.[79]

Social life in these frontier settlements was spiced occasionally by the visits of foreign vessels, celebrations of religious or other special holidays, and sporting events, as well as periodic scandals and love affairs. Before 1786 only Spanish vessels visited the province, but foreign visitors later included Frenchmen, Englishmen, Spaniards, Russians, and "Bostonses," or merchantmen from the new United States of America (the Spaniards assumed that all of them came from Boston). The Comte de la Pérouse of France was among the first of the foreign visitors to pause in Alta California; he stopped at Monterey and visited nearby Carmel during his voyage along the California coast in the late summer of 1786. His journey, although opening communications for Californians with the outside world and providing excellent descriptions of the northern part of the province, is misleading when the civil settlements are considered. La Pérouse never visited any of them and his reports concerning such communities are often erroneous and incomplete. For instance, he noted that there was only one Spanish *pueblo* in all of Alta California, when in reality there were two at that time. Again, he noted incorrectly that "New California, in spite of its fertility, has not yet a single colonist,"[80] when indeed hundreds of them had settled there in the decade preceding his visit.

Malaspina visited Alta California on his extensive exploratory and scientific voyage to the Pacific in 1791. He and his two small vessels remained in port for two weeks, in which period the meticulous Malaspina and his officers noted much about the presidios, missions, and *pueblos* of Alta California. Malaspina described the presidio of Monterey in detail, noted its personnel, and concluded that it was a fully developed military establishment. He praised the mission system, especially the self-sacrifice of the Franciscan missionaries and the economic achievements of each mission. However, he was not impressed with the Indians. Although he noted that they were skillful hunters, they had no concept of private property and he thought the "Indians of the Mission of Monterey are the stupidest, as well as the ugliest and filthiest, that can be found."[81] During this visit, Malaspina's men observed daily *novilladas* (bullfights with young bulls) in the plaza of the presidio of Monterey, purchased fruit from the settlers of San José, buried an American sailor from one of their own ships, and compiled statistics on population, livestock, and food prices within the province.[82] When they departed on September 26, 1791, the Catholic fathers gave benedictions on their behalf, cannons were fired, and the people crowded to the dockside to give the visitors a rousing send-off.[83] From this visit and its report one may gather that Californians welcomed such an opportunity for diversion from the routine of everyday life.

The famous English navigator George Vancouver spent considerable time in Alta California on his Pacific voyages in the period from 1792 to 1794. His three visits in the province took him from San Francisco to San Diego, although his comments upon life there principally dwelt upon the missions and presidios. However, he did note that the *pueblos* differed notably from the other settlements. They were composed, according to Vancouver, principally of old Spanish or Creole soldiers who had served their time and had no further military obligations. Grants of land were made to them to raise corn and cattle, to support the neighboring presidios as well as themselves. In general, he noted that each *pueblo* had thirty or forty old soldiers, together with their families; he added that they could be considered as a citizen militia to help in the defense of the province.[84]

Visits from United States ships began in 1788 with the arrival at Monterey of the *Columbia* and *Lady Washington*, commanded by Captains James Kendrick and Robert Gray, respectively. (Unreported trading vessels may have visited Monterey earlier.) Thereafter, many vessels stopped in Alta California, and the residents became quite familiar with New Englanders—so familiar, in fact, that the term "Boston" became synonymous with the United States, as noted earlier.[85] Yet, few if any of these visitors ever managed to see San José and Los Angeles, remaining largely in the port communities.

These visits broke the monotony of life in Alta California and provided residents their initial contact with the outside world. They were also opportunities to celebrate, to relax from daily pursuits, and participate in dancing, gambling, musical presentations, and sporting events. The presence of foreigners was sometimes exciting in other ways. Two notable examples occurred during the early nineteenth century.

Nikolai Petrovitch Rezanov of the Russian American Company at Sitka, Alaska, came to San Francisco on April 5, 1805, in search of supplies to relieve the severe food shortage of his own colony and to try to open a regular trade with Spanish California. When the governor of Alta California, José Joaquín de Arrillaga, came up from Monterey to meet Rezanov and prevent him from trading with the Spanish settlements, his efforts were interrupted by Concepción, the sixteen-year-old daughter of the presidial commandant of San Francisco. Rezanov was attracted by her beauty and sparkling personality. Also, he saw a way to win the desired commercial concessions through her. He courted her openly for six weeks, finally asking for her hand in marriage. Concepción consented, but her family and the Franciscan friars objected, principally because of the differing faiths of the lovers. A marriage contract was drawn up, but the sacrament was never consummated. Rezanov, having by now obtained the needed provisions, sailed for Sitka on May 21, and died two years later in Russia. Concepción did not learn of his death until 1842; she had never married, long awaiting his return. Finally, she entered a convent at Benicia and died there in 1857.[86] The entire episode captured public interest in a matter of considerable social significance for its time.

Excitement of a different sort came with the arrival of Hippolyte de Bouchard during the period of the Latin-American wars for independence. He conducted a naval raid on Alta California in November and December, 1818. Two vessels entered Monterey bay on November 21, and a battle ensued. Bouchard demanded the surrender of the entire province. His force landed, stayed on shore a week, and then ruthlessly pillaged and burned the settlement before departing. He landed again at Santa Bárbara and later threatened the coastal settlements to the south. The episode aroused Californians to defend themselves and brought the distant fighting of the Latin-American patriots to the very doorstep of this remote province. Yet, it was the only episode when Californians became directly involved in these struggles, and the residents were more alarmed at Bouchard's actions than interested in becoming patriots and helping overthrow the royal government.[87]

Foreign visits were not the only occasions for great celebrations. Picnics, folk dances accompanied by violins and guitars, *fandangos*, bullfights, horse races, rodeos, and sporting events were held to celebrate certain holidays or achievements. The arrival of a new governor was often the occasion for extensive ceremonies. The last Spanish governor of Alta California, Pablo Vicente de Solá, was greeted with gala festivities in 1815. When he reached Monterey there was a military reception in his honor held in the plaza of the presidio, followed by a formal reception where twenty *señoritas* advanced to kiss his hand. Next, a great feast was served. Then a space was cleared for the popular presidial and *pueblo* sport of fighting between bulls and bears. This was a common pastime in both San José and Los Angeles, where a wooden barrier was erected around the sides of the plaza, and a platform for spectators was built outside the barrier. The bull and the bear were then introduced into the enclosure, with the hind foot of the bear attached by a rope to the forefoot of the bull. Although the bull was often urged on by *toreadores*, the bear was usually the victor in such encounters. Processions, cockfighting, horse racing, and gambling were other popular forms of entertainment among the colonists in Alta California.[88]

Women occasionally contributed to the local gossip and excitement on the social scene. Concepción Arguello's love affair with Rezanov already has been noted. The decade of the 1780s was dominated by the actions of the tempestuous Doña Eulalia de Callis, wife of Pedro Fages, governor of the province from 1782 to 1791. A fiery Catalan like her husband, she at first refused to accompany her spouse to his new post and did not make the long journey from Loreto to Monterey until six months after he took office. Her coming was a great occasion for the settlers, and many receptions were held in her honor. Doña Eulalia, however, was shocked by the nakedness of the Indians and began giving away her clothes, but stopped when she was reminded that she could not replenish her wardrobe. After the birth of a daughter in August, 1784, she insisted that her husband send her back to civilization in New Spain. He refused, and she threw him out of her apartments for three months. Accusing him of "playing" with a servant girl, she publicly proclaimed his infidelity to the populace from the streets of Monterey. She announced that she would get a divorce, but at this point the friars intervened. They said they could find no grounds for divorce, whereupon Doña Eulalia locked herself in her rooms with her son and daughter, vowing not to return to her husband. Governor Fages in a fit of rage broke down the door and threatened to tie her up if she would not go to the mission at San Carlos of her own will. She finally consented to go, but after her arrival there she still proved an unruly female, to say the least. She displayed frequent public outbursts during the conduct of church services, for which the friars threatened to flog her and put her in chains. At long last, she became convinced that the charges she had made against her husband were untrue, and the two were reconciled in September, 1785. Later she petitioned authorities to remove her husband from office on the grounds of ill health, but nothing came of her request, and Governor Fages initiated his own request for removal early in 1790.[89]

Education during the Spanish period in Alta California was sporadic and rudimentary in content. Secular schools were established to supplement those at the missions, which were mostly for Indians, in the latter part of the eighteenth century and the early years of the nineteenth. Parental indifference and Franciscan opposition to popular education had to be overcome by persistent effort. Only two governors of Alta California, Diego de Borica (1794 to 1800) and Pablo Vicente de Solá (1815 to 1822), conscientiously pushed the cause of secular education. They did succeed in establishing some schools, providing at least a foundation for popular education, even though the schools seem to have barely existed from one year to the next, and their academic competence was indeed questionable.

Much of the early population of the frontier province was unlettered. Few of the original settlers in any of the civil communities could write their names or read a single line, and in the case of the first colonists in Los Angeles, none could do so. About one-third of the soldiers at the presidios and in the mission garrisons could read and write.[90]

King Carlos IV of Spain in 1793 ordered that all towns of the Spanish viceroyalties in the Americas should establish schools, primarily to teach the Indians to read and write. Governor Borica tried hard to establish primary schools in all the presidios and *pueblos* of Alta California, hiring teachers from the military forces if necessary. He ordered that each *vecino* in the *pueblos* contribute two pesos a year to support the school and the teacher's salary. These schools were "to teach the Christian doctrine" and to provide fundamental training in reading and writing at such hours that the children might be free part of the time to help with work in the fields.[91]

Governor Borica's order prompted the establishment of the first primary schools in Alta California. San José led the way in December, 1794, founding a school in a public granary, where a retired sergeant named Manuel Vargas taught. Although attendance was compulsory and a tax of thirty-one cents per month per scholar was ordered for the maintenance of the school, San Diego evidently lured Vargas away with an annual salary of 250 pesos to teach their children on a regular basis. The government supplied the paper for the schools; the curriculum consisted largely of learning the catechism, reading, and writing. Strangely, there is no evidence of Alta California children studying simple arithmetic in these early schools, making their curriculum somewhat different from that in other frontier regions. Corporal Manuel Boranda, a carpenter by trade, taught the children of the San Francisco presidio gratuitously. In February, 1796, there were twenty-seven children attending Ramón Lasso de la Vega's school at San José; four of them paid nothing and the remainder, two and one-half *reales* a month. The *pueblo* provided a house for the teacher and his family. At Santa Bárbara there were thirty-two children in school, and the teacher earned an annual salary of 125 pesos, whereas Vargas at San Diego had twenty-two pupils and a reduced salary of $100 by that time. These schools continued at least until 1797, but their existence and progress in the years thereafter is unknown.[92]

These four schools seem to have been the only ones before the turn of the nineteenth century. Parental opposition to having children removed from their charge, the lack of trained teachers, inadequate facilities, and financial support consisting almost entirely of family contributions seem to have made each school's existence highly precarious. Governor José Joaquín de Arrillaga (1800 to 1814) was neither interested in promoting colonization (except for twenty foundlings, ten boys and ten girls who were "fond of cigars") nor furthering popular education in the province.[93]

There seems to have been no early school in Los Angeles, but the one in San José apparently continued on a yearly basis. A contract between the residents of that community and one Rafael Villavicencio as teacher in 1811 outlines the responsibilities of the instructor as well as those of the citizens and provides a detailed list of operational procedures at the school. Villavicencio was to be paid eighteen *reales* a year by each householder (the payment could be made in grain or flour) in return for his teaching the Christian doctrine, reading, and writing to their sons. Authorities were instructed to assemble the eligible children and bring them to the teacher for instruction. Six hours of school—three in the morning from eight to eleven o'clock and three more in the afternoon from two to five o'clock—were provided for, and attendance was compulsory. In the event of any child's absence, the teacher was instructed to inform the parents, who, in turn, were to provide reasons for his missing school. If any child missed twice, village authorities were to force the parents to send their negligent child to school immediately. While there, pupils were responsible "to God" only under the supervision of the teacher, but parents were advised to examine the children at home to see if they were making progress. If no improvement was noted, then parents should complain to the authorities, since Villavicencio was to devote himself exclusively to the instruction for which he was being paid.[94]

Governor Solá showed considerable interest in public education during his term in office, re-establishing primary schools at each of the four presidios and in both *pueblos* by 1817–1818. Settlers or retired soldiers taught reading, writing, and ciphering. There were also separate schools for boys and girls in Santa Bárbara. Solá urged the establishment of a college for Indian boys along the lines of others in New Spain, but he received no encouragement from Mexico City. Undaunted, he then turned to recommending books for use in the schools, furnished students copies of the *Gaceta de Mexico*, decrees of the Spanish Cortes, fiction such as *Don Quijote*, and even a copy of the liberal Spanish Constitution of 1812. These works were intended primarily for developing the student's reading ability, but their contents would be of doubtful value in a primary school. Governor Solá often visited the schools and had students come to his office in Monterey to discuss what they had read and learned.[95]

Mariano Guadalupe Vallejo, later one of Alta California's most important landowners and political figures, received his primary education in the Spanish period at one of these schools, the one in Monterey where Corporal Miguel Archuleta was the teacher. Vallejo described the school, its curriculum, and the methods of instruction. A one-room adobe house with crude benches along the walls served as a schoolhouse; the teacher sat on a raised platform at one end. Students began the day by kissing the hand of the schoolmaster and saying a *bendito* (prayer beginning with a blessing) to a picture of a saint. They recited their lessons when called upon by the teacher, usually standing and repeating in a loud voice what they had learned by rote. They studied a primer for six months to a year and then spent the next six months reading a book pertaining to Christian doctrine. Also, they read manuscript letters, learned to make straight marks and write basic words, studied the four fundamental rules of arithmetic, and learned the Christian doctrine by heart, repeating it in a singsong manner. The teacher beat the student's hand with a ferrule for mistakes. He used a hemp lash with iron points for more serious offenses, such as laughing aloud, running in the street, truancy, spilling ink, or failure to know the Christian doctrine. Instruction took place every weekday, with Saturday reserved for examinations.[96]

Although these schools provided some primary education for a limited number of people in Alta California, most of the population remained unlettered to the end of the Spanish period. An example of this lack of education may be found in the Vallejo documents in the Bancroft Library, where records of the presidio of San Francisco in the period from 1799 to 1812 show that only eight of fifty-one soldiers, some of whom came from the civil communities, could even sign their names. Not one person from the whole *villa* of Branciforte could read or write.[97]

Medical practices and developments were primitive throughout Alta California during the Spanish era. Epidemics of one disease or another were evident as early as the first decade of settlement. Smallpox, perhaps introduced by foreign visitors, apparently became a yearly menace after 1781, when it was reported at Loreto in Baja California and at San Gabriel in Alta California.[98] Some military and naval physicians, frequently called "surgeons," were present at times. Pedro Prat on the *San Carlos* participated in the initial occupation of the region in 1769, and he helped treat the scurvy that broke out on that voyage. Other physicians came to reside principally at San Francisco and Monterey, but only one doctor was noted among the civil population at the *pueblo* of Los Angeles in 1790.[99] Manuel Gutiérrez de Quijano, originally from Madrid, was a private practitioner in Monterey from 1807 to 1824, treating a wide variety of illnesses and injuries, ranging from wounds inflicted by bears to vaccination against smallpox.[100] Guitérrez de Quijano had a license to practice medicine from Spanish authorities as early as 1799.[101]

Without any doubt the most significant single medical achievement in the entire Spanish period was the introduction of vaccination against smallpox. Five years after Edward Jenner's original publication in Europe of his theories concerning smallpox vaccination, Spain organized its extensive expedition, under the direction of the court physician Francisco Xavier de Balmis, to carry vaccine to the Spanish colonies in the New World. Although some inoculation was performed as early as 1806 in Alta California, José Veredia brought the first vaccine to the province in 1817, considerably later than it was introduced into the provinces of the central and eastern portions of the northern frontier. He and resident physician Gutiérrez de Quijano vaccinated a "large number of persons", including forty children, during the last year of Spanish administration in the province.[102]

Transportation and communications for colonists in Alta California were generally primitive and a hindrance to development of the region. Sea traffic with San Blas and other ports of New Spain was so infrequent and undependable that there were serious food shortages in the early years of settlement.[103] After the founding of the agricultural *pueblos* of San José and Los Angeles, however, one hears less about this problem. Land transportation between Alta California and the rest of New Spain was not only a lengthy proposition but an arduous one. Two major routes existed, one overland to Loreto in Baja California, and the other to Sonora and Sinaloa via the junction of the Colorado and Gila rivers. The latter route was closed after the Yuma Indians rose in rebellion in 1781. Within the province itself there were public highways called *caminos reales*, but they were mere trails. Also, colonists could not travel without a passport authorizing each trip. Transportation on roads or in villages was by foot, horse, mule, or cart. Bridges over *arroyos*, creeks, and rivers were constructed of either wooden poles or earth. Most were between Monterey and San Francisco, and the greatest bridge-building era seems to have been from 1797 to 1816.[104] However, neither the viceregal nor provincial government built or financed bridges, as governments today do. Authorities might order the building of bridges or roads, but they regarded them as being of local interest, use, and benefit; therefore, local labor and community funds or assessments were used to construct and maintain such public works.[105]

Communications were largely restricted to the official postal service and irregular contacts by sea with the mainland of New Spain. The large number of people who could neither read nor write reduced the importance of this problem, but official correspondence and local exchanges of information were still necessary. Soldier-couriers had begun carrying the mail between Monterey and Loreto as early as 1775. By 1793 this service had been regularized so that the distance of approximately fourteen hundred miles could be covered in twenty days, and an extension to San Francisco had been established. Soldiers left the San Francisco presidio on the first of every month and were replaced at Monterey by others who carried the mail southward. There was a regular schedule by day and hour of arrival for each mission, presidio, and *pueblo*, and couriers generally had an hour of rest at each station. In fact, this mail service resembled the famous Pony Express from Saint Joseph, Missouri, to Sacramento, which operated in the period from 1860 to 1861. *Habilitados* (paymasters) acted as postmasters at the Spanish presidios and received eight per cent of the gross receipts for their services; *alcaldes* or other administrative officials of communities performed the task of local postmasters. These persons were responsible for the official franking of letters, except for those sent by the friars, which were allowed to go free, a privilege reportedly abused by the padres. Mail service between the missions was usually provided by Indian runners, not by soldiers. Dispatches by sea were often delayed by lack of shipping, although both Spanish and foreign vessels were employed for mail service. In 1783 a contract was let with a privately owned company to provide regular mail service by sea between Loreto and Santa Cruz. Small boats made twelve round trips a year over this route, thus helping to overcome the problem of communications between Alta California and the center of viceregal authority.[106]

Civilian settlers in Alta California seem not to have developed local handicrafts and arts to any advanced degree, such as that achieved in the folk art of the New Mexican *paisanos*. Perhaps the sparse population, the hard agricultural work, the lack of a ready market for locally produced items, and the contact with foreigners who could supply most needed goods all retarded such development. Nothing is known about the existence of early painting and sculpture in the *pueblos*, although religious art objects and paintings are mentioned occasionally. Yet, it is obvious that music, principally that of violin and guitar, was readily available and that dancing was a popular pastime. The architecture of the *pueblos* was like that of the presidios, although the civil communities were not walled cities laid out in a square and they were less compact than were the presidios. Single-storied adobe houses with whitewashed walls and roofs of asphalt or red tiles predominated. Small barred windows allowed some light to penetrate interiors. Houses in town usually did not have interior courtyards or gardens, although some of the more pretentious homes did.[107]

Alta California's two *pueblos* and single *villa* were beset with all sorts of problems and internal disorders. Crime was a constant threat. Civil settlements seemed prone to four kinds of crime or transgression: gambling, immorality, and slothfulness on the part of the colonists and horse-stealing on the part of the Indians.[108] Gambling was common, and adultery was frequent. Settlers Sebastián Alvitre of Los Angeles and Francisco Ávila of San José spent considerable time in prisons, exile, or at forced labor because of their illicit relations with Indian women or the wives of their neighbors. Despite legal restrictions on their local production, wine and brandy were produced, especially in the vicinity of San José, and one settler obviously operated a still.[109] More serious crimes such as murder and incest were punishable by death (the sentence executed usually by firearms), exile, and hard labor. Flogging and confinement to the stocks for a designated number of hours were the usual punishments for lesser offenses. The *villa* of Branciforte was evidently a haven for dissolute, immoral characters and petty criminals. Regulations issued for this settlement on July 17, 1797, prohibited gambling, drunkenness, concubinage, and communications with the nearby Indian villages. Residents were required to attend mass on all holy days of obligation, and every Sunday they had to stand a general inspection of themselves, their arms and implements, and all of their possessions to ensure that stolen articles were returned to their rightful owners.[110]

Idleness in the civil settlements was a constant concern to outside observers, especially the Franciscan missionaries. Colonists at Branciforte in 1798–1799 were rebuked for their laziness.[111] Father Isidro Alonso Salazar wrote Viceroy Branciforte in May, 1796, to advise him of conditions at San José and Los Angeles. He reported:

> The two towns founded twenty years ago have made no advancement. The people are a set of idlers. For them, the Indian is an errand boy, *vaquero* [cowboy], and digger of ditches . . . . Confident that the Gentiles are working, the settlers pass the day singing. The young men wander on horseback through the *rancherías* soliciting the women to immorality.[112]

In the same month and year another clerical official observed the nature of life in the *pueblos*. Unimpressed, he wrote:

In Alta California the pueblos hardly deserve the name, so formless and embryonic is their state. The cause is scant relish for work on the part of the settlers. One is more likely to find in their hands a deck of cards than the spade or the plow. For them the Gentile sows, ploughs, reaps, and gathers the harvest. . . .[113]

Missionary opposition to civil settlements and their colonists neither prevented their establishment nor their continued existence and growth. The above comments reflect exaggeration and bias, yet they are useful also in pointing out that the *paisanos* of California competed for the use of Indian labor and contributed to the immorality of the province. Settlements endured not only missionary criticism, but natural disasters, such as floods, earthquakes, plagues, epidemics, and invasions of locusts, yet they continued to exist. San José and Los Angeles, founded to raise crops and livestock as a contribution to the agricultural self-sufficiency of Alta California,[114] not only seemed to resolve the problem of food shortages but survived to grow into great cities. Branciforte, although not nearly so successful a community as the other two, eventually became a part of Santa Cruz.

The *paisanos* of Alta California were principally agriculturalists and ranchers. They succeeded in establishing the agricultural and stock-raising industries in the province long before Spanish control ended. Because the interior valleys and mountain regions were largely ignored by settlers, there was no major mining activity during the colonial years. The Spanish population, originally fewer than one hundred, swelled to over three thousand people by the end of fifty years of Spanish occupation. This figure equaled the total number of colonists living in Texas at the same time, but was far less than that of New Mexico, Nueva Vizcaya, Sinaloa, and Sonora. However, the number of Spanish and mixed-blood residents in Alta California easily outstripped the civilian population of either Baja California or Pimería Alta.

In addition to establishing permanent civil communities and *ranchos* in northern and southern portions of the province, the Spanish settlers of Alta California helped to hold it for the mother country. Isolated from the rest of New Spain, they were exposed to foreign encroachment, largely through trade. This encouraged the development of a feeling of self-sufficiency; although not as pronounced as in New Mexico, there was an attitude of frontier independence, a disdain or lack of concern with the course of events in Spain or in Mexico City. Civilian settlers in Alta California easily accepted Mexican independence in 1821, just as their descendants welcomed the arrival of the Anglo-Americans twenty-five years later.

The two *pueblos* and lone *villa* of Alta California, along with the *ranchos* of the countryside, were permanent products of the Spanish colonial era. They occupied a significant place beside the mission and the presidio in the settlement, growth, and continuance of frontier California.

PART V
Conclusions

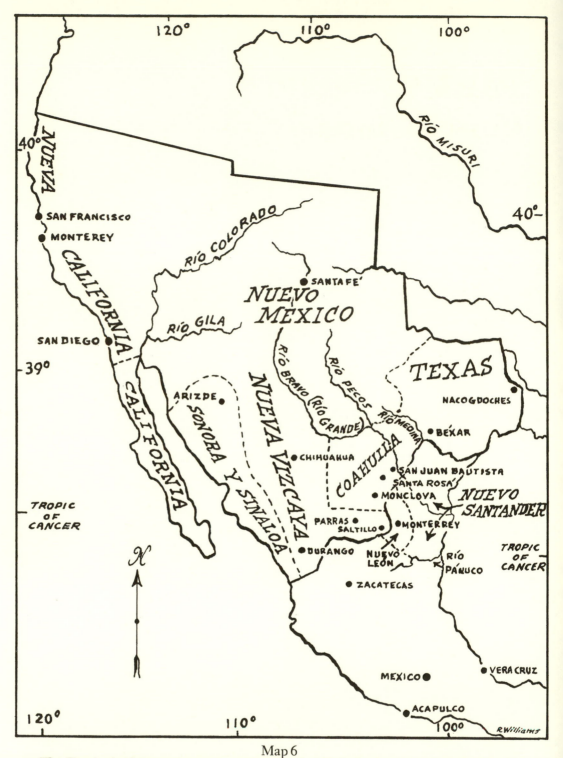

Map 6

The Provincias Internas, according to Fray Juan Agustín de Morfi. Adapted from
Fray Juan Agustín de Morfi, *Viaje de indios y diario del Nuevo México*, ed. Vito
Alessio Robles, 2d ed (México, D.F., Antigua Libreria Robredo y José Porrúa e
Hijos, 1935), frontispiece.

11. Los Paisanos

Spanish-speaking settlers of the frontier communities in northern New Spain were an important part of centuries-long Spanish expansion. Unfortunately, their role has been neglected, while historians have emphasized that of explorers, missionaries, government officials, and presidial soldiers. Yet settlers and their communities were integral parts of the Spanish frontier experience. They were closely related to familiar institutions, especially the presidio, because of the use of soldier-settlers to colonize remote regions. Still they provided a more permanent settlement base in the long run, usually outliving both the mission and the presidio.

Within a few years after a new region had been opened to missionary and military establishments, royal authorities permitted the founding of civil settlements. Often, as in the cases of Culiacán in Sinaloa, La Bahía del Espíritu Santo in Texas, and most locations in Sonora, the first settlers were presidial soldiers and their families. These soldier-settlers provided the nucleus around which the community expanded. Population was augmented by immigration and natural increase. Also soldiers who subsequently retired from active duty at nearby presidios frequently settled in these towns. Within a generation or two, the number of civilian colonists came to exceed that of other Spanish representatives on the frontiers of New Spain.

Not only were these citizens more numerous than members of military and religious establishments, but they contributed in many ways to the expansion and consolidation of Spain's holdings in America. First, they were the initial true frontiersmen on the continent of North America, in the sense of coming into new regions for the purpose of establishing permanent homes. Their frontier experience preceded that of the Anglo-Americans by anywhere from a few years to as much as a century. Second, they transmitted the rudiments of European civilization, especially the characteristics of Spanish culture, to a far-flung region over three times the size of Spain itself. They brought their language, social customs, traditions, religion, working habits, crops, and livestock to the frontiers ranging from Nuevo Santander and Texas to the two Californias. Third, they proved to be innovators, adapting to their environment on each frontier. Their isolation from the earlier settled regions of New Spain and from each other forced them to adjust, and this often led, as in New

Mexico, to the development of folk art and a culture of their own. Farming methods, labor, architecture, vehicles, public works, and even local celebrations were all affected by the new circumstances. Settlers of a Spanish heritage had to adapt to the frontier's peculiar conditions. Fourth, confronted with isolation, constant threats from marauding Indians, and foreign encroachment, they developed personal characteristics and an entire culture that differed markedly from those elsewhere in the viceroyalty, particularly from the residents of Mexico City. On the one hand, they were more dependent upon royal authority to assist in founding their settlements and to supply them with the necessary goods to begin life in a new environment. On the other hand, they became more self-reliant, more individualistic, less class conscious, and more conservative in their political outlook than the people of central New Spain. Fifth, they established and maintained permanent settlements that served not only as urban centers for each province but as focal points for administration, economic activity, and further expansion. Indeed, Spanish settlements were truly urban-rural communities, in that the town was where the colonists resided, while the gardens, agricultural plots, and livestock pastures outside them were where they worked. Finally, these settlers became the nucleus of the Spanish-speaking population in what is today northern Mexico as well as the southwestern United States. When waves of Mexican immigrants came later to the United States, particularly in the period from 1900 to 1930, it was only natural that these people should locate at least in part near such older Spanish-speaking communities as San Antonio, Albuquerque, Santa Fé, Los Angeles, and San José.

There were many types of civil settlements on the frontier of New Spain. They ranged from the important *ciudades* and *villas* to the smaller communities variously called *pueblos, poblaciones, plazas,* and *puestos. Reales de minas,* such as Durango, Parral, and Chihuahua, sometimes became important civil settlements. It should be noted, however, that this kind of community was significant mostly in Nueva Vizcaya and to a lesser extent in Sonora. Farming and livestock raising dominated the lives of most colonists in frontier New Spain. *Haciendas* and *ranchos* also became important centers of Spanish civilization, especially in Coahuila, Texas, Nuevo Santander, New Mexico, Nueva Vizcaya, Sonora, Sinaloa, and Alta California. However, it should be noted that the *hacienda* system was not as widespread as were the *ranchos;* the *hacienda* flourished in the Central Plateau region, but never in the area north of the present Mexican boundary.

Although there were all sorts of regulations to promote standardization in the founding and administration of frontier communities, the fact is that they were not all alike. The detailed laws served only as guidelines for the basic orientation of towns, the location and sizes of plazas, and the allotment of lands to individuals. Beyond that, the locations of settlements, sizes of plots, street measurements and orientations, and erection of public buildings varied from one community to another, and indeed from one frontier to the next.

With the exception of New Mexico, the northern frontier of New Spain was settled by a process of gradual expansion. On the Pacific frontier, Baja California was occupied almost a century before Alta California; indeed, the older province became the point of departure for the settlement of the newer one. In the northwest, settlement of Sinaloa began in 1531 at Culiacán, the oldest frontier community considered in this book. Once Sinaloa had been settled, pacified, and consolidated, colonists moved into Sonora, and finally into Pimería Alta, a district of Sonora then, but today divided between Sonora and Arizona. The north central frontier, composed of Nueva Vizcaya and New Mexico, was first settled in the southern portion near Durango, with colonization reaching northward to the *real de minas* of Parral by 1631. However, by then Spanish settlers had already advanced into New Mexico, occupying it until 1680, when the Pueblo revolt forced them to retreat southward, thereby contributing to the growth of El Paso del Norte, today comprising Ciudad Juárez and its neighboring towns downriver along the Río Grande. In the eighteenth century settlers from southern Nueva Vizcaya moved northward into the present state of Chihuahua. Finally, on the northeastern frontier the process of gradual expansion is illustrated by the early occupation of southern Coahuila (the Saltillo-Parras district) and Nuevo León almost simultaneously, followed by the later settling of northern Coahuila, near Monclova. Then came the occupation of Texas, and finally the filling in of the unoccupied region known then as Nuevo Santander—today's Tamaulipas and southern Texas. All in all, the predominant direction of Spanish expansion was from south to north. Although the frontier moved steadily northward, vast spaces between settlements were left unoccupied.

It is obvious that the greatest burst of activity occurred in the eighteenth century. Sonora, Pimería Alta, Texas, Alta California, northern Nueva Vizcaya (Chihuahua), and Nuevo Santander were settled during the last one hundred years of the viceroyalty of New Spain. When we consider that Coahuila was also detached from Nueva Vizcaya, and Sinaloa and Sonora from the same province in 1734, it is evident that over one-half of the provinces considered in this study were either occupied originally or established administratively during the eighteenth century. Yet, the population growth of the older, more established provinces probably meant that the majority of the Spanish-speaking settlers on the northern frontier lived in these more pacified and consolidated regions.

Total population, although sparse in some areas, was in reality much larger than has been supposed. Naturally, the original number of settlers in each community, district, or province was quite small. Since all regions were not occupied until the latter half of the eighteenth century and reliable census figures are not available until then, no over-all estimate of the whole frontier population is possible until that time. If we allow for slight differences of years in the period from 1760 to 1800, when figures were given for separate provinces, and take into account some estimates derived from miscellaneous reports, it would appear that the population of the northern frontier of New Spain was approximately 417,000 persons. Since Alexander von Humboldt reported the total inhabitants of New Spain at 4,483,559 in 1794,[1] it may, therefore, be concluded that the frontier provinces accounted for almost ten per cent of the population.

Of course, the colonists were concentrated largely in certain regions, some being far more populous than others. By province, the total population in the period from 1760 to 1800 is indicated in Table 13.

Table 13
Population in Frontier Provinces
1760–1800

Province/Region	Year	Population
Nueva Vizcaya	1780	228,000
Sonora	1783	46,077
Sinaloa	1783	41,567
New Mexico	1790	30,953
Nuevo Santander	1795	30,450
Nuevo León	1760	20,523
Coahuila	1787	15,272
Texas	1792	2,992
Alta California	1790–1800	1,000
Baja California	1790–1800	500
Total		417,334

By 1821 the total had risen to approximately 474,000 people, or about eight per cent of New Spain's total population of 5,877,420.[2] This expansion is shown for the period from 1815 to 1821 in Table 14.

Table 14
Population in Frontier Provinces
1815–1821

Province	Year	Population
Nueva Vizcaya	1815	190,564
Sonora and Sinaloa	1815	123,854
Nuevo León	1815	26,000
Coahuila	1815	50,600
Nuevo Santander	1815	38,000
New Mexico	1817	36,579
Texas	1815	4,051

Table 14 (*continued*).

Province	Year	Population
Alta California	1821	3,270
Baja California	1821	800
Total		473,718

In general, most people lived in frontier communities, many of them small hamlets or villages. Spanish towns and their jurisdictions had certain established limits, within which were the residential districts, areas reserved for government and ecclesiastical buildings, agricultural lands allotted to individuals, and common properties, which included royal as well as grazing lands owned by the community as a whole. People were not dispersed over the countryside; some were in small communities and on rural properties, but within the limits of jurisdiction assigned to a major center of settlement. This was true in New Mexico both in the region between Taos and Socorro and in the vicinity of El Paso del Norte. Neither did towns develop from the clustering together of rurally oriented frontiersmen. Communities were established first; settlers subsequently spread into the surrounding area. Yet they always remained dependent upon that community, of which they were considered a part. What developed, then, was a settlement pattern that stressed both urban life and rural work. The jurisdiction of any particular community might include subordinate communities of many kinds, including nearby *haciendas, ranchos*, and settlements for pacified, Christianized Indians as well.

Since there were many communities in each province and they were settled at different times, it might be helpful to compare the populations of some of the more important ones. A closer look at their recorded and estimated figures is provided in Table 15 for the years indicated.

Table 15
Populations of Civil Communities in
Frontier New Spain

Province and Settlement	Year	Population
Coahuila		
Santiago de Saltillo	1575	approx. 20
	1785	8,174
	1810	12,000
Santa María de las Parras	1787	7,028
	1810	10,000
Santiago de Monclova	1689	approx. 100
	1810	6,000
San José de Palafox	1815	203
	1816	277

Table 15 (*continued*).

Province and Settlement	Year	Population
Nuevo León		
Monterrey	1605	approx. 100
Texas		
San Fernando de Béxar	1731	approx. 250
	1777	2,060
	1783	1,248
	1804	1,998
	1820	1,814
Real Presidio del Espíritu Santo	1777	696
	1784	496
	1804	924
	1809	405
Nacogdoches	1783	349
	1793	810
	1809	655
Nuevo Santander		
Villa de Aguayo (today Victoria)	1757	more than 400
Villa de Santander (today Jiménez)	1757	approx. 450
	1795	806
Soto la Marina	1757	221
Reynosa	1757	289 (290?)
	1795	1,191
Camargo	1757	637 (678?)
	1795	1,174
Laredo	1757	85
	1795	636
	1819	1,418
Nueva Vizcaya		
Durango	1563	approx. 65
	1604	approx. 400
	1760	9,000
	1780	12,800
	1815	8,919
San José del Parral and San Bartolomé	1632	more than 300
	1780	7,400
	1815	9,931
San Felipe el Real de Chihuahua	1788	more than 5,000
	1807	7,000
	1815	4,895
San Juan del Río	1815	10,371
New Mexico		
Santa Fé	1630	approx. 750
	1744	approx. 600
	1752	605
	1760	1,285

Table 15 (*continued*).

Province and Settlement	Year	Population
	1776	2,014
	1789	2,901
	1790	3,733
	1793	4,346
	1817	6,728
Santa Cruz de la Cañada	1695	approx. 200
	1744	approx. 500
	1752	556
	1760	1,515
	1789	1,301
	1790	8,895
	1793	10,185
	1817	12,903
Villa de Alburquerque	1706	252
	1744	approx. 500
	1752	476
	1760	1,814
	1789	1,347
	1790	5,959
	1793	6,255
	1817	8,160
El Paso del Norte	1680	approx. 2,200
	1684	1,030
	1744	approx. 3,000
	1784	4,101
	1789	5,310
	1790	5,244
	1800	6,163
	1805	6,209
Sinaloa		
San Miguel de Culiacán	1531	60–100
	1605	approx. 150
	1700	approx. 2,125
	1760	2,216
	1783	10,490
	1803	13,800
El Fuerte de Montesclaros	1760	1,886
	1783	6,151
	1803	10,100
San Felipe y Santiago de Sinaloa	1605	approx. 100
	1700	approx. 150
	1760	3,500
	1783	9,178
	1803	12,000
Rosario	1760	2,459
	1783	5,627
	1803	7,200

Table 15 (*continued*).

Province and Settlement	Year	Population
Sonora		
Alamos	1760	3,400
	1783	7,837
	1803	9,000
San Miguel de Horcasitas	1684	36
	1778	approx. 125
Arizpe	1778	1,534
	1815	9,600
Tubac	1752	52
	1757	411
San Agustín del Tucson	1777	77
	1804	approx. 300
	1819	approx. 500
Baja California		
Loreto	1697	18
	1767	approx. 500
	1800	450–600
Alta California		
San José	1777	68
	1790	80
	1800	170
	1810	110
	1820	240
Los Angeles	1781	44
	1790	109
	1800	315
	1810	365
	1820	650
Branciforte	1797	17
	1800	66
	1820	75

Urban centers on the frontier seem to have fallen into three basic categories: (1) those permanent settlements where the initial population grew to more than one thousand people and sometimes to many thousands, (2) the permanent communities that never seemed to expand beyond a few hundred residents, and (3) establishments that remained at less than one hundred people or eventually were abandoned, moved to other sites, or absorbed into other settlements. In the first category may be found Durango, Parras, Saltillo, Monclova, San Fernando de Béxar (San Antonio), Reynosa, Camargo, Laredo, San José del Parral, San Bartolomé del Valle, San Felipe el Real de Chihuahua, Santa Fé, El Paso del Norte, Alburquerque, Santa Cruz de la Cañada, San Miguel de Culiacán, Rosario, El Fuerte, Arizpe, and Alamos. These twenty settlements all exceeded one thousand in population, some reaching ten or twelve thousand, by the last half century of Spanish administration. In fact, some had more people than did whole provinces such as Texas, Baja California, or Alta California. However, it should also be pointed out that figures for these urban concentrations may be somewhat misleading for they often include subordinate districts and settlements (for example, Santa Cruz de la Cañada in New Mexico).

In the second category of communities having a few hundred settlers we find La Bahía del Espíritu Santo, Nacogdoches, Soto la Marina, Loreto, San José, and Los Angeles, as examples, while Branciforte, Tubac, San José de Palafox, and San Miguel de Horcasitas illustrate the third category, the very small or temporary community. It is notable that there are fewer examples of civil communities in the latter two categories and that most of them seem to have been in the far northeast and northwest regions, particularly in Texas, Sonora, and the Californias.

Finally, when considering settlement patterns, it should be observed that at least one civil community developed within each province, no matter how strong the missionary and presidial establishments might be. Furthermore, although there were occasional population losses over short periods, each of these civil settlements increased in size, as shown by a comparison of late colonial statistics with early figures. Even the least populated of the northern frontier provinces—Baja California—developed a civil center around Loreto. *Ciudades*, such as Durango, and *villas*, such as San Fernando de Béxar (later a *ciudad* itself), Santa Fé, Saltillo, El Paso del Norte, and Alburquerque, in most cases were not only centers of administration, economic activity, and clerical activities, but had the greatest concentrations of civil inhabitants as well. Branciforte in Alta California was an exception, as it never became a center of political activities or of populations. The rapid growth of some of these communities in the latter half of the eighteenth century is shown in Table 15. This increase was brought about by the pacification of large sectors of the frontier, the probable reduction in the death rate through the introduction of smallpox vaccination, and increased immigration into the older, more settled regions protected by the actual frontiers to the northward, and natural increase of the civilian population. Yet, this growth only reflects the increase of the entire area and that for all of New Spain toward the end of the eighteenth century.[3]

Spanish-speaking people came to the northern frontiers of New Spain at different times for a variety of purposes. In almost every case royal authorities had to offer rewards, privileges, or support to obtain colonists who would move from their established homes to frontier provinces.[4] In the early years—most of the sixteenth century—explorers searched for wealth and highly developed Indian civilizations. These ventures seldom created permanent civil settlements. The discovery of precious metals in Nueva Vizcaya and to a lesser extent in Sinaloa and Sonora did promote occupation and led to the establishment of what became prominent civil communities. Farming and stock raising were essential to the survival of the miners and of the soldiers brought in to protect miners, stockmen, and farmers.[5] Stockmen advanced largely because of the competition for lands with farmers in central New Spain, a situation which resulted in overcrowded conditions. The attraction of available large tracts of pastureland on the northern frontier was an impetus for the move northward, in addition to the demand for livestock and their by-products among miners and settlers in that remote region. The animals introduced into the northern regions revolutionized the way of life, as did farming in the river valleys. Indeed, as Silvio Zavala has observed, Spanish towns, agricultural properties, and stock ranches were "frontier institutions" of equal importance to missions, presidios, and mining districts.[6] Finally, many settlers moved to the northern frontier as part of Spain's eighteenth century defensive expansion, to hold her claims against the threats of marauding Indians and encroaching foreigners.

Class distinctions did not, as a general rule, seem as marked on the frontier as they were elsewhere in New Spain and South America. A few families of the lesser nobility in Spain reached the northern frontier, primarily in the early years of settlement. Some original colonists included soldiers and government officials from Europe, as well as Canary Islanders, but the foreign-born became a decided minority on the frontier, more so with each passing generation as racial and class distinctions became less marked. "Spaniard" came to mean anyone of Spanish heritage or of "civilized" life style. The few Europeans in any frontier province were overwhelmed by the numbers of native-born whites. There were mixed bloods of all classifications and kinds, who along with the Spaniards became part of the over-all generic category known as *"gente de razón."* Differentiation by color was apparent in the use of various terms to describe mixed bloods: "mestizo" usually meant a mixture of Indian and Spaniard originally, but came to mean a mixed blood who appeared white; *color quebrado,* or "broken color," was used for people who showed in their appearance some nonwhite ancestry. Negroes and Indians living according to the Spanish way of life were accepted into the majority group, leaving only the unpacified Indians as a separate class in the last half century of Spanish occupation. Census lists, governmental and ecclesiastical reports, and observations of visitors tried faithfully to list the numbers of each category, yet family listings within each community listed names without any racial identification. There are hardly any notable cases of class rivalry on the frontier, an exception being the early clash of Canary Island colonists with older residents of San Fernando de Béxar. Physical isolation, community ties, the ever-present danger of Indian attack, the rigors of everyday life, and royal grants of land, tools, seeds, and privileges to settlers all influenced the development of a society in which class rivalry and distinction had little place except for statistical purposes. When the struggle for Mexican independence occurred, there was little if any class conflict on the frontier between *peninsular* and *criollo*.

Settlers in the frontier regions came largely from earlier-settled adjacent provinces. At first there were immigrants from Spain and central New Spain, especially in Sinaloa, southern Nueva Vizcaya, and New Mexico. As the decades passed and expansion continued, however, settlers for new ventures were recruited elsewhere on the frontier itself. Sinaloa supplied colonists for Sonora, and it, in turn, populated Pimería Alta. Sinaloa and Sonora furnished most of the soldiers and settlers for the occupation of Alta California. El Paso del Norte was occupied first in small numbers from Nueva Vizcaya, but principally by New Mexicans after 1680, when the Pueblo revolt forced them to retreat from New Mexico proper. The province was repopulated after 1693 from El Paso del Norte and Nueva Vizcaya. Chihuahua, then northern Nueva Vizcaya, was established and settled by New Mexicans and Nueva Vizcayans, the latter also contributing to the early settlement of southern Coahuila near Parras and Saltillo. Nuevo León and Coahuila furnished settlers for both Texas and Nuevo Santander, although the latter province also obtained some of its initial colonists from regions below the Pánuco River. In all cases, therefore, most of the colonists either had passed through the frontier experience themselves recently or were still in that stage.

Spanish settlers were primarily small farmers, stockmen, day laborers, and artisans of many types. Unlike the later frontier in the United States, there were no fur traders, trappers, or land speculators, and the Spanish frontier lacked cattle trails and developed systems of transportation and communications. Whereas the settlement of the western United States by farmers and cattlemen came relatively late in the over-all frontier experience, the Spanish northern frontier was occupied intentionally almost from the beginning by agriculturists. They raised crops on their own lands within community grants or they developed the widespread livestock industry on large private holdings, smaller *ranchos*, or within the communal pasturage set aside for each town. In addition, there were also merchants, muleteers, artisans—such as blacksmiths, tailors, bakers, masons, carpenters, and silversmiths—government officials, soldiers, and even a few professionals, such as teachers, surgeons, and an occasional dentist, on the frontier.

Hired day labor and slave labor existed on almost every frontier, but slavery was by no means a major institution of northern New Spain. The number of slaves in any province at any given time was very small, not exceeding one or two per cent of the total population. Furthermore, slave status was not restricted to persons of any particular class or color and might be inflicted on Spaniards and mixed bloods as well as Indians and Negroes. Family listings in census returns for the latter part of the eighteenth century in New Mexico, for example, show clearly that persons of any category might be slaves and domestic servants, depending more upon economic circumstances than anything else. Moreover, these people were considered integral parts of the colonial family and were listed with the other members of the household.

Land was owned both communally and privately. In theory, the king possessed all the land of New Spain and other viceroyalties, and by his authority the viceroy or governor of a province provided communal grants to colonizers and groups of settlers. Within each grant certain lands were reserved for government and ecclesiastical use, for common pasturage and recreation, and for the crown. Each settler received a building lot and at least one agricultural plot. If he met the conditions—living on his assigned land, building a house, planting crops, and otherwise developing the land—the property became his, usually after a four-year probationary period. He could then sell his lands, will them to his heirs, or buy other plots as he desired and was able. Outside of the towns, individuals could petition for and obtain title to large or small tracts of unsettled land, generally for the purpose of raising livestock. *Haciendas* and *ranchos* were private grants, obtained for a nominal fee and usually subject to the condition that they be developed, else the individual faced possible revocation of the grant. The owners of these grants were not given tools, seeds, livestock, or any other government support. The land itself was considered sufficient; it was up to the individual to provide the stock and other necessities, quite unlike the government support provided colonists in the towns. Private land ownership, therefore, became more important in northern New Spain than it did in the southern part of the viceroyalty, where the communal *ejido* was prevalent.

The lifestyle of the settlers was simple by modern standards, family and community oriented, and characterized by hard work with little time for diversion. Most people lived in unpretentious homes built from materials available locally. Adobe brick was the most common, but stone was used where it could be found, as in Texas; straw and wood were used to build primitive *jacales* almost everywhere, but especially on the northeastern frontier. This practice was commonly employed to build dwellings, but sometimes it lasted for longer periods, as in Coahuila and Texas. Usually consisting of a single story, frontier homes had few rooms, often only one or two in use at a given time. With earthen floors (occasionally brick), flat roofs, few if any windows, and wooden beams extending along the roof line in New Mexico, it is no wonder that Lieutenant Pike described the homes of Santa Fé as "resembling a fleet of flat-bottomed boats . . . descending the Ohio River."[7]

Material possessions were few and necessarily primitive. Furniture was both crude and scarce, especially beds and chairs. Low tables, *trasteros* (cupboards), and chests seem to have been the most common articles. Locally manufactured pottery was supplemented by imported majolica in some homes; cooking vessels were generally of copper and many utensils, of wood. Occasionally colonists had crude looms, especially in New Mexico. Clothing was generally simple and wardrobes meager. Dresses, shawls, blouses, and petticoats were usually made of cotton and silk; some ladies even had silk stockings. Men wore short jackets, shirts, knee breeches, and silk stockings. Footwear consisted of leather shoes, *guaraches* (sandals), or sometimes boots. Round hats completed the ensembles. Farm tools and livestock constituted the principal possessions of the settlers, along with their land and their dwellings. However, many owned religious objects such as crosses, medallions, paintings, and *bultos*. Some had jewelry, and others owned books, but neither in great quantity.

Education, where it was available, was rudimentary and within the grasp of only a few settlers, even with the establishment of some primary schools in the period from 1790 to 1821. *Comandante-general* Nemesio Salcedo was primarily responsible for the founding and encouragement of frontier schools in the first decade of the nineteenth century. These institutions were generally supported on a subscription basis by citizens who had sons enrolled in them; they did not receive provincial, viceregal, or other royal funds. They had limited numbers of male students only and often were conducted in community buildings or in the homes of teachers. The curriculum consisted mostly of reading, writing, simple arithmetic, and religious doctrine. It is evident that learning was principally by memorization and recitation. Teachers were hired by local authorities on one-year contracts. They were not professionally trained and were usually hired from a nearby presidio or from the local citizenry. Compensation ranged from one hundred to five hundred pesos annually. It should be emphasized that these educational facilities were available in only a few population centers and over short periods of time. Although some families had books in their homes, there were no community libraries and nowhere was there a printing press on the frontier in the Spanish years. It is apparent that for most of the colonial period settlers received little education, if any. The majority could not read or write; in fact, large numbers could not even sign their names. Parental opposition to schooling of children was common; it was believed that education was a waste of valuable time that could more properly be spent helping to raise crops and livestock. Consequently, most children obtained what education they had in the home. Yet, the fact that there were some secular schools at the end of the colonial period should not be overlooked. They provided the rudiments of education, preparing some children for positions of responsibility in their communities and others for higher instruction elsewhere. Under difficult circumstances, at least a beginning toward a school system was made.

Diseases took heavy toll among the people of the frontier communities. Frequent smallpox epidemics were the greatest threat. Medical facilities and combative medicine either were lacking or were insufficient to meet the needs.

Hospitals, although called for in the *Recopilación de leyes de los reynos de las indias,* were few in number until relatively late in the colonial period. The introduction of vaccination during the first decade of the nineteenth century had an enormous impact upon the settlers. Control of smallpox was a major factor in the population growth of the frontier regions of the early nineteenth century. Reduction in the impact of the disease increased the normal life span as well as the survival rate of infants and children. There were only a few doctors on the frontier. Usually, they were recruited from the complement of the presidios and were general physicians rather than surgeons, as they were often called. Dentists were almost nonexistent until the latter years of Spanish administration; even then they appeared only occasionally in certain provinces.

Transportation and communications between settlements, regions, and provinces and with the rest of New Spain were both primitive and irregular. Horses, mule trains, and crude *carretas* (carts) dominated the field of transportation throughout the long colonial experience. Travel was no faster at the end of almost three centuries than it was at the beginning. Roads and bridges existed, but the former were only trails through long stretches of uninhabited territory, and the latter frequently washed away when rivers flooded. Building and maintenance of roads and bridges were the responsibility of nearby communities, since they were intended for local benefit. With a shortage of both funds and labor, roads lacked uniformity and generally remained unimproved. Communications consisted primarily of the mail service, a unified system which was established in the final decades of the eighteenth century by Teodoro de Croix. However, it should be remembered that most people on the frontier had no need for a regular transportation or communications system. Once established in a particular settlement, they could not depart without a royal passport and then only for a specific purpose. They did not travel anywhere except locally, from community to farm, for example. Since they could not read or write, they had no pressing need for a mail service or other system of communications. Except for merchants, muleteers, supply-train personnel, and government officials, colonists generally remained within their districts or provinces, thus preserving their isolation and encouraging the growth of intense regionalism on the frontier. Although efforts were made to locate and mark trails between provinces in the late eighteenth century, the fact remains that Texans, New Mexicans, Californians, and residents of Pimería Alta had virtually no contact with each other.

Crime was a major problem, and it covered a wide variety of wrongdoing. Murder, adultery, rape, theft of livestock, prostitution, indebtedness, gambling, drunkenness, and heresy were evidently the most common crimes on the frontier. By the end of the eighteenth century the most serious problem seemed to be what to do with the increasingly large number of vagabonds in the northern provinces. Idleness and vagrancy had little place where the overwhelming majority of the populace was dedicated to hard work. Laws were passed to outlaw vagabondage, yet the frequent and repeated use of the term *"sin oficio"* (without an occupation) in the census reports seems to indicate that this social problem was not solved. Punishments ranged from the death penalty and exile from the community to varying periods in jail, confinement to the stocks, whipping, fines, and loss of property.

Actually, gambling was both a crime and an ever-present diversion among colonists on the frontier. There were few opportunities for relaxation and recreation, but celebrations were held whenever a pretext existed. Communities honored saints' days and other religious holidays, welcomed and bade good-by to important visitors, and commemorated important events. The *fandango* and dancing, music, horseracing, bullfights, other games involving both large and small livestock, drinking, and gambling seem to have been the principal diversions on these occasions. Although religious and civil officials infrequently protested the dances and other special celebrations and tried to establish laws to regulate the recreation of the settlers, it is evident that these special celebrations not only continued but perhaps became more intensive toward the end of the colonial era. They helped to break the monotony of everyday life and established lasting customs in some of the communities. This was true of the worship of the Virgin of Guadalupe in many places, the ceremony honoring La Conquistadora in Santa Fé, and the annual performance of such plays as *Los Pastores* and *Las Posadas* throughout New Mexico.

Folk art seems to have developed in some frontier regions, reaching a particularly high level in New Mexico. Isolated by vast stretches of uninhabited land between themselves and not only Nueva Vizcaya but Texas, Pimería Alta, and Alta California as well, the *paisanos* of New Mexico were forced to improvise. This they did in many ways, often preserving styles and practices originally brought from Spain or older regions of New Spain long after they had vanished or been significantly altered there. New Mexican settlers in the mountain villages and valleys north of Santa Fé, particularly near Santa Cruz de la Cañada, preserved the *penitente* ceremonies in association with Holy Week. In fact, lacking ordained priests, they developed their own form of worship; *penitente* customs in certain ways became more severe than those in Andalucia itself. The *paisanos* made their own *santos*, staged simple plays on religious occasions, and preserved the lyrical musical traditions of an earlier Spain. They also developed their own architectural forms, carved their own furniture, and wove blankets and carpets of *yerga*. Thus, thousands of miles from Spain and the capital of New Spain, there developed a folk culture with crude yet appealing artistic expression that both preserved old Spanish customs and adapted to conditions on the frontier. In their pocket of settlement, removed from contact with other centers of Spanish culture, the *paisanos* proved to be great innovators.

Once established in a frontier settlement, the greatest problem the *paisano* and his family faced was eking out an existence. Subsistence in the far reaches of New Spain's northern frontier required hard work and perseverance in the face of both natural and man-made difficulties. Droughts, floods, erosion, epidemics, insects, and soil exhaustion were only some of the natural problems faced by the settlers. Man-controlled problems that seriously affected the development of frontier communities included close regulation by royal authorities; intensive squabbles among civil, military, and religious officials; extreme geographic isolation from other communities and provinces; internal moral and criminal difficulties; and lack of commerce between settlements. Of utmost importance, however, was the common problem experienced by all such settlements at one time or another—the threat of Indian attack. Such an event might occur at any time and place, and its menace hung continually over the heads of Spanish colonists for varying periods of time. Some provinces, such as Sinaloa and southern Nueva Vizcaya, were free of this threat by the end of the eighteenth century, but New Mexico, Pimería Alta, Sonora, northern Nueva Vizcaya, Coahuila, and Texas still had to live with the thought that any day might mean the end for a particular group of settlers or community. During approximately the last century of Spanish administration, colonists also had to contend with the advancing threat of foreigners—Frenchmen, Englishmen, Russians, and finally the Anglo-Americans from the newly established United States of America. Isolation, the Indian threat and open warfare, and foreign encroachments probably were the most important factors in the development of frontier society. Furthermore, this society became indelibly planted in remote areas, such as New Mexico, where it seems unlikely that its characteristics can ever be completely eradicated. As one noted scholar of Spanish-American society in the present United States has observed, the qualities of "The Spanish character" have survived the test of time and are "part of the cultural landscape of the Southwest."[8]

Spanish settlers developed a society that was simultaneously centered in community, family, and individual. They had a real sense of identification with their environment,[9] and consequently their land, whether communally or individually owned, was of great importance to them. It served as a form of security for those who originally received the grant and cultivated it or grazed livestock on it. In fact, the land along with the crops and stock constituted the major possessions that parents enjoyed during their lifetimes and could pass on to their children. Their struggle for survival stamped the *paisanos* with energy and a temperament of their own.[10] They learned to work for themselves on their own properties and thereby developed self-reliance, a feeling of independence, and identification with their own domains. They had little to identify with in the society of central New Spain, its classes, occupations, and rivalries. With the exception of some settlers in Texas and Coahuila, there was little interest in the Mexican war for independence from Spain, especially its class struggle between *criollos* and *peninsulares*; indeed, most of the people were apathetic or resisted the movement of patriots begun, continued, and ended in central and southern New Spain.

Yet, later this same region was seen as the guardian of liberty and promoter of the democratic way of life.[11] Why? Individualism, regional isolation, village orientation, resistance to outside control, innovations and a reliance upon themselves, family cohesiveness, and the preservation of the Catholic religion as a unifying force all set the colonists of northern New Spain apart from the people elsewhere. The devotion to one's extended family, intermarriage among classes and races, and dependence upon one another also contributed to the homogeneity and feeling of separateness of frontier people. It is, therefore, understandable that certain communities and provinces in the northern region stood in opposition to what their citizens thought was an unfair, tyrannical influence from outside sources, an effort to regulate their affairs and life style. The North became the bulwark of resistance to Antonio López de Santa Anna's centralizing policies in the period from the 1830s to the 1850s, to the Mexican conservatives of the nineteenth century, to French intervention, to the Second Empire under Maximilian von Hapsburg, to *porfirismo* at the end of the century, and to the regime of General Victoriano Huerta in 1913–1914. In reality, this region played an enormous role, furnishing leaders, armies, and ideas, in the initiation, continuation, and achievement of the Mexican Revolution in the twentieth century.

Although there are some similarities between the settlers of the frontier in New Spain and the Anglo-Americans who pushed westward across the North American continent, there are significant differences between the two frontier societies that help to explain the singular nature of the Spanish-speaking civilization. The Spanish frontier from Culiacán to Pimería Alta, Durango to Santa Fé, Saltillo to San Fernando de Béxar and Nacogdoches, and Loreto to San Francisco was older than the Anglo-American one, especially the one in the Trans-Mississippi West. Settlers reached some parts of the northern frontier as much as two centuries before Anglos crossed the Mississippi. When British colonists began to occupy the Trans-Appalachian country in Kentucky, Tennessee, and Ohio following the Great War for the Empire (French and Indian, or Seven Years', War) and just before the so-called American Revolution, New Spain's northern frontier had already reached its approximate limits. Alta California and Pimería Alta were just then being settled, but all the other provinces considered in this study had already undergone a long frontier experience, sometimes spanning several centuries. By 1821, when Mexico established her independence, Spanish settlers were firmly entrenched in civil communities scattered from Nacogdoches in the east to San José and Los Angeles in the west. About the same time the westward expanding Anglos had reached the Mississippi Valley and were sending out exploring expeditions into the area west of the "Father of Waters." Sinaloa, parts of Nueva Vizcaya, and the southern portion of Sonora had by then passed beyond the frontier stage and were more heavily populated than most of the other northern provinces. The real problem was that the few Spanish settlers of Texas, Alta California, and the region between stood in the direct path of Anglo-American expansion to the Pacific Ocean. Within a few decades the new frontiersmen from the United States came in direct contact with the Spanish settlers in the more desirable locations of what today constitutes the southwestern United States. The result was a confrontation of frontier societies in which neither really understood the ways of the other.

Spanish expansion differed in many other ways from the Anglo-American experience of the nineteenth century. First, Spanish civil communities were established in the initial occupation, and dispersal into the surrounding countryside occurred only after areas were pacified and consolidated. The community always remained the center of population, economic activity, political administration, and social as well as cultural life. This was true from the founding of the first settlement to the end of the Spanish period. Towns were where *paisanos* first lived in Spanish frontier regions; they did not come about as a result of rural settlers finally establishing a community, as occurred in Anglo-American regions. Second, the Spanish communities were planned in advance, their locations specified and mapped, and the settlers brought in by royal officials. Plazas, streets, public buildings, house lots, agricultural plots, and common lands were all specifically designated before any movement took place. Third, settlers had to be recruited to come to frontier communities; they did not simply wander out into unsettled districts and begin life anew. Royal officials provided gifts of livestock, seed, tools, and even financial subsidies as inducements, and they also specified the privileges and responsibilities of the settlers. Fourth, Spanish colonists were not allowed to travel freely on the frontier or to move from one community to the next without official approval and the granting of a special license. They not only did not have the opportunity to establish new homesteads but could not visit other towns and provinces. Fifth, the northern frontier did not serve as a "safety valve" for settlers escaping from population pressures elsewhere, except perhaps for stockmen who occupied the pasturelands of the north in preference to the more crowded area of central New Spain. Finally, there were few if any land speculation ventures in Spanish frontier provinces, such as there were in the westward expansion of the United States. Land was transferred directly from the king's appointed agents to communities and individuals, thus leaving no area of operation for the land speculator.

According to Carey McWilliams, the true settlers of New Mexico were the villagers, the people who established themselves with community or family grants. He noted that "these are the real peasants, the *paisanos*, the men of the country. . . ."[12] Adelina Otero Warren added that "my people are a simple people," possessing vigor and "a background of culture, of loyalty."[13] These observations apply not only to the people of Spanish heritage in New Mexico, but to those who established a frontier society over the course of centuries and in an area extending over what is today one-half of Mexico and about one-fifth of the United States.

Indeed, the true settlers of the northern frontier were not missionaries, soldiers, aristocrats, great landowners, European immigrants, or even government officials. Some of these were present, but they were at all times a decided minority. The *paisanos*, commonplace countrymen, were overwhelmingly the backbone of Spanish settlement on almost all frontiers. They were a hardworking, home-loving, innovative people. They were the real founders of Spanish civilization on the far-flung frontier of New Spain, the forebears of today's Spanish-speaking population of northern Mexico and the southwestern United States.

Like the presidial soldier and the missionary, the *paisano* is entitled to recognition of his role in the expansion of New Spain. As a permanent *poblador*, he and his descendents created a society that outlived all other institutions of the Spanish frontier experience.

Chronology

1521 (August 13)	Cortés recaptured Mexico City from Aztecs.
1530–36	Cabeza de Vaca in Texas and northern Borderlands.
1531	San Miguel de Culiacán, Sinaloa, founded by Nuño de Guzmán.
1535	Cortés established temporary colony at La Paz, Baja California.
	Antonio de Mendoza became first viceroy of New Spain.
1540–42	Coronado's expedition to southwestern region of present United States.
1542–43	Cabrillo-Ferrelo expedition along coast of California.
	Conclusion of De Soto-Moscoso expedition to Florida and present southeastern United States.
	New Laws issued in Spain.
1548	Opening of silver mines at Zacatecas.
1562	Province of Nueva Vizcaya created with Francisco de Ibarra as first governor.
1563 (November–December)	Durango founded in Nueva Vizcaya by Ibarra; became capital of frontier regions in north.
1564 (May–June)	San Juan de Sinaloa founded on Fuerte River.
1565 (September)	San Agustín, Florida, founded by Pedro Menéndez de Avilés.
1573 (July 3)	Philip II promulgated colonization laws.
1575	Santiago de Saltillo founded in Coahuila by Alberto del Canto.
	Santa Bárbara and San Bartolomé already founded and prosperous in southern Chihuahua.
1584	Carbajal occupied new province of Nuevo León (created in 1579); León (Cerralvo) and San Luis (near Monterrey) founded.
1585	San Felipe de Sinaloa founded.
1588	Spanish armada defeated by English.
1591 (September 13)	Tlaxcaltecan Indian town of San Esteban de Nueva Tlaxcala, Coahuila, founded.
	Jesuits arrived and began work in Sinaloa.
1594–98	Santa María de las Parras, Coahuila, founded.
1596 (September 20)	Diego de Montemayor founded Nuestra Señora de Monterrey in Nuevo León.
1598 (July)	Juan de Oñate colonized New Mexico at San Juan de los Caballeros.

257

1603	Sebastián Vizcaíno expedition to coast of California.
1610 (Spring)	Santa Fé, New Mexico, founded by Governor Pedro de Peralta.
1621	Durango became first frontier community to receive status of a *ciudad*.
1626 (September 4)	San Gregorio de Cerralvo, Nuevo León, founded.
1629–31	*Real de minas* of San José del Parral founded.
1637	San Juan Bautista de Cadereita, Nuevo León, founded.
1659 (December)	Mission of Nuestra Señora de Guadalupe del Paso founded on Río Grande.
1680 (August)	Pueblo Indian revolt in New Mexico forced Spaniards to retreat to El Paso del Norte.
1681	*Recopilación de leyes de los reynos de las indias* published.
1683	Presidio of El Paso del Norte established.
1683–85	Atondo-Kino temporary colonization of Baja California at La Paz and San Bruno.
1685–87	La Salle's temporary colony at Fort Saint Louis in southern Texas.
1687–1711	Father Eusebio Francisco Kino in Pimería Alta.
1689 (August 12)	Santiago de Monclova, Coahuila, founded.
1690–93	Franciscan missions temporarily established in East Texas.
1693 (December)	Reconquest and resettlement of New Mexico begun by Diego de Vargas; Santa Fé resettled and presidio established.
1695 (April 21–23)	Santa Cruz de la Cañada, New Mexico, founded by Diego de Vargas.
1697 (October)	Loreto founded in Baja California.
1699–1701	Mission of San Juan Bautista established on Río Grande; presidio erected.
1703–1704	Two *reales de minas* of Chihuahua and Santa Eulalia established in Chihuahua.
1706 (January–June)	Villa of Alburquerque, New Mexico, established by Governor Francisco Cuervo y Váldes.
1712 (January 29)	San Felipe de Linares, Nuevo León, founded.
1716 (July 3)	Domingo Ramón and St. Denis reoccupied East Texas.
1718 (May 1)	Martín de Alarcón established mission of San Antonio de Valero; presidio begun on May 5.
1718 (October 1)	San Felipe el Real de Chihuahua elevated to *villa* status from two earlier *reales de minas*.
1721–22	Marqués de Aguayo colonizing expedition to Texas; La Bahía established as a presidio.
1731 (March)	Villa of San Fernando de Béxar established in San Antonio, Texas, region; Canary Islanders settled.
1734	Sonora and Sinaloa detached from Nueva Vizcaya and made into separate province.

1736–41	Discovery of silver at Arizonac in Pimería Alta led to mining rush and establishment of *real de minas*; abandoned when silver ores gave out.
1740	Yaqui Indian revolt in Sonora.
1741–42	Pitic initially founded in Sonora; abandoned before end of decade.
1748–55	José de Escandón occupied Nuevo Santander (Tamaulipas), and established towns of Jiménez, Reynosa, Camargo, Mier, Revilla, and Laredo, among others.
1751 (November 20)	Pima Indian uprising in Pimería Alta.
1752 (March 7)	Presidio of Tubac established in Pimería Alta.
1753 (March 1)	Founding of San Fernando de Austria, Coahuila.
1755 (May 15)	Laredo founded in Nuevo Santander on north bank of Río Grande.
1758	Settlement of Carrizal established.
1760	Bishop Tamarón visited New Mexico.
1762 (November 3)	France ceded Louisiana to Spain in first Treaty of San Ildefonso.
1766–68	Marqués de Rubí and Nicolás de Lafora inspected frontier of New Spain.
1767	Expulsion of Jesuits from Spanish kingdoms.
1768	Settlement of Loreto by civilians encouraged by José de Gálvez.
1768–71	Gálvez-Elizondo pacification campaign in Sonora.
1769 (April–July)	Occupation of Alta California by Governor Portolá and Father Serra: San Diego founded.
1770	Mission and presidio at Monterey, Alta California, established.
1772	New Regulations for Presidios issued.
1773 (June–September)	East Texas abandoned; settlers moved to San Antonio.
1774 (September)	East Texas reoccupied; community of Bucareli founded.
1775–76 (October–March)	Juan Bautista de Anza led settlers to Alta California.
1776	Comandancia-general de las Provincias Internas del Norte established, with Teodoro de Croix as first *comandante-general*.
1776 (Summer–Fall)	Presidio and pueblo of San Agustín del Tucson founded in Pimería Alta.
1776 (September 17)	Presidio of San Francisco established in Alta California.
1777 (November 29)	Pueblo of San José in Alta California founded.
1777–78	Fray Juan Agustín de Morfi visited northeastern frontier and New Mexico.
1779 (January–April)	Pueblo of Nacogdoches, Texas, founded.
1781 (July)	Yuma Indian uprising at junction of Colorado and Gila rivers.
1781 (September 4)	Pueblo of Los Angeles founded in Alta California.

1783	Villa of Pitic, Sonora, founded (present Hermosillo); garrison from presidio at San Miguel de Horcasitas moved there.
1787 (July 27)	Northern Coahuila and Saltillo-Parras region of Nueva Vizcaya combined into province of Coahuila.
1789?	Plan of Pitic officially approved and promulgated.
1790–95	Spain established military garrison (no families) at Nootka Sound on Vancouver Island.
1797 (July)	Villa of Branciforte founded near mission Santa Cruz in Alta California.
1804	Alta California and Baja California made into separate provinces with own governors and capitals.
1804–1805	Smallpox vaccination process introduced into Nueva Vizcaya and New Mexico.
1807 (March–June)	Lieutenant Zebulon Montgomery Pike in New Mexico, Chihuahua, and San Antonio.
1810 (April 27)	San José de Palafox, Coahuila, founded (abandoned after 1818).
1810 (September 16)	Hidalgo revolt at Dolores began Mexico War for Independence.
1811	Father Hidalgo taken prisoner in Coahuila, sent to Chihuahua, where he was defrocked, tried, and shot.
	Antiroyalist insurrection at San Antonio, Texas.
	San Antonio, Texas, elevated to status of *ciudad* (only one within limits of present United States).
1812–13	Magee-Gutiérrez filibustering expedition into Texas; ended with Battle of the Medina.
1818 (November–December)	Hippolyte de Bouchard raided and sacked Alta California at Monterey and Santa Bárbara.
1821 (September)	Mexico achieved its independence from Spain.

Glossary

Acequia	Irrigation ditch; *acequia madre*, main irrigation ditch.
Adarga	Bullhide shield of oval form.
Administrador de correos	Postmaster.
Adobe	Clay or mud formed into bricks with straw as a binder and used for building homes, walls, public buildings, etc.
Agregados	Concentration or collection of recent settlers in a community.
Aguardiente	Locally manufactured whisky or brandy.
Alabado	Religious hymn of praise.
Alcabala	Excise or sales tax paid on goods when they changed hands.
Alcalde-mayor	Chief magistrate of town or district; a civil official.
Alcaldía	District or local jurisdiction of an alcalde.
Alférez	The chief ensign (standard-bearer, or junior official) of a town.
Alhóndiga	Public granary or market.
Almojarifazgo	Export and import duty.
Almud	Half of a *fanega*; about one and one-quarter bushels of grain.
Alta California	Upper California; region of present state of California.
Arriero	Muleteer.
Arroba	Weight of about twenty-five pounds.
Atole	Boiled, strained corn in a porridge or gruel form.
Audiencia	High Spanish court with executive as well as judicial functions.
Ayuntamiento	Town council of Spanish community; municipal government.
Baja California	Lower California; that part of California south of the international boundary between Mexico and the United States.
Barrio	Ward or district of a city or town.
Bendito	Prayer beginning with this word as a blessing.
Bulto	Religious image usually carved in the round from pine or cottonwood.
Caballería	A house and farm lot in Spanish community; usually larger than a *peonía*, measuring approximately 100–125 acres.
Caballero	Gentleman or horseman.

261

Cabildo	Town council or municipal form of government; building in which the council met.
Calidad	Class, race, or condition of person's character.
Camino	Road or highway; *camino real,* royal or king's highway.
Camposanto	Cemetery or holy ground.
Cantador	Singer of ballads.
Cantor	Singer who composes hymns or ballads.
Cañada	Canyon or glen between the mountains.
Capitulación	Agreement or contract.
Cardador	Carder or comber of wool.
Carreta	Crude wooden cart, drawn by oxen or mules.
Casas reales	Royal or government buildings.
Casta	A caste or mixed blood of any type.
Cédula	Decree or dispatch from the king; royal order.
Cigarro	Frontier cigarette rolled by smoker.
Ciudad	A major Spanish city or civil community, usually possessing a charter and having extensive rights and privileges.
Cofradía	Confraternity, or brotherhood, established for a specific purpose.
Colcha	Coverlet or blanket, sometimes with geometric designs.
Colono	Colonist, or settler.
Color quebrado	Of broken color; person of mixed blood showing definite color strain.
Comandante-general	Commandant-general, usually used in connection with chief administrative official of Provincias Internas del Norte after 1776.
Comunero	Joint holder of town lands and defender of the municipality against encroachments of crown and other centralizing agencies.
Congregación	An Indian settlement, usually established after a conquest.
Conquistador	Conqueror.
Coplas populares	Popular, common, or everyday quatrain; stanzas of four lines.
Correos conductores	Mailmen, often presidial soldiers performing this duty.
Corrida	Bullfight.
Coyote	Derogatory word for one of mixed Indian and mestizo blood; native of the country.
Criado	Domestic servant.
Criollo (Creole)	A person of Spanish or European heritage born in America.
Cuera	Short leather jacket worn by soldiers and settlers on military campaigns; usually made up of several thicknesses.
Cura	Parish priest, curate, or rector; member of secular clergy.
Ejido	Common lands allotted by crown to each settlement.
Encomendero	Owner of an encomienda.
Encomienda	A grant of Indians to some deserving Spaniard, generally for labor purposes.

Esclavo	Slave or captive.
Escopeta	Firelock or gun.
Escuela de primeras letras	Primary school.
Español	Technically a Spaniard, but on the frontier an all-embracing term to describe anyone of Spanish heritage or appearance, even those born in America; synonymous with "Creole" as used elsewhere.
Estancia	Landed property; a stock-raising estate or farm for grazing cattle.
Europeo	In theory a European, but on the frontier it meant a Spaniard from the mother country.
Fandango	Lively public or private dance enjoyed by settlers on the frontier.
Fanega	Measurement of grain and seed; usually equal to about two and one-half bushels, but varied according to locale.
Farolito	Small lantern of New Mexico made by setting candle inside paper bag and in base of sand.
Fiesta	Public celebration; holiday or feast.
Fiesta de toros	Bullfight.
Gachupín	A derogatory term used in New Spain to describe a native of Spain.
Ganado mayor	Larger livestock, such as cattle, horses, and mules.
Ganado menor	Smaller livestock, such as sheep and goats.
Genízaro	Localism used in New Mexico to describe an Indian of a nomadic tribe captured or ransomed by New Mexicans and then employed by them or settled in an established community; non-Pueblo Indians peaceably settled under Spanish control.
Gente decente	"Decent," reasonable, or civilized people.
Gente de razón	"People of reason"; civilized people, or Spanish settlers; educated or rational persons in distinction to unconquered Indians.
Guaracha	Leather sandal.
Habilitado	Paymaster or presidial quartermaster.
Hacienda	Large, privately owned estate, usually embracing smaller properties and employing many families in raising crops or livestock; also, the royal treasury.
Hidalgo	Member of lesser nobility, by birth or through process of being ennobled; in theory, a "son of somebody."
Hilandero	Spinner of wool.
Hoja	Leaf of paper; therefore, cigarette paper.
Horno	Beehive-shaped oven brought by Spaniards to America.
Indio	Indian.
Indios bárbaros	Wild, or unpacified, Indians.
Intendencia	Administrative district of New Spain after 1786.
Isleño	Literally an islander; in Texas a settler from the Canary Islands at San Fernando de Béxar.
Jacal	Hut of straw and wooden sticks.

Labor	Land measurement of approximately 177 acres.
Labrador	One who works with plow or spade; a small farmer or peasant.
Latifundio	Large landholding.
Leyenda negra	The "Black Legend" that Spaniards were ruthless, corrupt, and inferior people, particularly in relation to English-speaking ones; not true settlers, as the English were.
Libro de marcas	Cattle-brand register.
Limpieza de sangre	Purity of blood.
Lobo	A mixture of Indian and mulatto; usually employed in a derogatory manner.
Lugar	Small place or village; a hamlet.
Luminaria	Small bonfire; often confused with a *farolito*.
Maestro de primeras letras (maestro de escuela)	Teacher of the primary grades; schoolmaster.
Marco	Mark, or weight of about one-half pound.
Mayordomo	Overseer, or supervisor, of some activity.
Mercader	Merchant or shopkeeper.
Merced	Spanish land grant or gift.
Mescal	Liquor prepared from agave cactus.
Mestización	Racial amalgamation or crossbreeding.
Mestizo	Mixed blood; an offspring of two or more races, usually Indian and white.
Metate	Grinding stone used for crushing corn.
Miniestras	Provisions, general ingredients, or greens for a person's daily consumption and subsistence.
Mulatto	Offspring of white and Negro.
Natural	Native of a place or country.
Novillada	Bullfight with young bulls.
Obraje	Mill, factory, or workshop.
Padrón	A Spanish census; often a listing of families.
Paisano	Literally a person of the country, a countryman; the civilian settler of the Spanish frontier.
Paraje	Place or campsite.
Partido	District.
Pastor	Shepherd.
Patrón	Landlord or protector.
Peninsular	Spaniard born in Spain.
Penitente	Popular name for member of religious brotherhood which administered ceremonies in New Mexico and practiced penance by scourging, carrying crosses, etc.; one who practiced a folk religion in New Mexico.
Peonía	A house and farm lot in a Spanish community smaller than a *caballería*.
Pimería Alta	Upper Pimería, or land of the Pima Indians; northern Sonora, including that part of Arizona below the Gila River.
Piñon	Small pine tree with edible nuts widely consumed by settlers.

Plaza	An open square (usually a rectangle) in center of Spanish town; also, a small village or community.
Población	Unchartered frontier village of Spanish-speaking people.
Poblador	Spanish settler or founder of a community.
Porción	Lot or allotment of land, especially in the Lower Río Grande Valley.
Posole	A stew made from meat, hominy, and chile, boiled together.
Provincias Internas del Norte	Internal Provinces of the North, referring to New Spain's northern provinces, particularly in the eighteenth century.
Pueblo	Unchartered frontier village or town under direct royal control and administration; usually composed of Spanish settlers; in New Mexico, however, an established community of sedentary Indians; also, the Spanish name for Indians living in this manner.
Puesto	A place, post, or small town.
Punche	Native tobacco grown in New Mexico.
Puro	Frontier cigar made from rolled tobacco leaves.
Quintal	Weight of approximately one hundred pounds.
Quinto Real	Duty paid to crown by individuals in return for right to operate mines; theoretically one-fifth of mine's output, but often less.
Ranchería	Camp or temporary settlement of Indians; collection of huts.
Ranchero	Owner of a small farm.
Rancho	Small, privately owned farm for raising crops, livestock, or both; a subsistence-type farm; in New Mexico a small settlement or place with few dwellings.
Real	One-eighth of a peso.
Real de minas	A mining district consisting of a principal community, its lesser settlements, and the surrounding environs.
Reata	Rope.
Rebozo	Scarf worn over the head or around the shoulders by women.
Reconquista	Spanish reconquest of the Iberian Peninsula from the Moslems, sometimes described as covering the period 711–1492.
Reducción	Mission station for congregating Indians and converting them to Christianity.
Regidor	Member of a town council; a representative or alderman.
Retablo	Painted wooden religious image, usually on a flat surface.
Romance	Traditional ballad or poetry.
Santero	Maker of religious images.
Santo	Image of a saint, carved or painted.
Sembrador	One who sows, thus a small farmer.
Serape	A woolen shawl or narrow blanket.
Sirviente	Domestic servant.
Sitio	Spanish square league of land (measurement varies according to use).

Solar	A house lot in a Spanish community.
Subdelegado de correos	Postmaster.
Suerte	Farm lot allocated to settlers in vicinity of a town; field separated from house lot.
Tabaquera	Miniature tobacco flask.
Tejedor	Weaver.
Tenatero	Nueva Vizcayan localism to describe an ore carrier in the mines.
Tierra caliente	Hot or humid lands.
Tierra despoblada	Uninhabited or deserted lands.
Tierra de guerra	Land of warfare.
Tierra de paz	Land of peace; pacified land.
Título	Title, article, or heading.
Toreador	Bullfighter.
Tortilla	Flat cake made of corn meal; usually eaten instead of bread.
Trastero	Large wooden cupboard.
Vagabundo	Vagabond, idler, loiterer; one without a home, job, or occupation (*"sin oficio"*).
Vara	Spanish yard; about thirty-three inches in length.
Vecino	Spanish settler or resident of a town; generally restricted to a family or householder; a citizen.
Verso	Spanish verse of four parts; a saying, philosophy, or idea sung by a *cantador*.
Viga	Wooden beam.
Villa	Chartered frontier settlement with limited rights and privileges such as right to self-government; next in importance to a *ciudad*.
Vino	Wine.
Visita general	General inspection or examination conducted by royal officials.
Visitador-general	Royal inspector with extensive powers.
Yerga (jerga)	Coarse woolen cloth woven in New Mexico.

Abbreviations

AASF	Archives of the Archdiocese of Santa Fé, microcopy in State Records Center and Archives, Santa Fé, New Mexico.
AGI	Archivo General de Indias, Sevilla, Spain.
AGN	Archivo General de la Nación, Mexico City.
AHP	El Archivo de Hidalgo del Parral (Parral Archives), microcopy at Fort Lewis College, Durango, Colorado.
BA	Béxar Archives, University of Texas Library, Austin, Texas.
BL	Bancroft Library, University of California, Berkeley, California.
BNM	Biblioteca Nacional de México, Mexico City.
CR-UNM	Coronado Room, Zimmerman Library, University of New Mexico, Albuquerque, New Mexico.
HAHR	*Hispanic American Historical Review.*
HL	Huntington Library and Art Gallery, San Marino, California.
JA	Archives of the City of Juárez (Juárez Archives), microcopy in University of Texas at El Paso Library Special Collections.
LA	Laredo Archives, Special Collections, St. Mary's University Library, San Antonio, Texas.
NA	Nacogdoches Archives, Texas State Library, Austin, Texas.
NMHR	*New Mexico Historical Review.*
SANM	Spanish Archives of New Mexico, State Records Center and Archives, Santa Fé, New Mexico.
SWHQ	*Southwestern Historical Quarterly.*
THRL (Alamo)	Texas History Research Library, The Alamo, San Antonio, Texas.

Notes

INTRODUCTION

1. Charles Gibson (ed.), *The Black Legend: Anti-Spanish Attitudes in the Old World and the New* (New York: Alfred A. Knopf, 1971), pp. 4, 22–23; Herbert I. Priestley, *The Coming of the White Man, 1492–1848* ([New York]: Macmillan Company, 1929), p. 139.

2. L. S. Stavrianos, *The World since 1500: A Global History*, 2d ed. (Englewood Cliffs, N.J.: Prentice-Hall, 1971), p. 388.

3. *Ibid.*, pp. 163–64, 388–89.

4. Fray Angelico Chávez, Book Review of *Southwestern Indian Ceremonials*, by Tom Bahti, *New Mexico*, Vol. 48, Nos. 5–6 (May–June, 1971), p. 56; Carey McWilliams, *North from Mexico: The Spanish-Speaking People of the United States* (New York: Greenwood Publishers, 1968), p. 71. I also discussed the current use of the term with Spanish-American people in Colorado, Texas, and New Mexico and observed its use for names of shops such as those of wood carvers in Chimayó, New Mexico. These people recognize the word *paisano* to mean a fellow Spanish-American or a description, appropriately enough, of the roadrunner, frequently seen in the Southwest.

5. John W. Reps, *Town Planning in Frontier America* (Princeton, N.J.: Princeton University Press, 1970), p. 35.

6. *Ibid.*, pp. 35–36.

7. *Ibid.*, p. 19.

8. *Ibid.*, p. 66.

9. Priestley, *Coming of White Man*, p. 96.

10. Reps, *Town Planning in Frontier America*, p. 68.

11. Zelia Nuttall, "Royal Ordinances Concerning the Laying Out of New Towns," *HAHR*, Vol. 4, No. 4 (November, 1921), pp. 743, 745; Reps, *Town Planning in Frontier America*, p. 41.

12. The contention of Reps, p. 41, that these regulations "remained virtually unchanged throughout the entire period of Spanish rule in the Western Hemisphere" is in error in view of subsequent legislation and localized regulations promulgated by the crown and its authorized agents.

13. Nuttall, "Royal Ordinances," pp. 750–51; Reps, *Town Planning in Frontier America*, p. 42.

14. Nuttall, "Royal Ordinances," p. 750, and *HAHR*, Vol. 5, No. 2 (May, 1922), p. 250; Reps, *Town Planning in Frontier America*, pp. 42–43.

15. Nuttall, "Royal Ordinances," 750–51; Reps, *Town Planning in Frontier America*, pp. 43–44.

16. Nuttall, "Royal Ordinances," pp. 751–53; Reps, *Town Planning in Frontier America*, pp. 44–45.

17. *Recopilación de leyes de los reinos de las Indias*, 3 vols. ([Madrid]: Consejo de la Hispanidad, 1943), tomo II, libro IV, título I, ley iv.

18. *Ibid.*, título VII, ley i.

19. *Ibid.*, ley ii, and título VIII, leyes i and vi.

20. *Ibid.*, título VII, ley II.

21. *Ibid.*, ley vii.

22. *Ibid.*, título XII, ley i; see also Priestley, *Coming of White Man*, p. 97, for sizes of the *peonía* and the *caballería*.

23. *Recopilación*, tomo II, libro IV, título XII, leyes i, iii, and xi.

24. *Ibid.*, título VII, ley viii.

25. *Ibid.*, leyes xii and xv.

26. *Ibid.*, título V, ley v.

27. *Ibid.*, libro VII, título I, leyes i and ii; título IV, leyes i, ii, iv, and v; título V, leys i, iv, vii, xii, xiv, and xv.

28. *Ibid.*, libro IV, título III, leyes xix, xx, and xxi; título V, ley viii; título VI, leyes ii, iii, and vi.

29. "Instructions for the Establishment of the New Villa of Pitic in the Province of Sonora, Approved by his Majesty and Ordered Adopted for Other Projected New Villas To Be Established in This General Commandancy," in Mattie A. Hatcher, *The Opening of Texas to Foreign Settlement, 1801–1821* (Austin: University of Texas Press, 1927), Appendix, Doc. 12, p. 314. See also Carlos E. Castañeda, *Our Catholic Heritage in Texas, 1519–1936*, 7 vols. (Austin, Texas: Von Boeckmann-Jones Company, 1936), Vol. 5, p. 311.

30. "Instructions," p. 315.

31. *Ibid.*, pp. 315–16; Castañeda, *Our Catholic Heritage*, Vol. 5, pp. 311–12.

32. "Instructions," p. 317.

33. *Ibid.*

34. *Ibid.*, pp. 317–20; Castañeda, *Our Catholic Heritage*, Vol. 5, pp. 312–13.

35. Reps, *Town Planning in Frontier America*, p. 51.

36. *Ibid.*, p. 48.

37. *Ibid.*, pp. 52, 54.

38. *Ibid.*, p. 58.

39. *Ibid.*, pp. 63–64.

40. See Priestley, *Coming of White Man*, pp. 94–95, for a description of frontier mining conditions.

41. James Lockhart, "Professional Notes," *HAHR*, Vol. 51, No. 2 (May, 1971), p. 424.

42. *Ibid.*

43. T. H. Hollingsworth, *Historical Demography* (Ithaca, N.Y.: Cornell University Press, 1969), pp. 108, 298.

44. Sherburne F. Cook and Woodrow Borah, *Essays in Population History: Mexico and the Caribbean, Volume One* (Berkeley and Los Angeles: University of California Press, 1971), p. v.

45. *Ibid.*, p. 1.

46. *Ibid.*, p. 15.

47. *Ibid.*, pp. 43–44.

48. *Ibid.*, pp. 121–22, 448.

49. *Ibid.*, pp. 445–46.

50. *Ibid.*, p. 128.

51. Lyle N. McAlister, "Social Structure and Social Change in New Spain," *HAHR*, Vol. 43, No. 3 (August, 1963), p. 365.

52. *Ibid.*, p. 368.

53. Alexander von Humboldt, *Political Essay on the Kingdom of New Spain* (ed. by Mary Maples Dunn), (New York: Alfred A. Knopf, 1972), p. 25.

54. *Ibid.*, p. 31.

55. *Ibid.*, p. 33.

56. *Ibid.*, p. 67.

57. *Ibid.*, pp. 71–72.

58. *Ibid.*, p. 125.

59. McAlister, "Social Structure," pp. 354–55.

60. *Ibid.*, p. 358.

61. *Ibid.*, p. 355.

62. See *ibid.*, p. 362, for a detailed classification of these groups. However, I have added some groups and moved others to reflect my own findings.

63. Herbert Eugene Bolton was the first to suggest that the Spanish advance occurred in three columns: the East Coast Corridor, West Coast Corridor, and Central Plateau. Both he and his student, the noted Spanish Borderlands historian Father John Francis Bannon, have adhered to this theory in Bolton, "The Northward Movement in New Spain," in John Francis Bannon (ed.), *Bolton and the Spanish Borderlands* (Norman: University of Oklahoma Press, 1964), pp. 67, 71, and John Francis Bannon, *The Spanish Borderlands Frontier, 1513–1821* (New York: Holt, Rinehart, and Winston, 1970).

CHAPTER 1

1. Hubert H. Bancroft, *History of the North Mexican States and Texas*, 2 vols. (San Francisco: The History Company, 1886–1889), Vol. I, pp. 375, 603–604.

2. Vito Alessio Robles, *Coahuila y Texas en la época colonial* (México, D.F.: Editorial Cultural, 1938), pp. 84, 88–89, 109; Herbert E. Bolton, "The Northward Movement in New Spain," in Bannon, *Bolton and the Spanish Borderlands*, p. 82; Herbert E. Bolton and Thomas M. Marshall, *The Colonization of North America, 1492–1783* (New York: Macmillan, 1922), p. 59; Alonso de la Mota y Escobar, *Descripción geográfica de los reinos de Nueva Galicia, Nueva Vizcaya, y Nuevo León*, 2nd ed. (México, D.F.: Editorial Pedro Robredo, 1940), p. 162. Francisco de Ibarra was not the founder of Saltillo, as stated by Bancroft, *North Mexican States*, Vol. I, p. 126, and by Bolton in earlier works such as *Colonization of North America*, p. 59.

3. Alessio Robles, *Coahuila y Texas*, p. 125.

4. *Ibid.*, pp. 123–24.

5. *Ibid.*, p. 124.

6. *Ibid.*, pp. 126, 135; Bolton and Marshall, *Colonization of North America*, p. 60; Marc Simmons, "Tlascalans in the Spanish Borderlands," *NMHR*, Vol. 39, No. 2 (April, 1964), p. 103.

7. Simmons, "Tlascalans in the Spanish Borderlands," pp. 104–109.

8. Alessio Robles, *Coahuila y Texas*, p. 137; Mota y Escobar, *Descripción geográfica*, p. 166; Bolton and Marshall, *Colonization of North America*, p. 60.

9. Alessio Robles, *Coahuila y Texas*, p. 354.

10. *Ibid.*, pp. 285, 353.

11. *Ibid.*, pp. 302–304.

12. *Ibid.*, pp. 354–58; Luis Navarro García, *Don José de Gálvez y la comandancia general de las provincias internas del norte de Nueva España* (Sevilla, Spain: Escuela de Estudios Hispano-Americanos, 1964), p. 33. Bancroft, *North Mexican States*, Vol. I, p. 376, maintains that Monclova was established in 1687 and that 150 families and 270 armed men were sent there.

13. Herbert E. Bolton, *Guide to Materials for the History of the United States in the Principal Archives of Mexico* (Washington, D.C.: Carnegie Institution, 1913, and New York, Kraus Reprint Corporation, 1966), p. 421.

14. Alessio Robles, *Coahuila y Texas*, pp. 571–72.

15. For the establishment of this mission, presidio, and nearby settlement, see Robert S. Weddle, *San Juan Bautista: Gateway to Spanish Texas* (Austin and London: University of Texas Press, 1968), pp. 18–28.

16. Alessio Robles, *Coahuila y Texas*, pp. 572–73.

17. Bancroft, *North Mexican States*, Vol. I, p. 607.

18. Alessio Robles, *Coahuila y Texas*, p. 590; Lawrence Kinnaird (ed. and trans.), *The Frontiers of New Spain: Nicolás de Lafora's Description, 1766–1768* (Berkeley, Calif.: The Quivira Society, 1958), p. 154.

19. Bancroft, *North Mexican States*, Vol. II, p. 79.

20. Carmen Perry (ed. and trans.), *San José de Palafox: "The Impossible Dream" by the Río Grande* (San Antonio, Texas: St. Mary's University Press, 1971), p. xii; Weddle, *San Juan Bautista*, p. 325.

21. Perry, *San José de Palafox*, p. iv.

22. *Ibid.*, pp. iv, 1.

23. *Ibid.*

24. *Ibid.*, pp. 28, 87.

25. *Ibid.*, p. 90.

26. *Ibid.*, p. v.

27. Alessio Robles, *Coahuila y Texas*, p. 88; Mota y Escobar, *Descripción geográfica*, p. 163; Woodrow Borah, "Francisco de Urdiñola's Census of the Spanish Settlements in Nueva Vizcaya, 1604," *HAHR*, Vol. 35, No. 3 (August, 1955), p. 402.

28. Alessio Robles, *Coahuila y Texas*, pp. 389, 406; Fray Juan Agustín de Morfi, *Viaje de indios y diario del Nuevo México*, 2d ed. (México, D.F.: Antigua Librería Robredo de José Porrúa e Hijos, 1935), p. 138.

29. Alessio Robles, *Coahuila y Texas*, p. 357.

30. Bancroft, *North Mexican States*, Vol. I, p. 606.

31. Alessio Robles, *Coahuila y Texas*, p. 407.

32. Cook and Borah, *Essays in Population History*, p. 168. Navarro García, *José de Gálvez*, p. 115, gives the Spanish population for Coahuila in 1760 as 4,600 persons.

33. Alessio Robles, *Coahuila y Texas*, p. 590; Kinnaird, *Frontiers of New Spain*, pp. 142, 154.

34. Alessio Robles, *Coahuila y Texas*, p. 541. Navarro García, *José de Gálvez*, p. 406, gives the total as 8,000 for the province.

35. Morfi, *Viaje de indios*, p. 245; Alessio Robles, *Coahuila y Texas*, p. 573; Bancroft, *North Mexican States*, Vol. I, p. 606.

36. Archivo del Ayuntamiento de Saltillo, Año de 1785, Carpeta No. 42, as published in Morfi, *Viaje de indios*, pp. 281–82. The printed totals do not agree with my own addition of each column, and therefore the recomputed figures are used in this book. It is interesting to note that there were only 51 slaves in the total population of 8,174 persons, thus amounting to only six-tenths of one per cent of the total number of inhabitants.

37. Alessio Robles, *Coahuila y Texas*, pp. 590, 595.

38. Bancroft, *North Mexican States*, Vol. II, pp. 78–79.

39. Navarro García, *José de Gálvez*, p. 118.

40. Borah, "Francisco de Urdiñola's Census, 1604," pp. 401–402.

41. Robert C. West, *The Mining Community in Northern New Spain: The Parral Mining District* (Berkeley and Los Angeles: University of California Press, 1949), pp. 59–60.

42. Morfi, *Viaje de indios*, p. 140ff.; Alessio Robles, *Coahuila y Texas*, p. 503 and map on p. 504.

43. Charles H. Harris, "The North Mexican *Hacendado*: The Case of Sánchez Navarro Family" (paper delivered at the annual meeting of the Southwest Social Science Association, San Antonio, Texas, March 30, 1972), p. 4. Dr. Harris has since published a full-length work on the history of this important *latifundio*.

44. *Ibid.*, pp. 5–7.

45. *Ibid.*, pp. 6, 10.

46. *Ibid.*, pp. 2, 12.

47. *Ibid.*, pp. 9–10.

48. Archivo del Ayuntamiento de Saltillo, Año de 1785, in Morfi, *Viaje de indios*, pp. 281–82.

49. West, *Mining Community in Northern New Spain*, p. 69; Alessio Robles, *Coahuila y Texas*, p. 607; Mota y Escobar, *Descripción geográfica*, pp. 163–67.

50. West, *Mining Community in Northern New Spain*, pp. 80, 127; Alessio Robles, *Coahuila y Texas*, pp. 402, 410, 608.

51. West, *Mining Community in Northern New Spain*, p. 127.

52. Morfi, *Viaje de indios*, p. 142; Bancroft, *North Mexican States*, Vol. II, p. 81; West, *Mining Community in Northern New Spain*, p. 127.

53. Alessio Robles, *Coahuila y Texas*, p. 36.

54. *Ibid.*, p. 608; Bancroft, *North Mexican States*, Vol. II, pp. 80–81.

55. Alessio Robles, *Coahuila y Texas*, p. 605.

56. *Ibid.*, p. 165.

57. *Ibid.*, p. 606. Bancroft, *North Mexican States*, Vol. II, p. 95, mentions the presence of a schoolmaster in Saltillo in 1811.

58. Alessio Robles, *Coahuila y Texas*, pp. 392, 609.

59. *Ibid.*, pp. 389–90, 392–93.

60. *Ibid.*, p. 606; Bancroft, *North Mexican States*, Vol. II, pp. 81–82.

61. Harris, "The North Mexican *Hacendado*," pp. 9–10.

62. Bolton, *Guide to Materials in the Archives of Mexico*, p. 410.

63. Vito Alessio Robles, *Monterrey en la historia y en la leyenda* (México, D.F.: Antigua Librería Robredo de José Porrúa e Hijos, 1936), pp. 93, 97; Hubert H. Bancroft, *History of Mexico*, 6 vols. (San Francisco: A. L. Bancroft and Company and The History Company, 1883–88), Vol. II, p. 777; Bolton and Marshall, *Colonization of North America*, pp. 60–61.

64. Alessio Robles, *Monterrey*, pp. 101, 109; Genaro García (ed.), *Historia de Nuevo León: con noticias sobre Coahuila, Texas, y Nuevo México* (México, D.F.: Librería de la Vda. de Ch. Bouret, 1909), p. 75.

65. Bancroft, *History of Mexico*, Vol. II, pp. 778–79; Rodrigo Mendirichaga, *Origenes y formación de Nuevo León: según dos cronicas del siglo XVII* (Monterrey, México: Ediciones Pauraque, 1954), p. 33.

66. Garcia, *Historia de Nuevo León*, p. 75; Bolton and Marshall, *Colonization of North America*, p. 60; Santiago Roel, *Nuevo León: apuntes históricas*, 4th ed. (Mon-

terrey, México: [Universidad de Nuevo León], 1952), p. 7; Mendirichaga, *Origenes y formación de Nuevo León*, p. 34.

67. Bolton and Marshall, *Colonization of North America*, p. 61; García, *Historia de Nuevo León*, p. 89.

68. Alessio Robles, *Coahuila y Texas*, p. 150; Roel, *Nuevo León*, p. 21; Bolton and Marshall, *Colonization of North America*, p. 61; Bancroft, *History of Mexico*, Vol. II, p. 780; Navarro García, *José de Gálvez*, p. 17. Mendirichaga, *Origenes y formación de Nuevo León*, p. 40, notes that the complete title of the city was Ciudad Metropolitana de Nuestra Señora de Monterrey.

69. Roel, *Nuevo León*, p. 8. Bancroft, *History of Mexico*, Vol. II, p. 780, erroneously claims that León was renamed Monterrey.

70. Roel, *Nuevo León*, p. 22.

71. *Ibid.*, p. 28; García, *Historia de Nuevo León*, pp. 125–26.

72. Roel, *Nuevo León*, p. 29; Navarro García, *José de Gálvez*, p. 17.

73. Mendirichaga, *Origenes y formación de Nuevo León*, p. 44.

74. Roel, *Nuevo León*, p. 30; Navarro García, *José de Gálvez*, p. 17. Bolton, *Guide to Materials in the Archives of Mexico*, p. 419, is in error when he states that Cadereita was founded in 1626. Mendirichaga, *Origenes y formación de Nuevo León*, p. 65, says that the date of the founding was March 12, 1637.

75. Roel, *Nuevo León*, p. 44.

76. Don Joseph Fernández de Jáuregui Urrutía, *Description of Nuevo León, Mexico (1735–1740)* (ed. and trans. by Malcolm D. McLean and Eugenio del Hoyo), (Monterrey, México: Instituto Tecnológico y de Estudios Superiores, 1964), pp. 88–95.

77. Kinnaird, *Frontiers of New Spain*, pp. 190, 195; Vito Alessio Robles (ed.), *Relación del viaje que hizo a los presidios internos situados en la frontera de America septentrional, por Nicolás de Lafora* (México, D.F.: Editorial Pedro Robredo, 1939), p. 250.

78. Bancroft, *History of Mexico*, Vol. II, p. 338n.

79. Nettie Lee Benson (ed. and trans.), *Report that Dr. Miguel Ramos de Arizpe . . . Presents to the August Congress on the Natural, Political, and Civil Conditions of the Provinces of Coahuila, Nuevo León, Nuevo Santander, and Texas . . .* (Austin: University of Texas Press, 1950), pp. 12–13.

80. Bancroft, *History of Mexico*, Vol. II, p. 777; Bolton and Marshall, *Colonization of North America*, p. 60; García, *Historia de Nuevo León*, pp. 74–75; Alessio Robles, *Monterrey*, pp. 101, 109.

81. Roel, *Nuevo León*, pp. 21, 23. These first settlers were listed by name, with the number of family members following each *vecino*. Bancroft, *History of Mexico*, Vol. II, p. 780, maintains that there were thirty-four families who settled Monterrey.

82. Mota y Escobar, *Descripción geográfica*, p. 208; Alessio Robles, *Monterrey*, p. 135.

83. Fernández de Jáuregui Urrutía, *Description of Nuevo León*, pp. 88–95. These figures did not include the numbers of children and servants.

84. Cook and Borah, *Essays in Population History*, p. 168.

85. Kinnaird, *Frontiers of New Spain*, p. 195; Alessio Robles, *Relación del viaje por Nicolás de Lafora*, p. 250.

86. Kinnaird, *Frontiers of New Spain*, p. 193.

87. Roel, *Nuevo León*, p. 65.

88. Bancroft, *History of Mexico*, Vol. II, p. 338n. Arizpe's estimate of seventy

thousand people for the province in 1811 seems high. See Benson, *Report that Miguel Ramos de Arizpe Presents*, p. 12.

89. Roel, *Nuevo León*, p. 65.

90. *Ibid.*

91. Bancroft, *History of Mexico*, Vol. II, pp. 335–36.

92. Alessio Robles, *Monterrey*, p. 137.

93. *Ibid.*, pp. 126, 129; Kinnaird, *Frontiers of New Spain*, p. 192.

94. Kinnaird, *Frontiers of New Spain*, p. 196; Benson, *Report that Miguel Ramos de Arizpe Presents*, pp. 20, 22.

95. Kinnaird, *Frontiers of New Spain*, p. 196. Mota y Escobar, *Descripción geográfica*, p. 209, reported that there was no news of any mines in the province in the early seventeenth century.

96. Roel, *Nuevo León*, p. 64.

97. Mota y Escobar, *Descripción geográfica*, p. 208, notes that the people lived in homes of "smeared palisades," and that they did not have adobe houses. Other references to *jacales* occur in Mendirichaga, *Origenes y formación de Nuevo León*, p. 4, and García, *Historia de Nuevo León*, p. 149.

98. Roel, *Nuevo León*, p. 53.

99. Mendirichaga, *Origines y formación de Nuevo León*, p. 64.

100. Roel, *Nuevo León*, pp. 26, 50, 53.

101. Bolton and Marshall, *Colonization of North America*, p. 61.

102. Mendirichaga, *Origenes y formación de Nuevo León*, p. 34; Bancroft, *History of Mexico*, Vol. II, p. 334; Bolton and Marshall, *Colonization of North America*, p. 60; Alessio Robles, *Coahuila y Texas*, p. 179; Fernández de Jáuregui Urrutía, *Description of Nuevo León*, p. 11.

103. Roel, *Nuevo León*, p. 49.

CHAPTER 2

1. There are many general studies of these explorations, as well as particular works on each one. For a good overview, see Rupert N. Richardson, *Texas: The Lone Star State* (New York: Prentice-Hall, 1943), pp. 19–21.

2. Fear of French aggression in Texas is noted by many authors as the principal reason for the settlement of the province. See, for example, *ibid.*, pp. 23–25; Lino Gómez Canedo, *Primeras exploraciones y poblamiento de Texas (1686–1694)* (Monterrey, México: Publicaciones del Instituto Tecnológico y de Estudios Superiores, 1968), p. xiv; T. R. Fehrenbach, *Lone Star: A History of Texas and the Texans* (New York: Macmillan, 1968), p. 40.

3. Richardson, *Texas*, p. 23.

4. Gómez Canedo, *Primeras exploraciones*, pp. xiv–xvii; Richardson, *Texas*, p. 25; Thomas P. O'Rourke, *The Franciscan Missions in Texas, 1690–1693* (Washington, D.C.: The Catholic University of America Studies in American Church History, 1927), p. 22. Fehrenbach, *Lone Star*, p. 41, states that the mission was located in Caddo County along the Trinity River.

5. Gómez Canedo, *Primeras exploraciones*, pp. xxvii, 310–13; Fehrenbach, *Lone Star*, p. 48.

6. Gómez Canedo, *Primeras exploraciones*, p. 314.

7. *Ibid.*, p. 274.

8. *Ibid.*, p. xxvii; Richardson, *Texas*, p. 25. Fehrenbach, *Lone Star*, pp. 41, 48, erroneously gives the date of abandonment as 1692.

9. Gómez Canedo, *Primeras exploraciones*, p. xxv.

10. Carlos E. Castañeda, *Our Catholic Heritage in Texas, 1519–1936,* 7 vols. (Austin, Texas: Van Boeckmann-Jones Co., 1936), Vol. II, pp. 45–47; Alessio Robles, *Coahuila y Texas,* p. 434. Odie B. Faulk, *A Successful Failure* (Austin, Texas: Steck-Vaughn Co., 1965), p. 78, states that the expedition consisted of sixty-five persons.

11. Richardson, *Texas*, p. 28; O'Rourke, *Franciscan Missions*, p. 22.

12. Fray Francisco Céliz, *Diary of the Alarcón Expedition into Texas, 1718–1719* (trans. and ed. by Fritz L. Hoffman), 2 vols. (Los Angeles: The Quivira Society, 1935), Vol. I, pp. 17–18, 38; Fritz L. Hoffman, "Martín de Alarcón and the Founding of San Antonio, Texas," in Thomas E. Cotner and Carlos E. Castañeda (eds.), *Essays in Mexican History* (Austin, Texas: Institute of Latin American Studies, 1958), p. 25; Carlos E. Castañeda, *A Report on the Spanish Archives in San Antonio, Texas* (San Antonio, Texas: Yanaguana Society, 1937), p. 19.

13. Céliz, *Diary of the Alarcón Expedition*, Vol. I, p. 23; Hoffman, "Martín de Alarcón and the Founding of San Antonio," pp. 26–27; Castañeda, *Our Catholic Heritage*, Vol. II, p. 91.

14. Céliz, *Diary of the Alarcón Expedition*, Vol. I, p. 23; Hoffman, "Martín de Alarcón and the Founding of San Antonio," pp. 27–28; Castañeda, *Our Catholic Heritage*, Vol. II, p. 92; Faulk, *Successful Failure*, p. 83.

15. Hoffman, "Martín de Alarcón and the Founding of San Antonio," p. 30.

16. Castañeda, *Our Catholic Heritage*, Vol. II, p. 91.

17. *Ibid.*, p. 144; Alessio Robles, *Coahuila y Texas*, p. 467; Richardson, *Texas*, p. 29; Gerald Ashford, *Spanish Texas: Yesterday and Today* (Austin and New York: Pemberton Press, 1971), pp. 125–26.

18. Castañeda, *Report on Spanish Archives*, p. 20; Richardson, *Texas*, pp. 29–30.

19. Alessio Robles, *Coahuila y Texas*, p. 470; Richardson, *Texas*, p. 30.

20. Alessio Robles, *Coahuila y Texas*, pp. 470–71. Castañeda, *Our Catholic Heritage*, Vol. II, p. 268, maintains that the Council of the Indies, not the Marqués de Aguayo, recommended that Canary Islanders be sent to Texas to settle San Fernando de Béxar. This is probably true in that Council of the Indies was the final authority, but the initial suggestion seems to have come much earlier from the marqués.

21. Castañeda, *Our Catholic Heritage*, Vol. II, pp. 278, 285; Robert S. Weddle, *San Juan Bautista: Gateway to Spanish Texas* (Austin and London: University of Texas Press, 1968), pp. 191–92.

22. Castañeda, *Our Catholic Heritage*, Vol. II, pp. 291–93; Weddle, *San Juan Bautista*, p. 191; Alessio Robles, *Coahuila y Texas*, p. 471.

23. Weddle, *San Juan Bautista*, p. 192; Castañeda, *Our Catholic Heritage*, Vol. II, p. 301. Castañeda, *Report on Spanish Archives*, p. 21, is in error when he states that only ten families reached San Antonio, for the documents in the Béxar Archives clearly give the number as fifteen and list each of the families.

24. Isaac J. Cox, "The Early Settlers of San Fernando," *Quarterly of the Texas State Historical Association*, Vol. 5, No. 2 (October, 1901), p. 147.

25. Don Juan de Acuña, Marqués de Casafuerte, Mexico City, November 28, 1730, BA, B24/142.

26. Testimonio de las diligencias echas por el S.ᵒʳ factor D.ⁿ Manuel Angel de Villegas Puente para el despacho y aviso de las familias que de orden de S. M. passan

apoblar ala provincia de los Tejas, Cuautitlán, November 5, 1730, BA, B12/113. J. Villasana Haggard has made a translation of this document and it is located in the same box of this collection.

27. *Ibid*.

28. Don Juan Antonio Peres de Almasan, Presidio de San Antonio de Béxar, March 10, 1731, BA, B12/114. A Haggard translation accompanies this document also.

29. Representaz.ⁿ hecha al S.ᵒʳ Barón de Riparda [*sic*] por el Cabildo . . ., February 7, 1771, NA; Castañeda, *Report on Spanish Archives*, pp. 21–22.

30. See Robert S. Weddle, *The San Sabá Mission: Spanish Pivot in Texas* (Austin: University of Texas Press, 1964), for a thorough study of this settlement; Richardson, *Texas*, p. 35.

31. Weddle, *San Juan Bautista*, pp. 544–47.

32. *Ibid*., pp. 339–44.

33. *Ibid*., p. 562.

34. Castañeda, *Our Catholic Heritage*, Vol. IV, pp. 66–98.

35. Herbert E. Bolton, *Texas in the Middle Eighteenth Century: Studies in Spanish Colonial Administration* (Berkeley: University of California Press, 1915, and New York, Russell and Russell, 1962), pp. 377–80.

36. *Ibid*., pp. 387–92; Castañeda, *Our Catholic Heritage*, Vol. IV, pp. 297–301.

37. Bolton, *Texas in the Middle Eighteenth Century*, pp. 394–96. The claim that there was no room for the Adaesanos at San Fernando is, according to Bolton, "absurd."

38. *Ibid*., pp. 401–402, 404.

39. *Ibid*., pp. 405–16, 426–40; Castañeda, *Our Catholic Heritage*, Vol. IV, pp. 313–27, 332–35.

40. Bolton, *Texas in the Middle Eighteenth Century*, p. 445.

41. Marqués de Altamira to Viceroy, February 29, 1752, in *ibid*., p. 309.

42. D. W. Meinig, *Imperial Texas: An Interpretive Essay in Cultural Geography* (Austin: University of Texas Press, 1969), p. 23.

43. *Ibid*., pp. 24–25.

44. El Barón de Ripperdá, Béjar, November 6, 1777, Estado general que manifiesta el número de vasallos y habitantes que tiene el Rey en esta Provincia de Texas, con distinción de clases, estados, y castas de todas las personas de ambos sexos, sin excluir los parvalos, BNM, in Morfi, *Viaje de indios*, Appendix II, pp. 275–80. These statistics are repeated by Alessio Robles, *Coahuila y Texas*, pp. 525–27.

45. Dom.ᵒ Cabello, Estado que manifiesta el número de vasallos y habitantes que tiene el Rey en esta Provincia . . ., Provincia de Texas, Real Presidio de San Antonio de Béxar, December 31, 1784, NA. Castañeda, *Our Catholic Heritage*, Vol. V, p. 32, sums up the figures for 1783 from this census.

46. Manuel Muñoz, Estado general de la Provincia de los Texas, Año de 1792, San Antonio de Béxar, December 31, 1792, NA.

47. O'Rourke, *Franciscan Missions*, p. 76; Castañeda, *Report on Spanish Archives*, p. 24.

48. Juan Baut.ª de Elguezábal, Estado que manifiesta el número de habitantes en la dicha provincia en el año 1804, Provincia de Texas, San Antonio de Béxar, January 30, 1805, BA, B24/133.

49. Nettie Lee Benson, (ed. and trans.), "A Governor's Report on Texas in 1809," *SWHQ*, Vol. 71, No. 4 (April, 1968), p. 611. For the Salcedo administration, see

Félix D. Almaráz, Jr., *Tragic Cavalier: Governor Manuel de Salcedo of Texas, 1808–1813* (Austin and London: University of Texas Press, 1971). Zebulon Pike's estimate of seven thousand people in the entire province is high. See Donald Jackson (ed.), *The Journals of Zebulon Montgomery Pike: with Letters and Related Documents*, 2 vols. (Norman: University of Oklahoma Press, 1966), Vol. II, p. 79. However, it should be noted that Pike visited only San Antonio and then for only six days, from June 7 to June 13, 1807.

50. David M. Vigness, *The Revolutionary Decades, 1810–1836* (Austin, Texas: Steck-Vaughn Co., 1965), p. 24, notes that in all there may have been some 2,500 people of European descent in Texas by 1820.

51. Barón de Ripperdá, Estado general que manifiesta el número de vasallos . . ., Béjar, November 6, 1777, BNM, in Morfi, *Viaje de indios*, p. 275.

52. Compiled from the following sources: Castañeda, *Our Catholic Heritage*, Vol. V, p. 32; Dom.º Cabello, Estado que manifiesta el número de vasallos . . ., December 31, 1784, NA; Antonio Gil Ybarbo, [Padrón] del Pueblo y Jurisdición de Nacogdoches, January 23, 1793, NA; Juan Baut.ª Elguezábal, Estado que manifiesta el número de habitantes . . ., San Antonio de Béxar, January 30, 1805, BA, B24/133; Jackson, *Journals of Zebulon Pike*, Vol. II, pp. 78–79; Benson, "Governor's Report on Texas in 1809," p. 611; Mattie A. Hatcher, *The Opening of Texas to Foreign Settlement, 1801–1821* (Austin: University of Texas Press, 1927), pp. 356–57.

53. Real Presidio de la Bahía de el Espíritu Santo, Extracto general de la tropa y vecindario de dicho presidio, January 12, 1780, photostat, THRL (Alamo).

54. Bernardo Serñi and Fr. Th.ᵉ Fran.ᶜᵒ López, Padrón de almas que existen en 31 de diciembre de 1792, Año de 1792, San Antonio de Béxar, December 31, 1792, NA.

55. Translations of Census Reports of Eastern Texas from the Nacogdoches Archives, University of Texas Archives, B14/4, Vol. 8, pp. 199–201.

56. *Ibid.*, pp. 216–18.

57. Barón de Ripperdá, Estado general que manifiesta el número de vasallos . . ., November 6, 1777, BNM, in Morfi, *Viaje de indios*, p. 276.

58. Real Presidio de la Bahía de el Espíritu Santo, Extracto general de la tropa y vecindario . . ., January 12, 1780, THRL (Alamo).

59. Dom.º Cabello, Estado que manifiesta el número de vasallos . . ., December 31, 1784, NA.

60. Antonio Gil Ybarbo, [Padrón] del pueblo y jurisdición de Nacogdoches, January 23, 1793, NA.

61. Manuel Muñoz, Estado general de la provincia de los Texas, San Antonio de Béxar, December 31, 1792, NA.

62. *Ibid.*; Bisente Amador y Salvador Rodrígues, Villa de San Fernando, Jurisdición de la Provincia de Texas, Año de 1792, NA; Hatcher, *Opening of Texas*. p. 357.

63. Castañeda, *Report on Spanish Archives*, pp. 21–22; Cox, "Early Settlers of San Fernando," pp. 152–58.

64. Representaz.ⁿ hecha al S.ᵒʳ Barón de Riparda [*sic*] por el Cabildo . . ., February 7, 1771, NA.

65. Cox, "Early Settlers of San Fernando," p. 159.

66. Barón de Ripperdá, Estado general que manifiesta el número de vasallos . . ., November 6, 1777, BNM, in Morfi, *Viaje de indios*, p. 276.

67. Real Presidio de la Bahía de el Espíritu Santo, Extracto general de la tropa y vecindario . . ., January 12, 1780, THRL (Alamo).

68. Manuel Muñoz, Estado general de la provincia de los Texas, San Antonio de Béxar, December 31, 1792, NA; Bisente Amador y Salvador Rodríguez, Villa de San

Fernando, Año de 1792, NA; Bernardo Serñi and Fr. Th.ᵉ Francisco López, Padrón de almas que existen en 31 de diciembre de 1792, Villa de San Fernando de Béxar, NA.

69. Tomás de Arocha and Manuel Barrera, List of Families in the Villa of San Fernando and Presidio of Béxar Made by the Two Alcaldes for the Year 1804, December 31, 1804, BA, B24/133.

70. Hatcher, *Opening of Texas*, pp. 357–58.

71. Castañeda, *Our Catholic Heritage*, Vol. V, p. 24; Faulk, *Successful Failure*, p. 145.

72. Sandra L. Myres, *The Ranch in Spanish Texas* (El Paso: Texas Western Press, 1969), p. 11.

73. *Ibid.*; Faulk, *Successful Failure*, p. 146.

74. Myres, *Ranch in Spanish Texas*, p. 12.

75. *Ibid.*, p. 14.

76. *Ibid.*, pp. 16–19.

77. *Ibid.*, p. 21.

78. *Ibid.*, p. 22; Padrón de los ranchos comprehendidos en la jurisdición del sindico D. Joaquín Leal, San Fernando de Béxar, December 18, 1810, NA.

79. Myrcs, *Ranch in Spanish Texas*, pp. 23–47, 52, 55–56.

80. Faulk, *Successful Failure*, p. 151; Castañeda, *Our Catholic Heritage*, Vol. III, pp. 84–86; Lt. Col. Don Juan Bautista Elguezábal to Comandante-General, June 20, 1803, in Hatcher, *Opening of Texas*, pp. 303–305.

81. Castañeda, *Our Catholic Heritage*, Vol. III, p. 78, discusses one of these shortage periods in 1736.

82. Meinig, *Imperial Texas*, p. 26; Almaráz, *Tragic Cavalier*, p. 11; O'Rourke, *Franciscan Missions*, p. 88; Castañeda, *Our Catholic Heritage*, Vol. III, p. 53; Benson, "Governor's Report on Texas in 1809," pp. 612–15; Manuel Salcedo, Béxar, May 7, 1809, University of Texas Archives, B12/127.

83. Teodoro de Croix, Chihuahua, February 15, 1779, BA, B24/151; Noticia de producto de estafeta de esta villa, 804 a 08 inclusivos, Béxar, June 25, 1809, NA.

84. Joseph Padrón, Villa de San Fernando, July 7, 1733, BA, B24/112.

85. Isaac J. Cox, "Educational Efforts in San Fernando de Béxar," *Quarterly of the Texas State Historical Association*, Vol. 6 (1902), p. 28; Faulk, *Successful Failure*, p. 165.

86. Cox, "Educational Efforts in San Fernando de Béxar," p. 29; Faulk, *Successful Failure*, pp. 165–67.

87. Nemesio Salcedo to Governor of Texas, Chiguagua, February 11, 1805, BA, B24/133.

88. Dionisio Valle to Don Juan Bautista Elguezábal, Nacogdoches, June 3, 1805, BA, B24/133.

89. Cox, "Educational Efforts in San Fernando de Béxar," pp. 29–30; Padre Mariano Sosa, Curate of Nacogdoches, to the Governor of Texas, Nacogdoches, May 26, 1810, BA, B12/127, translation, Vol. 830, pp. 79, 82–83.

90. Cox, "Educational Efforts in San Fernando de Béxar," pp. 30–32.

91. Governor Don Manuel de Salcedo and Settlers of San Antonio, Béxar, March 1, 1812, THRL (Alamo).

92. Padre Mariano Sosa to Governor of Texas, Nacogdoches, May 26, 1810, BA, B12/127, Volume 830, pp. 79–83.

93. Francisco Viana to Governor Don Juan Bautista Elguezábal, Bahía del Espíritu Santo, June 24, 1805, BA, B24/133.

94. Don Antonio Gil Ybarbo, Lieutenant Governor, Nuestra Señora del Pilar de Nacogdoches, [1783?], BA, B12/127, translation, Vol. 830, p. 32.

95. *Ibid.,* pp. 33–44.

96. Faulk, *Successful Failure,* pp. 172–75; Castañeda, *Our Catholic Heritage,* Vol. V, pp. 414–15.

97. Castañeda, *Our Catholic Heritage,* Vol. III, p. 71 and Vol. V, p. 204; Faulk, *Successful Failure,* pp. 167–68.

98. Castañeda, *Our Catholic Heritage,* Vol. V, pp. 203–204, 409–10; Faulk, *Successful Failure,* pp. 167–68.

99. Antonio Cordero, Béxar, April 8, 1806, BA, B24/135; Faulk, *Successful Failure,* p. 168; Don Antonio Cordero y Bustamente, Béxar, November 23, 1805, BA, B24/134.

100. Castañeda, *Our Catholic Heritage,* Vol. III, p. 78.

101. *Ibid.,* Vol. IV, p. 18.

102. Fray Juan Agustín de Morfi, *History of Texas, 1673–1779* (trans. and ed. by Carlos E. Castañeda), 2 vols. (Albuquerque, N.Mex.: Quivira Society, 1935), Vol. I, pp. 79, 92.

103. Jackson, *Journals of Zebulon Pike,* Vol. II, p. 78.

104. Faulk, *Successful Failure,* pp. 176–77; Jackson, *Journals of Zebulon Pike,* Vol. I, p. 437; Bessie L. Fitzhugh, *Bells over Texas* (El Paso: Texas Western Press, 1955), pp. 39–47.

105. Richardson, *Texas,* pp. 50–53; Almaráz, *Tragic Cavalier,* p. 124; Juan Manuel Lambrano to Comandante-General, Ciudad de San Fernando, June 19, 1811, NA.

CHAPTER 3

1. Florence Johnson Scott, "Spanish Colonization on the Lower Río Grande, 1747–1767," in Cotner and Castañeda, *Essays in Mexican History,* pp. 4–9; Lawrence F. Hill, *José de Escandón and the Founding of Nuevo Santander: A Study in Spanish Colonization* (Columbus: Ohio State University Press, 1926), pp. 4–5; Seb S. Wilcox (comp.), "Data on Laredo History to 1820," folder in Special Collections, St. Mary's University Library, San Antonio, Texas, p. 1.

2. Scott, "Spanish Colonization on the Lower Río Grande," pp. 10–11; Hill, *José de Escandón,* pp. 5–6.

3. Hill, *José de Escandón,* pp. 6–7; Wilcox, "Data on Laredo History to 1820," p. 2.

4. Wilcox, "Data on Laredo History to 1820," p. 2; Scott, "Spanish Colonization on the Lower Río Grande," pp. 12–14. Wilcox maintains that Mier was founded in 1753, but Mrs. Scott states that the exact date of its founding was March 6, 1752.

5. Hill, *José de Escandón,* pp. 7–8; Bolton, *Texas in the Middle Eighteenth Century,* p. 298. Navarro García, *José de Gálvez,* p. 96, estimates that more than five thousand settlers came to Nuevo Santander over a seven-year period, while Wilcox, "Data on Laredo History to 1820," p. 2, claims that only thirty-six hundred Spaniards were settled in this region by Escandón.

6. Scott, "Spanish Colonization on the Lower Río Grande," p. 12, reports that Camargo had sixty-five families and Reynosa, forty-three in 1750; the two communities also possessed thirty-six thousand head of livestock.

7. Bolton, *Texas in the Middle Eighteenth Century,* p. 298. Hill, *José de Escandón,* p. 104, states that there were 6,383 persons in the twenty-three communities by 1755. In addition, there were 2,857 Indians congregated near the province's fifteen missions by that time.

8. Hill, *José de Escandón*, pp. 106–107.

9. *Ibid.*, p. 9.

10. *Ibid.*, pp. 112–38.

11. *Ibid.*, pp. 9–10.

12. Myres, *Ranch in Spanish Texas*, p. 60, citing document titled Estado general de la colonia del Seno Mexicano . . ., in *Estado general de las fundaciones hechas por D. José de Escandón*, 2 vols. (México, D.F., 1929). I have added the totals. There are minor differences in the figures reported for Reynosa and Camargo in the text of Hill, *José de Escandón*, pp. 128, 130.

13. Félix Calleja, Informe gral. sobre colonia de Nuevo Santander y Nuevo Reyno de León, Villa Capital de Santander, July 25, 1795, photostat, University of Texas Archives, B12/124, Vol. 805. In this document the total population of Nuevo Santander is given in one place as 30,450 civilized persons, while in two others it is shown as 30,318 and 30,435, respectively.

14. Seb S. Wilcox, "The Spanish Archives of Laredo," *SWHQ*, Vol. 49, No. 3 (January, 1946), pp. 342, 346.

15. "Inventory of the County Archives of Texas," No. 240, Webb County, St. Mary's University Library, p. 10, citing *Estado general de las fundaciones hechas por D. José de Escandón en la colonia del Nuevo Santander*, 2 vols. (México, D.F.: Archivo General de la Nación, 1929), Vol. I, pp. 448–49.

16. Wilcox, "Spanish Archives of Laredo," p. 346.

17. Estado que manifiesta los vecinos de esta villa de S.ⁿ Agustín de Laredo, Villa de Laredo, January 29, 1789, LA.

18. Calleja, Informe gral., Villa Capital de Santander, July 25, 1795, University of Texas Archives, B12/124, Vol. 805.

19. Yldefonso Ramón, Padrón, Villa de Laredo, Provincia de Nuevo Santander, Intendencia de San Luis Potosí, April 30, 1819, LA.

20. Hill, *José de Escandón*, pp. 70, 113; Scott, "Spanish Colonization on the Lower Río Grande," pp. 8–9; Florence Johnson Scott, *Royal Land Grants North of the Río Grande, 1777–1821: Early History of Large Grants Made by Spain to Families in the Jurisdiction of Reynosa* ([n.p.]: Texian Press, 1969), pp. 3, 6.

21. Hill, *José de Escandón*, p. 70; "Inventory of the County Archives of Texas," No. 240, Webb County, St. Mary's University Library, p. 10; Estado que manifiesta los vecinos, Villa de Laredo, January 29, 1789, LA; Ramón, Padrón, Villa de Laredo, April 30, 1789, LA.

22. Hill, *José de Escandón*, pp. 6–9; Calleja, Informe gral., Villa Capital de Santander, July 25, 1795, University of Texas Archives, B12/124, Vol. 805.

23. "Inventory of the County Archives of Texas," No. 240, Webb County, St. Mary's University Library, pp. 10, 11, 13.

24. Calleja, Informe gral., Villa Capital de Santander, July 25, 1795, University of Texas Archives, B12/124, Vol. 805; Scott, Royal Land Grants, p. 5; Ramón, Padrón, Villa de Laredo, April 30, 1789, LA; Don Estevan Grande to Justicia Mayor, Villa de Laredo, February 18, 1809, LA.

25. Hill, *José de Escandón*, p. 9; Scott, "Spanish Colonization on the Lower Río Grande," p. 16.

26. Bolton, *Texas in the Middle Eighteenth Century*, p. 299.

27. General Visitation of the Villa de Laredo, 1767 (trans. by J. Villasana Haggard), University of Texas Archives, B12/117, pp. 5–6, 56; Scott, "Spanish Colonization on the Lower Río Grande," pp. 17–19; Scott, *Royal Land Grants*, pp. 13, 15; Wilcox, "Data on Laredo History to 1820," pp. 49–50.

28. *Ibid.*, p. 51.

29. *Ibid.*, p. 2.

30. General Visitation of the Villa de Laredo, 1767, University of Texas Archives, B12/117, pp. 22, 55; Scott, "Spanish Colonization on the Lower Río Grande," p. 19; Scott, *Royal Land Grants*, pp. 14–15; Wilcox, "Data on Laredo History to 1820," pp. 38–46, 50. Fehrenbach, *Lone Star*, p. 76, erroneously calls these grants "*mercedes*," and says that they were one-half-mile wide along the riverfront. In general, Spanish land grants were called *mercedes*, but in this instance the term *porción* was used.

31. Wilcox, "Data on Laredo History to 1820," p. 2.

32. Hill, *José de Escandón*, pp. 115, 138; Calleja, Informe gral., Villa Capital de Santander, July 25, 1795, University of Texas Archives, B12/124, Vol. 805.

33. Santiago de Jesús Sánchez, Villa de Laredo, March 22, 1783, LA. There is a summary of the contents of this document in Wilcox, "Spanish Archives of Laredo," p. 349.

34. Miguel Ponse Borrego, The. Justisia Mallor, Villa de S.ⁿ Agustín de Laredo, July 5, 1788, LA; Don José Gonsáles, Teniente Justicia Mayor, Villa de Laredo, August 22, 1790, LA; Tomás Sánchez, San Agustín de Laredo, May 29, 1779, LA.

35. Santiago de Jesús Sánchez, Villa de S.ⁿ Agustín de Laredo, May 30, 1784. This document is also summarized in Wilcox, "Spanish Archives of Laredo," pp. 349–50.

36. Diego de Lasaga, Gov. de N. Santander, April 18, 1781, LA; Gonsáles, Villa de Laredo, August 22, 1790, LA; Santiago de Jesús Sánchez, Villa de S.ⁿ Agustín de Laredo, May 6, 1799, and José Jesús de la Garza, Laredo, [n.d.], LA.

37. Ponse Borrego, Villa de S.ⁿ Agustín de Laredo, July 5, 1788, LA; Gonsáles, Villa de Laredo, August 22, 1790, LA; José Jesús de la Garza, Capitán de Milicias y Justicia, Villa de S.ⁿ Agustín de Laredo, March 28, 1796, LA.

38. Ponse Borrego, Villa de S.ⁿ Agustín de Laredo, July 5, 1788, LA; Gonsáles, Villa de Laredo, August 22, 1790, LA.

39. Miguel Ponze Borrego, Estado que manifiesta el N. de Yndios y Yndias . . . de que se compone la nación de los Carrisos agregados a la Villa de Laredo . . ., Laredo, July 14, 1788, LA.

40. Wilcox, "Spanish Archives of Laredo," pp. 355–56; Ramón Perea, Laredo, August 1, 1815, LA.

41. Seb S. Wilcox, "Laredo during the Texas Republic," SWHQ, Vol. 42, No. 2 (October, 1938), p. 88.

42. Calleja, Informe gral., Villa Capital de Santander, July 25, 1795, University of Texas Archives, B12/124, Vol. 805.

43. José Gonsáles, San Agustín de Laredo, July 4, 1790, LA.

44. José Antonio García Davila, Villa de Laredo, December 31, 1814, LA.

45. Joseph Trebiño y Nicolás de Ybarra, Villa de S.ⁿ Agustín de Laredo, February 27, 1771, LA.

46. Santiago de Jesús Sánchez, [Laredo, 1782?], LA. Señora Uriburu also declared that she had married D. Juan Guerra (deceased) in the Valle de Salinas and had borne three daughters and a son (deceased). She was forty-eight years old, "*poco más o menos*" (more or less), and did not know how to sign her name.

47. José M.ᵃ Tovar, Alcalde, Laredo, August 24, 1815, LA.

48. José María Elizondo, Villa de San Agustín de Laredo, May 11, 1811, LA.

49. Yldefonso García, Laredo, July 12, 1811, LA.

50. José María Tovar, Alcalde, Inventorio de los bienes de D.ᵃ Alexandra Sánchez, Laredo, May 22, 1815, LA.

51. Hill, *José de Escandón*, p. 71; Ramón, Padrón, Villa de Laredo, April 30, 1819, LA.

52. Hill, *José de Escandón*, p. 103.

53. Seb S. Wilcox, "Data on Laredo History, 1821 to Date," folder in St. Mary's University Library, p. 177; Wilcox, "Spanish Archives of Laredo," p. 356; "Inventory of the County Archives of Texas," No. 240, Webb County, St. Mary's University Library, pp. 42–45.

54. Wilcox, "Spanish Archives of Laredo," pp. 353–55.

INTRODUCTION TO PART II

1. Herbert E. Bolton, "The Northward Movement in New Spain," in Bannon, *Bolton and the Spanish Borderlands*, p. 79.

CHAPTER 4

1. West, *Mining Community in Northern New Spain*, p. 6.

2. *Ibid.*, p. 3.

3. J. Lloyd Mecham, *Francisco de Ibarra and Nueva Vizcaya* (Durham, N.C.: Duke University Press, 1927), pp. 59, 61; Mota y Escobar, *Descripción geográfica*, p. 186.

4. Mecham, *Francisco de Ibarra*, p. 3.

5. Florence C. Lister and Robert H. Lister, *Chihuahua: Storehouse of Storms* (Albuquerque: University of New Mexico Press, 1966), p. 19.

6. Mecham, *Francisco de Ibarra*, p. 71.

7. *Ibid.*, pp. 102–109.

8. *Ibid.*, pp. 113–23; Bancroft, *North Mexican States*, Vol. I, pp. 103–11.

9. Mecham, *Francisco de Ibarra*, p. 141.

10. *Ibid.*, p. 127; Lister and Lister, *Chihuahua*, p. 20; West, *Mining Community in Northern New Spain*, p. 10.

11. Vito Alessio Robles, *Francisco de Urdiñola y el norte de la Nueva España* (México, D.F.: Imprenta Mundial, 1931), pp. 171–85; Bolton, "The Northward Movement in New Spain," in Bannon, *Bolton and the Spanish Borderlands*, p. 82; Bancroft, *North Mexican States*, Vol. I, pp. 112, 126. For Coahuila's early settlement in the vicinity of Saltillo and Parras, see Chap. 1.

12. Bancroft, *North Mexican States*, Vol. I, pp. 305–306.

13. Mota y Escobar, *Descripción geográfica*, pp. 190–97.

14. Francisco R. Almada, *Resumen de historia del estado de Chihuahua* (México, D.F.: Libros Mexicanos, 1955), p. 57; West, *Mining Community in Northern New Spain*, pp. 12–13, 83.

15. Almada, *Historia del estado de Chihuahua*, p. 58.

16. Charles W. Hackett (ed.), *Historical Documents Relating to New Mexico, Nueva Vizcaya, and Approaches Thereto, to 1773*, 3 vols. (Washington, D.C.: Carnegie Institution, 1923–37), Vol. II, p. 7.

17. Lister and Lister, *Chihuahua*, p. 33. A *marco* is approximately one-half of a pound, according to J. Villasana Haggard and Malcolm D. McLean, *Handbook for Translators of Spanish Historical Documents* ([Austin]: University of Texas Archives Collections, 1941), p. 80.

18. Hackett, *Historical Documents*, Vol. II, p. 7.

19. *Ibid.*, pp. 4, 389. Marín's report of September 30, 1693, is contained in this volume, pp. 387–410.

20. Navarro García, *José de Gálvez*, p. 60.

21. Almada, *Historia del estado de Chihuahua*, pp. 89–95; Bancroft, *North Mexican States*, Vol. I, p. 600.

22. Almada, *Historia del estado de Chihuahua*, pp. 111–12.

23. Lista de subjetos que denominan para que quedan salir desta jurisdiz.ⁿ del Paso del Río del Norte a poblaz.ⁿ el Paraje del Carrizal, JA, microcopy, University of Texas at El Paso Library, reel 42, frames 062ff.

24. Manuel Antonio S.ⁿ Juan, Paso del Norte, November 1, 1758, JA, microcopy, reel 42, frames 113–15.

25. Indice, o descripción plano del pueblo, que se pretende hazer en el paraje llamado del Carrizal, Documentos de 1758, JA, microcopy, reel 42, frame 061.

26. Bancroft, *North Mexican States*, Vol. I, pp. 103–104.

27. *Ibid.*, p. 111.

28. Lister and Lister, *Chihuahua*, p. 20; Mota y Escobar, *Descripción geográfica*, pp. 198–99.

29. Borah, "Francisco de Urdiñola's Census, 1604," *HAHR*, pp. 398–402. For other references to this same census, see Cook and Borah, *Essays in Population History*, p. 131, and Alessio Robles, *Francisco de Urdiñola*, pp. 286–89.

30. Hackett, *Historical Documents*, Vol. II, pp. 16, 393.

31. *Ibid.*, pp. 8–13.

32. *Ibid.*, p. 391.

33. *Ibid.*, pp. 74–78, 405.

34. Navarro García, *José de Gálvez*, pp. 114–16.

35. Bancroft, *North Mexican States*, Vol. I, pp. 596–97.

36. *Ibid.*, p. 598; Lister and Lister, *Chihuahua*, pp. 66.

37. Navarro García, *José de Gálvez*, p. 112, states that there were five presidios in 1755, but he includes the one at El Paso del Norte which then belonged to New Mexico.

38. Kinnaird, *Frontiers of New Spain*, p. 76.

39. *Ibid.*, pp. 8, 10, 59, 66, 69.

40. Alonso Pedro O'Crouley, *A Description of the Kingdom of New Spain*, 1774 (trans. and ed. by Seán Galvin), ([San Francisco]: John Howell Books, 1972), p. 18.

41. *Ibid.*

42. *Ibid.*, p. 128.

43. Navarro García, *José de Gálvez*, pp. 405–406.

44. *Ibid.*, p. 409.

45. *Ibid.*, p. 408.

46. *Ibid.*, pp. 410–13.

47. *Ibid.*, p. 368.

48. Almada, *Historia del estado de Chihuahua*, pp. 127–33, presents the population figures for the Chihuahuan region, but the author errs in accepting the total of 100,752 for the *villa* of Chihuahua. Such a figure is impossible, for it would cause the sum of the figures for each community to exceed the total of 124,151 for the province as a whole. The settlement listings, although they do not so state, must include only Spaniards and mixed bloods, for the total is only 62,578, when all the communities are added together. If we subtract the 5,233 inhabitants given for El Paso del Norte (properly considered with New Mexico) and add Croix's estimated 70,050 Christianized Indians shown eight years earlier, we then have a figure of 127,395 for the province, quite closely approximating the total figure given by Almada.

49. Bancroft, *North Mexican States*, Vol. I, p. 691.

50. Jackson, *Journals of Zebulon Pike*, Vol. I, pp. 409, 411, 422.

51. *Ibid.*, Vol. II, p. 65.

52. Almada, *Historia del estado de Chihuahua*, p. 131; Lister and Lister, *Chihuahua*, p. 88.

53. Memoria sobre el Reyno de Nueva España, Provincias Internas y Californias; formado por el Coronel del Real Cuerpo de Ingenieros del Exército D.ⁿ Juan Camargo y Cavallero en Veracruz, á 24 de Octubre de 1815, microcopy, Servicio Histórico Militar (Madrid) doc. 5-2-4-3. I am indebted to Dr. Janet Fireman of Fresno State College for bringing this manuscript to my attention.

54. Padrón del vecindario q.ᵉ tiene este R.ˡ de Minas de S.ⁿ José del Parral y su jurisdición, Año de 1788, AHP, microcopy, Center of Southwest Studies, Fort Lewis College, Durango, Colorado, reel 1788A, doc. 2.

55. *Ibid.*; Navarro García, *José de Gálvez*, p. 117. O'Crouley, *Kingdom of New Spain*, plate 13, facing p. 19, defines a *coyote* as a combination of an Indian and a mestizo.

56. West, *Mining Community in Northern New Spain*, p. 5.

57. Padrón del vecindario, 1788, AHP, microcopy, reel 1788A, doc. 2.

58. Navarro García, *José de Gálvez*, pp. 116–17.

59. *Ibid.*, p. 116.

60. Padrón de los vecinos de esta demarcación, July 10, 1649, AHP, microcopy, reel 1649A.

61. Juan Fran.ᶜᵒ Antonio Gijón Váldez, Padrón formado de este Real de Señor S.ⁿ Josef del Parral y su jurisdiz.ⁿ, Año de 1768, AHP, microcopy, reel 1768, doc. 1.

62. Padrón del vecindario, 1788, AHP, microcopy, reel 1788A, doc. 2.

63. West, *Mining Community in Northern New Spain*, pp. 23, 25.

64. Autos de Visita General . . . del D.ⁿ Juan Francisco de Córdoba, Governador y Cap.ⁿ Gral., Nueva Vizcaya, Año de 1707, AHP, microcopy, reel 1707, doc. G-19. Most of the *haciendas* and *ranchos* are simply listed for the date when the *visitador* and the owner went over the books and papers of the establishment. The *visitador* reminded the owner of his obligations to treat his workers well and educate them in the mysteries of the Catholic faith.

65. Mecham, *Francisco de Ibarra*, p. 204; West, *Mining Community in Northern New Spain*, pp. 5, 9, 11, 57, 61–62.

66. Borah, "Francisco de Urdiñola's Census, 1604," pp. 399–402.

67. Mecham, *Francisco de Ibarra*, pp. 204–206.

68. Lister and Lister, *Chihuahua*, p. 48.

69. *Ibid.*

70. Haggard and McLean, *Handbook for Translators*, p. 77.

71. Lister and Lister, *Chihuahua*, p. 49.

72. Alessio Robles, *Francisco de Urdiñola*, p. 66.

73. Donald D. Brand, "The Early History of the Range Cattle Industry in Northern Mexico," *Agricultural History*, Vol. 35, No. 3 (July, 1961), p. 134.

74. Autos de Visita General . . . del D.ⁿ Juan Francisco de Córdoba, Año de 1707, AHP, microcopy, reel 1707, doc. No. G-19.

75. Padrón de este año de 1788 fecho por orden del senor subdelegado D.ⁿ Manuel Rodrígues, Haz.ᵈᵃ de S.ᵗᵃ Rosa, AHP, microcopy, reel 1788A, doc. 2.

76. See, for example, Bando para que se alisten todos los vecinos del Real, Las Minas del Parral, May 12, 1641, AHP, microcopy, reel 1641A, for an early order, followed by two lists, one with 142 names and another with 61 *vecinos* thereon. Also,

see Autos y lista de algunos vecinos de este Real, Real de Minas del Parral, June 1, 1614, AHP, microcopy, reel 1648; Bando para que se alisten los vecinos de este Real, AHP, microcopy, reel 1668A; and Revista de vecinos de S.ta Bárbara y de El Oro mandada pasar por el Gobernador de Santa Bárbara, July 30, 1719, AHP, microcopy, reel 1716A. These are only a small sample of the many muster lists compiled in the civil settlements.

77. Autos pronunciados por el S.or Gen.l Don Carlos de Mendoza, April 17, 1666, AHP, microcopy, reel 1666A.

78. Lista y muestra de los vecinos del Parral y su jurisdiz.on, Año de 1672, AHP, microcopy, reel 1672A, doc. 7.

79. AHP, Administrativa y de Guerra, microcopy, reel 1707. For specific lists of *vecinos*, see documents on this reel of microfilm numbered G-4, G-8, G-10, G-14, G-15, G-17, and G-18.

80. Lista y reseña de vecinos y armas fechas por el alcalde de Santa Bárbara, Don Miguel García Ordóñez y Vecloia, en esa villa San José de la Ciénega y su jurisdición de habitantes de 14 a.s a 50 a.s, AHP, Administrativa y de Guerra, microcopy, reel 1731A, doc. G-6.

81. Borah, "Francisco de Urdiñola's Census, 1604," p. 401; Padrón formado de este Real, Año de 1768, AHP, microcopy, reel 1768, doc. 1; Almada, *Historia del estado de Chihuahua*, pp. 106–107, 131, 138.

82. Expediente instruido por el H.ble Ayuntamiento sobre establecimiento de una escuela pública, Villa y Minas de San José del Parral, May 21, 1810, AHP, Administrativa y de Guerra, microcopy, reel 1809, doc. G-4.

83. Eleanor B. Adams and Keith W. Algier, "A Frontier Book List—1800," *NMHR*, Vol. 43, No. 1 (January, 1968), pp. 50–53.

84. Borah, "Francisco de Urdiñola's Census, 1604," p. 401; Bancroft, *North Mexican States*, Vol. I, p. 313; Padrón formado de este Real, Año de 1768, AHP, microcopy, reel 1768, doc. 1; Padrón del vecindario, 1788, AHP, microcopy, reel 1788A, doc. 2; Almada, *Historia del estado de Chihuahua*, pp. 77–78; Jackson, *Journals of Zebulon Pike*, Vol. II, p. 66.

85. Almada, *Historia del estado de Chihuahua*, pp. 136–37.

86. Hackett, *Historical Documents*, Vol. II, p. 391; Lister and Lister, *Chihuahua*, p. 33.

87. Fernando B. Sandoval, *El correo en las provincias internas*, 1779 (México, D.F.: Junta Mexicana de Investigaciones Históricas, 1948), p. 4; Instrucciones que deberan observar los administradores de las estafetas de este Reyno de Nueva España, Vera Cruz, July 30, 1766, HL, José de Gálvez Collection, GA 185; Copia del reglamento original que por quenta de S. M. se debe observar en el Oficio de Correo General, Vera Cruz, July 30, 1766, HL, Gálvez Collection, GA 189.

88. Sandoval, *El correo en las provincias internas*, pp. 6–8.

89. *Ibid.*, p. 42.

90. *Ibid.*, pp. 22–23.

91. *Ibid.*, pp. 11–15.

92. *Ibid.*, pp. 19, 40.

93. *Ibid.*, pp. 8, 40.

94. Jackson, *Journals of Zebulon Pike*, Vol. II, pp. 62, 64.

95. *Ibid.*, pp. 65–66.

96. Lister and Lister, *Chihuahua*, pp. 62–63.

97. Jackson, *Journals of Zebulon Pike*, Vol. II, p. 81.

98. *Ibid.*, Vol. I, p. 415.

99. *Ibid.*, Vol. II, pp. 81–82.

100. *Ibid.*, p. 83.

101. West, *Mining Community in Northern New Spain*, pp. 63, 65, 67, 70–72, 77, 79, 81–83.

102. Jackson, *Journals of Zebulon Pike*, Vol. II, pp. 82–83.

103. Lister and Lister, *Chihuahua*, p. 79; Autos para la fiesta de toros, Real de Minas de San Josef del Parral, February 11, 1649, AHP, Administrativa y de Guerra, microcopy, reel 1679 [document is misfiled on the wrong reel], doc. G-107; Ayuntamiento del Parral, Sobre corridas de toros anuales, October 8, 1802, AHP, Administrativa y de Guerra, microcopy, reel 1802, doc. G-5.

104. AHP, Causas Criminales, microcopy, reels 1633C (doc. G-46), 1637B (doc. G-12), 1642B (document dated October 26, 1642), 1648 (doc. 109), 1652D (doc. 25), 1665B (doc. 37), and 1703 (doc. G-31).

105. Contra el capitán Alonso García por haber traido algunas indias de la Provincia de la [*sic*] Nuevo Mexico a vender en este Real, Real de Minas de San Josef del Parral, January 12 and 22, 1665, AHP, Causas Criminales 37, microcopy, reel 1665B; Contra Mateo de la Cruz, indio, por indicios de brujería, AHP, Causas Criminales, reel 1703, doc. G-31; Jackson, *Journals of Zebulon Pike*, Vol. II, p. 89; Lister and Lister, *Chihuahua*, p. 60.

106. Lister and Lister, *Chihuahua*, pp. 84–86.

107. Navarro García, *José de Gálvez*, pp. 116–17; Hackett, *Historical Documents*, Vol. II, pp. 17, 407.

108. Kinnaird, *Frontiers of New Spain*, p. 74.

109. *Ibid.*, p. 11.

CHAPTER 5

1. See two major works on Castaño's unsuccessful venture: Albert H. Schroeder and Dan S. Matson, *A Colony on the Move: Gaspar Castaño de Sosa's Journal* ([Santa Fé]: School of American Research, 1965), pp. 5–15; and George P. Hammond and Agapito Rey, *The Rediscovery of New Mexico, 1580–1594* (Albuquerque: University of New Mexico Press, 1966), pp. 28–39, 245–95.

2. George P. Hammond and Agapito Rey, *Oñate: Colonizer of New Mexico, 1595–1628*, 2 vols. (Albuquerque: University of New Mexico Press, 1953), Vol. I, pp. 7–14, 150–68, 289–308; George P. Hammond and Agapito Rey, "Oñate and the Colonization of New Mexico," in Richard N. Ellis (ed.), *New Mexico Past and Present: A Historical Reader*, (Albuquerque: University of New Mexico Press, 1971), pp. 22–28.

3. Hammond and Rey, *Oñate*, Vol. I, pp. 17–18, 34.

4. Throughout this book the Spanish colonial spelling of Alburquerque has been used. The *villa* was named for the viceroy of New Spain, the Duque de Alburquerque, and all references to it in letters, censuses, diaries, and reports use that spelling. The middle *r* was dropped from the name in local use about the time the Atchison, Topeka, and Santa Fe Railroad reached New Mexico in 1880 and an Anglo-American community grew up near the railroad. The family name of descendants of the Duke of Alburquerque is still spelled as it was in the colonial era.

5. Priestley, *Coming of White Man*, pp. 56–57; Hackett, *Historical Documents*, Vol. III, pp. 327–28.

6. Anne E. Hughes, *The Beginnings of Spanish Settlement in the El Paso Dis-*

trict (Berkeley: University of California Press, 1914), pp. 303–308. Hughes describes the two missions as those of Nuestro Padre San Francisco de las Sumas and La Soledad de los Janos, both on the right bank of the river and located below the mission at Guadalupe. For other accounts of El Paso's origins, see Armando B. Chávez M., *Historia de Ciudad Juárez, Chih.*, 2d ed. (Juárez, Chihuahua: [n.p.], 1951), p. 38; C. L. Sonnichsen, *Pass of the North: Four Centuries on the Rio Grande* (El Paso: Texas Western Press, 1968), p. 23; Vina Walz, "History of the El Paso Area, 1680–1692," (Ph.D. dissertation, University of New Mexico, 1951), pp. 7, 18; Castañeda, *Our Catholic Heritage*, Vol. I, p. 249.

7. Hughes, *Spanish Settlement in the El Paso District*, pp. 311–12; Castañeda, *Our Catholic Heritage*, Vol. I, p. 251; Walz, "History of the El Paso Area," pp. 23–25.

8. J. Lawrence McConville, "A History of Population in the El Paso-Ciudad Juárez Area," (M.A. thesis, University of New Mexico, 1966), p. 22; Hughes, *Spanish Settlement in the El Paso District*, p. 315; Castañeda, *Our Catholic Heritage*, Vol. I, pp. 254–63; Walz, "History of the El Paso Area," pp. 75–76, 80.

9. Sonnichsen, *Pass of the North*, p. 34.

10. *Ibid.*, pp. 45–46; Walz, "History of the El Paso Area," p. 87.

11. Hughes, *Spanish Settlement in the El Paso District*, pp. 322–27, 329; Sonnichsen, *Pass of the North*, p. 47.

12. Hughes, *Spanish Settlement in the El Paso District*, pp. 344–69; Walz, "History of the El Paso Area," p. 121, 143–45.

13. Hughes, *Spanish Settlement in the El Paso District*, p. 361.

14. *Ibid.*, pp. 383, 387.

15. *Ibid.*, p. 370. Walz, "History of the El Paso Area," p. 161, maintains that the total was 1,051 persons.

16. Walz, "History of the El Paso Area," p. 264.

17. Sonnichsen, *Pass of the North*, p. 70; Ellis, *New Mexico Past and Present*, p. 64; Bannon, *Spanish Borderlands Frontier*, pp. 88–89. For a detailed account of Vargas' second expedition into New Mexico based upon documentary evidence, see J. Manuel Espinosa, *Crusaders of the Río Grande* (Chicago: Institute of Jesuit History, 1942).

18. Testimonio de los Auttos que se han hecho en este R.ⁿᵒ de nu.ᵃ Mex.ᵒ en consta de la nu.ᵃ Villa y Poblazion fundado por el S.ʳ Gov.ᵒʳ Cap.ⁿ Gen.ˡ D.ⁿ Diego de Vargas Zapatta Lujan Ponze de Leon . . ., Archivo General de la Nación, México, D.F., historia 39, doc. 5, photostat, CR-UNM.

19. *Ibid.*

20. Pettizion q.ᵉ presentaron los Vez.ᵒˢ Mexicanos de la Villa Nueba de S.ᵗᵃ Cruz en 25 de sep.ᵉ de 1695 a.ˢ al s.ʳ Gov.ᵒʳ y Cap.ⁿ Gen.ˡ de este R.ⁿᵒ y prov.ᵃ de la nueba Mex.ᶜᵒ . . ., AGN, historia 39, doc. 6, photostat, CR-UNM.

21. Lansing B. Bloom (ed.), "Albuquerque and Galisteo: Certificate of Their Founding," *NMHR*, Vol. 10, No. 1 (January, 1935), p. 48; Richard E. Greenleaf, "The Founding of Albuquerque, 1706: An Historical-Legal Problem," *NMHR*, Vol. 39, No. 1 (January, 1964), p. 13.

22. Richard E. Greenleaf, "Atrisco and Las Ciruelas, 1722–1769," *NMHR*, Vol. 42, No. 1 (January, 1967), p. 6.

23. Bloom, "Albuquerque and Galisteo," pp. 49–50.

24. See Myra Ellen Jenkins, "The Baltasar Baca 'Grant': History of an Encroachment," *El Palacio*, Vol. 61 (1961), pp. 47–64, for an excellent study of Spanish encroachment on Indian lands and the hostility resulting from the two people living in

such close proximity. Dr. Jenkins' recent article on "Spanish Land Grants in the Tewa Area," *NMHR*, Vol. 47, No. 2 (April, 1972), pp. 113–34, also provides valuable insights into Spanish land practices in New Mexico, with particular reference to encroachment on Indian lands north of Santa Fé.

25. E. Boyd, "The Plaza of San Miguel del Vado," *El Palacio*, Vol. 77, No. 4 ([1971?]), pp. 17–19.

26. Marc Simmons, "Settlement Patterns and Village Plans in Colonial New Mexico," *Journal of the West*, Vol. 8, No. 1 (January, 1969), pp. 12–14.

27. *Ibid.*, pp. 15–20.

28. Hammond and Rey, *Oñate*, Vol. I, pp. 289–308; Fray Angelico Chávez, *Origins of New Mexico Families in the Spanish Colonial Period* (Santa Fé: Historical Society of New Mexico, 1954), p. xi; France V. Scholes, "Civil Government and Society in New Mexico in the Seventeenth Century," *NMHR*, Vol. 10, No. 2 (April, 1935), p. 96; Hackett, *Historical Documents*, Vol. III, p. 133.

29. Declaration of Fray Miguel de Menchero, Santa Bárbara, May 10, 1744, in Hackett, *Historical Documents*, Vol. III, pp. 406–407. McConville, "History of Population in the El Paso-Ciudad Juárez Area," reports that there were fifty Indian families at Nuestra Señora de Guadalupe del Paso, basing his information on the same Menchero report.

30. Sonnichsen, *Pass of the North*, p. 78.

31. Kinnaird, *Frontiers of New Spain*, p. 83.

32. Description of . . . El Paso del Río del Norte, as Given by One of Its Citizens, after Seven Years Residence There, September 1, 1773, in Hackett, *Historical Documents*, Vol. III, pp. 506–508.

33. Descripción geográfica del Nuevo México, escrita por el R. P. Fr. Juan Agustín de Morfi, Año de 1782, AGN, historia 25, doc. 6, photostat, CR-UNM.

34. These figures have been compiled from the following documents and archives: Padrón Gral. de los Pueblos de esta Jurisdicción del Passo, echo por el Ten.te Gobernador Eugenio Fernández, Año de 1784, Passo, December 31, 1784, JA, microcopy, reel 46, frames 0159–95; Padrón Gral. de los Pueblos de la Jurisdicción del Passo, Fray Damian Martínez and Nicolás Soler, Paso, May 9, 1787, JA, microcopy, reel 46; Alberto Maynez, Prov.ª de N.ª México, Jurisd.ⁿ del Passo del Norte, SANM, microcopy, reel 11, frames 1239–43; Francisco Xavier de Uranga, Prov. del Nuevo México, Jurisdicción del Passo, December 31, 1789, SANM, microcopy, reel 12, frame 242; Estado que manifiesta el número de vasallos y habitantes . . ., Provincia del Nuevo México, Santa Fé, November 20, 1790, SANM, microcopy, reel 12, frame 428; Estado que manifiesta el número de vasallos y habitantes . . ., Santa Fé, November 20, 1793, SANM, microcopy, reel 13, frame 428; Estado que muestra las Jurisdicciones . . ., Santa Fé, SANM, microcopy, reel 14, frames 654–57; Noticia de las misiones . . ., Paso, December 31, 1804, JA, microcopy, reel 48, Frame 0083; and Relación o Padrón del Número de Vezinos y Personas que hai en cada uno de los Partidos, Pueblos, y Ranchos de esta Jurisdicción, Año de 1805, JA, reel 48, frames 0174 and 0195 (duplicate).

35. Noticia de las misiones que ocupan los Clerigos y Religiosos de la Provincia del Santo Evangelio de la dicha Jurisdiccion . . ., Paso, December 31, 1804, JA, microcopy, reel 48, frame 0083. This document indicates a total of 5,407 Spaniards and mixed bloods, along with only 783 Indians in the total population of 6,190 persons for the Paso del Norte region.

36. Estado que manifiesta el número de Vasallos y havitantes, Prov.ª del Nuevo México, fin de Diciembre de 1817, SANM, microcopy, reel 18, frame 870.

37. Menchero, Declaración, May 10, 1744, BNM, legajo 8, doc. 17, photostat, CR-UNM. Hackett, *Historical Documents*, Vol. III, pp. 398–99, states that the same document is in AGN, historia 25, but in the BNM version Santa Fé had 127 families; Rancho de Chama and Río del Oso, about 17 families; Ojo Caliente, 46 families; and Las Bocas, only 10 families. Bernalillo is not listed in the BNM document.

38. Menchero, Declaration, May 10, 1744, in Hackett, *Historical Documents*, Vol. III, pp. 401–402.

39. Menchero, Declaración, May 10, 1744, BNM, legajo 8, doc. 17, photostat, CR-UNM; Menchero, Declaration, May 10, 1744, in Hackett, *Historical Documents*, Vol. III, pp. 402–405.

40. Menchero, Declaración, BNM, legajo 8, doc. 17, photostat, CR-UNM.

41. Estado general y particular del Número de Familias y Personas que contienen las 16 Poblaciones Españoles, y gente de razón establecidas, y pobladas en el Reyno del Nuevo México . . ., Año de 1752, AGN, Provincias Internas 102, Part 3, Expediente 3, photostat, CR-UNM.

42. *Ibid.*

43. Eleanor B. Adams (ed.), *Bishop Tamarón's Visitation of New Mexico*, 1760 (Albuquerque: Historical Society of New Mexico, 1954), pp. 35, 39, 43, 46, 63.

44. Kinnaird, *Frontiers of New Spain*, pp. 90–91, 93.

45. Francisco Atanasio Domínguez, *The Missions of New Mexico*, 1776 (trans. by Eleanor B. Adams and Fr. Angelico Chávez), (Albuquerque: University of New Mexico Press, 1956), p. 6.

46. *Ibid.*, p. 42.

47. *Ibid.*, p. 84.

48. *Ibid.*, pp. 151, 154.

49. *Ibid.*, p. 217.

50. Descripción geográfica del Nuevo México, escrita por el R. P. Fr. Juan Agustín de Morfi, Año de 1782, AGN, historia 25, doc. 6, photostat, CR-UNM.

51. Fernando de la Concha, Santa Fé, August 21, 1789, Ritch Collection, RI 62, HL.

52. Fernando de la Concha, Visita General, September 11–December 9, 1789, Ritch Collection, RI 40, HL.

53. Analysis of the 1790 census in New Mexico is based upon the following documents, all originals in the SANM, State Records Center and Archives, Santa Fé, New Mexico, microcopy in possession of the author: Provincia del Nuevo Mexico, Estado que manifiesta el número de Vasallos, y havitantes que tiene el Rey en esta Prov.ª con distinción de Estados, Clases, y Castas, de todas las Personas de ambos sexos, con inclusión de los Parbulos, Santa Fé, Nov.ʳᵉ 20 de 1790, reel 12, frame 428; Prov.ª del Nuevo México, Jurisdicción de esta Villa de Santa Fé, Padrón del vecindario q.ᵉ tiene esta Villa, Partidos, y Pueblos, 9 de Nob.ᵉ de 1790, reel 12, frames 372–407; Padrón General de esta Jurisdicción de la Alcaldía de S.ⁿ Phelipe de Alburquerque, Provincia del Nuevo México, 22 de Octubre de 1790, reel 12, frames 319–53; Census returns for the northern jurisdictions, reel 12, frames 459–62; Pueblos of San Juan and San Lorenzo de Pecuries, Jurisdiction of Santa Cruz, reel 12, frames 486–96; Padrón General, San Carlos de la Alameda, Año de 1790 [incomplete], reel 12, frames 501–502; and Pádron de Todas las gentes del Pueblo de Zuñi . . . y sus Ranchos, veinte y tres de Octubre de 1790, reel 12, frames 355–62.

54. Estado que manifiesta el número de Vasallos y havitantes . . ., Santa Fé, November 20, 1790, SANM, microcopy, reel 12, frame 428.

55. Padrón General de . . . San Phelipe de Alburquerque, October 22, 1790, SANM, microcopy, reel 12, frames 319–53.

56. Estado que manifiesta el Número de Vasallos y avitantes . . ., Santa Fé, November 20, 1793, SANM, microcopy, reel 13, frame 428.

57. Estado que muestra las Jurisdicciones . . ., November 24, 1800, SANM, microcopy, reel 14, frames 654–57. I have had to recompute totals by adding individual jurisdictions, since the document itself has errors in total numbers of Indians and Spaniards as well as jurisdictional errors.

58. Jackson, *Journals of Zebulon Pike*, Vol. II, p. 50.

59. *Ibid.*, Vol. I, p. 391.

60. *Ibid.*, p. 392.

61. Fr. Josef Benito Pereyra, Noticia de las misiones que ocupan . . . dicha Provincia de Nuevo México, December 31, 1810, Ritch Collection, RI 68, HL.

62. Estado que manifiesta el número de Vasallos y havitantes, Prov.ª del Nuevo México, fin de Diciembre de 1817, SANM, microcopy, reel 18, frame 870. For comparison, Colonel Juan Camargo reported in 1815 that New Mexico had a population of 35,750 persons, or about two people per square league. See Memoria sobre el Reyno de Nueva España . . ., Veracruz, October 24, 1815, microcopy, Archivo Historico Militar (Madrid), doc. 5-2-4-3.

63. Hammond and Rey, *Oñate*, Vol. I, pp. 289–308.

64. Scholes, "Civil Government and Society in New Mexico," p. 97.

65. Padrón del Vecindario que tiene el Pueblo de el Passo, No. 1, Jurisdicción del Passo, JA, microcopy, reel 47.

66. Padrón del Vecindario . . ., Santa Fé, November 9, 1790, SANM, microcopy, reel 12, frames 372–407; Padrón General de . . . San Phelipe de Alburquerque, SANM, microcopy, reel 12, frames 319–53.

67. Simmons, "Tlascalans in the Spanish Borderlands," pp. 107–109.

68. Scholes, "Civil Government and Society in New Mexico," p. 97.

69. Chávez, *Origins of New Mexico Families*, p. xv.

70. Scholes, "Civil Government and Society in New Mexico," p. 98.

71. For examples of Indians living in Spanish communities, see Padrón del Vecindario que tiene el Pueblo del Passo, No. 1, Jurisdicción del Passo, JA, microcopy, reel 47; Padrón del Vecindario . . ., Santa Fé, November 9, 1790, SANM, microcopy, reel 12, frames 372–407; and Padrón General de . . . San Phelipe de Alburquerque, SANM, microcopy, reel 12, frames 319–53.

72. Padrón General de . . . San Phelipe de Alburquerque, SANM, microcopy, reel 12, items 25 and 113.

73. Padrón Gral. de los Pueblos de esta Jurisdicción del Passo, echo por el Ten.te Governador Eugenio Fernández, Año de 1784, Passo, December 31, 1784, JA, microcopy, reel 46, frames 0159–95.

74. Padrón del Vecindario . . ., Santa Fé, November 9, 1790, SANM, microcopy, reel 12, frames 372–407; Padrón General de . . . San Phelipe de Alburquerque, October 22, 1790, SANM, microcopy, reel 12, frames 319–53; Census returns for the northern jurisdictions, SANM, microcopy, reel 12, frames 459–62; Padrón General de San Carlos de la Alameda, Año de 1790, SANM, microcopy, reel 12, frames 501–502.

75. Padrón General de . . . San Phelipe de Alburquerque, October 22, 1790, SANM, microcopy, reel 12, items 556, 622, and 723; Padrón del Vecindario . . ., Santa Fé, November 9, 1790, SANM, microcopy, reel 12, items 45 and 571.

76. Padrón General de San Carlos de la Alameda, Año de 1790, SANM, micro-copy, reel 12, frames 501–502; Padrón del Vecindario . . ., Santa Fé, November 9, 1790, SANM, microcopy, reel 12, items 309–13.

77. Padrón General de . . . San Phelipe de Alburquerque, October 22, 1790, SANM, microcopy, reel 12, frames 319–53; Padrón del Vecindario . . ., Santa Fé, November 9, 1790, SANM, microcopy, reel 12, frames 372–407; Padrón Gral. del vecindario de la Villa de Sta. Cruz de la Cañada, Año de 1790, SANM, microcopy, reel 12, frames 463–86; and Padrón General de San Carlos de la Alameda, Año de 1790, SANM, microcopy, reel 12, frames 501–502.

CHAPTER 6

1. Scholes, "Civil Government and Society in New Mexico," pp. 99–101.

2. *Ibid.*, pp. 102–103; France V. Scholes, "Church and State in New Mexico, 1610–1650," *NMHR*, Vol. 12, No. 1 (January, 1937), pp. 102–106.

3. Hackett, *Historical Documents*, Vol. III, pp. 109–10; Lesley B. Simpson, *The Encomienda in New Spain* (Berkeley: University of California Press, 1950), p. 121; Ruth K. Barber, "Indian Labor in the Spanish Colonies," *NMHR*, Vol. 7, No. 2 (April, 1932), p. 141 n.

4. Lansing B. Bloom, "The Vargas Encomienda," *NMHR*, Vol. 14, No. 4 (October, 1939), pp. 367–71.

5. *Ibid.*, pp. 372–95, 412, 416.

6. Nemesio Salcedo to Ayudante Inspector de Nueva Vizcaya, Chihuahua, April 6, 1803, SANM, Mrs. James Seligman Papers, microcopy, reel 21, frames 584–86.

7. Relación de los niños que . . . [están] en la Escuela en este Pueblo del Socorro, Diciembre 20 de 1805, JA, microcopy, reel 48.

8. School Summary, Pueblo del Passo, January, 1805 [*sic*], JA, microcopy, reel 48, frames 086, 089, 095. The cover date should be January, 1806, since the summary contains the date of December 31, 1805.

9. Estado General que manifiesta el número de niños que asisten a las Escuelas assi en este Pueblo como a los demas de los Pueblos de su Jurisdicción, Passo, 1806, SANM, microcopy, reel 16, frame 194.

10. Estado General . . ., Passo del Norte, June 30, 1807, SANM, microcopy, reel 16, frame 363.

11. Padrón General de . . . San Phelipe de Alburquerque, October 22, 1790, SANM, microcopy, reel 12, items 622 and 723; Padrón del Vecindario . . ., Santa Fé, November 9, 1790, SANM, microcopy, reel 12, item 45; Nemesio Salcedo to S. Gobernador interino del Nuevo México, Chihuahua, August 10, 1808, SANM, micro-copy, reel 16, frames 592–93; H. Bailey Carroll and J. Villasana Haggard (trans. and eds.), *Three New Mexico Chronicles: The Exposición of Don Pedro Bautista Pino, 1812; the Ojeada of Lic. Antonio Barreiro, 1832; and the Additions by Don José Agustín de Escudero, 1849* (Albuquerque, N.Mex.: Quivira Society, 1942), p. 94; Juan Ruiz de Apodaca, Mexico, December 23, 1816, SANM, microcopy, reel 22, frame 640; Governor of New Mexico to Audiencia of Guadalajara, Santa Fé, June 15, 1820, SANM, microcopy, reel 20, frame 219.

12. Rufus A. Palm, Jr., "New Mexico's Schools from 1581 to 1846," (M.A. thesis, University of New Mexico, 1930), pp. 38–40. George I. Sánchez, *Forgotten People: A Study of New Mexicans* (Albuquerque, N.Mex: Calvin Horn Publisher, 1967), p.

49n., maintains that in 1811 there were two public schools, at Las Vegas and Santa
Fé, but he shows no documentary evidence to support this statement.

13. Eleanor B. Adams and France V. Scholes, "Books in New Mexico, 1598–
1680," *NMHR*, Vol. 17, No. 3 (July, 1942), pp. 227–52, and book lists on pp. 256–
70; Eleanor B. Adams and France V. Scholes, "Two Colonial New Mexico Libraries,
1704, 1776," *NMHR*, Vol. 19, No. 2 (April, 1944), pp. 135–46, and book lists on
pp. 149–67; Domínguez, *Missions of New Mexico*, pp. 220–33.

14. Ralph E. Twitchell, "Captain Don Gaspar de Villagrá," *El Palacio*, Vol. 17,
No. 9 (November 1, 1924), pp. 208–209, 216.

15. Marc Simmons, "New Mexico's Smallpox Epidemic of 1780–1781," *NMHR*,
Vol. 41, No. 4 (October, 1966), pp. 320–24.

16. *Ibid.*, p. 320; Lansing B. Bloom, *Early Vaccination in New Mexico* (Santa
Fe: Historical Society of New Mexico, 1924), p. 3; Joseph Antonio Cavallero to
Governor of New Mexico, Aranjuez, May 20, 1804, SANM, microcopy, reel 22,
frames 436–38.

17. Bloom, *Early Vaccination in New Mexico*, pp. 4–8; Nemesio Salcedo to Governor of New Mexico, Chiguagua, November 14, 1804, SANM, microcopy, reel 15,
frame 350; Cristóval María Larrañaga, Estado que manifiesta el Num.º de Niños
Vacunados de Orn. del Sr. Com.ᵗᵉ Gral. en esta Provincia de Nuevo México por el
Cirujano de la Tropa, D.ⁿ Cristóval M.ª Larrañaga, en el presente año, Santa Fé,
May 24, 1805, SANM, microcopy, reel 15, frames 639–40; Cristóbal M.ª Larrañaga
to Gov. and Lt. Col. D.ⁿ Joaquín del Real Alencaster, Sebiyeta (Sevilleta), March
24, 1805, SANM, microcopy, reel 15, frames 405–407; Francisco Obispo de Durango
(Fray Manuel Francisco de Cruzealegui), Durango, December 2, 1804, AASF,
Patentes IV, Box 6, microcopy, reel 48, frames 888–89.

18. Bloom, *Early Vaccination in New Mexico*, pp. 9, 12; SANM, microcopy, reel
16, frames 758 and 975; Joseph Larrañaga, Record of Vaccinations, 1815, Ritch Collection, RI 70, HL.

19. Carroll and Haggard, *Three New Mexico Chronicles*, pp. 35, 97; Lawrence
Kinnaird, "The Spanish Tobacco Monopoly in New Mexico, 1766–1767," *NMHR*,
Vol. 21, No. 4 (October, 1946), pp. 328–37; E. Boyd, "The Uses of Tobacco in
Spanish New Mexico," *El Palacio*, Vol. 65, No. 3 (June, 1958), p. 103. There is a
splendid example of a *tabaquera* in the shape of a pouch with its stopper on display
in the Museum of New Mexico, Palace of the Governors, Santa Fé, New Mexico.

20. Carroll and Haggard, *Three New Mexico Chronicles*, p. 35; Scholes, "Civil
Government and Society in New Mexico," p. 105; Donald E. Worcester, "The
Spread of Spanish Horses in the Southwest," *NMHR*, Vol. 19, No. 3 (July, 1944),
p. 225, and Vol. 20, No. 1 (January, 1945), pp. 1, 10.

21. William W. Long, "A History of Mining in New Mexico during the Spanish
and Mexican Periods," (M.A. thesis, University of New Mexico, 1964), pp. 78,
101–102.

22. Scholes, "Civil Government and Society in New Mexico," pp. 110–11; Carroll
and Haggard, *Three New Mexico Chronicles*, p. 106; Max L. Moorhead, "The
Presidio Supply Problem of New Mexico in the Eighteenth Century," *NMHR*, Vol.
36, No. 3 (July, 1961), pp. 210–13.

23. Moorhead, "The Presidio Supply Problem," pp. 214–29; Carroll and Haggard,
Three New Mexico Chronicles, p. 63; Matricula Cofrades, Cuenta General, Book
79, Santa Fé, AASF, microcopy, reel 44, frame 1037.

24. Domínguez, *Missions of New Mexico*, pp. 252–53. The author also provides

a table of values for the produce and animals sold in New Mexico on pp. 245–46.

25. Max L. Moorhead, "Spanish Transportation in the Southwest, 1540–1846," *NMHR*, Vol. 32, No. 2 (April, 1957), pp. 107–11.

26. *Ibid.*, pp. 112–13; France V. Scholes, "The Supply Service of the New Mexico Missions in the Seventeenth Century," *NMHR*, Vol. 5, Nos. 1 and 2 (January and April, 1930), pp. 94, 115; Adams, *Bishop Tamarón's Visitation of New Mexico*, p. 40. *Carretas* of this type may be seen today in the courtyard of the Museum of New Mexico, Palace of the Governors, Santa Fé, in Old Town, Albuquerque, and in the plaza of the Kit Carson Museum, Taos.

27. Moorhead, "Spanish Transportation in the Southwest," p. 121; Lansing B. Bloom, "Early Bridges in New Mexico," *Papers of the American School of Research* ([Santa Fé], 1925), pp. 9–19.

28. Moorhead, "Spanish Transportation in the Southwest," pp. 121–22.

29. *Ibid.*, p. 116; Marqués de Grimaldi, Aranjuez, May 22, 1768, SANM, micro-copy, reel 10, frames 1013–14; Teodoro de Croix, Chihuahua, February 15, 1779, SANM, microcopy, reel 10, frames 1092–1100; and Derrotero que deve seguir el Nuevo Correo mensual desde la Bahía del Espíritu Santa en la Provincia de Texas h.^{ta} Arizpe en Sonora, Chihuahua, February 15, 1779, SANM, microcopy, reel 10, frames 1101–10. The last two documents are copies of those used by Sandoval, *El Correo en las Provincias Internas*. See Chap. 4 on Nueva Vizcaya for the route and instructions governing the operation of this mail service.

30. Joseph de Gálvez, San Lorenzo el Real, November 5, 1781, SANM, micro-copy, reel 22, frames 210–12; Phelipe de Neve to Juan Bautista de Anza, Arispe, December 18, 1783, SANM, microcopy, reel 11, frames 616–18.

31. [Fernando de Chacón] to Manuel de Ochoa, Santa Fé, August 29, 1801, SANM, microcopy, reel 14, frame 862; [Chacón] to [José] Joaquín Ugarte, Santa Fé, June 14, 1802, SANM, microcopy, reel 14, frame 984; José Joaquín Ugarte to Sor. Coronel D. Fernando de Chacón, San Elceario, August 18, 1802, SANM, micro-copy, reel 14, frame 1011; [Manrrique] to S. Com.^{te} del Presidio de S. Eleceario, Santa Fé, March 31, 1810, SANM, microcopy, reel 17, frame 85; [Manrrique] to Sr. Com.^e del Presidio de S. Eleceario, Santa Fé, October 6, 1810, SANM, microcopy, reel 17, frames 194–95; Nemesio Salcedo to Governor of New Mexico, Chihuahua, July 10, 1804, SANM, reel 15, frame 301.

32. Real Cédula, Madrid, August 28, 1789, SANM, microcopy, reel 11, frames 1169–74; Don Félix María Calleja, Real Palacio de México, March 3, 1815, SANM, microcopy, reel 17, frames 1049–52; Rafael Sarracinoz (?), Compañia de S.ⁿ Elceario, Santa Fé, September 17, 1819, SANM, microcopy, reel 19, frame 957.

33. Simmons, "Settlement Patterns and Village Plans in Colonial New Mexico," pp. 7–8; Jenkins, "The Baltasar Baca 'Grant'," pp. 47–50; Richard E. Greenleaf, "Land and Water in Mexico and New Mexico, 1700–1821," *NMHR*, Vol. 47, No. 2 (April, 1972), pp. 85, 93, 96; Myra Ellen Jenkins, "Spanish Land Grants in the Tewa Area," *NMHR*, Vol. 47, No. 2 (April, 1972), p. 114; Frankie McCarty, *Land Grant Problems in New Mexico* (Albuquerque, N.Mex.: Albuquerque *Journal*, 1969), p. 2.

34. W. A. Keleher, "Law of the New Mexico Land Grant," *NMHR*, Vol. 4, No. 4 (October, 1929), pp. 352–53, 368; Lansing B. Bloom, "Instructions to Peralta by Vice-Roy," *NMHR*, Vol. 4, No. 2 (April, 1929), pp. 179–81, 187.

35. Petitions for travel, licenses, and passports abound in the SANM. See, for example: reel 1, frame 434; reel 3, frames 924–26, 974–81, and 1037–38; reel 4, frames

110 and 1006–1008; reel 5, frames 140–64; reel 9, frames 1025–28; reel 11, frames 610–13, 679–86, and 715–18; reel 12, frames 209 and 303–14; reel 13, frames 196–97; reel 14, frame 245; reel 15, frame 185; reel 18, frames 137–38; reel 19, frame 441; and reel 21, frame 480 (an actual printed passport form with seal and official signatures).

36. Keleher, "Laws of the New Mexico Land Grant," p. 355.

37. Louis H. Warner, "Conveyance of Property the Spanish and Mexican Way," *NMHR*, Vol. 6, No. 4 (October, 1931), p. 339.

38. Antonio de Salazar to Governor Mogollón, Santa Fé, August 25, 1714, Ritch Collection, RI 52, and Francisca Antonia de Gijosa to Governor Mogollón, Ritch Collection, RI 54, both in HL.

39. J. J. Brody and Anne Colberg, "A Spanish-American Homestead Near Placitas, New Mexico," *El Palacio*, Vol. 73, No. 2 (Summer, 1966), p. 12.

40. See Francisca Antonia de Gijosa, Ritch Collection, RI 54, HL, for subsequent disposition of property following the original ownership; see Greenleaf, "Atrisco and Las Ciruelas, 1722–1769," pp. 7–10, for a controversy arising over land between two branches of one family; also, see Jenkins, "The Baltasar Baca 'Grant'," pp. 52–58, and Jenkins, "Spanish Land Grants in the Tewa Area," for two excellent, detailed descriptions of Spanish-speaking settlers trespassing on Laguna and Tewa Indian lands in the eighteenth century.

41. Barber, "Indian Labor in the Spanish Colonies," pp. 140–141, 336, 346; Fray Juan de la Peña, January 4, 1710, Patentes I, Book I, Box 1, AASF, microcopy, reel 47, frames 14–15; Viceroy Diego Fernández de Córdova, marqués de Guadalcazar, to Governor Juan de Eulate, February 5, 1621, in Lansing B. Bloom, "A Glimpse of New Mexico in 1620," *NMHR*, Vol. 3, No. 4 (October, 1928), pp. 366–67; Fray Juan de Zavaleta, July 2, 1700, Patentes I, Book I, Box 1, AASF, microcopy, reel 47, frame 5.

42. Fray Angelico Chávez, "The Penitentes of New Mexico," *NMHR*, Vol. 29, No. 2 (April, 1954), pp. 109–20; Marta Weigle, *The Penitentes of New Mexico* (Santa Fé, N.Mex.: Ancient City Press, 1970), pp. 3, 5–13, 15. Two other excellent works on the *penitentes* are: Alice C. Henderson, *Brothers of Light: The Penitentes of the Southwest* (New York: Harcourt and Brace, 1937, and Chicago: Río Grande Press, 1962), and Dorothy Woodward, "The Penitentes of New Mexico," (Ph.D. dissertation, Yale University, 1935). The reader should be warned that there are many popularized accounts of this sector of Spanish society, some of which are erroneous and based upon insufficient original research.

43. Hester Jones, "Uses of Wood by the Spanish Colonists in New Mexico," *NMHR*, Vol. 7, No. 3 (July, 1932), pp. 280–83. Cottonwood, pine, juniper, piñon, red cedar, oak, Douglas fir, and aspen were all used in the making of various wooden products.

44. Mitchell A. Wilder and Edgar Breitenbach (eds.), *Santos: The Religious Folk Art of New Mexico* (Colorado Springs, Colo.: Taylor Museum, 1943), pp. 13, 22–28, 31; Jones, "Uses of Wood by the Spanish Colonists," pp. 284–85; E. Boyd, *The New Mexico Santero* (Santa Fé: Museum of New Mexico Press, 1969), pp. 5–6; E. Boyd, *Popular Arts of Colonial New Mexico* (Santa Fé: Museum of International Folk Art, 1959), pp. 29–33; José E. Espinosa, *Saints in the Valleys: Christian Sacred Images in the History, Life, and Folk Art of Spanish New Mexico*, 2d ed. rev. (Albuquerque: University of New Mexico Press, 1967), pp. 51–55, 61–64; Robert L. Shalkop, *Wooden Saints: The Santos of New Mexico* ([Colorado Springs, Colo.]: Taylor Museum, [n.d.]), pp. 13–14.

45. Espinosa, *Saints in the Valleys*, p. 21; Boyd, *The New Mexico Santero*, pp. 4–5; Shalkop, *Wooden Saints*, p. 14; Boyd, *Popular Arts of Colonial New Mexico*, pp. 16–20; Lansing B. Bloom, "Early Weaving in New Mexico, *NMHR*, Vol. 2, No. 3 (July, 1927), pp. 235–38. A crude, locally made Spanish loom and spinning wheel may be seen today at the Museum of New Mexico, Palace of the Governors, Santa Fé, New Mexico.

46. Castañeda, *Our Catholic Heritage*, Vol. I, p. 245; Espinosa, *Saints in the Valleys*, p. 86; Sister Joseph Marie, *Role of the Church and the Folk* (privately published Ph.D. dissertation); W. Thetford Leviness, "In the Christian Tradition," *Empire Magazine, Denver Post*, December 20, 1970, pp. 10–11.

47. Lota M. Spell, "Music Teaching in New Mexico in the 17th Century," *NMHR*, Vol. 2, No. 1 (January, 1927), pp. 30–31; Lincoln B. Spiess, "Church Music in Seventeenth Century New Mexico," Vol. 40, No. 1 (January, 1965), pp. 5, 14–16; Aurelio M. Espinosa, "Spanish Folk-Lore in New Mexico," *NMHR*, Vol. 1, No. 2 (April, 1926), pp. 136, 139, 142–143, 146, 149–152; Espinosa, *Saints in the Valleys*, p. 85.

48. George Kubler, *Religious Architecture of New Mexico: In the Colonial Period and Since the American Occupation* (Colorado Springs, Colo.: Taylor Museum and Fine Arts Center, 1940, and Chicago, Río Grande Press, 1962), p. 7.

49. *Ibid.*, pp. 24–25; William Lumpkins, "A Distinguished Architect Writes on Adobe," *El Palacio*, Vol. 47, No. 4 (n.d.), pp. 3–4; Warner, "Conveyance of Property," p. 340.

50. Lumpkins, "A Distinguished Architect Writes on Adobe," p. 3; Boyd, *Popular Arts of Colonial New Mexico*, pp. 7–16; Jackson, *Journals of Zebulon Pike*, Vol. I, p. 392; William W. Plowden, Jr., "Spanish and Mexican Majolica Found in New Mexico," *El Palacio*, Vol. 65, No. 6 (December, 1958), p. 212; David H. Snow, "The Chronological Position of Mexican Majolica in the Southwest," *El Palacio*, Vol. 72, No. 1 (Spring, 1965), pp. 25–26. For a good description of the origins of majolica in Spain and Mexico, see Florence C. Lister and Robert H. Lister, "Majolica: Ceramic Link between Old World and New," *El Palacio*, Vol. 76, No. 2 (Summer, 1969), pp. 1–15.

51. Espinosa, *Saints in the Valleys*, p. 19; Domínguez, *Missions of New Mexico*, p. 245 and note. For records of baptisms and burials, see AASF, microcopy, reels 5 and 37, depicting numerous occasions when special ceremonies were held.

52. Roland F. Dickey, *New Mexico Village Arts*, 2d ed. (Albuquerque: University of New Mexico Press, 1970), p. 21; Alberto Maynez, El Paso del Norte, JA, microcopy, reel 45, frames 131 and 138, and reel 46, frames 82–84; A. Von Wuthenau, "The Spanish Military Chapels in Santa Fé and the Reredos of Our Lady of Light," *NMHR*, Vol. 10, No. 3 (July, 1935), pp. 176, 188; Eleanor B. Adams, "The Chapel and Cofradía of Our Lady of Light," *NMHR*, Vol. 22, No. 4 (October, 1947), pp. 329–30, 333–34. This reredos has survived, although the military chapel in which it was originally placed has long since been destroyed. The reredos was moved by Bishop Lamy to the parish church, from which it was transferred in 1940 to the church of Cristo Rey in Santa Fé, where it is today.

53. Fray Angelico Chávez, "Nuestra Señora del Rosario, La Conquistadora," *NMHR*, Vol. 23, Nos. 2 and 3 (April and July, 1948), pp. 95–97, 104, 119–21, 125–26, 192.

54. Dickey, *New Mexico Village Arts*, pp. 21–23; Adams, *Bishop Tamarón's Visitation of New Mexico*, pp. 50–51.

55. Fray José de la Prada, Custos, Pojoaque, February 5, 1786, AASF, Patentes

III, Book III, Box 3, microcopy, reel 47, frames 267–69; Jackson, *Journals of Zebulon Pike*, Vol. I, p. 387.

56. Eleanor B. Adams, "Viva el Rey!," *NMHR*, Vol. 35, No. 4 (October, 1960), pp. 284–92.

57. Espinosa, *Saints in the Valleys*, p. 82.

58. France V. Scholes, "Troublous Times in New Mexico, 1659–1670," *NMHR*, Vol. 12, Nos. 2 and 4 (April and October, 1937), pp. 136–40, 380; France V. Scholes, "The First Decade of the Inquisition in New Mexico," *NMHR*, Vol. 10, No. 3 (July, 1935), pp. 206, 215–22.

59. For witchcraft proceedings, see Autos y Diligencias, Villa de Santa Fé, Año de 1708, May 13–31, 1708, SANM, microcopy, reel 4, frames 74–109; Santa Fé, July 2–August 1, 1715, SANM, microcopy, reel 5, frames 165–83; Santa Fé, January 12–21, 1732, SANM, microcopy, reel 6, frames 977–96; and Santa Fé, February 11–19, 1733, SANM, microcopy, reel 7, frames 35–46.

60. Desordenes que se advierten en el Nuevo México . . ., escritas por el mismo R. P. Fr. Juan Agustín de Morfi, AGN, doc. 8, photostat, CR-UNM.

61. Scholes, "Church and State in New Mexico," pp. 335–42. Ortiz was arrested and tried in Santa Fé. His wife testified that she had committed adultery, but had been urged to do so by Rosas, who also wanted her to run away with him and kill her husband if he would provide the means of committing such an act. On May 8, 1642, Ortiz was acquitted.

62. For banishments, see SANM, microcopy, reel 3, frames 1048 and 1065–67; reel 5, frames 448–50; reel 17, frames 174 and 1045. For regulations to control vagabonds, see Phelipe de Neve, Arispe, December 10, 1783, and Juan Bautista de Anza, Santa Fé, April 15, 1784, SANM, microcopy, reel 11, frames 610–13 and 679–86; Fernando de la Concha, Santa Fé, September 17, 1790, SANM, microcopy, reel 12, frames 303–14; and Viceroy Conde de Revilla Gigedo, December 31, 1791, SANM, microcopy, reel 22, frame 349.

63. Ralph E. Twitchell, *The Leading Facts of New Mexican History*, 2 vols. (Cedar Rapids, Iowa: Torch Press, 1911–12, and Albuquerque, N.Mex., Horn and Wallace, 1963), Vol. I, p. 475.

64. D. W. Meinig, *Southwest: Three Peoples in Geographical Change* (New York: Oxford University Press, 1971), p. 27.

65. Dickey, *New Mexican Village Arts*, p. 5. This same observation is made in different words by Simmons, "Settlement Patterns and Village Plans in Colonial New Mexico," p. 19.

66. Simmons, "Settlement Patterns and Village Plans in Colonial New Mexico," p. 19. Nancie L. González, *The Spanish Americans of New Mexico* (Albuquerque: University of New Mexico Press, 1969), p. 45, notes that there were no *patrones* in New Mexico during the Spanish period and that there was no extreme dependence upon one single authority.

67. Dickey, *New Mexico Village Arts*, pp. 6–8, 20; González, *Spanish Americans of New Mexico*, pp. 62–65, 69.

68. Sánchez, *Forgotten People*, p. 10.

CHAPTER 7

1. Bolton, "The Northward Movement in New Spain," in Bannon, *Bolton and the Spanish Borderlands*, p. 76; Bancroft, *North Mexican States*, Vol. I, pp. 28–29, 37–38, 59. Mota y Escobar, *Descripción geográfica*, p. 98, notes that there were

sixty original settlers of Culiacán, not one hundred, but he erroneously states that the date of the *villa's* founding was 1532.

2. Bancroft, *North Mexican States*, Vol. I, pp. 113–15, 206; Charles A. Chapman, *A History of California: The Spanish Period* (New York, Macmillan, 1921), p. 156. Mota y Escobar, *Descripción geográfica*, p. 108, states that San Felipe y Santiago de Sinaloa, thirty leagues from Culiacán, was founded by Pedro Almindez Chirinos, who had been sent there by Governor Guzmán. This early settlement evidently did not last, although the location was a good one and was resttled in 1585 with a garrison of soldiers.

3. Plan que manifiesta el número de Vasallos que tiene el Rey en esta Provincia con distinción de clases, castas, y destinas, y bienes que poseen expresando por notas lo correspondiente a el estado, situación, y circumstancias de dha. Provincia, Provincia de Sonora o Nueva Andalucía, El Cav.ᵗᵒ de Croix, Arispe, June 2, 1783, AGI Guadalajara 284. I am indebted to Max L. Moorhead, Professor of History at the University of Oklahoma, for making this document available to me.

4. Chapman, *History of California*, p. 204.

5. Bancroft, *North Mexican States*, Vol. I, pp. 115–16; Mota y Escobar, *Descripción geográfica*, p. 99.

6. Luis Navarro García, *Sonora y Sinaloa en el siglo XVII* (Sevilla, Spain, Publicaciones de la Escuela de Estudios Hispano-Americanos de Sevilla, 1967), p. 11.

7. *Ibid.*, pp. 45–47; Mota y Escobar, *Descripción geográfica*, pp. 98, 108–109.

8. Navarro García, *Sonora y Sinaloa*, p. 55. Bancroft, *North Mexican States*, Vol. I, p. 207, states that there were perhaps eighty *vecinos* residing at San Felipe de Sinaloa alone by mid-seventeenth century.

9. Chapman, *History of California*, p. 156; Bannon, *The Spanish Borderlands Frontier*, p. 61.

10. Bancroft, *North Mexican States*, Vol. I, pp. 573–74. Chapman, *History of California*, p. 205, maintains that the total population of Sonora and Sinaloa about 1760 was thirty-two thousand, with the greater majority of them living in Sinaloa.

11. Chapman, *History of California*, p. 205.

12. Plan que manifiesta el número de Vasallos . . ., AGI, Guadalajara 284; Navarro García, *José de Gálvez*, p. 417.

13. Plan que manifiesta el número de Vasallos . . ., AGI, Guadalajara 284.

14. Humboldt's figures are given in Bancroft, *North Mexican States*, Vol. I, p. 721.

15. Memoria sobre el Reyno de Nueva Espana . . ., Veracruz, October 24, 1845, microcopy, servicio Histórico Militar (Madrid), doc. 5-2-4-3.

16. Bancroft, *North Mexican States*, Vol. I, pp. 635, 646–649.

17. Mota y Escobar, *Descripción geográfica*, p. 99; Plan que manifiesta el número de Vasallos . . ., AGI, Guadalajara 284.

18. Bancroft, *North Mexican States*, Vol. I, p. 207.

19. Navarro García, *Sonora y Sinaloa*, p. 53.

20. Bancroft, *North Mexican States*, Vol. I, p. 546, citing observations from Villaseñor y Sánchez's monumental 1745 publication, *Teatro Americano*.

21. Plan que manifiesta el número de Vasallos . . ., AGI, Guadalajara 284; Navarro García, *Sonora y Sinaloa*, pp. 48–51; Mota y Escobar, *Descripción geográfica*, p. 100.

22. Bancroft, *North Mexican States*, Vol. I, p. 546.

23. Plan que manifiesta el número de Vasallos . . ., AGI, Guadalajara 284; Petition of Father Andrés Pérez, September 12, 1638, in Hackett, *Historical Documents*, Vol. III, p. 96.

24. Navarro García, *José de Gálvez*, p. 417.

25. Mota y Escobar, *Descripción geográfica*, p. 99; Plan que manifiesta el número de Vasallos . . ., AGI, Guadalajara 284.

26. Opinion of Don Francisco de Bustamente, México, February 18, 1639, in Hackett, *Historical Documents*, Vol. III, pp. 121–22; Navarro García, *Sonora y Sinaloa*, p. 12. Both Mota y Escobar and the caballero de Croix report of 1783 mention the intense heat of the province; the extremes of temperature in Sonora are noted as well in the footnotes to the Plan que manifiesta el número de Vasallos . . ., AGI, Guadalajara 284.

CHAPTER 8

1. Chapman, *History of California*, pp. 156–57.

2. Eduardo W. Villa, *Historia del estado de Sonora*, 2d ed. (Hermosillo: Editorial Sonora, 1951), p. 93.

3. Donald Rowland, "The Sonora Frontier of New Spain, 1735–1745," in *New Spain and the Anglo-American West: Historical Contributions Presented to Herbert Eugene Bolton*, 2 vols. (Lancaster, Penna.: Lancaster Press, 1932), Vol. I, p. 147.

4. Navarro y García, *Sonora y Sinaloa*, pp. 67–69.

5. *Ibid.*, p. 277.

6. *Ibid.*, pp. 252–53.

7. Rowland, "The Sonora Frontier of New Spain," pp. 148–49.

8. Chapman, *History of California*, p. 196; Villa, *Historia del estado de Sonora*, p. 113; Bancroft, *North Mexican States*, Vol. I, pp. 526–27. Some pieces of silver at Arizonac were reported to weigh one hundred *arrobas*, or about twenty-five hundred pounds.

9. See Luis Navarro García, *La sublevación yaqui de 1740* (Sevilla, Spain: Escuela de Estudios Hispano-Americanos, 1966), for an account of the causes, course, and results of the Yaqui uprising in 1740.

10. Bancroft, *North Mexican States*, Vol. I, p. 531.

11. *Ibid.*, p. 534.

12. Chapman, *History of California*, pp. 204–205.

13. *Ibid.*, p. 205.

14. [Father Juan Nentuig], *Rudo Ensayo* (Tucson, Ariz.: Arizona Silhouettes, 1951), pp. 128–42.

15. *Ibid.*, pp. 144–45.

16. Kinnaird, *Frontiers of New Spain*, p. 125.

17. Villa, *Historia del estado de Sonora*, pp. 145–48.

18. Plan que manifiesta el número de Vasallos . . ., AGI, Guadalajara 284.

19. Bancroft, *North Mexican States*, Vol. I, pp. 721–22. Navarro García, *José de Gálvez*, p. 419, gives the population of Arizpe in 1777 as 1,540 residents, with 500 adults included. Of these adults, 335 had occupations, but only 22 were farmers and some 50 were gold-seekers.

20. Mario Hernández Sánchez-Barba, *La última expansión española en américa* (Madrid: Instituto de Estudios Políticos, 1957), pp. 71–74. Wheat was reported to yield in a ratio of 21 to 1; corn, 80 to 1; and beans, 45 to 1. In spite of the misleading title of the Hernández work, the occupation of Sonora was not "the last Spanish expansion in America."

21. "Instructions for the Establishment of the New Villa of Pitic in the Province of Sonora . . .," in Hatcher, *Opening of Texas*, pp. 314–22; Castañeda, *Our Catholic*

Heritage, Vol. V, pp. 311–13; Greenleaf, "Land and Water in Mexico and New Mexico, 1700–1821," pp. 97–102, 111. Greenleaf points out that the Plan of Pitic was given royal approval in 1789, six years after the official establishment of the *villa* and the removal of the presidio from Horcasitas to Pitic. He notes that the crown may have assigned the date of 1789 arbitrarily to the document or waited to approve the articles as models for future settlements even though the community of Pitic was already in being.

22. Ynstrucción practica que han de observar los comisionados para el reparti-miento de tierras, AGN, Historia 16, photostat, CR-UNM, paragraph 14. Note that in the total for the *reales* column eight of the sum fourteen have been carried over to the pesos column, since eight *reales* were the equivalent of one peso. This leaves a sum of six *reales* in the proper column.

23. Chapman, *History of California*, p. 205; Bancroft, *North Mexican States*, Vol. II, p. 647; Villa, *Historia del estado de Sonora*, p. 161; Plan que manifiesta el número de Vasallos . . ., AGI, Guadalajara 284.

24. Navarro García, *Sonora y Sinaloa*, p. 162; Plan que manifiesta el número de Vasallos . . ., AGI, Guadalajara 284.

25. Navarro García, *La sublevación yaqui de 1740*, pp. 15–16.

26. *Ibid.*, p. 33.

27. Ignaz A. Pfefferkorn, *A Description of Sonora* (ed. and trans. by Theodore E. Treutlein), 2 vols. in one (Albuquerque: University of New Mexico Press, 1949). The section of this work entitled "Concerning the Spaniards in Sonora," pp. 284–95, is particularly valuable for the study of civilian settlers in the province.

28. *Ibid.*, pp. 284–85. Father Pfefferkorn's use of the term "*criollo*" is the only instance of its use on the northern frontier. Later he contradicts his use of the term by talking about Sonoran-born Spaniards, who indeed would have been Creoles in the conventional use of the word, but he does not apply that term to describe them.

29. *Ibid.*, p. 286.

30. Navarro García, *Sonora y Sinaloa*, p. 169.

31. *Ibid.*

32. Pfefferkorn, *Description of Sonora*, pp. 87–92; Plan que manifiesta el número de Vasallos . . ., AGI, Guadalajara 284. Father Pfefferkorn also discusses the earlier silver discovery at Arizonac, erroneously noting that it yielded a huge quantity of that metal in 1730, six years before its discovery.

33. Pfefferkorn, *Description of Sonora*, pp. 286–87.

34. *Ibid.*, pp. 287–88.

35. *Ibid.*, pp. 52–54.

36. *Ibid.*, p. 288; Plan que manifiesta el número de Vasallos . . ., AGI, Guadalajara 284.

37. [Nentuig], *Rudo Ensayo*, p. 23.

38. *Ibid.*, pp. 27–28; Pfefferkorn, *Description of Sonora*, pp. 98–103; Plan que manifiesta el número de Vasallos . . ., AGI, Guadalajara 284. The census of 1783 showed a total of 46,916 head of cattle in the four jurisdictions of Cosala, Alamos, Ostimuri, and Sonora, with the last-named having 20,647 head. In addition, there were 29,828 sheep, 15,480 mares, 10,026 goats, 7,937 tame horses, and 7,682 mules and burros in the province. The only other animals raised extensively were oxen and swine, noted in the same document.

39. Pfefferkorn, *Description of Sonora*, pp. 195–97, 288–89.

40. *Ibid.*, p. 48.

41. *Ibid.*, p. 49.

42. *Ibid.*, p. 289.

43. *Ibid.*, pp. 289–90.

44. *Ibid.*, p. 56.

45. *Ibid.*, pp. 219–21; [Nentuig], *Rudo Ensayo*, p. 25.

46. Pfefferkorn, *Description of Sonora*, pp. 134, 177–178.

47. *Ibid.*, p. 289.

48. Father Eusebio Francisco Kino to Baltasar de Mansilla, Nuestra Señora de Dolores, June 30, 1687, HL, HM 9987; Kino to Duquesa d'Aveiro, Mission of Conicari, February 15, 1687, HL, HM 9986. For an excellent, detailed analysis of Kino's work in Pimería Alta, see Herbert E. Bolton (ed.), *Kino's Historical Memoir of Pimería Alta*, 2 vols. (Cleveland, Ohio: Arthur H. Clark Company, 1919). For an authoritative, readable biography of Kino, see Herbert E. Bolton, *Rim of Christendom: A Biography of Eusebio Francisco Kino, Pacific Coast Pioneer* (New York: Macmillan, 1936).

49. Hubert H. Bancroft, *History of Arizona and New Mexico, 1530–1888* (San Francisco: The History Company, 1889), pp. 369, 383; Ray H. Mattison, "Early Spanish and Mexican Settlements in Arizona," *NMHR*, Vol. 21, No. 4 (October, 1946), p. 281; Rufus K. Wyllys, *Arizona: The History of a Frontier State* (Phoenix, Ariz.: Herr and Herr, 1950), pp. 48, 53; Odie B. Faulk, *Arizona: A Short History* (Norman, University of Oklahoma Press, 1970), pp. 28–30.

50. Wyllys, *Arizona*, p. 48.

51. Bancroft, *History of Arizona and New Mexico*, p. 381.

52. Sidney R. Brinckerhoff, "The Last Years of Spanish Arizona, 1786–1821," *Arizona and the West*, Vol. 9, No. 1 (Spring, 1967), p. 7.

53. Faulk, *Arizona*, p. 43.

54. *Ibid.*, p. 29.

55. Bancroft, *North Mexican States*, Vol. I, p. 723.

56. Brinckerhoff, "Last Years of Spanish Arizona," p. 15; Mattison, "Early Spanish and Mexican Settlements in Arizona," p. 282.

57. Brinckerhoff, "Last Years of Spanish Arizona," pp. 15–16.

58. *Ibid.*, p. 17.

59. Bancroft, *History of Arizona and New Mexico*, p. 382; Wyllys, *Arizona*, p. 61.

60. Brinckerhoff, "Last Years of Spanish Arizona," p. 17.

61. *Ibid.*, p. 15.

62. *Ibid.*, p. 16; Mattison, "Early Spanish and Mexican Settlements in Arizona," pp. 285–87.

63. Faulk, *Arizona*, p. 48.

64. Brinckerhoff, "Last Years of Spanish Arizona," p. 14.

CHAPTER 9

1. These failures are discussed in Bancroft, *North Mexican States*, Vol. I, pp. 50–51, 173–74.

2. Father Eusebio Francisco Kino to Duchess d'Aveiro, Real de Nuestra Señora de Rosario, June 3, 1682, HL, HM 9997.

3. Father Eusebio Francisco Kino to Father Francisco [Ximénez], April 20, 1683, HL, HM 9995; Kino to [Ximénez], *San Lucas*, July 27, 1683, HL, HM 9998; Chapman, *History of California*, pp. 168–69.

4. Father Eusebio Francisco Kino to Duchess d'Aveiro, San Bruno, December 15, 1683, HL, HM 9994.

5. *Ibid.*; Father Eusebio Francisco Kino to Duchess d'Aveiro, San Bruno, October 25, 1684, HL, HM 9979; same to same, San Bruno, December 8, 1684, HL, HM 9976.

6. Kino to Duchess d'Aveiro, San Bruno, December 8, 1684, HL, HM 9976, and Father Eusebio Francisco Kino, Relación de la segunda entrada de las Californias, de este año de 1685, HL, HM 9974; Chapman, *History of California*, p. 169; Bancroft, *North Mexican States*, Vol. I, pp. 190–93.

7. See Kino to Duchess d'Aveiro, México, November 16, 1686, HL, HM 9989, for this suggestion.

8. Chapman, *History of California*, pp. 172–84; Bancroft, *North Mexican States*, Vol. I, pp. 277–304, 421–491; Irving B. Richman, *California Under Spain and Mexico, 1535–1847* (New York: Cooper Square Publications, 1965), pp. 45–47, 57–58.

9. Bancroft, *North Mexican States*, Vol. I, p. 474.

10. *Ibid.*, p. 760n.

11. *Ibid.*, pp. 487–88, 726–27; Don Francisco Javier Clavigero, *The History of [Lower] California* (trans. by Sara E. Lake, ed. by A. A. Gray), (Stanford, Calif.: Stanford University Press, 1937, and Riverside, Calif., Manessier Publishing Co., 1971), p. 367; Richman, *California Under Spain and Mexico*, p. 76.

12. Bancroft, *North Mexican States*, Vol. I, p. 762.

13. *Ibid.*, pp. 488, 762.

14. *Ibid.*, p. 762; Peveril Meiggs, *The Dominican Mission Frontier of Lower California* (Berkeley: University of California Press, 1935), p. 144.

15. Bancroft, *North Mexican States*, Vol. I, pp. 461, 467.

16. *Ibid.*, Vol. II, pp. 706–707.

CHAPTER 10

1. For thorough, accurate studies of the exploration of the California coastline, see Henry R. Wagner, *Spanish Voyages to the Northwest Coast of America in the Sixteenth Century* (San Francisco, 1928), and the same author's two-volume study, *Cartography of the Northwest Coast of America to 1800* (Berkeley: University of California Press, 1937).

2. Chapman, *History of California*, p. 223; Richman, *California Under Spain and Mexico*, pp. 68–70. Chapman notes that one of the men on the *San Carlos* was a baker for the proposed settlement.

3. Chapman, *History of California*, p. 223; Richman, *California Under Spain and Mexico*, p. 75.

4. Estado general que comprehende las Personas, Armamento, y respetos ornamentos . . . que han ido en las dos expediciones de Mar, y entrada por tierra a los puertos de San Diego y Monterey, Real de los Alamos, August 1, 1769, HL, José de Gálvez Collection, GA 532. This document contains an excellent fold-out table in five columns listing the specific items under various subheadings. Richman, *California Under Spain and Mexico*, p. 70, lists the goods in general and states that the *San Carlos* carried only one thousand pesos in currency for financial support.

5. Chapman, *History of California*, p. 224, states that about one-quarter of the estimated three hundred men who began the expeditions lost their lives, and others deserted, so that only about one-half of the original total actually reached Alta California.

6. *Ibid.,* p. 385.

7. Hubert H. Bancroft, *History of California,* 7 vols. (San Francisco, A. L. Bancroft Company and The History Company, 1884–90), Vol. I, pp. 199–201. Only the first two volumes of this set pertain to the Spanish period in Alta California.

8. *Ibid.,* Vol. II, p. 158. Richman, *California Under Spain and Mexico,* p. 452, gives this number as 1,200, but Governor Borica's figures for 1797 would exceed that total. He reported on July 24, 1797, a total of 832 Spaniards, 464 mestizos, 385 persons of *color quebrado,* and one slave, or 1,682 persons in all among the *gente de razón.* Together with 11,060 Christianized Indians at the missions, this provided a grand sum of 12,742 people living in the Spanish communities.

9. Chapman, *History of California,* p. 385.

10. *Ibid.,* pp. 150–53, 386–87. See also Herbert E. Bolton, "The Mission as a Frontier Institution in the Spanish American Colonies," in Bannon, *Bolton and the Spanish Borderlands,* pp. 187–211. Bolton's article appeared originally in the *American Historical Review,* Vol. 23 (October, 1917), p. 42–61.

11. Chapman, *History of California,* p. 389.

12. *Ibid.,* pp. 389–91. On the successes and failures of the presidio in general, see Odie B. Faulk, "The Presidio: Fortress or Farce?" *Journal of the West,* Vol. 8, No. 1 (January, 1969), pp. 22–28, and Sidney R. Brinckerhoff and Odie B. Faulk, *Lancers for the King* (Phoenix: Arizona Historical Foundation, 1965). Neither work, however, devotes much attention to the California presidios.

13. Bancroft, *History of California,* Vol. I, p. 218.

14. Richard F. Pourade, *Anza Conquers the Desert: The Anza Expeditions from Mexico to California and the Founding of San Francisco, 1774 to 1776* (San Diego, Calif.: Union Tribune Publishing Company, 1971), pp. 79–80. For a full account of the Anza expeditions, see Herbert E. Bolton, *Anza's California Expeditions,* 5 Vols. (Berkeley: University of California Press, 1930).

15. Pourade, *Anza Conquers the Desert,* pp. 92–93, citing Anza's diary.

16. *Ibid.,* pp. 91, 93.

17. *Ibid.,* pp. 97–98, 168.

18. Quoted in *ibid.,* p. 152.

19. *Ibid.*

20. *Ibid.,* p. 163.

21. *Ibid.,* pp. 184, 187.

22. *Ibid.,* p. 197.

23. Richman, *California Under Spain and Mexico,* pp. 133–35. These settlements were primarily to support missionary activity among the Indians at the junction of the Colorado and Gila rivers and were never regularized as civil communities before the uprising.

24. *Ibid.,* p. 124; Bancroft, *History of California,* Vol. I, pp. 310–11.

25. Phelipe de Neve to S.°r D.n Teodoro de Croix, Monte Rey, April 15, 1778, AGN, Provincias Internas 121, HL, California File, HM16781; Oscar O. Winther, *The Story of San José: California's First Pueblo, 1777–1869* (San Francisco: California Historical Society, 1935), pp. 2–3. Richman, *California Under Spain and Mexico,* p. 125, states erroneously that the original population was sixty-six people. Bancroft, *History of California,* Vol. I, p. 312, also commits the same mistake.

26. Neve to Croix, Monte Rey, April 15, 1778, HL, HM16781; Winther, *Story of San José,* p. 4.

27. D.n Phelipe de Neve, Reglamento Provincial para la Peninsula de Californias, San Carlos de Monterrey, June 1, 1779, AGN, Provincias Internas 121, no. 12, HL,

HM 16781. There is also an incomplete copy of this lengthy document of 240 pages, missing *títulos* 13, 14, and 15, in the Vallejo documents of the Bancroft Library, Berkeley, California.

28. *Ibid.*

29. One *vara* is about equal to thirty-three inches, or approximately one yard.

30. One *fanega* is equal to approximately 2½ bushels.

31. Neve, Reglamento, San Carlos de Monterrey, June 1, 1779, HL, HM16781.

32. Richman, *California Under Spain and Mexico*, p. 125; Bancroft, *History of California*, Vol. I, p. 340.

33. Richman, *California Under Spain and Mexico*, p. 126; Bancroft, *History of California*, Vol. I, pp. 342–43.

34. Phelipe de Neve, Mission San Gabriel, August 26, 1788 [*sic*], photostat, BL, doc. C-A178; Richman, *California Under Spain and Mexico*, p. 126.

35. Teodoro de Croix to Joseph de Gálvez, Arizpe, February 28, 1782, AGI, Guadalajara 267, typescript, BL, doc. C-A178; Thomas W. Temple II (trans.), "First Census of Los Angeles," *Historical Society of Southern California: Annual Publications*, Vol. 15, Part 2 (1931), pp. 148–49. Bancroft, *History of California*, Vol. I, p. 345, appends the names of the original settlers in a footnote.

36. Chapman, *History of California*, p. 391.

37. Bancroft, *History of California*, Vol. I, p. 388.

38. Winther, *Story of San José*, p. 5.

39. Bancroft, *History of California*, Vol. I, pp. 477–78.

40. *Ibid.*, pp. 460–61.

41. *Ibid.*, pp. 565–68; Richman, *California Under Spain and Mexico*, pp. 170ff.

42. Richman, *California Under Spain and Mexico*, pp. 172–73; Bancroft, *History of California*, Vol. I, pp. 568–70.

43. Robert G. Cowan, *Ranchos of California: A List of Spanish Concessions, 1775–1822, and Mexican Grants, 1822–1846* (Fresno, Calif.: Academy Library Guild, 1956), p. 139. Richman, *California Under Spain and Mexico*, p. 347, is in error in the statement that the number of *ranchos* in the Spanish period was "not more than twenty."

44. Cowan, *Ranchos of California*, pp. 4, 139.

45. One *sitio*, or square league, was equal to approximately 4,428 acres, or about seven square miles.

46. Cowan, *Ranchos of California*, pp. 3–4; Ruth Staff, "Settlement in Alta California before 1800" (M.A. thesis, University of California, Berkeley, 1931), pp. 96–97; Richman, *California Under Spain and Mexico*, pp. 347–48.

47. Chapman, *History of California*, p. 249.

48. Richman, *California Under Spain and Mexico*, p. 226.

49. Chapman, *History of California*, p. 385.

50. Table compiled from Richman, *California Under Spain and Mexico*, p. 174; Winther, *Story of San José*, p. 7; Donald C. Cutter, *Malaspina in California* (San Francisco: John Howell Books, 1960), Appendix E, pp. 83–84; Estado que manifiesta el número de vasallos, Jurisdicción de Santa Bárbara, December 31, 1803, Vallejo Documentos, No. 28:7, BL; Resumen general que manifiestan . . . los Nuevos Establicimientos, Probincia de Californias, Loreto, August 1, 1804, Vallejo Documentos, No. 28:98, BL; Resumen Gral. que manifiesta el estado en que se hallan los nuebos establicimientos de esta Prov.ª, Provincia de la Nueva California, Vallejo Documentos, No. 28:101, BL; Bancroft, *History of California*, Vol. I, pp. 569, 659,

715, and Vol. II, pp. 111, 349, 377, and 390. Both Bancroft and Winther maintain that the population of San José in 1810 was about 125 people, but the Vallejo documents in the Bancroft Library clearly show only 110 persons for that date.

51. Bancroft, *History of California*, Vol. I, p. 601.

52. *Ibid.*, Vol. II, p. 155.

53. *Ibid.*, p. 413.

54. *Ibid.*, Vol. I, pp. 605–606.

55. *Ibid.*, Vol. II, p. 413. Staff, "Settlement in Alta California," pp. 46–47, states that the orphans went to San Diego, Monterey, Santa Bárbara, and San José.

56. See, for example, Estado que manifiesta el número de vasallos, Jurisdicción de Santa Bárbara, December 31, 1803, Vallejo Documentos, No. 28:7, BL. No slaves were indicated in this document or any other.

57. Chapman, *History of California*, p. 392.

58. Pourade, *Anza Conquers the Desert*, p. 80.

59. Phelipe de Neve to S.ᵒʳ D.ⁿ Teodoro de Croix, Monte Rey, April 15, 1778, AGN, Provincias Internas 121, HL, California File, HM16781.

60. Teodoro de Croix to Joseph de Gálvez, Arizpe, February 28, 1782, AGI, Guadalajara 267, BL, doc. C-A178; Temple, "First Census of Los Angeles," pp. 148–49.

61. Cutter, *Malaspina in California*, pp. 83–84. Malaspina also noted that the citizens of San José came to Monterey on September 23, 1791, to sell fruit to the crews of his vessels. See *ibid.*, p. 37.

62. See maps in Bancroft, *History of California*, Vol. I, pp. 348, 350, depicting the *acequias madres* running from the respective rivers to the *suertes* of the settlers in each town.

63. Cutter, *Malaspina in California*, pp. 83–84.

64. Richman, *California Under Spain and Mexico*, p. 452.

65. Resumen Gral. que manifiesta el estado en que se halla los Nuebos Establicimientos de esta Prov.ᵃ, Provincia de la Nueva California, Vallejo Documentos, No. 28:101, BL.

66. Richman, *California Under Spain and Mexico*, pp. 207–208.

67. *Ibid.*, p. 452; Staff, "Settlement of Alta California," p. 58.

68. Richman, *California Under Spain and Mexico*, p. 453.

69. *Ibid.*

70. Staff, "Settlement of Alta California," pp. 75–76; Richman, *California Under Spain and Mexico*, p. 127.

71. Staff, "Settlement of Alta California," pp. 96–97; Chapman, *History of California*, p. 393.

72. Cowan, *Ranchos of California*, p. 4.

73. For an example, see John W. Caughey, *California*, 2d ed. (Englewood Cliffs, N.J.: Prentice Hall, 1953), p. 135.

74. Chapman, *History of California*, p. 395.

75. Richman, *California Under Spain and Mexico*, p. 339; Frank W. Blackmar, *Spanish Institutions of the Southwest* (Baltimore, Md.: Johns Hopkins Press, 1891), p. 261.

76. Richman, *California Under Spain and Mexico*, p. 339.

77. Chapman, *History of California*, p. 401.

78. Cutter, *Malaspina in California*, pp. 80–82. Appendix C on these pages lists the prices established for animals, grains, and basic foods consumed by Californians about 1790. An *arroba* is about twenty-five pounds, and a *fanega* about 2½ bushels.

79. Felipe de Neve, Bando, Real Presidio de Monterey, January 1, 1781, BL, doc. C-A178; Cutter, *Malaspina in California*, pp. 80–82.

80. Charles N. Rudkin (trans. and ed.), *The First French Expedition to California: La Pérouse in 1786* (Los Angeles: Glen Dawson, 1959), pp. 49, 79.

81. Cutter, *Malaspina in California*, pp. 49–53.

82. *Ibid.*, pp. 29, 31, 37, 80–83.

83. *Ibid.*, p. 39.

84. Marguerite E. Wilbur (ed.), *Vancouver in California, 1792–1794: The Original Account of George Vancouver*, 2 vols. (Los Angeles: Glen Dawson, 1953), Vol. II, pp. 231–33.

85. Chapman, *History of California*, p. 403.

86. *Ibid.*, pp. 411–17; Richman, *California Under Spain and Mexico*, pp. 197–99. The latter reference states that Concepción was the sister of Luis Arguello, the commandant of the Presidio at San Francisco, and that she was fourteen years old at the time of Rezanov's visit.

87. Chapman, *History of California*, pp. 441–49.

88. Richman, *California Under Spain and Mexico*, pp. 342–45.

89. Chapman, *History of California*, pp. 397–400.

90. Staff, "Settlement in Alta California," p. 103.

91. *Ibid.*, pp. 103–104.

92. Bancroft, *History of California*, Vol. I, pp. 642–44.

93. Richman, *California Under Spain and Mexico*, p. 209.

94. Winther, *Story of San José*, p. 12, citing José M.ª Estudillo al Comd. de S.ⁿ José, Contrato sobre instrucción pública, Monterey, October 26, 1811.

95. Bancroft, *History of California*, Vol. II, pp. 425–29.

96. *Ibid.*, pp. 427–28.

97. Vallejo Documentos, Vol. 15, Nos. 1–85, BL.

98. Sherburne F. Cook, "Smallpox in Spanish and Mexican California, 1700–1845," *Bulletin of the History of Medicine*, Vol. 7, No. 2 (February, 1939), pp. 154–55.

99. Sherburne F. Cook, "The Monterey Surgeons during the Spanish Period in California," *Bulletin of the Institute of Medicine*, Vol. 5, No. 1 (January, 1937), pp. 43–49; Richman, *California Under Spain and Mexico*, p. 453.

100. Cook, "Monterey Surgeons," p. 70.

101. Doctor de M. José Ignacio García Jove, February 28, 1799, Vallejo Documentos, No. 28:6, BL.

102. Cook, "Monterey Surgeons," p. 70; Cook, "Smallpox in Spanish California," pp. 167, 170–71.

103. Staff, "Settlement in Alta California," p. 16.

104. J. N. Bowman, "The Bridges of Provincial California," *El Palacio*, Vol. 68, No. 4 (Winter, 1961), pp. 223–29.

105. *Ibid.*, p. 230.

106. J. M. Guinn, "Early Postal Service of California," *Publications of the Historical Society of Southern California*, Vol. 4 (Los Angeles: Historical Society of Southern California, 1898), pp. 18–19; Staff, "Settlement in Alta California," p. 104.

107. Richman, *California Under Spain and Mexico*, p. 338.

108. *Ibid.*, p. 152.

109. Bancroft, *History of California*, Vol. I, pp. 640–41.

110. *Ibid.*, p. 638; Richman, *California Under Spain and Mexico*, p. 173.

111. Richman, *California Under Spain and Mexico*, p. 173.
112. Quoted in *ibid.*, p. 171.
113. Quoted in *ibid.*
114. Phelipe de Neve to Viceroy Antonio María de Bucareli y Ursúa, Monte Rey, June 6, 1777, AGN, Provincias Internas 121, HL, California File, HM16781.

CHAPTER 11

1. Von Humboldt, *Political Essay on the Kingdom of New Spain*, p. 33. Note that Von Humboldt's figures show only 272,881 people in the frontier provinces which he did not visit. His figures for Nueva Vizcaya (Durango) and Coahuila are low, those for the Californias are too high, and those for Sonora and New Mexico are about right. He made no report of the population in Nuevo León, Nuevo Santander, and Sinaloa.

2. Memoria sobre el Reyno de Nueva España . . ., Veracruz, October 24, 1815, microcopy, Archivo Histórico Militar (Madrid), doc. 5-2-4-3.

3. For example, see Von Humboldt, *Political Essay on the Kingdom of New Spain*, pp. 31, 238. Von Humboldt observed that the population had increased in Nueva Vizcaya "with the rapidity everywhere . . . where a nation of shepherds is replaced by agricultural colonists." He noted that the entire population of New Spain in 1804 was 5,840,000, whereas it had been 4,483,559 only ten years earlier. See also, on population growth in the eighteenth century, McAlister, "Social Structure," p. 368.

4. Silvio Zavala, "The Frontiers of Hispanic America," in W. D. Wyman and C. B. Kroeber (eds.), *The Frontier in Perspective* (Madison: University of Wisconsin Press, 1957), p. 45.

5. *Ibid.*, pp. 40–41.
6. *Ibid.*, pp. 41–43, 47.
7. Jackson, *Journals of Zebulon Pike*, Vol. I, p. 391.
8. McWilliams, *North from Mexico*, p. 11.
9. *Ibid.*, p. 9.
10. Zavala, "Frontiers of Hispanic America," p. 48.
11. *Ibid., pp.* 49–50
12. McWilliams, *North from Mexico*, pp. 70–71.
13. Adelina Otero Warren, "The Spell of New Mexico," in Wayne Moquín and Charles Van Doren (eds.), *A Documentary History of the Mexican Americans* (New York: Bantam Books, 1972), p. 374.

Bibliographical Essay

Much has been written in the past fifty years on specific subjects within the over-all field of the Spanish Borderlands. Often these works have made major contributions to the advancement of knowledge in the more general fields of Latin American, Mexican, United States, and Western history. Professor Charles Gibson of the University of Michigan recognized this fact when he noted in his *Spain in America* (New York: Harper and Row, 1966) that "it is probable that no other part of colonial Spanish America has stimulated so extensive a program of research." (p. 189) Unfortunately, there are still many historians both in Latin America and the United States who fail to take note of these intensive studies, which are frequently based upon more detailed analysis of authentic Spanish sources than those commonly used in contemporary books and articles.

No effort is made here to provide a comprehensive reading list pertaining to the whole subject of the Spanish Borderlands. Major attention is devoted to the important sources, primary and secondary, relating to the civil communities and the Spanish frontier settlers. Yet, because of the relationship between Spanish settlements and other frontier institutions and the occasional mention of settlers in other works, the general field of Borderlands history has not been completely excluded. A short section on works treating other topics has, therefore, been added, following the main part of this essay, which in general parallels the text.

GENERAL WORKS

Father John Francis Bannon recently provided the field of Spanish Borderlands history with something his mentor, Herbert Eugene Bolton, never got around to doing. Father Bannon's masterful synthesis, *The Spanish Borderlands Frontier, 1513–1821* (New York: Holt, Rinehart, and Winston, 1970), furnishes an excellent overview of Spain's long centuries of frontier experience, although it concentrates upon the regions now a part of the United States and is primarily concerned with exploratory, military, ecclesiastical, and political activities. Earlier, Father Bannon edited a series of Bolton's essays under the title *Bolton and the Spanish Borderlands* (Norman: University of Oklahoma Press, 1965). This is a provocative study, revealing once again the importance of Bolton's research and also suggesting all sorts of topics and approaches to the study of New Spain's northern frontier.

Although Bolton is rightly considered a pioneer in the study of the Borderlands, he is not the only one. *The Works of Hubert Howe Bancroft,* a series published in thirty-nine volumes at San Francisco in the 1880s, may be considered somewhat dated, but the historian cannot afford to ignore its individual volumes. Particularly valuable for this study were Bancroft's *History of the North Mexican States and Texas,* 2 vols. (San Francisco: The History Company, 1886–89), *History of Arizona and New*

Mexico, 1530–1888 (San Francisco: The History Company, 1889, and Albuquerque, N.Mex., Horn and Wallace, 1962), *History of Mexico,* 6 vols. (San Francisco: A. L. Bancroft Company and The History Company, 1883–88), especially the second through the fourth volumes, and *History of California,* 7 vols. (San Francisco: The History Company and A. L. Bancroft Company, 1884–90), particularly the first two volumes, which cover the period 1542–1824.

Outside of these three authors, few have dealt with the Spanish frontier over all, and no general study of the civil settlements and their inhabitants exists. Herbert E. Bolton, *The Spanish Borderlands: A Chronicle of Old Florida and the Southwest* (New Haven, Conn.: Yale University Press, 1921), still provides a good introduction and overview of institutions developed on the frontier, but only for that portion within the present United States; the book hardly mentions the role of the Spanish settler. Edward Gaylord Bourne, *Spain in America, 1450–1580* (New York: Harper and Brothers, 1904, and Barnes and Noble, 1962), is useful only for exploration, conquest, and early colonization, although it does have six chapters on Spanish institutions planted in the Americas. Chapter 9 of Charles Gibson, *Spain in America* (New York: Harper and Row, 1966), is a well-written, up-to-date summary of the Spanish Borderlands and their place in the over-all history of Latin America and of the United States. Edward H. Spicer, *Cycles of Conquest: The Impact of Spain, Mexico, and the United States on the Indians of the Southwest, 1533–1960* (Tucson: University of Arizona Press, 1962), pp. 298–306, treats the Spanish town as an important frontier institution through which European influence was exerted, but most of the work concentrates upon the interrelationship and influence of other institutions upon the Indians of northern New Spain. D. W. Meinig, *Southwest: Three Peoples in Geographical Change, 1600–1700* (New York and Toronto: Oxford University Press, 1971), examines the Spanish period in one short chapter and is restricted to the southwestern United States, but it is a splendid analysis of the influence of one culture upon another.

Other general works concerned with Spanish expansion and influence in North America include Herbert E. Bolton and Thomas M. Marshall, *The Colonization of North America, 1492–1783* (New York: Macmillan, 1922); Herbert I. Priestley, *The Coming of the White Man, 1492–1848* ([New York]: Macmillan, 1929); and Dario Flores Fernández, *The Spanish Heritage in the United States* (Madrid: Publicaciones Españolas, 1965).

Various general histories of the western and southwestern United States provide some coverage of the Spanish Borderlands in summary form, but give little if any information concerning the civil settlements. Professional journals have published many articles on specific topics relevant to the region. Special issues of the *Journal of the West* (January, 1969), and the *Southwestern Historical Quarterly* (April, 1968) have been devoted entirely to the Spanish Borderlands, but only one of the thirteen articles in these two issues deals with the Spanish settlers and their communities. Occasional articles on the northern frontier have appeared in *The Americas, New Mexico Historical Review, Arizona and the West,* and the *Western Historical Quarterly;* except for the ones in the *New Mexico Historical Review,* relatively few have discussed subjects relating to Spanish society and settlement on the frontier. Those that do are mentioned in the appropriate frontiers discussed later in this essay.

Most of the above works concentrate on the Spanish Borderlands in general. The civil community itself has been studied by only a few historians. The monumental

Recopilación de leyes de los reynos de las indias, 4 vols. (Madrid, 1681), and 3 vols. (Madrid: Consejo de la Hispanidad, 1943), provides in the fourth book, second volume, a good codification of Spanish law regarding discoveries, settlements, commerce, and local government. However, this compilation of Spanish law should not be considered alone, as it deals with only a part of the colonial period, and Spanish practice often differed greatly from theory. Zelia Nuttall, "Royal Ordinances Concerning the Laying Out of New Towns," *Hispanic American Historical Review*, Vol. 4, No. 4 (November, 1921), pp. 743–53, and Vol. 5, No. 2 (May, 1922), pp. 249–54, furnishes an excellent study and a translation of Philip II's colonization laws of 1573, although the second article is but a corrected translation of the first. Mattie A. Hatcher, *The Opening of Texas to Foreign Settlement, 1801–1821* (Austin: University of Texas Press, 1927) contains translated royal instructions for the establishment of the *villa* of Pitic in Sonora during the 1780s, a body of regulations that served also for later civil communities, especially in Alta California and Texas. Richard E. Greenleaf, "Land and Water, 1700–1821," *New Mexico Historical Review*, Vol. 47, No. 2 (April, 1972), pp. 85–112, not only discusses land practices but stresses the Instructions for Pitic, analyzing selected paragraphs and concluding that the actual document came into existence after the founding of the *villa*. The best secondary source for the study of the civil community is John W. Reps, *Town Planning in Frontier America* (Princeton, N.J.: Princeton University Press, 1970), especially Chapter 2, "Pueblo and Presidio: Spanish Planning in Colonial America." Settlement plans for individual communities are also illustrated in this soundly researched text.

For studies of population history, see Sherburne F. Cook and Woodrow Borah, *Essays on Population History: Mexico and the Caribbean, Volume One* (Berkeley and Los Angeles: University of California Press, 1971), for insights and problems concerning census studies and other demographic sources. Although the work deals mainly with central New Spain, it provides helpful information relating to analysis of such documents and occasionally comments on settlements along the northern frontier. Lyle N. McAlister, "Social Structure and Social Change in New Spain," *Hispanic American Historical Review*, Vol. 43, No. 3 (August, 1963), pp. 349–70, not only outlines the basic social classifications of eighteenth-century New Spain, but emphasizes that the whole system was more dynamic and subject to change than has been supposed. Population and racial characteristics of society at the turn of the nineteenth century are advanced by Alexander von Humboldt, *Political Essay on the Kingdom of New Spain* (ed. by Mary Maples Dunn), (New York: Alfred A. Knopf, 1972). Charles Gibson (ed.), *The Black Legend: Anti-Spanish Attitudes in the Old World and the New* (New York: Alfred A. Knopf, 1971), is an excellent collection of readings and analysis of the growth of anti-Spanish bias and prejudice among English-speaking people, stressing their opposition to Spain, her kingdoms, and her culture in general.

On the over-all subject of the Spanish frontier in America, little has been written in the way of general interpretation or in comparison to the Anglo-American expansion. Silvio Zavala's pioneering essay, "The Frontiers of Hispanic America," in W. D. Wyman and C. B. Kroeber (eds.), *The Frontier in Perspective* (Madison: University of Wisconsin Press, 1957), pp. 35–58, concentrates on the northern expansion of New Spain in a general way and advances some interesting points of comparison between the Spanish and Anglo frontiers. It is essentially an introductory study, however, by no means a conclusive one. Víctor Andrés Belaúnde, *The Frontier in His-*

panic America (Rice Institute Pamphlets, No. 10 [October, 1923]), pp. 202–13, is a short, introductory study maintaining that the frontier appeared only rarely in the Spanish colonies because of the lack of free land.

BIBLIOGRAPHIES AND GUIDES

Almost sixty years after its original publication, Herbert E. Bolton, *Guide to Materials for the History of the United States in the Principal Archives of Mexico* (Washington, D.C.: Carnegie Institution, 1913, and New York: Kraus Reprint Corporation, 1966), remains the basic tool for the serious researcher in Mexican archives. It should be consulted very early in the research process for both national and state collections of documents. The "Bibliographical Notes" in Father Bannon's *The Spanish Borderlands Frontier*, pp. 257–87, are extensive and well organized by subject matter. Oakah L. Jones, Jr. "The Spanish Borderlands: A Selected Reading List," *Journal of the West*, Vol. 8, No. 1 (January, 1969), pp. 137–42, is a summary of the major books and articles.

Special manuscript collections often have valuable guides to assist the researcher in locating materials within their holdings. Of particular importance for two major collections at the University of Texas are the works of Chester V. Kielman: *The University of Texas Archives: A Guide to the Historical Manuscripts Collections in the University of Texas Library* (Austin: University of Texas Press, 1967), and the same author's *Guide to the Microfilm Edition of the Béxar Archives, 1717–1803* (Austin: University of Texas Archives Microfilm Publication, 1967). Carlos E. Castañeda, *A Report on the Spanish Archives in San Antonio, Texas* (San Antonio, Texas: Yanaguana Society, 1937), not only provides a good summary of that city's history but assistance in locating and using that part of the Béxar Archives not transferred to the University of Texas in 1896.

In New Mexico there are three major guides for collections of manuscript material located in Santa Fé. Fray Angelico Chávez, *Archives of the Arch-diocese of Santa Fé* (Washington, D.C.: Academy of American Franciscan History, 1957), is a useful aid in consulting an important but too often ignored collection. The extensive Spanish Archives of New Mexico recently have been completely microfilmed and a guide was prepared under the direction of Myra Ellen Jenkins with the title of *Calendar of the Spanish Archives of New Mexico* (Santa Fé: State of New Mexico Records Center, 1968). Ralph E. Twitchell, *The Spanish Archives of New Mexico*, 2 vols. (Cedar Rapids, Iowa: The Torch Press, 1914), is an older but still useful guide to the same collection, although it must be used with caution, since the translations are occasionally misleading and sometimes incorrect.

Doris M. Wright, *A Guide to the Mariano Guadalupe Vallejo Documentos para la historia de California, 1780–1875* (Berkeley: University of California Press, 1953), is helpful, especially for the Mexican period, since the Vallejo papers in the Bancroft Library are bound into thirty-six volumes. Also useful for California history is Dale L. Morgan and George P. Hammond (eds.), *A Guide to the Manuscript Collections of the University of California* (Berkeley: University of California Press, 1963).

Of general interest in locating manuscript collections is Philip M. Hamer (ed.), *A Guide to Archives and Manuscripts in the United States* (New Haven, Conn.: Yale University Press, 1961). It provides short summaries of the major holdings in some thirteen hundred depositories in the United States, including those possessing Spanish manuscripts.

In addition to dictionaries, card catalogues, local guides to archival collections, and specialized reference works, one of the most useful aids for anyone doing research in Spanish manuscripts is J. Villasana Haggard and Malcolm D. McLean, *Handbook for Translators of Spanish Historical Documents* ([Austin]: University of Texas Archives Collections, 1941). It provides helpful hints in deciphering paleography, tables of equivalent measures, monetary standards and their values, weights and measures, and a key to abbreviations often cited in manuscripts, but the book has become so scarce now that it needs to be reprinted.

THE NORTHEASTERN FRONTIER

Principal archival collections for this region (Texas, Coahuila, Nuevo León, and Tamaulipas) are located at San Antonio, Austin, Saltillo, and Monterrey. The Laredo Archives in the Special Collections room of the St. Mary's University Library in San Antonio, Texas, provide extensive and intensive coverage of Laredo from its founding in 1755. Originals, typescripts, and microfilm are available in this well-maintained collection. Some viceregal folders, census information, and royal *cédulas* for Spanish Texas are available at the Texas History Research Library, The Alamo, also in San Antonio. The University of Texas Archives at Austin contain the extensive original manuscripts of the Béxar Archives, originally located in San Antonio and amounting now to some 80,795 documents comprising an estimated total of 205,500 pages in all. Some translations and complete rolls of microcopy are also available. The Latin American Collection at the University of Texas and the Nacogdoches Archives, Archives Division, Texas State Library, both in Austin, have considerable holdings of manuscript material, some of which pertain to civil settlements during the Spanish period. Of special importance are the many census reports for various communities in Texas among the papers of the Nacogdoches Archives.

Published primary works should be consulted for the study of civil settlements and their inhabitants in this region. Texas has received far better coverage for the Spanish period than have the other states. Fray Francisco Céliz, *Diary of the Alarcón Expedition into Texas, 1718–1719* (trans. by Fritz L. Hoffman), 2 vols. (Los Angeles: The Quivira Society, 1935), is an excellent study of the Spanish colonizing expedition sent to San Antonio and East Texas. Fray Juan Agustín de Morfi, *History of Texas, 1673–1779* (trans. and ed. by Carlos E. Castañeda), (Albuquerque, N.Mex.: The Quivira Society, 1935), and the same author's *Viaje de indios y diario del Nuevo México* (ed. by Vito Alessio Robles), 2d ed. (México: Antigua Librería Robredo y José Porrúa e Hijos, 1935), both provide population statistics and eyewitness observations of frontier settlements about the end of the eighteenth century. Ernest Wallace and David M. Vigness (eds.), *Documents of Texas History* ([Austin, Texas]: The Steck Company, [1960]), is a splendid source book containing selected documents, especially a translated and annotated version of a census for Spanish Texas in 1783. Virginia H. Taylor (trans. and ed.), *The Letters of Antonio Martínez: Last Spanish Governor of Texas, 1817–1822* (Austin: Texas State Library, 1957), deals with social and political problems, particularly the growing contraband trade, at the end of the Spanish administration of Texas.

There is no single secondary work that covers the history of the entire northeastern frontier. However, there are some important studies relating to individual states or provinces and others on special topics that furnish valuable information about the settlers and the communities of the region.

For Texas the best single-volume history with good coverage of the Spanish period is still the widely used Rupert N. Richardson, *Texas: The Lone Star State* (New York: Prentice Hall, 1943). T. R. Fehrenbach's more recent work, *Lone Star: A History of Texas and the Texans* (New York: Macmillan, 1968), is less satisfactory because of its errors and misleading generalizations concerning the Spanish experience on this frontier. Of enormous value to the researcher studying the Spanish period is the detailed, highly accurate Carlos E. Castañeda, *Our Catholic Heritage in Texas*, 1519–1936, 7 vols. (Austin, Texas: Von Boeckmann-Jones Company, 1936). Volumes I–V and part of Volume VI cover the period of Spanish administration, with much attention to civil settlements and society based upon a lifetime of the author's own meticulous archival research. Herbert E. Bolton, *Texas in the Middle Eighteenth Century: Studies in Spanish Colonial Administration* (Berkeley: University of California Press, 1915, and New York: Russell and Russell, 1962), is a sound study of the San Sabá experiment and the many transfers of settlers in and out of East Texas during the decade of the 1770s.

Works dealing with specific periods of Spanish administration supplement the more general ones. Odie B. Faulk, *The Last Years of Spanish Texas*, 1778–1821 (The Hague: Mouton and Company, 1964), provides a general chronological overview with occasional comment on the society of Spanish Texas, including some subjects not treated elsewhere. Information on the period before 1778 is covered in Faulk, *A Successful Failure* (Austin, Texas: Steck Vaughn Company, 1965). David M. Vigness, *The Revolutionary Decades*, 1810–1836 (Austin, Texas: Steck Vaughn Company, 1965) summarizes the final decade of Spain's administration in Texas and supplies a fine analysis of conditions in Texas prior to the achievement of Mexican independence. Gerald Ashford, *Spanish Texas: Yesterday and Today* (Austin, Texas, and New York: The Pemberton Press, 1971), although not strictly a period history, is a popularly written account emphasizing exploratory ventures and foreign visitors, not the actual Spanish population of the frontier province. D. W. Meinig, *Imperial Texas: An Interpretive Essay in Cultural Geography* (Austin, University of Texas Press, 1964), stresses the fact that there was little cohesion or stability in the three centers of settlement in Texas. Although most of Meinig's work deals with a later period, he reaches some sound conclusions relating to Spanish Texas as a remote, dangerous, vaguely defined, underdeveloped, and sparsely settled frontier. Walter P. Webb (ed.), *The Handbook of Texas*, 2 vols. (Austin: Texas State Historical Association, 1952), is a handy reference work organized alphabetically and covering the entire history of the state, not just the Spanish period. However, its observations on the Spanish era must be used with caution in view of its many errors.

Special topics are discussed by some of the leading historians of the Spanish period. Lino Gómez Canedo, *Primeras exploraciones y poblamiento de Texas (1686–1694)* (Monterrey, Nuevo León: Publicaciones del Instituto Tecnológico y de Estudios Superiores de Monterrey, Serie: Historia, 1968), is a masterful, soundly researched study of the exploration northward from Coahuila and Nuevo León, mostly in search of the French under La Salle, and of the establishment, problems, and abandonment of the Franciscan missions in East Texas at the end of the seventeenth century. The same subject, with an extension to 1793, is treated in Thomas P. O'Rourke, *The Franciscan Missions in Texas*, 1690–1793 (Washington, D.C.: Studies in American Church History, 1927), a monograph which arose out of a doctoral dissertation at Catholic University. Sandra L. Myres, *The Ranch in Spanish Texas* (El Paso: Texas Western Press, 1969), is a thoroughly documented, well-organized, interesting account of the origins, adaptations, methods, and influence of Spanish ranching in colonial Texas and Nuevo Santander as well as upon the later cattle industry in Texas. Robert S. Weddle, *The San Sabá Mission: Spanish Pivot in Texas* (Austin: University of Texas Press, 1964), and the same author's *San Juan Bautista: Gateway to Spanish Texas* (Austin and London: University of Texas Press, 1968), are both splendid local studies, soundly researched, and written in great detail, but they do not say much about civilian settlers in the province. Two works pertain largely to the last decade of Spanish administration. Mattie A. Hatcher, *The Opening of Texas to Foreign Settlement, 1801–1821* (Austin: University of Texas Press, 1927), concentrates on the efforts made by Spanish officials to erect barriers against the advancing Anglo-American occupation of Texas. An excellent study of a royalist governor who opposed the insurgents in Texas during the war for independence and made sound recommendations for the consolidation of Spain's hold on Texas (which, incidentally, were not followed by the mother country) is provided by Félix D. Almaráz, Jr., *Tragic Cavalier: Governor Manuel Salcedo of Texas, 1808–1813* (Austin and London: University of Texas Press, 1971).

The Southwestern Historical Quarterly and its predecessor, *The Quarterly of the Texas State Historical Association*, contain many articles pertaining to Spanish Texas, some of which pertain to the civilian settlements and their residents. Isaac J. Cox, "The Early Settlers of San Fernando," Vol. 5, No. 2 (October, 1901), pp. 142–60, the same author's "Educational Efforts in San Fernando de Béxar," Vol. 6, No. 1 (July, 1902), pp. 27–63, and Robert S. Weddle, "San Juan Bautista: Mother of Texas Missions," Vol. 71, No. 4 (April, 1968), pp. 542–63, are only a few of the more important articles for the present study. Fritz L. Hoffman, "Martín de Alarcón and the Founding of San Antonio," in Thomas E. Cotner and Carlos E. Castañeda (eds.), *Essays in Mexican History* (Austin, Texas: Institute of Latin American Studies, 1958), is a soundly researched article, complementing the author's earlier work in the Quivira Society Publications. Livestock and early ranching are the topics of three significant articles: Donald Brand, "The Early History of the Range Cattle Industry in Northern Mexico," *Agricultural History*, Vol. 35, No. 3 (July, 1961), pp. 132–39; Odie B. Faulk, "Ranching in Spanish Texas," *Hispanic American Historical Review*, Vol. 44, No. 2 (May, 1965), pp. 257–66; and Donald E. Worcester, "The Spread of Spanish Horses in the Southwest," *New Mexico Historical Review*, Vol. 19, No. 3 (July, 1944), pp. 225–32, and Vol. 20, No. 1 (January, 1945), pp. 1–13). Finally, an unpublished M.A. thesis by Helen M. Dixon, "The Middle Years of the Administration of Juan María Barón de Ripperdá, Governor of Texas, 1773–1775" (University of Texas, 1934), is illustrative of the many events and problems in the frontier province during the 1770s, especially the problem of the East Texas settlers and Governor Ripperdá's support of their resettlement in that region.

For Coahuila, Vito Alessio Robles, *Coahuila y Texas en la época colonial* (México: Editorial Cultural, 1938), is a splendid overview of the province's colonial experience, including its settlement and social aspects pertaining to the principal civil communities. Alessio Robles, *Francisco de Urdiñola y el norte de la Nueva España* (México: Imprenta Mundial, 1931), provides a thorough account of Coahuila's origins, at least of its southern region, and details the ventures undertaken by the noted explorer and colonizer. Carmen Perry (ed. and trans.), *San José de Palafox: "The Impossible Dream" by the Río Grande* (San Antonio, Texas: St. Mary's University Press, 1971), is a recent, well-researched, handsomely printed study of an unsuccessful Spanish effort to colonize permanently a location on the north bank of the Río Grande in the decade before Mexican independence was established. Miss Perry provides photostats of documents pertaining to the settlement, along with useful translations, in a well-organized format. Florence Johnson Scott, *Royal Land Grants North of the Río Grande, 1777–1821* ([n.p.]: Texian Press, 1969), is an interesting study of large land grants made to families in the Reynosa district on the south bank of the Río Grande, more properly associated with the province of Nuevo Santander. Marc Simmons' article, "Tlascalans in the Spanish Borderlands," *New Mexico Historical Review*, Vol. 39, No. 2 (April, 1964), pp. 101–10, stresses the importance of the Tlaxcaltecan settlement near Saltillo and the spread of its inhabitants to other frontiers. An excellent study of the establishment, growth, and influence of a single *hacienda* in Coahuila is presented in a work by Charles H. Harris, III, "The North Mexican *Hacendado*: The Case of the Sánchez Navarro Family," an unpublished paper read at the meeting of the Southwest Social Science Association in Dallas, Texas, March 30, 1972. In planning a major work on this important family and the growth of the *hacienda* system, Harris published an article on the same subject, "Empire of the Sánchez Navarro," *Américas*, Vol. 24, No. 4 (April, 1972), pp. 12–18.

Nuevo Santander, or present Tamaulipas, was the last province occupied by Spanish settlers on the northeastern frontier, and it was a true civil colony. Lawrence F. Hill, *José de Escandón and the Founding of Nuevo Santander: A Study in Spanish Colonization* (Columbus: Ohio State University Press, 1926), is a basic early work on the occupation of this province and is one of the more notable studies to have appeared on the subject of civil settlements on the frontier of New Spain. Florence Johnson Scott, "Spanish Colonization of the Lower Río Grande, 1747–1767," in Cotner and Castañeda [eds.], *Essays in Mexican History*, concentrates on an important subregion of the province and provides extensive information on the establishment, composition, and nature of the settlements on both banks of the Lower Río Grande region. Seb S. Wilcox has supplied a series of works pertaining to one of these settlements—Laredo—and its archives. His two articles in the *Southwestern Historical Quarterly*, "The Spanish Archives of Laredo," Vol. 49, No. 3 (January, 1946), pp. 341–60, and "Laredo during the Texas Republic," Vol. 42, No. 2 (October, 1938), provide a chronological review and analysis of documents pertaining to major events, population figures, and problems covered in the Laredo Archives. Finally, his unpublished paper in the St. Mary's University Library, "Data on Laredo History to 1820," although only a working study, is of considerable value to those interested in using the archival collection there.

For Nuevo León the secondary accounts of the colonial experience are not as full as they might be. However, there are a few important works that provide general information concerning the province, containing scattered information about the settlers there and the civil communities, particularly the most important settlement, Monterrey. For the over-all history of the province one will not find any information in Bancroft, *History of the North Mexican States and Texas*; instead, it is necessary to consult the same author's *History of Mexico*, particularly the second volume of that six-volume study. Genaro García (ed.), *Historia de Nuevo León: con noticias sobre Coahuila, Texas, y Nuevo México* (México: Librería de la Vda. de Ch. Bouret, 1909), and Santiago Roel, *Nuevo León: apuntes historicas*, 4th ed. (Monterrey, México: [Universidad de Nuevo León], 1952), contain the most detailed information concerning the establishment of civil settlements and the nature of society therein. Vito Alessio Robles, *Monterrey en la historia y en la leyenda* (México: Antigua Librería Robredo de José Porrúa e Hijos, 1936), is a general history of Monterrey which contains reliable information on the establishment and early experiences of that important community. Rodrigo Mendirichaga, *Origenes y formación de Nuevo León: según dos cronicas del siglo XVII* (Monterrey, México: Ediciones Pauraque, 1954), is an important work based upon two original sources concerning the early history of the province. Two studies provide firsthand descriptions of Nuevo León at different periods within the colonial era: Don Joseph Fernández de Jáuregui Urrutía, *Description of Nuevo León, México (1735–1740)*, (trans. and ed. by Malcolm D. McLean and Eugenio del Hoyo) (Monterrey, México: Instituto Tecnológico y de Estudios Superiores, 1964), and Nettie Lee Benson trans. and ed., *Report that Dr. Miguel Ramos de Arizpe . . . Presents to the August Congress on the Natural, Political, and Civil Conditions of the Provinces of Coahuila, Nuevo León, Nuevo Santander, and Texas . . .* (Austin: University of Texas Press, 1950). Substantial information concerning the province and its settlers may also be found in other works pertaining to the northern frontier in general and cited in full elsewhere in this essay.

THE NORTH CENTRAL FRONTIER

Archival collections of importance for the region of Nueva Vizcaya (Durango and Chihuahua) and New Mexico are located in Hidalgo del Parral, Chihuahua, El Paso, Texas, and Santa Fé and Albuquerque, New Mexico—although much was lost in the fire that damaged the city of Chihuahua in the early 1940s. These are only the major depositories; the microfilm copies of original documents make important collections in this region more readily available at various locations both in the United States and in Mexico.

El Archivo de Hidalgo del Parral is an extensive collection of manuscripts located in the former *real de minas* of San José del Parral. It is composed of thousands of documents spanning the period from the town's founding in 1631 to achievement of Mexican independence in 1821 and beyond. Census returns for the district, settlement information relating to Parral and San Bartolomé del Valle, and reports concerning local events and problems are particularly valuable for a study of Spanish society on the frontier. Microcopy of these documents is also available at Fort Lewis College in the Center of Southwest Studies, Durango, Colorado, and at the University of Texas at El Paso. This microfilming project was accomplished in 1959–60 and included a general index. However, researchers will find that the only way to uncover information on specific subjects is to proceed slowly through each year's roll of microfilm in a frame-by-frame search.

The Spanish Archives of New Mexico are in the State Records Center and Archives at Santa Fé, New Mexico. They constitute a major repository of colonial documents in the United States and are well maintained in individual folders for each document. Photostatic copies of these thousands of documents are in bound volumes in the Coronado Room, Zimmerman Library, University of New Mexico, Albuquerque. The State Records Center and Archives also has microcopy of the entire collection, available for sale to researchers and institutions. Furthermore, this same agency has microcopy of the records of the Archdiocese of Santa Fé, a collection which should be consulted by all interested in the social history of colonial New Mexico. The Coronado Room of the University of New Mexico also has photostatic copies of selected documents from the Archivo General de la Nación, Mexico City (particularly the *ramos* of Historia, Provincias Internas, Californias, Inquisición, and miscellaneous other sections); the Archivo General de Indias, Sevilla, Spain (especially Audiencia de Mexico, Guadalajara, Indiferente General, and a half-dozen other special sections); the Biblioteca Nacional de México, Mexico City; and the Museo Nacional, Mexico City. None of these collections is complete, but they are occasionally extensive, having been assembled over almost half of the present century and bound into volumes.

At the University of Texas at El Paso the Archives Division of the library possesses ninety-one reels of microfilm from the Archives of the City of Juárez (the Juárez Archives). These are extensive holdings containing census returns, town plans, and settlement information on the establishment and growth of the Paso del Norte region. Some indexes to specific rolls in this collection have been prepared by seminar students under the direction of Dr. Wilbert H. Timmons. They facilitate the location of specific documents, but should be used only in that way, not as a substitute for studying the manuscript itself, since the index descriptions are brief. In addition, the same institution has microcopy of the Chihuahua Collection, which emphasizes the period after 1824, with only a few scattered documents before that date. Baptismal certificates, marriage petitions, bishop's decrees, and matter pertaining to the Juárez Cathedral are also found in this collection.

Original documents, transcriptions, and some translations of manuscripts pertaining to New Mexico and the northern frontier are also found in the William G. Ritch Collection, Huntington Library and Art Gallery, San Marino, California. This collection contains 2,274 items, including documents covering the period 1539–1890, although only the first three boxes in the collection contain materials relative to the colonial era.

Published collections of documents, reports of various officials, and other primary materials such as diaries and letters are particularly important for the north central frontier and nearby areas as well. A few of those used in the present study are described here. Charles W. Hackett (ed.), *Historical Documents Relating to New Mexico, Nueva Vizcaya, and Approaches Thereto, to 1773*, 3 vols. (Washington, D.C.: Carnegie Institution, 1923–37), is particularly valuable. Alonso de la Mota y Escobar, *Descripción geográfica de los reinos de Nueva Galicia, Nueva Vizcaya, y Nuevo León*, 2d ed. (México: Editorial Robredo, 1940), supplies an excellent description of frontier Nueva Vizcaya, as well as comments on Nuevo León, within a half century after initial occupation. A handsomely printed recent publication of Pedro Alonso O'Crouley, *A Description of the Kingdom of New Spain*, 1774, trans. and ed. by Seán Galvin ([San Francisco]: John Howell Books, 1972), provides some interesting information on population, races, and frontier communities, including Durango and New Mexico in general. H. Bailey Carroll and J. Villasana Haggard, trans. and eds., *Three New Mexico Chronicles: The Exposición of Don Pedro Bautista Pino, 1812; the Ojeada of Lic. Antonio Barreiro, 1832; and the Addition by Don José Agustín de Escudero, 1849* (Albuquerque, N.Mex.: The Quivira Society, 1942), contains extensive primary information on social life and society in New Mexico, although only the Pino report pertains to the colonial era.

Travel reports of contemporary ecclesiastical and civil officials are also helpful in determining the nature of colonial society in Nueva Vizcaya and New Mexico. Eleanor B. Adams (ed.), *Bishop Tamarón's Visitation of New Mexico, 1760* (Albuquerque: Historical Society of New Mexico *Publications in History*, 1954), not only furnishes one of the earliest comprehensive observations of the New Mexico scene but also comments at length on the individual Spanish settlements, as well as the Indian pueblos. Miss Adams has cooperated with Fray Angelico Chávez in editing *The Missions of New Mexico, 1776: A Description by Fray Francisco Atanasio Domínguez* (Albuquerque: University of New Mexico Press, 1956), a masterful study describing the *villa* of Santa Fé, Santa Cruz de la Cañada, and Albuquerque in considerable detail, along with other Spanish and Indian settlements in New Mexico. Two outstanding works explain the role and observations of Nicolás de Lafora, who accompanied the Marqués de Rubí on his expedition to and inspection of the northern frontier of New Spain in the period from 1766 to 1768. Nicolás de Lafora, *Relación del viaje que hizo a los presidios internos situados en la frontera de la américa septentrional*, ed. by Vito Alessio Robles, (México: Editorial Pedro Robredo, 1939), provides a splendid editorial introduction, Lafora's comments on military matters, and significant observations concerning the settlers of Nueva Vizcaya and New Mexico, as well as those of Sonora, Nueva Extremadura (Coahuila), Texas, and Nuevo León. Lawrence Kinnaird, ed. and trans., *The Frontiers of New Spain: Nicolás de Lafora's Description, 1766–1768* (Berkeley, Calif.: Quivira Society, 1958), contains an excellent introduction by the editor and a useful translation of Lafora's record of the journey, complete with observations relating to the civil communities as well as the society and the presidios along the northern frontier. Francisco R. Almada follows this visit with the useful *Informe de Hugo O'Conor sobre el estado de las Provincias Internas del Norte, 1771–1776* (México, 1952), and Donald Jackson, ed., *The Journals of Zebulon Montgomery Pike: with Letters and Related Documents*, 2 vols., (Norman: University of Oklahoma Press, 1966) is a superlative study and collection of materials, providing Pike's firsthand observations on society and population in Santa Fé, Chihuahua, and San Antonio during his 1807 "visit" to northern New Spain.

As with the northeastern frontier, there is no single secondary work that pertains to both Nueva Vizcaya and New Mexico. Francisco R. Almada provides the best general history of the state of Chihuahua in his *Resumen de historia del estado de Chihuahua* (México: Libros Mexicanos, 1955). Florence C. Lister and Robert H. Lister, *Chihuahua: Storehouse of Storms* (Albuquerque: University of New Mexico Press, 1966), is a thoughtful, well-balanced history of the state with emphasis on the period after independence but also with some perceptive analysis of the colonial way of life. Luis Navarro García, the noted Spanish historian of the colonial experience in northern New Spain, has provided a factual, well-organized study of eighteenth-century conditions on the frontier as well as the nature of society there in his indispensable *Don José de Gálvez y la comandancia general de las Provincias Internas del Norte de Nueva España* (Sevilla: Escuela de Estudios Hispano-Americanos, 1964). Of the many histories of New Mexico, the most recent and scholarly is Warren A. Beck, *New Mexico: A History of Four Centuries* (Norman: University of Oklahoma Press, 1962). Still useful as a reference work is Ralph E. Twitchell, *The Leading Facts of New Mexican History*, 2 vols. (Cedar Rapids, Iowa: The Torch Press, 1911–12, and Albuquerque, N.Mex.: Horn and Wallace, 1963), although there is little information on colonial society, civil communities, or everyday settlers contained therein. Richard N. Ellis has edited *New Mexico Past and Present: A Historical Reader* (Albuquerque: University of New Mexico Press, 1971), an outstanding collection of essays by many scholars pertaining to important events and controversial happenings in the over-all history of the state, yet emphasizing its Spanish and Indian heritages.

Specialized works pertaining to this frontier include studies on a wide diversity of topics. Probably the leading study of mining activity in Nueva Vizcaya is Robert C. West, *The Mining Community in Northern New Spain: The Parral Mining District* (Berkeley and Los Angeles: University of California Press, 1949), a work which fully discusses mining methods, settlements, and the inter-relationship of miners, stockmen, and farmers not only in Nueva Vizcaya but all over the frontier. J. Lloyd Mecham has examined the early conquest, colonization, and growth of Nueva Vizcaya in his interesting and highly accurate *Francisco de Ibarra and Nueva Vizcaya* (Durham, N.Car.: Duke University Press, 1927). A little-known topic, but one of great importance to the improved communications of the later eighteenth century, is examined in Fernando B. Sandoval, *El correo en las Provincias Internas, 1779* (México: Junta Mexicana de Investigaciones Historicas, 1948). Woodrow Borah's article on "Francisco de Urdiñola's Census of the Spanish Settlements in Nueva Vizcaya, 1604," *Hispanic American Historical Review*, Vol. 35, No. 3 (August, 1955), pp. 398–402, is an invaluable document and analysis for early use in determining the composition of society in early seventeenth-century Nueva Vizcaya, as well as the occupations and possessions of the settlers.

For the history of the Paso del Norte region four published works provide general comments and other information on social conditions and inhabitants of the civil settlements there during the colonial era. C. L. Sonnichsen, *Pass of the North: Four Centuries on the Río Grande* (El Paso, Texas: Texas Western Press, 1968), is a recent, readable overview. Armando B. Chávez M., *Historia de Ciudad Juárez, Chih.* (Juárez, Chihuahua: [n.p.], 1951), is less detailed and of limited value. Two splendid studies by one of El Paso's most renowned citizens, Cleofas Calleros, are *La antorcha del Paso del Norte* (El Paso, Texas: American Printing Company, 1951), and *El Paso's Missions and Indians* (El Paso, Texas: McMath Company, 1951). On the founding, early growth, and problems of El Paso del Norte, see Anne E. Hughes, *The Beginnings of Spanish Settlement in the El Paso District* (Berkeley: University of California Press, 1914), and an unpublished Ph.D. dissertation at the University of New Mexico (1951) by Vina Walz, entitled "History of the El Paso Area, 1680–1692," which updates, revises, and expands upon the earlier Hughes work. J. Lawrence McConville, "A History of Population in the El Paso-Ciudad Juárez Area" (M.A. thesis, University of New Mexico, 1966), is a demographic study of some use, although its scope is wider than the colonial period.

New Mexico has received more attention from scholarly writers than any other region or province on the entire frontier of New Spain. In addition to the general works mentioned earlier, there are many special studies, only a handful of which can be mentioned here as especially valuable in the study of Spanish settlers and civil communities in the colonial period. An excellent, well-researched work on the local administration of the province is Marc Simmons, *Spanish Government in New Mexico* (Albuquerque: University of New Mexico Press, 1968). It is not only a study of government, as its title implies, but shows considerable understanding of local Spanish society and the nature of life in the civil settlements. Fray Angelico Chávez, *Origins of New Mexico Families: in the Spanish Colonial Period* (Santa Fé: Historical Society of New Mexico, 1954), provides not only an excellent general summary of settlement patterns and family origins by century, but is an exhaustive reference work on individual families who resided in the province at any time during the colonial experience. On early efforts to occupy New Mexico, see Albert H. Schroeder and Dan S. Matson, *A Colony on the Move: Gaspar Castaño de Sosa's Journal* ([Santa Fé]: School of American Research, 1965); George P. Hammond and Agapito Rey, *The Rediscovery of New Mexico, 1580–1594* (Albuquerque: University of New Mexico Press, 1966); and George P. Hammond and Agapito Rey, *Oñate: Colonizer of New Mexico, 1595–1628*, 2 vols. (Albuquerque: University of New Mexico Press, 1953). For the Pueblo Indian revolt of 1680 and the reconquest by Diego de Vargas, see Charles W. Hackett, ed., *Revolt of the Pueblo Indians of New Mexico and Otermín's Attempted Reconquest, 1680–1682*, 2 vols. (Albuquerque: University of New Mexico Press, 1942); Jesse B. Bailey, *Diego de Vargas and the Reconquest of New Mexico* (Albuquerque, N.Mex., 1940); J. Manuel Espinosa, *First Expedition of Vargas into New Mexico* (Albuquerque: University of New Mexico Press, 1940); and Espinosa, *Crusaders of the Río Grande* (Chicago: Institute of Jesuit History, 1942). Nancie L. González, *The Spanish Americans of New Mexico; a Heritage of Pride* (Albuquerque: University of New Mexico Press, 1969), is the best over-all history of the Spanish and Mexican heritage of the province and state, although it concentrates mostly on the character and behavior of the people, as well as associations of New Mexicans in the 1960s. The author does recognize that the prevailing type of settlement in colonial New Mexico was "the small agricultural and livestock-raising village" (p. 36), not the *hacienda* with its often-cited *patrón* system of society. George I. Sánchez, *Forgotten People: a Study of New Mexicans* (Albuquerque, N.Mex.: Calvin Horn Publishers, 1967), was originally published in 1940. It is a general study of the Spanish-speaking people, with little on the colonial era and much emphasis upon the citizens of Taos County.

Much has been written on the subject of the *penitentes* of New Mexico, probably because of their spectacular ceremonies, the fact that they differed from Anglo-American norms, and a preoccupation of popular writers with violence. However, Fray Angelico Chávez separated fact from fiction with his article "The Penitentes of New Mexico," *New Mexico Historical Review*, Vol. 29, No. 2 (April, 1954), pp. 97–123, pointing out that they probably originated from *cofradías*, or religious brotherhoods, during the "secular period" from 1790 to 1830. Alice C. Henderson, *Brothers of Light: The Penitentes of the Southwest* (New York: Harcourt, Brace, and Company, 1937, and Chicago: Río Grande Press, 1962), and Marta Weigle, *The Penitentes of the Southwest* (Santa Fé, N.Mex.: Ancient City Press, 1970), are the most reliable, well-balanced single works available on the subject. An unpublished Ph.D. dissertation at Yale University in 1935 by Dorothy Woodward, "The Penitentes of New Mexico," is probably the most thoroughly researched, comprehensive account, and its publication with an updated editorial introduction would be invaluable.

The culture and folk arts of Spanish settlers in New Mexico are covered in an excellent work by Roland F. Dickey, *New Mexico Village Arts*, 2d ed. (Albuquerque: University of New Mexico Press, 1970). The late E. Boyd, noted colonialist and authority on Spanish folk arts of the Museum of New Mexico, has published three important works on this subject. Her *Popular Arts of Colonial New Mexico* (Santa Fé: Museum of International Folk Art, 1959) provides a splendid, readable analysis of furniture-making, weaving, and carving of religious images in colonial New Mexico. *Saints and Saint Makers of New Mexico* (Santa Fé: Laboratory of Anthropology, 1946), and *The New Mexican Santero* (Santa Fé: Museum of New Mexico Press, 1969), both by the same accomplished author, are indispensible sources for an examination of the general subject of the making of *santos* in New Mexico. José E. Espinosa, *Saints in the Valleys: Christian Sacred Images in the History, Life, and Folk Art of Spanish New Mexico*, rev. ed. (Albuquerque: University of New Mexico

Press, 1967), is a well-written, handsomely printed study of *santos* and *santeros*. Two publications of the Taylor Museum, Colorado Springs Fine Arts Center, not only discuss the origins, practice, and development of this art, but portray numerous *santos* from that collection in extensive illustrations. These works are: Robert L. Shalkop, *Wooden Saints: The Santos of New Mexico* (Colorado Springs: Taylor Museum of The Colorado Springs Fine Arts Center, [1967?]), and Mitchell A. Wilder and Edgar Breitenbach, *The Religious Folk Art of New Mexico* (Colorado Springs: Taylor Museum, 1943). Two works pertaining to aspects of Spanish culture in New Mexico are Arthur L. Campa, *Spanish Folk Poetry in New Mexico* (Albuquerque: University of New Mexico Press, 1946), and Aurelio M. Espinosa, *The Spanish Language in New Mexico and Southern Colorado* (Santa Fé: Historical Society of New Mexico *Publications*, 1911).

The *New Mexico Historical Review* and *El Palacio* are two leading scholarly journals which have published articles on a wide variety of subjects pertaining to civil settlements and society in colonial New Mexico. It is not possible to cite all of them here, but some of the more important contributions to specific topics can be emphasized. France V. Scholes, "Civil Government and Society in New Mexico in the Seventeenth Century," *New Mexico Historical Review* (journal title omitted hereafter), Vol. 10, No. 2 (April, 1935), pp. 71–111), is particularly appropriate to the present study and valuable in understanding the nature of Spanish society in the century before the Pueblo revolt. Scholes's other contributions should be consulted: "Church and State in New Mexico, 1610–1650," scattered articles from Vol. 11, No. 1 (January, 1936), pp. 9–76, to Vol. 12, No. 1 (January, 1937), pp. 78–106; "Troublous Times in New Mexico, 1650–1670," scattered articles from Vol. 12, No. 2 (April, 1937), pp. 134–74, to Vol. 16, No. 3 (July, 1941), pp. 313–27; and "The First Decade of the Inquisition in New Mexico" Vol. 10, No. 3 (July, 1935), pp. 195–241.

Transportation and trade have been treated by three leading historians. France V. Scholes, "The Supply Service of the New Mexican Missions in the Seventeenth Century," Vol. 5, Nos. 1, 2, 4 (January, April, October, 1930), pp. 93–115, 186–210, 386–404, deals with the organization, financing, and problems of the "regular" supply trains from Chihuahua to New Mexico. Max L. Moorhead's "Spanish Transportation in the Southwest, 1540–1846," Vol. 33, No. 2 (April, 1957), pp. 107–22, is probably the best single source available concerning the methods and problems of primitive transportation not only in New Mexico but on the entire frontier. Moorhead's "The Presidio Supply Problem of New Mexico in the Eighteenth Century," Vol. 36, No. 3 (July, 1961), pp. 210–29, treats the never-resolved problem of supplying the frontier presidios adequately, even by employing private contractors. Lansing B. Bloom, "The Chihuahua Highway," Vol. 12, No. 3 (July, 1937), pp. 209–16, is a short piece examining the origins of the modern highway below El Paso and explaining the use of the route from Zacatecas to Chihuahua and El Paso del Norte in colonial times. Bloom adds appropriately that "culture knows no international boundary." (p. 216) The same author's "A Trade Invoice of 1638: For Goods Shipped by Governor Rosas from Santa Fé," Vol. 10, No. 3 (July, 1935), pp. 242–48, tells of some of the goods either used by settlers or shipped in trade at an early time in the province's history.

Marc Simmons' lead article, "Settlement Patterns and Village Plans in Colonial New Mexico," *Journal of the West*, Vol. 8, No. 1 (January, 1969), pp. 7–21, stresses the fact that Spanish settlers were dispersed along the Río Grande in small communities, creating all sorts of military problems in defending the province properly.

The *New Mexico Historical Review* contains many articles devoted to the founding of specific settlements. Among these are: Richard E. Greenleaf, "The Founding of Albuquerque, 1706: An Historical-Legal Problem," Vol. 39, No. 1 (January, 1964), pp. 1–15; Greenleaf, "Atrisco and Las Ciruelas, 1722–1769," Vol. 42, No. 1 (January, 1967), pp. 5–25; Lansing B. Bloom, "Albuquerque and Galisteo: Certificate of Their Founding," Vol. 10, No. 1 (January, 1935), pp. 48–50; and Ireneo L. Cháves, trans., "Instructions to Peralta by Vice-Roy," Vol. 4, No. 2 (April, 1929), pp. 170–87.

W. A. Keleher presents an excellent legal analysis of New Mexico's land system in his "Law of the New Mexico Land Grant," Vol. 4, No. 4 (October, 1929), pp. 350–71, and Louis H. Warner discusses the manner of transferring property between individuals in his "Conveyance of Property, the Spanish and Mexican Way," Vol. 6, No. 4 (October, 1931), pp. 334–59. A recent summary of New Mexico's land problems and the development of grants made by Spain and Mexico, by staff writer Frankie McCarty, appeared in the Albuquerque *Journal* from September 28 to October 10, 1969. Reprinted in pamphlet form under the title *Land Grant Problems in New Mexico* (Albuquerque: Albuquerque *Journal*, 1969), it provides a good overview and historical perspective concerning the present land conflict in New Mexico. Two excellent articles by Myra Ellen Jenkins depict the degree of gradual Spanish encroachment upon Indian lands in the Laguna district and in the region north of Santa Fé during the eighteenth century and afterward. They are: "Spanish Land Grants in the Tewa Area," *New Mexico Historical Review*, Vol. 47, No. 2 (April, 1972), pp. 113–34, and "The Baltasar Baca 'Grant'; History of an Encroachment," *El Palacio*, Vol. 61 (1961), pp. 47–64. A good review of the many labor systems employed by Spain is Ruth K. Barber, "Indian Labor in the Spanish Colonies," *New Mexico Historical Review*, Vol. 7, No. 2 (April, 1932), pp. 105–42, No. 3 (July, 1932), pp. 233–72, and No. 4 (October, 1932), pp. 311–47, but little of the text pertains to New Mexico. The failure of the *encomienda* system there and the non-implemented grant to Diego de Vargas are examined by Lansing B. Bloom, "The Vargas *Encomienda*," *New Mexico Historical Review*, Vol. 14, No. 4 (October, 1939), pp. 366–417.

Economic life in Spanish New Mexico is portrayed in a few scholarly articles in the *New Mexico Historical Review*. Lansing B. Bloom, "Early Weaving in New Mexico," Vol. 2, No. 3 (July, 1927), pp. 228–38, and Hester Jones, "Uses of Wood by the Spanish Colonists of New Mexico," Vol. 7, No. 3 (July, 1932), pp. 273–91, are particularly valuable in studying two of the local industries that simply grew up in the province. Royal efforts to establish a monopoly on the growth and trade of tobacco by prohibiting local tobacco crops are examined in Lawrence Kinnaird, "The Spanish Tobacco Monopoly in New Mexico, 1766–1767," Vol. 21, No. 4 (October, 1946), pp. 328–39. Nevertheless, New Mexicans continued to grow tobacco locally, a subject treated by Leslie A. White in *"Punche*: Tobacco in New Mexico History," Vol. 18, No. 4 (October, 1943), pp. 386–93. William W. Long, "A History of Mining in New Mexico during the Spanish and Mexican Periods" (M.A. thesis, University of New Mexico, 1964), reveals how small mining activity in Spanish New Mexico was until the opening of the copper mines in the southwestern part of the province near Santa Rita el Cobre.

Three articles in the *New Mexico Historical Review* and one master's thesis treat the subject of early education and learning in the province. Eleanor B. Adams and France V. Scholes, "Books in New Mexico, 1598–1680," Vol. 17, No. 3 (July, 1942), pp. 226–70, and "Two Colonial New Mexico Libraries, 1704, 1776," Vol. 19, No. 2

(April, 1944), pp. 135–67, clearly demonstrate that books did reach the remote New Mexican frontier and that there were at least some literate persons there at all times. Miss Adams and Keith W. Algier, "A Frontier Book List—1800," Vol. 43, No. 1 (January, 1968), pp. 49–59, is an interesting study, a compilation of both religious and secular books as well as an analysis of their contents where known. From these three articles it is obvious that books certainly entered the colonies, an idea advanced almost one-quarter of a century ago by Professor Irving Leonard, and reached even the most distant frontiers. The general subject of religious and secular education in colonial New Mexico forms a part of the text for Rufus A. Palm, Jr., "New Mexico's Schools from 1581 to 1846," (M.A. thesis, University of New Mexico, 1930).

The achievements and problems of the settlers are treated in a variety of articles. The cycles of smallpox epidemics and their impact, for example, are discussed by Marc Simmons, "New Mexico's Smallpox Epidemic of 1780–1781," *New Mexico Historical Review*, Vol. 41, No. 4 (October, 1966), pp. 319–26. Lansing B. Bloom, *Early Vaccination in New Mexico* (Santa Fé: Historical Society of New Mexico, 1924), is a reprint in pamphlet form of an article appearing earlier in the *New Mexico Historical Review*. It treats the little-discussed subject of the introduction of cowpox vaccine in the first decade of the nineteenth century, the methods of treating children, and the numbers of people vaccinated.

Since the first printing press was not introduced into New Mexico until 1834, there was no publication of written work during the entire Spanish period. Henry W. Kelly, "Franciscan Missions of New Mexico, 1740–1760," *New Mexico Historical Review*, Vol. 15, No. 4 (October, 1940), pp. 345–68, Vol. 16, Nos. 1 and 2 (January and April, 1941), pp. 41–69, 148–83, studies the organization of the Custodia de San Pablo, the establishment of missions from the Conchos River to the Río Arriba country of New Mexico, and the relationship between the missions and nearby Spanish settlements. Early music and instruments used in the province are examined by Lota M. Spell, "Music Teaching in New Mexico in the Seventeenth Century," Vol. 2, No. 1 (January, 1927), pp. 27–36, and Lincoln B. Spiess, "Church Music in Seventeenth Century New Mexico," Vol. 40, No. 1 (January, 1965), pp. 5–21. George Kubler, "The Religious Architecture of New Mexico in the Colonial Period and Since the American Occupation," *Contributions of the Taylor Museum* (Colorado Springs, Colo.: The Taylor Museum, 1940), is a good general overview of the architectural amalgamation that occurred between Spanish and Indian styles. Specific churches and chapels for settlers in Santa Fe during the eighteenth century are discussed by Eleanor B. Adams, "The Chapel and *Cofradía* of Our Lady of Light in Santa Fé," *New Mexico Historical Review*, Vol. 22, No. 4 (October, 1947), pp. 327–41; A. Von Wuthenau, "The Spanish Military Chapels in Santa Fé and the Reredos of Our Lady of Light," Vol. 10, No. 3 (July, 1935), pp. 175–94; and Colonel José D. Sena, "The Chapel of Don Antonio José Ortiz," Vol. 13, No. 4 (October, 1938), pp. 347–59.

Spanish folklore, legends, drama, and special celebrations are also discussed in five scholarly articles published in professional journals. Arthur L. Campa, "Religious Spanish Folk Drama in New Mexico," *New Mexico Quarterly*, Vol. 2 (February, 1932), pp. 3–13, and Aurelio M. Espinosa, "Spanish Folk-Lore in New Mexico," *New Mexico Historical Review*, Vol. 1, No. 2 (April, 1926), pp. 135–55, provide general studies of their subjects, while a specific legend is treated by José Manuel Espinosa, "The Legend of Sierra Azul," Vol. 9, No. 2 (April, 1934), pp. 113–58, emphasizing the constant search for mythical wealth that did not materialize in New

Mexico but whose legend was used to promote official interest in the region. Two of New Mexico's leading authorities on the colonial history of the province have authored articles pertaining to local ceremonies, their origins, practices, and impact upon the Spanish settlers. These are Eleanor B. Adams, "Viva el Rey!," Vol. 35, No. 4 (October, 1960), pp. 284–92, and Fray Angelico Chávez, "Nuestra Señora del Rosario, La Conquistadora," Vol. 23, Nos. 2 and 3 (April and July, 1948), pp. 94–128, 177–216.

THE NORTHWESTERN FRONTIER

Primary source material on the Spanish administration and settlers of Sinaloa and Sonora are neither so plentiful nor so readily available as that pertaining to other frontiers, such as New Mexico and Nueva Vizcaya. Manuscripts are principally located in the Archivo General de Indias, Sevilla, Spain, and the Archivo General de la Nación in Mexico City, yet neither collection is so extensive for the northwestern region as it is for others. Provincial archives are not nearly so full as those for other frontier provinces. Perhaps the Bancroft Library at the University of California in Berkeley is the only institution in the United States having "adequate" collections of materials relative to these two provinces in the Spanish period. Were it not for the extensive records and reports of the Jesuits prior to 1767, the historian would be confronted with an even greater problem in approaching this region, because the secular records are both sketchy and scanty.

Fortunately, some original records and letters have been discovered and subsequently published. The best documentary account of the nature of society among Spanish settlers in the whole region is Ignaz Pfefferkorn, *Sonora: A Description of the Province*, trans. and ed. by Theodore E. Treutlein, (Albuquerque: University of New Mexico Press, 1949). The *Rudo Ensayo*, by an anonymous author believed to be another Jesuit named Juan Nentuig, has been translated and annotated by Eusebio Guiteras and published by Arizona Silhouettes at Tucson in 1951. It emphasizes the problems of soldiers and settlers in Pimería Alta and does not say much about either Sonora proper or Sinaloa in the latter part of the eighteenth century. Early information on Sinaloa is available in Mota y Escobar's *Descripción geográfica*, cited earlier among the works for the North Central Frontier. Other published primary materials pertinent to this frontier are: Herbert E. Bolton, *Kino's Historical Memoir of Pimería Alta*, 2 vols. (Cleveland, Ohio: Arthur H. Clark Company, 1919), and Juan Mateo Mange, *Unknown Arizona and Sonora, 1693–1721* [*Luz de Tierra Incognita*], trans. by Harry J. Karns (Tucson, 1954).

There is no general history of both Sinaloa and Sonora, the latter region including Pimería Alta, a portion of which today comprises the state of Arizona. The best general history of that state is Rufus K. Wyllys, *Arizona: the History of a Frontier State* (Phoenix, Arizona: Herr and Herr, 1950), and a recent study is Odie B. Faulk, *Arizona: a Short History* (Norman: University of Oklahoma Press, 1970), the first fifty-five pages of which cover the period before the war between Mexico and the United States began in 1846. Eduardo M. Villa, *Historia del estado de Sonora*, 2d ed. (Hermosillo: Editorial Sonora, 1951), is an acceptable, informative over-all history of the state with some material in its early chapters devoted to the colonial era.

Period studies and investigations of special topics are available, but not in great quantity. The previously mentioned Spanish historian of the frontier of New Spain, Luis Navarro García, has provided two excellent works pertaining to the northwestern frontier. His *Sonora y Sinaloa en el siglo XVII* (Sevilla: Publicaciones de la Escuela de Estudios Hispano-Americanos, 1967), is a comprehensive work on the two provinces in a little-studied century, employing materials from the Archivo General de Indias, while his *La sublevación yaqui de 1740* (Sevilla: Escuela de Estudios Hispano-Americanos, 1966), treats a specialized topic concerned with the causes, events, and results of the Yaqui Indian revolt of 1740. Theodore E. Treutlein, *Missionary in Sonora: The Travel Reports of Joseph Och, S.J.*, 1755–1767 (San Francisco: California Historical Society, 1965), is not only an excellent account of missionary activity, Indian characteristics, and Spanish settlements in the province, but a splendid eyewitness report on the expulsion of the Jesuits. Mario Hernández Sánchez-Barba, professor at the University of Madrid, has written about José de Gálvez and the campaign to pacify Sonora in the late 1760s in his La *última expansión española en América* (Madrid: Instituto de Estudios Políticos, 1957). Unfortunately, there is little here on Spanish settlers and communities in Sonora, and the title is misleading, for Sonora did not represent "the last Spanish expansion in America" by any means. James M. Murphy, *The Spanish Legal Heritage in Arizona* (Tucson: Arizona Pioneer's Historical Society, 1966), hardly touches the Spanish period at all in its analysis of the survival of Spanish-Mexican law in Arizona. Some comments on civil communities and their settlers may be found in John Francis Bannon, *The Mission Frontier in Sonora* (New York, 1955), and the many works of Peter Masten Dunne, including *Pioneer Black Robes on the West Coast* (Berkeley: University of California Press, 1940), *Jacobo Sedelmayr, Missionary, Frontiersman, Explorer* (Tucson, 1955), and *Juan Antonio Balthasar, Padre Visitador to the Sonora Frontier, 1744–1745* (Tucson, 1957). Although its title is misleading, Charles E. Chapman, *The Founding of Spanish California: The Northwestward Expansion of New Spain, 1687–1783* (New York: Macmillan, 1916), is a superb study of frontier Sonora in the important eighteenth century as Spanish settlements expanded northwestward on this frontier.

Professional articles relating to this region are much fewer in number than those pertaining to the New Mexican and Texan frontiers. Harry P. Johnson, "Diego Martínez de Hurdaide: Defender of the Northwestern Frontier of New Spain," *Pacific Historical Review*, Vol. 11, No. 2 (June, 1942), pp. 169–86, discusses the activities of this important civil official in Sinaloa, but the concentration is upon military activities against rebellious Indians. James R. Hastings, "People of Reason and Others: the Colonization of Sonora to 1767," *Arizona and the West*, Vol. 2 (Winter, 1961), pp. 321–40, is useful and pertinent to the social topics considered in this study. An important and informative work pertaining to Spain's final years of administration in Pimería Alta is Sidney B. Brinckerhoff, "The Last Years of Spanish Arizona, 1786–1821," *Arizona and the West*, Vol. 9 (Spring, 1967), pp. 5–20, while Ray H. Mattison, "Early Spanish and Mexican Settlements in Arizona," *New Mexico Historical Review*, Vol. 21, No. 4 (October, 1946), pp. 273–327, discusses the early settlements at Tubac and Tucson, in addition to those in the period following achievement of Mexican independence. Richard J. Morrisey, "The Early Range Cattle Industry in Arizona," *Agricultural History*, Vol. 24, No. 3 (July, 1950), pp. 151–56, hardly touches colonial Arizona at all. Lyle W. Williams, "The Northwest Frontier of New Spain, 1750–1800," (M.A. thesis, University of Texas, 1964), stresses the frontier society of the "little people" (soldiers, townsmen, missionaries, mission Indians, miners, ranchers, and *hacendados*) and the deterioration of the frontier because of Gileño Apache raids. Donald Rowland, "The Sonora Frontier of New

Spain, 1735–1745" in *New Spain and the Anglo-American West: Historical Contributions Presented to Herbert Eugene Bolton*, 2 vols. (Lancaster, Penna.: Lancaster Press, 1932), Vol. I, pp. 147–64, examines three Spanish documents and emphasizes the Apache threat to the established communities as well as their influence in retarding further expansion.

THE PACIFIC FRONTIER

The single most important repository for manuscripts and other materials pertaining to both Baja California and Alta California is the Bancroft Library, University of California, Berkeley. Begun with the extensive collection of Hubert Howe Bancroft, over the years it has added manuscripts relating to the western part of North America from Alaska to Panama. Its large microfilm holdings, including hundreds of reels from the Archivo General de la Nación in Mexico City, and huge photographic collection increase its over-all value to the researcher. Of great importance to this study were its holdings, particularly those of the Felipe de Neve Correspondence and Papers, 1781–82; California Mission Statistics, 1769–1834 (includes presidios and *pueblos*); the Archives of California, consisting of sixty-three bound volumes of documents, of which the first fourteen pertain to the Spanish period; and the Vallejo Documents, particularly those relating to the Spanish period and covering the years 1780 through 1821.

California also has a second major collection of Spanish documents pertaining to the frontier of New Spain. The Henry E. Huntington Library and Art Gallery, San Marino, California, has holdings known as the Kino Papers, 1680–1687, relating primarily to early efforts to establish missions and colonies in Baja California; the José de Gálvez collection of 734 manuscripts covering the period 1763–1794; the California File, 1731–1940, containing some 1,500 pieces dealing with California in general; and the Lower California-Church History Collection; in addition to the William G. Ritch Papers pertaining to New Mexico in the period 1539–1940.

These two important archival collections are supplemented by the publication of documentary accounts by government officials and visitors in the Californias during the last century of Spanish administration. Don Francisco Javier Clavigero, S.J., *The History of [Lower] California* (trans. by Sara E. Lake, ed. by A. A. Gray), (Stanford, Calif.: Stanford University Press, 1937, and Riverside, Calif.: Manessier Publishing Company, 1971), is one of the best contemporary accounts of missionary activity and observations concerning the Indians in Baja California. Originally published in 1786 with the title *Storia della California*, it emphasizes the role of the Jesuits in the pacification of that frontier before their expulsion in 1767. Only occasional comments, however, are made concerning the presidios at Loreto and San José del Cabo, and very little is said regarding families of the soldiers and the settlers in the vicinity of the presidios. One of the earliest descriptions of Alta California (1775) is provided by its later governor, Pedro Fages, in his *A Historical, Political, and Natural Description of California* (trans. by Herbert I. Priestley), (Berkeley: University of California Press, 1937), although this description occurs before many settlers had arrived in the province and before the civil settlements were founded. The Huntington Library has in bound form the 398 folios of the important report of the viceroy of New Spain, Conde de Revilla Gigedo, Ynstrucción reservada del Reyno de N.E. [Nueva España] que el Exmo. Senor Virrey Conde de Revilla-Gigedo dío a su sucesor, el Exmo. S.ʳ Marqués de Branciforte, México, 30 de junio de 1794. Herbert E. Bolton, *Anza's California Expeditions*, 5 vols. (Berkeley: University of California Press, 1930), is still one of the most authoritative accounts of the important colonizing venture of 1775–1776 and is entirely based upon primary documents. Some observations of Alta California by foreign visitors are provided by: Jean Francois Galaup de la Pérouse, *A Voyage Round the World, Performed in the Years 1785, 1786, 1787, and 1788* (London: G. G. and J. Robinson, 1798), and by George Vancouver, *A Voyage of Discovery to the North Pacific Ocean, and Round the World; in Which the Coast of North-West America Has Been Carefully Examined and Accurately Surveyed . . .*, 3 vols. (London: G. G. and J. Robinson, 1798). A specialized account of Vancouver's visit to and observations of Alta California is George Vancouver, *Vancouver in California, 1792–1794: The Original Account of George Vancouver*, ed. by Marguerite E. Wilbur, 2 vols., (Los Angeles: Glen Dawson, 1953). For the voyage of Nikolai Petrovich Rezanov to California, see T. C. Russell (ed.), *The Rezanov Voyage to Nueva California in 1806* (San Francisco, 1926), and *Langsdorff's Narrative of the Rezanov Voyage to Nueva California in 1806* (San Francisco, 1927).

Once again, as with the other frontiers discussed in this essay, there is no general work covering both of the Californias or the entire Pacific Frontier. Baja California is discussed in detail, although emphasis is placed on the Jesuit missions and not on the settlers who established themselves nearby, in Miguel Venegas, *Noticia de la California y de su conquista temporal y espiritual*, 3 vols. (Madrid, 1757, and México, 1943–44). Peter Masten Dunne, *Black Robes in Lower California* (Berkeley: University of California Press, 1952), also concentrates upon the Jesuit missions of the peninsula, while Peveril Meiggs, *The Dominican Mission Frontier of Lower California* (Berkeley: University of California Press, 1935), is the only major work on the significant period of Dominican administration, after 1769.

For Alta California some of the general state histories are valuable and contain well-researched parts on the Spanish settlement of the province. These include John W. Caughey, *California*, 2d ed. (Englewood Cliffs, N.J.: Prentice-Hall, 1953); Andrew F. Rolle, *California: A History* (New York, 1963); and W. H. Hutchinson, *California: Two Centuries of Man, Land, and Growth in the Golden State* (Palo Alto, Calif.: American West Publishing Company, 1969). Of particular value for the Spanish settlement of Alta California and the characteristics of its settlers are two excellent works by Charles E. Chapman, *The Founding of Spanish California: The Northwestward Expansion of New Spain, 1687–1783*, mentioned earlier in the portion of this essay devoted to Sinaloa and Sonora, and *A History of California: The Spanish Period* (New York: Macmillan, 1930), an outstanding work on civil as well as military and missionary settlements, in addition to a balanced study of Spanish institutions of the frontier province. Irving B. Richman, *California under Spain and Mexico, 1535–1847* (Boston, 1911, and New York: Cooper Square Publishers, 1965), is detailed and valuable for the study of colonial society, but bears a resemblance to material contained in the Bancroft volumes on California. Two studies by Frank W. Blackmar, *Spanish Colonization in the Southwest* (Baltimore: Johns Hopkins University Studies in History and Political Science, 1890), and *Spanish Institutions of the Southwest* (Baltimore: Johns Hopkins Press, 1891), concentrate mostly on California, in spite of their titles, and are now somewhat dated, although they make fine background reading. Blackmar provides insights into Spanish policy, the governmental system, missions, presidios, and the civil communities of Alta California.

Works on special topics relating to the Spanish settlement era and the development of Alta California cover a wide variety of subjects. Richard F. Pourade, *Anza Conquers the Desert: The Anza Expeditions from Mexico to California and the Founding of San Francisco, 1774 to 1776* (San Diego, Calif.: Union-Tribune Publishing Company, 1971), is a recent work on this important phase of settlement in California. It is a popularly written, interesting, authoritative account, stressing the daily events of both the exploratory venture and the colonizing expeditions of 1775 to 1776, the latter bringing hundreds of settlers to the province from Sinaloa, Sonora, and Pimería Alta. Oscar O. Winther, *The Story of San José: California's First Pueblo, 1777–1869* (San Francisco: California Historical Society, 1935), contains in its first chapter an excellent, well-researched account of the founding, population, early problems, and development of this important civil settlement, which indeed was Alta California's first real community for settlers other than presidial soldiers and missionaries. Charles N. Rudkin (trans. and ed.), *The First French Expedition to California: La Pérouse in 1786* (Los Angeles: Glen Dawson, 1959), includes early observations of California society (except for the *pueblos*, which were never visited) by the ill-fated La Pérouse expedition. A masterful work on the expedition of Alejandro Malaspina and official observations pertaining to California during his visit there in 1791 is Donald C. Cutter, *Malaspina in California* (San Francisco: John Howell Books, 1960). Henry R. Wagner, *Cartography of the Northwest Coast of America to 1800* (Berkeley: University of California Press, 1937), and *Spanish Voyages to the Northwest Coast of America in the Sixteenth Century* (San Francisco, 1928), are still the outstanding works available concerning the exploration of the Pacific Coast and especially the many achievements of the Spanish navigators.

Susanna B. Dakin discusses the tumultuous role of three women in Spanish California—Doña Feliciana Arballo, Doña Eulalia Fages, and Doña Concepción Arguello—in her *Rose or Rose Thorn? Three Women of Spanish California* (Berkeley: Friends of the Bancroft Library, 1963). Early *ranchos* and livestock-raising activities are treated by George P. Hammond, *Romance of the California Ranchos* ([n.p.], 1954), a pamphlet of an address delivered in Concord, California, and Robert G. Cowan, *Ranchos of California: A List of Spanish Concessions, 1775–1822, and Mexican Grants, 1822–1846* (Fresno, Calif.: Academy Library Guild, 1956). The latter work is particularly useful for its introduction and individual listing of Spanish concessions to individual Californians. Furthermore, its author emphasizes that there were comparatively few such grants made in the Spanish period, the large majority being during Mexican sovereignty.

Professional articles treating many subjects have been published in scholarly journals from time to time. Sherburne F. Cook wrote two, on smallpox epidemics and early medical practices, for the *Bulletin of the Institute of the History of Medicine* (title varies). "The Monterey Surgeons during the Spanish Period in California," Vol. 5, No. 1 (January, 1937), pp. 43–72, and "Smallpox in Spanish and Mexican California, 1700–1845," Vol. 7, No. 2 (February, 1939), pp. 153–91, are both particularly appropriate in the present study of everyday life and problems of settlers in Alta California. Thomas W. Temple II (trans.), "First Census of Los Angeles," *Historical Society of Southern California: Annual Publications*, Vol. 15, Part 2 (1931), reports on and analyzes the 1781 census for the founding of the civil *pueblo* of Los Angeles, particularly emphasizing original settlers, their families, and possessions of each. J. M. Guinn, "Early Postal Service of California," *Publications of the Historical Society of Southern California*, Vol. 4 (Los Angeles, 1898), and Mary F. Williams, "Mission, Presidio, and Pueblo," *California Historical Quarterly*, Vol. 1, No. 1 (July, 1922), pp. 23–35, are both useful in the study of improved communications and local institutions in Spanish California. Jean François Galaup de la Pérouse, "A Visit to Monterey in 1786," (no translator cited), *California Historical Society Quarterly*, Vol. 15, No. 3 (September, 1936), pp. 216–33, and George Vancouver, "San Francisco in 1792," *California Historical Society Quarterly*, Vol. 14, No. 2 (June, 1935), pp. 111–20, are extracts from larger works, with occasional comments on California society.

An excellent account of the arrival of settlers in Alta California, the establishment of early communities, and the depiction of daily life in the *pueblos* is Ruth Staff, "Settlement in Alta California before 1800," (M.A. thesis, University of California, 1931). The author not only portrays the establishment and development of civil communities but also discusses some of the major events and problems in the lives of the settlers. Spain's northernmost settlement, a presidial garrison without families at Santa Cruz de Nootka on Vancouver Island, is treated in my "The Spanish Occupation of Nootka Sound, 1790–1795," (M.A. thesis, University of Oklahoma, 1960).

RELATED SUBJECTS

Although it is not my intention in this book or this essay to discuss in full topics not primarily concerned with Spanish civilian settlements and the colonists who came to the northern frontier, some basic works should be mentioned here because of their relationship to the principal topics and their importance as background reading in developing an over-all understanding of the frontier region. A few selected source materials are, therefore, indicated here. They are mainly concerned with the role of the church, the presidio, government, Indian affairs, and the general history of the Mexican-American in the United States.

The mission was a prominent frontier institution often closely related to the civil settlement. Herbert Eugene Bolton, "The Mission as a Frontier Institution in the Spanish American Colonies," *American Historical Review*, Vol. 23, No. 4 (October, 1917), pp. 42–61, and reprinted in Bannon, *Bolton and the Spanish Borderlands* (pp. 187–211), is a superb pioneering overview of the church's important role in the spread of Spanish civilization northward. It supplies reasons for the missionary establishments, their composition, and their organization, and especially analyzes their great influence upon the Indians within their sphere as well as the frontier experience of Spaniards. Over the course of the past half-century there have been some excellent studies of missions, missionaries, and the role of the church, particularly for the provinces of the Californias, Pimería Alta, and the northwestern frontier, and less so for New Mexico, Texas, and the northeastern frontier. An excellent recent work concerning a little-known mission is the well-researched, readable account by John L. Kessell, *Mission of Sorrows: Jesuit Guevavi and the Pimas, 1691–1767* (Tucson: University of Arizona Press, 1970). Individual studies of prominent missionaries have tended to focus on the work of Fathers Eusebio Francisco Kino and Junípero Serra, with little about any of the other important members of the regular orders and practically nothing whatsoever on the secular clergy in frontier Spanish communities. Herbert E. Bolton, *Rim of Christendom: A Biography of Eusebio Francisco Kino, Pacific Coast Pioneer* (New York: Macmillan, 1936, and Russell and Russell, 1960), is a sound study. Bert M. Fireman, "Kino on the Arizona Border," *The American West*, Vol. 3 (Summer, 1966), pp. 16–21, and Fay Jackson Smith, John L. Kessell, and Francis Fox, *Father Kino in Arizona* (Phoenix, 1966), are particularly useful works—and authoritative—on an extensively covered subject. Probably the best studies on Serra are those by Maynard Geiger. He is the author of *The Life and Times of Fray Junípero Serra,* 2 vols. (Washington, D.C.: Academy of American Franciscan History, 1959), and edited *Palou's Life of Fray Junípero Serra* (Washington, D.C.: Academy of American Franciscan History, 1955), which is both a biography of the famous Franciscan and a history of the occupation and development of Alta California to the early 1780s. Zephyrin Engelhardt, *The Missions and Missionaries of California,* 4 vols. (San Francisco, 1908–15), and many shorter studies of particular missions by the same author are also useful in the over-all understanding of the church's role in California settlement. A handsomely printed, color-illustrated small volume of more than passing interest is José de Onís, *Las Misiones españolas en los Estados Unidos: tratado de Pablo Tac* (New York, 1958). It provides a good descriptive overview of the Spanish missions from Florida to California. Other studies of missions have been mentioned earlier for their respective frontiers, since they relate more clearly to the civil settlements and their inhabitants.

During the past decade the presidio as a frontier institution has received considerable attention from scholars. Some consideration of this military topic is necessary for a well-rounded understanding of Spanish society in frontier New Spain, since soldiers were often the original settlers of a civil community, and many retired soldiers and their families came to live in the settlements and thus brought with them some military characteristics and customs. Three articles in *Journal of the West,* Vol. 8, No. 1 (January, 1969) concentrate on the presidio and the soldier of the frontier. These are: Odie B. Faulk, "The Presidio: Fortress or Farce?"; Paige W. Christiansen, "The Presidio and the Borderlands: A Case Study"; and Max L. Moorhead, "The *Soldado de Cuera*: Stalwart of the Borderlands." Further studies of the military on the frontier and the presidio include Sidney R. Brinckerhoff and Odie B. Faulk, *Lancers for the King: A Study of the Frontier Military System of Northern New Spain, with a Translation of the Royal Regulations of 1772* (Phoenix: Arizona Historical Foundation, 1965), and Odie B. Faulk, *The Leather Jacket Soldier: Spanish Military Equipment and Institutions of the Late 18th Century* (Pasadena, Calif.: Socio-Technical Publications, 1971).

Spanish government and administration in the northern provinces have been the focal points of some excellent works. José de Gálvez, the *visitador-general* appointed by Carlos III, has had the attention of Herbert I. Priestley, *José de Gálvez: Visitador-General of New Spain* (Berkeley: University of California Press, 1916), and recently of Luis Navarro García of Spain, in a work that was cited earlier. Bernard E. Bobb, *The Viceregency of Antonio María Bucareli in New Spain, 1771–1779* (Austin: University of Texas Press, 1967), is a study of a controversial viceroy who devoted much of his attention to frontier problems and their resolution. In the past forty years there have been some excellent studies of frontier officials, beginning with Alfred B. Thomas, *Teodoro de Croix and the Northern Frontier of New Spain, 1776–1783* (Norman: University of Oklahoma Press, 1941). Bernardo de Gálvez, *Instructions for Governing the Interior Provinces of New Spain, 1786* (trans. and ed. by Donald E. Worcester) (Berkeley, Calif.: The Quivira Society, 1951), is an outstanding study of frontier conditions and regulations issued by a knowledgeable frontier official who became viceroy for a short time. John W. Caughey, *Bernardo de Gálvez in Louisiana, 1770–1783* (Berkeley: University of California Press, 1934), takes a look at an earlier phase of the same official's life, concentrating upon his intelligent leadership and realization of frontier problems. A superb study of one *comandante-general* of the Provincias Internas and his enforcement of new Indian policies against the Apaches after 1786 is Max L. Moorhead, *The Apache Frontier: Jacobo Ugarte and Spanish-Indian Relations in Northern New Spain, 1769–1791*

(Norman: University of Oklahoma Press, 1968). Hugo O'Conor, an experienced frontiersman of Irish heritage in New Spain, was assigned to carry out many of the provisions in the Royal Regulations of 1772. He has been studied by David M. Vigness, "Don Hugo Oconor and New Spain's Northeastern Frontier," *Journal of the West*, Vol. 6, No. 1 (January, 1967), pp. 27–40, and by Paige W. Christiansen, "Hugo Oconor's Inspection of Nueva Vizcaya and Coahuila," *Louisiana Studies*, Vol. 2 (Fall, 1963), pp. 157–75.

Although some of the previously mentioned works include information concerning Spanish-Indian relations on the northern frontier, there are additional studies that concentrate on that special subject. Edward H. Spicer, *Cycles of Conquest: The Impact of Spain, Mexico, and the United States on the Indians of the Southwest, 1533–1960*, previously mentioned in this essay for the Northwestern Frontier, is an excellent detailed overview not only of European relations with Indians in the southwestern United States but in Sonora as well. Herbert E. Bolton, *Athanase de Mézières and the Louisiana-Texas Frontier, 1768–1780*, 2 vols. (Cleveland, Ohio: Arthur H. Clark Company, 1914), is a study of a Frenchman employed by Spain to pacify and control the *"naciones del norte"* (nations of the north). In my *Pueblo Warriors and Spanish Conquest* (Norman, University of Oklahoma Press, 1966), I use the Pueblo Indians of New Mexico as an example of the regular Spanish policy of forming an "alliance" with friendly Indian nations to overcome the more rebellious ones. Joseph F. Park, "Spanish Indian Policy in Northern Mexico, 1765–1810," *Arizona and the West*, Vol. 4 (Winter, 1962), pp. 325–44, provides an excellent study of changing Spanish frontier policies in a critical period. Alfred B. Thomas has edited three major works on Indian policy relating to New Mexico that are indispensable for one studying this particular subject. These are: *After Coronado: Spanish Exploration Northeast of New Mexico, 1696–1727* (Norman: University of Oklahoma Press, 1935); *Forgotten Frontiers: A Study of the Spanish Indian Policy of Don Juan Bautista de Anza, Governor of New Mexico, 1777–1787* (Norman: University of Oklahoma Press, 1932); and *The Plains Indians and New Mexico, 1751–1778* (Albuquerque: University of New Mexico Press, 1940).

The recent awakening of Mexican-Americans in the United States and interest in their cultural heritage has led to publication of a wide variety of materials, some of which discuss the origins of Spanish-speaking people in the frontier provinces considered in this book. Carey McWilliams, *North from Mexico: The Spanish-Speaking People of the United States* (Philadelphia: J. B. Lippincott, 1949, and New York: Greenwood Press, 1968), is a pioneering study of the general subject, still in wide use in spite of its errors. So too, are Julian Samora (ed.), *La Raza: Forgotten Americans* (Notre Dame, Ind.: University of Notre Dame Press, 1966), and Herschel T. Manuel, *Spanish-Speaking Children of the Southwest: Their Education and Their Public Welfare* (Austin: University of Texas Press, 1965). Almost forty per cent of Wayne Moquín and Charles Van Doren (eds.), *A Documentary History of the Mexican Americans* (New York, Bantam Books, 1972), deals with the Spanish colonial period and is informative and useful for the reader interested in this subject. Manuel P. Servín, *The Mexican-Americans: An Awakening Minority* (Beverly Hills, Calif.: Glencoe Press, 1970), is an overview of the culture and conflicts of Mexican-Americans, although little of the text deals with the Spanish period. The works of George I. Sánchez and Nancie L. González, discussed in the portion of this essay pertaining to the North Central Frontier, are also useful for the study of this topic.

Index

INDEX   349